PURCHASE ORDER

OKS
INT

Cokesbury

Retail Division
The United Methodist Publishing

LITERARY LMII
ARKET ACE
ITH

American
Book Trade
Directory

Kroch's & Brentano's, Inc.
WHOLESALE BOOKSELLERS AND STATIONERS
South Wabash Ave   Chicago, Illinois 60603

G130071

IMPORTANT

PURCHASE ORDER   No.   N028

Ship To: SAN
enter   SAME

SHIPPING INSTRUCTIONS
Ship via: book post
Ship (XX)et once ,   Cancel back orders if not
( ) on _____19_____   shipped: (X X) at once
( ) Do (X X) Do NOT insure at our e

PUBLIC LAW 94-553—OCT. 19, 1976

The National Herald Review

ublic Law 94-553
4th Congress

An Act

for the general revision of the Copyright Law, title 17 of the United States
Code, and for other purposes.

Be it enacted by the Senate and House of Representatives of the
United States of America in Congress assembled,

TITLE I—GENERAL REVISION OF COPYRIGHT LAW

Sec. 101. Title 17 of the United States Code, entitled "Copyrights",
hereby amended in its entirety to read as follows:

TLE 17—COPYRIGHTS

erary Awards (13)

ARCHITECTURAL AESTHETICS—
Form or Function?

Snyder Tracy, a graduate of Yale's School of Architecture
(1939), admits openly, in his introduction to *GAUDI: The*
His Work, that his primary architectural influence
onio Gaudi i Cornet (1852-1926). Gaudi is
to be the most original genius of the art nouveau
wn as *modernismo* in Spain and his

he attracted a loyal following of stud
was denigrated by the majority of h

ORDER WITH THIS COU
KALICOMB PRESS
345 West 18th Street, N.Y. N.

Please send me ____ copies o
At $ ____ per copy plus $1.00 postage + h
Name _____
Address _____
City _____ State ___ Zip ___
☐ Check Enclosed   ☐ Visa   ☐ MasterCard
Card # _____
Signature _____
Exp. Date ___

GAUDI: The Man and His Art
By Snyder Tracy/Kalicomb Pres

THE BOOK MARKET

THE BOOK MARKET

How to
Write, Publish
and Market
Your Book

ARON MATHIEU

Andover Press, Inc. / *New York*

For Rosella

Library of Congress Cataloging in Publication Data
Mathieu, Aron M., 1981–
   The book market.
   I. Title
Z283.M37   070.5'2   81-562   AACR2

*An Andover Press book. Distributed to the
trade by Ingram Book Company.*

BOOK DESIGN BY FRANK JAMES CANGELOSI

FIRST EDITION

Copyright © 1981 by Aron Mathieu

Published by Andover Press, Inc.
516 West 34th Street, New York, New York 10001

Manufactured in the United States of America
ISBN 0-939014-00-9

Library of Congress Catalog Card No.: 80-71059

Contents

PART I
Royalty Publishing

1

Why Do Publishers Act the Way They Do?

EVERY BIG-NAME writer was once a newcomer without one printed line to his credit. Yet the best of us are part of a parade that moves on without us when our minds become dated or our energy lessens. Today's best-selling literary names will vanish soon, and the new crop that will bask in the glow of million-dollar advances is unknown this very moment.

To the writer of quality, the world is indeed his oyster. It applauds and celebrates him, yet, while this is going on, he has little opportunity to learn why things happen as they do in book publishing. The reason for this is that the publisher feels no need to explain his objectives to writers. The underlying purpose of these chapters is to give you a floor of understanding, a means of coping, as well as the reason to write your best line every time.

No one tries to keep book-publishing operations or attitudes secret from writers. It's just that it has always been easier for knowledgeable people in the business to discuss these among themselves, in the shorthand, conversational way that informed people use when communicating with one another, than to begin at the beginning and explain the whole process to each new writer.

Book publishers don't play dirty tricks, nor do they cheat. What they say they will do, they do—especially the written specifics. It does not suit their purpose to explain to authors the facts of life about book publishing that motivate their actions.

The black figures at the bottom line of the profit-and-loss statement of a book-publishing division owned by a big corporation keep the divisional management in power. From the bottom line come pensions, perks, power, status, and salary.

It wasn't always like this. Alfred Knopf did what he wanted to do. It was his business, and he enjoyed running it his way. So did Charles Scribner, Horace Liveright, Pat Covici, and a score of others who entered book publishing because of what Dick Simon, a founder of Simon & Schuster, called "the amenities of the business." To these men, book publishing was a means of expressing how they felt about the natural and political world and the human condition itself.

The book-publishing business today is less of a vehicle for the owner to express intellectual and philosophical attitudes and reveal personal taste than it once was. It's a world of hype and sell, risk and profit, and, sometimes, risk and retreat fast.

It is the attitude of risk and retreat fast that has physically and emotionally hurt so many good people who are writers. They are hurt because they do not understand what happened to their books or why.

The calculated, competitive attitude of publishers toward talent is the same that the oil and chemical people show toward natural resources. They want what they want, and they go after it without very much regard for the casualties. A lot of fine personal relationships do still exist in book publishing between writers and their editors and between publishers and their staffs. But, at the top, the heads of multinational corporations that own such a significant part of the book-publishing business have somewhat the same regard for a book as they have for a can of coffee. Why should we expect their divisional market managers to feel different?

Smaller publishers, living in the same world as their big, rich relations, have picked up the same attitude, and they are often as cavalier with a book as with a ring binder, treating either one as merchandise. This is the condition of book publishing today, and the author should seek to understand how his book will be treated and why. If he has this knowledge, the author is more secure, because he knows what is going on and is more capable of standing on his own two feet and taking care of himself in good style.

This bulks up both the author's psyche and his trading position. If, in addition to this, as an author, you can make your book better by utilizing your talents to the fullest, you help us all, no less yourself than the reader. An awful lot of junk is released today, and such books are quickly read and discarded. The author's name floats off. Your best work on every page is your gift to yourself and to publishing.

2

Is Your Book as Good as You Can Make It?

YOU KNOW, from what you have already been through, that writing a book asks much in time and energy and, especially, in putting your faith in yourself on the line. With this commitment, any way to reduce your risk is worth investigating. One way to tip the odds in your favor is to pretest the editorial value of your book before shipping it off to a publisher.

Editorial pretesting means submitting your book, before it goes to an editor or literary agent, to several individuals selected for their judgment. The purpose is to produce a manuscript that represents your best effort. You might ask: "Can't the editor help out?" Yes, but only to a limited degree.

Skillful editorial labor is scarce and expensive. An editor's salary with that of his secretary and their proportionate office expense is three thousand dollars or more for one month's work.* When a book requires two months' editorial work, the cost is at least six thousand dollars. This explains why authors, especially new ones, stand almost as alone after acceptance as during the creative period of writing their books. The

---

* This breaks down as follows: associate or assistant editor, $300 to $350 a week; editorial secretary (who assists in reading copy as well as transcribing mail), $160 to $210 a week; Social Security and state unemployment tax paid by the publisher, $35 to $40 a week; proportionate office cost for two people, including rent, light, heat, air conditioning, office supplies, and repairs, editorial travel, pensions, telephone, paid vacations and proportionate administrative cost, $140 to $160 a week; consultation time with senior editor or executive editor, $50 to $75 a week. Average: $3,000 for four weeks. Of that sum, the editor receives 40 percent, the remaining 60 percent being supportive costs.

patient editorial assistance that an author sometimes thinks will be forthcoming once a book is accepted may not materialize. It costs too much. Editorial pretesting makes you less dependent on an editor who has to argue for the privilege of putting more of his time into your book.

But isn't that what editors are for—to locate talented writers and improve and publish their works? Let's look more closely. If an author's book has a press run of ten thousand, which is a tad high for a new author, and an editor puts one full month's time on the project, the editorial cost riding on each printed copy of the book is 30 cents ($3,000 ÷ 10,000). If the editor puts two months of his time into one book, the cost is 60 cents. A balance sheet showing the cost of producing one book when the press run is ten thousand indicates the publisher's stance:

Expense per Book

Cost of printing and binding one cloth-bound book with a 10,000 press run	$1.40
Cost of editor's work for one month	.30
Author's average royalty on a book retailing at $8.00 and selling 10,000 copies	1.00
Sales and publicity cost per book	1.10
	$3.80

Income per Book

Book dealer pays the publisher 60% of the retail price of $8.00	$4.80

Profit per Book

$4.80 income less $3.80 expense	$1.00

Well, that's good. Here's a profit of one dollar for every book printed. Multiply it out for yourself: ten thousand books times one dollar profit per book is ten thousand dollars' profit. But will the publisher be able to sell each copy that is printed, or will the book bomb and sell only three thousand or plod along and sell five thousand?

Since the publisher doesn't know the answer to this question in advance of publication, he tries putting a sharper pencil to the expenses listed above. When expenses are three dollars and eighty cents per book, with a ten thousand press run, the publisher's gamble is thirty-eight thousand dollars. In return, he will take in forty-eight thousand dollars when all ten thousand books are sold.

That kind of math doesn't fascinate a publisher. What he wants is to invest less and make more. How does he go about doing this? One way is to stop publishing books that will bomb. At first blush, that doesn't look so hard. Anybody can tell the difference between a book that is literate and one that is plain dumb. But no one can tell which of the literate books will sell and which will not. That is the crux of why a book publisher tries to reduce his initial investment.

There are a number of things he can do, and he does most of them. First, he can print 10,000 copies, but, instead of folding, gathering, and binding all the sheets as they come off the press, he may hold 6,000 flat sheets on wooden skids and bind 4,000. That reduces his initial investment by $4,000. Second, instead of allowing one or two months' in-house editorial time on a book, he may allow only two to three weeks' editorial work. Third, he may hold the author's royalty advance to the amount of money the author would receive on a sale of 3,000 copies. And fourth, he will hold back much of the publicity and advertising expense. Thus, instead of starting off with a bang and spending $11,000 within sixty days of publication (10,000 × $1.10), he may initially spend only 20 percent of the sales budget, or $2,200. And, fifth, he may cut corners by reducing the quality of the printing and binding.

Is this usual?

It happens every day.

Why?

Because the publisher wants two things: (1) to reduce his wager; and (2) to wait for the book to give out a signal that it will be profitable to advertise. When a book starts to move off the dealer's shelves of its own accord (word-of-mouth advertising's being the major cause), that's a reasonable signal it is turning into a good seller and is worth the risk of additional and immediate paid advertising. When the same book fails to move of its own accord, this can be regarded as a signal that the cost of buying more advertising will translate itself into too many dollars needed to sell one book profitably. Sometimes such a book is simply allowed to trail off.

Are there times when a publisher goes ahead and spends considerable promotion money without the kind of "signal" first mentioned?

Yes, indeed.

When the author's agent can negotiate a respectable advance, say twenty thousand dollars, the publisher's hand is forced. To protect his investment, he now has to perform positively and sometimes may start off by asking his staff to give the book more editorial time.

Will he do the same for you?

In the last ten years, as one example, Doubleday published about five thousand new titles. I suspect that up to 10 percent, or five hundred books, barely nosed a sale over five thousand copies.

Let's ask an honest question. What if fifty of these had been advertised more and been given one month's more editorial time? Would these fifty each have reached a sale of eight thousand copies?

Possibly. Surely most of the fifty would have sold better. Then why didn't Doubleday do it?

It may surprise you to learn that this is not Doubleday's business. Nor that of any publisher. The job of a publisher isn't to sell the most copies he possibly can of each book. The publisher's job is to make a profit on the overall operation.

What does this attitude mean to you?

It means that, if you are relatively unknown, receive little or no advance, and the print order for your book is around ten thousand, the publisher is going to ask your book to prove itself on the dealers' shelves before he starts spending any real money—like five or ten thousand dollars in radio, TV, newspaper, and magazine advertising. Your book has to show definite signs of life. It has to earn good reviews and good word-of-mouth advertising and start selling of its own accord at bookstores before anything major is done to support it.

Well, you say, if the editor gives my book only two weeks' work, maybe three at the outside, and the publisher won't spend any real money on it unless the book starts to sell of its own accord, what chance do I have? The answer to that is that you are the one who offered to take a chance by writing your book. The publisher took a chance, too, in contracting with you to produce it. This contract calls for him to take financial risks in editing, printing, binding, advertising, and selling. When there is no heavy advance to the author to force his hand, he may try to reduce this risk. Think of it this way—can you expect him to spend the most he can on every new title? Usually, with a new author, the publisher waits to hear what the book is doing before opening his wallet wide.

What we're saying is that the game is up to you.

And that is what so few writers know.

They feel the editor is going to give their book time, affection, homework, and all kinds of thought and research. They feel he will invite many good editorial minds to read the book and give him ideas, and then he will work these out with the author in personal conference and by phone. Both of us should live so long!

The editor is going to give your book a two weeks' editing job, three weeks' at the outside. What can you do to protect yourself?

That's what this chapter is all about.

You can learn how to improve your book by pretesting it editorially. Then, make it as fine as you can by benefiting from the judgment of objective, competent people.

Do all authors do this?

Most do not.

What happens when an editor reports to his supervisor that he likes a new author's book but that it needs six weeks' editorial work?

One supervising editor sent me this comment:

> If I okay one of my editors putting two months' time on a book by a new author, it's not only a matter of adding extra costs to one book.
>
> Turning an editor loose for two months on one book makes me ask: Does this give me the most dollars back from that editor's time? I can't use the time of a first-class editor to make a so-so book move up in sales from four thousand to eight thousand. I have to put that editor's time on books that have a shot at the clubs, TV, paperbacks, and the movies.

Put the hat on yourself. Let's say you are publishing two hundred books a year and are aware that one hundred of them can be made better by adding one month's additional editorial time to each. That's three thousand dollars' additional annual costs. True, the books would probably sell better; some might sell very much better. Some might fall by the wayside if the author resists the changes, and some might end up with the same sales. Talented, experienced editors who can take a so-so book and, with diplomacy and skill, work with the author to improve it are hard to find unless you steal them. What do you do?

Chances are, you weigh the matter and continue to publish two hundred titles, half of which aren't as good as you can make them.

When the time comes for you to market your own completed book, it is up to you to make it as good as you know how. Purchasing an editorial evaluation of your book, before shipping it to a publisher, will tip the odds in your favor.

The cost of getting a professional opinion on an unpublished manuscript is about $150 for a script of 200 to 240 pages. If your manuscript is longer, you can figure on paying more. Pretesting your unpublished work with three different readers comes to about $450.

That is a lot of money. Especially after all the other expenses involved in writing a book. What if you just mail your book in and don't pretest? Will the publisher tell the editor to spend all day Thursday reading your book and all day Friday making notes on every chapter? Will he pay the editor's secretary for a day's work in transcribing the notes and send you a ten-page letter explaining how to improve your book?

When a book misses the mark, it comes back. What was wrong? "Sorry," they say. Sure, they're sorry, but not sorry enough to spend several hundred dollars educating you.

When you pretest, you learn the score and have a chance to alter it in your favor.

Here is a page of what one author received as part of a nine-page letter of comment from a pretester:

> I congratulate you on opening your novel with four pages of dialogue. This is a bold maneuver and you may find it reads easier if you piece small bits of action into the dialogue. I don't want you to alter your plan of using straight dialogue for your opening, but I suggest you give the reader a respite.
>
> Four pages of uninterrupted dialogue asks for close reader attention and takes more effort to read than twice that many pages

of description and action. So, let the reader take a foot off the gas, and rest the old engine. Slip in a little "business" (as it's called in playwriting) between the lines of dialogue. Your characters in the early pages are at poolside, so this should be easy for you.

Later in the same chapter, you describe a fight between Jane and Clark. A good fight will change my blood beat. It's not just tender kisses that excite me; fights do, too. And you have to do your part. When Jane pulls Clark's hair, have her yank so hard that some strands come out. Let Clark yowl with surprise, maybe more surprise than anger. When he hits Jane, let her lip bleed and drip on her dress. If I were to see a fight like that in a restaurant, I would get upset and move off. In a book, I want to move in closer. Can you do that for me?

In chapter one, pages 7, 9, and 11 of the nice Xerox copy you sent me, I have indicated where you might insert a hint of conflict to come, and included a suggestion for involving the reader right now with Cleo. The purpose of this is to pull the reader into chapter two. As an indication of what I'm talking about, I mailed you today the bound galleys of my own newest gothic title and marked several places in chapter one that (I hope) pull the reader into chapter two. I also marked on pages 7, 9, and 11 in your own chapter one where you might accomplish the same thing, and in the margin, I suggested how.

Will your readers prefer to see the characters' problems resolved? I suspect the editor may think so. With this in mind, I am offering three ideas to give your novel a form of resolution. The first two are "plants" for what is to come, and the latter is a suggested solution.

If you feel pretesting will improve your book, to whom should you send it? How much should you pay? We will deal first with the pretesting of nonfiction. The first thing is to select an individual with an authoritative position in the field of your book, someone who can communicate at your level. If knowing the subject is all that is necessary, then every Ph.D. in physics would be a great physics teacher, and none would be accused of "talking in shorthand." How do you find out if the person you have in mind not only knows the subject but also can explain to you what he has to say?

If you have completed a nonfiction book, you know something about research, and that's what you need here. Has your man written anything? Read it. Does he give lectures? Attend one. One way or another, you must check out this person's ability to communicate at your level, before you spend any part of your $450 for pretesting a nonfiction book. When you locate two or three experts in your field who you believe have these two qualities, here's the kind of letter you might send each:

Dear——:

I have completed a manuscript titled "The Social Bee," and, to give you the gist of it, a chapter outline is enclosed along with one chapter. I want to find out, before I send it to a publisher, whether the approach and facts are correct.

This brings me to you.

I am writing for permission to send "The Social Bee" to you with my check for one hundred and fifty dollars. The manuscript is typed, double spaced, on white paper, size 8½ by 11 inches. There are 230 pages.

Would you be willing to read this material and advise me whether or not you feel the facts are straight and the approach is valid?

When you find things to comment on, I would like you to number such passages (1, 2, 3, etc.) along the margin of the page and then attach a letter with comments on the numbered passages. The manuscript I send you will be a clean Xerox copy, and you can mark it up. I hope you will include a general appraisal as well.

The market I have in mind for this book would include bee-keepers, state and national bee associations, agricultural colleges teaching beekeeping, amateur beekeepers, health-food stores and gourmet shops that sell books as well as honey, individuals with a penchant for health foods, suppliers for beekeepers, honey buyers at chain stores, cooking-page editors, subsistence farmers, communes, and stores selling to the residents of these communes.

I agree to accept whatever you send me as full value for my $150. Enclosed is a stamped self-addressed envelope. May I send you the full manuscript of "The Social Bee"? Thank you for your time and courtesy.

Sincerely yours,

———————————

Enclosures: Three-page outline of "The Social Bee"
One chapter
One stamped, self-addressed envelope

14

The suggestion from here is that you mail one such letter and, if the person you select agrees to do the work, wait until you receive the completed response before going on to the next. What you learn may help you improve your manuscript before approaching Number Two. It's a sort of literary judo. You want at least two authorities to read your work, because their points of view and their emphasis might be different.

There is a cheaper and faster way of pretesting nonfiction, provided your manuscript is of an informative or "how-to" nature and you believe you will be satisfied with "spot testing" instead of a review of the entire book.

Take two chapters of your book, preferably two consecutive chapters, and circle a total of twelve paragraphs in red. Select paragraphs that make sense in themselves, and ask your pretester's advice on the paragraphs circled.

I used this method for fourteen years while publishing *The Farm Quarterly,* and I learned there is one built-in disadvantage. The technical expert looks at things strictly from his own point of view. For instance, in an article on increasing corn production, lots of things could be wrong, but the part that the seed-corn grower can be counted on to notice is the relationship between the corn-seed grower and the farmer. The botanist pays no attention to this but concentrates on any mention of stamen, pistil, or calyx. To prevent picky comments, we not only circled certain paragraphs but also asked a few questions that invited a practical, historical, or cultural response. We couldn't do this with every paragraph we circled, because it looked as if we were asking too much. But our questions, which were brief and specific, did indicate what we most wanted to know and took the expert off the dime.

The cost of buying this kind of "spot" pretesting is around fifteen to twenty-five dollars per chapter. A personal letter may sometimes get results, whereas the impersonal letter allows the receiver to turn it down without feeling he's saying no to a friend. Here is a letter I received from an author asking me to review a chapter.

Dear——:

While studying photography at the graduate school at Rochester, we were given oral history tapes as study material, and one of these was a lecture you delivered to the Society of Magazine Photographers.

THE BOOK MARKET

I thought of your tape this week when I completed my book "The Exact Image." It deals with new techniques in photography, most of which I picked up at Deluxe Fast Service, where I am chief lab technician. My lab technicians usually end up with a better print when they have some sort of cultural photographic background. Understanding Brassai, Strand, Atget, Man Ray, and a half-hundred others gives the lab men, I think, a certain intellectualism to draw upon.

In my book "The Exact Image," I have one chapter on cultural backgrounds of photography, and I explain how this relates to the lab technician. Enclosed is this one chapter (as well as a chapter outline of the entire book). In the enclosed chapter are ten paragraphs that I have numbered. In the margin alongside five of these paragraphs, I have asked several short specific questions; in the other paragraphs, no questions are asked.

I would like your comments on these ten paragraphs. If you have time to help me, I am sure my book will be improved. I have enclosed twenty dollars and agree to accept whatever comments you send me as full value for the twenty-dollar check.

Enclosed is an SASE. I look forward to hearing from you.

Sincerely yours,

When your correspondent replies and says: "Okay, I'll do it," send a short thank-you letter. Your original letter did the job, and you don't have to add anything.

If results from pretesting one or two chapters offer editorial benefits, you might want to continue with additional chapters.

You can parlay this experience to draw appreciative publishing attention to yourself. When submitting your manuscript to a publisher, you can enclose copies of your correspondence with the experts you consulted or give some quotes.

Not all nonfiction books are simple, how-to jobs. Many have an intellectual stature. Here, you have to submit the entire manuscript, because your book's viewpoint is equal in importance to the facts you present. And the person you select to review it should be more of a scholar, statesman, or social-science professor than a technical expert.

16

The price of $150 would remain the same for a book of 220 to 240 pages. If your book is 100 pages more, add $50. When your book is in an intellectual area, it's best to have three pretesters read the full manuscript. Your first pretester may have a bias or a residual loyalty that shades the judgment you will receive.

Then, in your own command post, after reviewing the remarks of each, you decide what to add, delete, or temper. By all means, get to the big people in your field, and find out what they have to say about your work. During the chore of editing one book, I sent a single chapter and a modest check to George Kennan, our former ambassador to Russia; Dr. Stephen F. Starr, head of the Russian American Institute; and Svetlana Alliluyeva, Stalin's daughter. In the domain of this particular chapter, these were the most knowledgeable people I could think of, and, although Alliluyeva bowed out, the responses of the other two were rewarding.

Will big people bother? I think so. It depends mostly on whether or not the material is up their alley.

You have two things working for you when you send nonfiction material to a professional. First, you show courtesy in recognizing the value of a professional's time and offering a modest check; and, second, you have entered the charmed circle of the professional man's main interest in life.

What if you have written a children's book and you happen to know a children's librarian? The kind that kids love because she knows the books they like? Will this librarian also know how to explain to you what she means by saying: "Your book needs more reader interest"? Can she tell you where this is needed, and offer alternate suggestions as to how you might go about getting it? If so, she's the reader you want. Fortunately, if you have actually written a juvenile, a bonanza awaits you. There's a monthly trade paper for librarians in charge of their juvenile department. It's called *The Horn Book*. In it, you'll find book reviews, articles, and letters from lively, knowledgeable, and sometimes feisty experts in this field. You can write them in care of *The Horn Book* (31 St. James Ave., Park Square Building, Boston, MA 02116). In some cases, the librarian's address is given. Few writers have such ready access to a wealth of first-class pretesters as does the juvenile writer.

Mostly, the pretesters you want to hire for fiction will come from the ranks of two kinds of people: book reviewers and creative-writing teachers.

Starting with book reviewers, which one should you choose? You'll find some good candidates in any major newspaper located in a cosmopolitan area or in high-quality national magazines that publish book reviews you enjoy. Select a reviewer whose literary opinions appeal to you, and try a letter of this nature:

Dear——:

I have enjoyed your reviews in _____ and because of this, I am writing to you. This month I completed a manuscript titled "_____," which I intend to offer to a book publisher.

Prior to doing this, I wish to pretest my book "_____" with some professional book reviewers whose columns I have read and enjoyed. What will I do with their suggestions, comments and conclusions? I can't answer that until I have read and studied them, but I believe the comments will be both sincere and helpful. My reasons for proceeding along these lines are simply that I don't want to go ahead on my own say-so. It's not that I am timid—you can't be timid and put two years of your life into a novel. Rather, I seek professional judgments before going further.

Would you be willing to review my book "_____"? If so, I will send it to you with my check for $150.00 on receipt of your "yes." To offer you some indication of the book, I have enclosed a three-page outline and the first chapter.

I'd like the work done in four weeks.

I want to learn whether, in your opinion, the book stacks up as something that many people would enjoy and be willing to recommend to their friends, or whether the better part of valor is to "stuff it." I would appreciate both general and specific comments. For example, if reader interest flags down, please tell me where, and, perhaps, make suggestions as to how it might be perked up. If you feel the plot is weak, you could tell me where and why. If my characters are one dimensional or not really credible, could you let me see this plainly with your eyes?

I agree in advance to accept your response to my manuscript as full value for the $150.00. I will pay in advance. Thank you for *your courtesy in reading this letter of inquiry. I look forward to hearing from you.*

Sincerely yours,

_____

P.S. If you want any personal data on me, please tell me and I will answer. My thinking is that my book must stand on its own merit.

The $150 is not going to make the reviewer say yes. A straightforward and sincere personality and being ready and willing to make and keep your part of the bargain are what you want to radiate. You want a letter that represents a clear-cut, one-time, business deal. Special pleading should be absent. If what you say in your letter makes the reviewer feel he can really help somebody, he will be more likely to comply.

Wait until you get your manuscript back with the response from the first reviewer before writing to the second. Again, you may receive some immediate editorial benefits from the first experience and want to make these changes before sending the manuscript on a second trip.

A payment of $150 is about right for a novel of 250 to 300 pages. If it goes to 400 pages, add $50.

Here's another source for pretesting a novel or an autobiography: Forty graduate schools offer a Master of Fine Arts degree in creative writing. The national secretary of Associated Writing Programs, Kathy Walton (Washington College, Chestertown, MD 21620), will send you the names of colleges in your state offering graduate degrees in creative writing and the names of the directors of the program. You want the program director to be your pretester, not the dean, as the latter might administer the entire arts program, but be short of experience in the area critical to you.

If your state is large and populous, you will probably have a choice of two or three nearby creative-writing programs and might care to visit the director in person. If you live in a less-populated state or if you want a wider choice, ask Miss Walton for her national list of directors of creative-writing programs. She is a generous and social person who has helped many writers and teachers of writing.

There are several ways to approach the person of your choice. Because faculty members come and go, ask the college switchboard operator whether the person you want is in residence and is currently the creative-writing-program director. Once you have the person's name confirmed, plus the fact that he is still teaching there, state your case in a letter. Here's one that almost worked. It was shown to me by a creative-writing director who pointed out its one drawback, which is easy enough to correct:

Dear———:

It was such a pleasure to type Athens on your envelope. The Homeric touch of the word still works its bit of magic for me.

My purpose in writing to you, Dr. L———, is to ask if you will review my latest novel, "Angelo, My Love," and for this help I offer you $150.

After leaving Ohio University, I did postgraduate work at Nova Scotia, where my aunt lived. I worked with Dr. ———. He said my writing "bristled with juvenilia."

Well, I am somewhat over that, having had two husbands, five babies, and lived with one man between the two marriages. From this, I should have learned a lot but I did not. While working in the Middle East, in Baluchistan, teaching English grammar to the children of oil engineers, I became interested in the Sufi philosophy. It offers an affirmative lifestyle. And practical. Practical in the sense that, as one becomes relatively nonmaterialistic, maturity starts to bloom.

I fell in love, really and truly, with a young colt of a girl—all of seventeen—and that, too, is behind me. But the patina of all this shows in "Angelo, My Love."

My oldest is now a high-school senior; my youngest is starting junior high. I sell real estate and support my family. People buying homes for eighty thousand dollars and up frightened and profited me.

What I would like you to do with my novel is this:

1. Read it.
2. Mark in the margins any code you want: like 1, 2, 3, 4, etc. And then in a letter give your comments as they refer to these numbers.

3. Include an overall criticism of the novel with reference to how it may be improved and where.

Would you be willing to help to this extent? My previous two novels have been rejected and on rereading them (years later), I agree with their critics.
I wish to know if my current novel is both readable and credible.
Please let me know if I may mail the novel and my check. I agree to accept whatever comments you send as full payment and will not "come back at you" with any ripostes.
Well, I have asked a lot. Thank you for considering it.

Sincerely yours,

———————————

The professor who showed me the above letter said he would have been better able to decide what to do, had the author enclosed one chapter and an outline of the novel. I asked why he felt this way.

"Well," he said, "we're a state university, and I don't want to accept $150 from a stranger whose manuscript could be more time consuming than I can handle. A chapter outline and one chapter would have told me more than the letter."

"Will you ask the author for this?"

"Well, maybe."

Enclosing an outline and one chapter with your letter may prevent a long pause in your communication with a pretester.

If you want to visit the program director in person, send a note asking permission to do this, stating why. It's possible to make a "cold call," and, if you do, take the complete manuscript and a chapter outline with you. The outline helps the teacher determine if your novel falls into an area of his competence and interest.

Talent scouts working for book publishers include some creative-writing graduate schools in their ports of call. As a result, it is not unlikely that the director of a graduate school of creative writing will be closer to understanding editorial requirements in the field of novels than the location of his college would indicate. There is one other special reason you might want to select the program director of a graduate school of creative writing. An experienced teacher whose students are working to establish themselves as writers is well equipped to communicate with you. The teacher's point of view will be different from that of a book-review editor, but it is usually a worthy one.

There's another good reason to pretest. If your book is accepted by a mainline royalty publisher, the choice is not yours as to whether the best editor in the shop will give it two weeks, one full month, or even two months of editorial time, but, while the book is still in your hands, *you* are the one who limits the reach for excellence. If you have the hots to get your script off to a publisher, if you "have had it up to here" and won't fool with your book anymore, your attitude is not dissimilar to that of the stranger, the mainline royalty publisher, who wants it in print and into the bookstores as fast as he can get it there or he wants it rejected, whichever is the quickest and seems most profitable.

All you ask of the pretester of your choice is that he spot a weakness and suggest some ways of repairing it.

This isn't too difficult for a pro.

You deserve to know what a couple of good pros think. Take a chance and go.

A list of contract editors who do editorial evaluating for mainline book publishers appears at the end of chapter 19.

3

The First Reader

THERE HE SITS, alone in a tiny office on the twenty-seventh floor. Facing him is a window that looks out on a court of high walls. He wonders about the grayish-white wall, twenty feet away, that is his view. Could he paint a scene on it? Ducks on a pond? No. How about the ladies of a sultan's court as they gather around their courtyard pool? . . .

"Found anything?"

The first reader turns in his chair to see his boss, one of the assistant editors.

"One cockroach. Dead."

"You can start a collection. Nothing else?"

"Not yet."

The assistant editor nods and keeps moving past the open door.

The first reader examines his fingernails. He picks up another manuscript and contents himself with the thought that this is how Ken McCormick started. And Jovanovich. And Jovanovich got so good that Harcourt took him in and put his name on the backbone of every book. What a way to go!

At age twenty-five, just out of college, where he received a master's degree in Modern American Lit., Raleigh, the first reader, was saved from going for a doctorate by answering an ad in *Publishers Weekly*. How long will he keep his job, he wonders, if he can't find something?

Each morning, some fifteen manuscripts arrive at his office from the shipping room. In a large, old-fashioned ledger, the first reader enters each manuscript's title, the day's date, and the name and address of the author. In the next column is space for the date returned. On this sun-dappled day in April, a dozen book manuscripts make a pile on his desk. On shelves around the office are two dozen manuscripts he wants to look at a second time, as well as a few long ones he doesn't want to return immediately, even though he knows they won't do. He remembers the story they told him about *Look Homeward Angel*. It came to the office in five typewriter boxes, with five hundred pages in each box. The editor read the first quarter-million words and then quit because nothing was happening. Later, when he met Max Perkins, the editor who "discovered" Thomas Wolfe, he asked when the script became interesting. "Just after the first quarter-million words," he answered. The first reader looked warily at the three long manuscripts, especially one that was stashed in three boxes.

"Don't let the stuff pile up," they keep telling him, "or you won't be able to get in or out. If it gets too much, take one home at night." He wonders, did they mean every night?

At this stage in his apprenticeship, only unsolicited book manuscripts come to the first reader. His company, however, also receives several complete book manuscripts daily from literary agents, along with a stream of queries from free-lance writers.

When the first reader was hired, Adam, the senior editor, explained the influx of editorial material. "Let's walk over to the mail desk," he said, "and see what we can learn."

At one end of a long sawbuck table, on which brown pads had been placed, a heavy-set, fast-working woman was sorting the mail—perhaps four hundred pieces of flat mail were in canvas mail sacks on the floor, just as they had arrived from the post office. She lifted a sack to the table and, starting to sort the mail, flipped envelopes into wire baskets that carried the names of people, or, in some cases, the names of departments. Bunner, the head of sales and publicity, stuck his head in the door and nodded at the mail clerk to give emphasis to his own private rule: "If my department's name is on the envelope, it's company mail and I see it first. We have no private mail here."

The credit manager was in and out of the mailroom every time he passed it on his way someplace else. "I've got some late babies," he said to Adam, "and I'm holding up their orders until they pay." He looked enviously at the unopened mail sacks on the floor, really wanting to up-end them and root around. Instead he asked the mail clerk, "If you spot an envelope from Markholm, will you call me?" The clerk nodded and looked at her watch. He'd be back in an hour.

Adam hoisted up one of the mail sacks. "Let's carry this over to a side table and look at the raw mail." What surprised the first reader most was the preponderance of business mail: orders and payments from dealers, wholesalers, libraries, and institutions; bills and correspondence from equipment suppliers, printers, and paper manufacturers; government forms and circulars offering trade-information data.

"Was this," Raleigh asked, "the way the mail sacks looked when you started here?"

"What's really changed is the editorial mail."

"How so?"

"Years ago, an author sat himself down and wrote a complete book. When it was finished, and it satisfied him, he sent it off to his agent or, sometimes, directly to a publisher. But today, authors expect a great deal of money for what they write, and they won't put one or two—let alone three—years into a book without some kind of favorable feedback. And by favorable feedback, they mean something they can eat. Agents show us bare outlines—without sample chapters—and ask for ten-thousand-dollar advances if the authors have a good track record or if they feel that a book is rolling with the tide. With a chapter outline and three sample chapters, their hands are out for twenty thousand dollars." Adam sighed. "Actually, that's the least of it. I've seen a zero added to these figures. It's chilling."

The first reader recognized who it was who got chilled and allowed his mind to dream up a vision of the agent phoning an author: "Big news, fella, big news. One hundred grand on that super outline you wrote." The first reader wondered if he were in the wrong end of the business.

Adam sat down at the mail table, put an elbow on it, and cupped his chin in his hand. "Talent is so short. Publishers bid fiercely against one another for books that aren't very good. We're bidding for the talent of semi-pros."

"What should book publishers do?" asked the first reader.

"I don't know. We hire first readers like you, and it's hard to justify their cost. There's so little that's rewarding in the slush pile. But it can come alive, too.

"Some publishers won't read it anymore. We do. If our name shines out to new writers, year after year, as a hospitable house, we may get their work first. If we close down on all unpublished, free-lance authors, we save the cost of reading unsolicited work, but we miss some winners. And it's the winners that carry you. You can't live on books that sell eight to ten thousand copies."

Adam kicked the mail sack. "There aren't enough good books written to supply book publishers with twenty thousand new titles a year. So what do we do?"

Adam answered his own question. "We publish the least bad and pay too much for what we get." He stopped short and looked at the first reader. "How does this make you feel?"

The first reader remembered a passage in *For Whom the Bell Tolls* in which young Robert Jordan slipped into the sleeping bag of Pablo, his mountaineer companion who had spent weeks in the same clothes, and, as Hemingway put it, "he got the full breath of Pablo." The first reader felt that, for the first time, he was getting the full breath of book publishing and said so.

"Talent," said Adam, "is expensive to buy. It's expensive to steal. We can't find enough of it. I mean a book that is well written and says something and is so satisfying that it pulls you into each succeeding page. What's true of us is true of every publisher. Too much money for a journeyman's work kills off the motivation to produce something fine. We know lots of our books aren't too good, and so we hype them with publicity and advertising."

"Would it be a good idea to start a small publishing company, issuing, say, three to six books a year, and pick only the best?"

"The best of what? Find me three titles that we can believe in strongly enough to back up with five or ten thousand dollars' advertising. Make that your assignment for the first six months here." Adam slapped the first reader lightly on the shoulder and turned to go into his own office.

The first reader stood looking at the heavy-set woman as she got down to the last mail sack. "Have you been here long?" he asked.

"Oh, yes. I worked for Mr. Sam, the publisher's father. I was the cleaning lady. They hired a janitorial company to do my work, and I've been sorting incoming mail for ten years and putting outgoing through the meter at night."

"Do you enjoy your job?"

"I enjoy payday."

The first reader walked back to his cubicle, his mind full of images of a world running short of literary talent, of hungry publishers, and of clever people who caused other people to want to buy a book.

He paused at the drinking fountain and looked at it. It wasn't that his job appeared so hard—it was just so different from what he expected on that first day. Returning to his office, he looked with renewed interest at the yellowed sheet of paper that had been tacked to the wall behind his chair by an unknown predecessor. At the top of the page, written with a grease pencil, a line read: "Who knows what lurks here?" At the bottom of the sheet another line read: "The first reader know." In between the two lines were the titles of unfortunate rejections made by various first readers.

The Family of Man	*Jonathan Livingston Seagull*
Up the Organization	*Ginger Man*
Day of the Jackal	*Lolita*
Lord of the Flies	*The Godfather*
84 Charing Cross Road	*Kon-Tiki*
The Diary of Anne Frank	*Topaz*
The Fodor Guidebooks	*The Peter Principle*

Underneath the list was a wry summary:

"Payment received by first readers for hours worked to reject above titles: sixty-two dollars and twelve cents."

A new head popped in the doorway. "Any happy news from home?"

"Yeah. Fellow just wrote and said if we bought his book he'd spend half the money to buy new bells for his church."

"What are you going to do?"

"Tell him it's the best offer I've had today and I'll have to consider it."

The head vanished down the hall, and the first reader turned back to his work. The easy banter of the editorial office sustains him, and he feels accepted when, after only four months on the job, people kid him on his failure to produce a winner. If they thought he was terrible, he knows darned well, they would either avoid him or pass by with a polite, touch-me-not smile. He has watched the vultures sit upon the doomed and knows, as long as they kid him, he is alive. Already, he thinks he has picked up a first reader's touch. Given a dozen book manuscripts, he can spend a half-hour with each and separate them into two piles, because

27

they are easy-ins and easy-outs and give him a feeling of having accomplished something when he carries a half-dozen book manuscripts down the hall to the shipping room.

The easy-ins, easy-outs have certain features he thinks he is beginning to sense. After unwrapping a novel, and before reading it, he checks the total number of pages, say four hundred, then cuts to where the first piece of action has to be going on. This usually means turning to pages 15 to 20, or 25 to 30, or 35 to 40. He looks for signs of dialogue, indications of action; he hopes to pick up some kind of feeling that flows off the page. He cuts again, this time to page 75, or 80 or 85, and looks for the same thing. A happily turned phrase quickly catches his eye, and he welcomes it. Two more cuts, and he has an inkling of whether the book is an easy-out or has to be read. If the former seems more likely, he goes at it at once. If the latter, he puts it aside to read the next morning. He does all his serious reading from nine till one, and, if he feels good, he reads again from two till three. The rest of the time he does his chores with what looked, at least at first glance, like easy-outs. Often he wants to write notes and explanatory letters, but they told him "correspondence breeds correspondence" and time costs money, and they spelled out what his job depends on. He has to discover talent.

No talent: pretty soon, a new first reader.

There was a light tap on his door, and Bertha, the mail sorter, offered a large yellow envelope. It contained copies of a chapter outline and two complete sample chapters along with the company's reply to the author and a note from Adam to him:

> *Raleigh:*
>
> We're going to start feeding you the company's position on general fiction. This won't be genre fiction: detective, Barbara-Cartland types, science fiction, but adult general fiction only.
>
> We want you to grasp our attitude so that pretty soon you can evaluate outlines and sample chapters of general-fiction books. For ten weeks, or so, we'll be sending you some outlines and sample chapters that we bought or rejected, or, sometimes, just encouraged, so you can run in step with our editorial position on general fiction. You'll also get our letters to these authors.
>
> In six weeks, I want you to write a one-page position paper for me in which you describe how the company evaluates the general fiction

we receive. I don't want a criticism. Just a report on the editorial attitude we have communicated to you. In one month, I'd like you to take all the material we will have sent you and discuss it with Jim. Show him where you agree or disagree with our decisions.

Perhaps you can take some of this work home with you to do. After you have discussed the reports with Jim, please see that all these duplicated book outlines and sample chapters from authors go to Bertha. She will shred it.

I do hope you will catch the spirit of what we are doing and, later, in your own way, extend and improve it.

Adam

The first reader, less overjoyed than he thought he would be, gave a short grunt. He clearly understood they wanted a statement describing the company's editorial position on general fiction.

Ha! What he really wanted to do was to take apart the nine general-fiction novels they had just published that were now sitting on his desk. "Forget-me books," he called them. A punch to the head but no follow-through. Important things left unresolved. Who was in charge of bringing the sweet, strong force of logic to these authors?

How smart of Adam to suggest he simply tell Jim what he thought instead of asking him to put it into writing. He realized he was saved from taking on the task of painting his peers into a corner.

In the window he saw his reflection. Coat off, shirt open, necktie slipped down, and a sober expression. Could he only find fault with a book, or could he help an author improve a manuscript? Well, letting him work with raw material, such as outlines and sample chapters, would show. He longed to leave his mark on every manuscript he worked on. He felt he was at the starting gate, the place everybody else broke from. "Please, God," he said softly, "please, baby, just one good manuscript." If only he could discover not one but two, and let each of his reports be glowing. Then let the company reject both, while he held fast to a carbon of his report. Then let someone else bring both out and have 'em sell a million each. Ha! Now his judgment would carry weight. After that, if he found something great, and wrote a big, strong "YES" report and the company published the book, the credit would go to him. Meanwhile, in the real world, if he found something, the credit would be divided. Most of it would go to the editor who handled the script, especially if there were heavy editing. He pursed his lips over a manuscript that failed to raise his pulse rate and decided to give it another twenty pages. After that, he skipped ahead to a later chapter and looked for action, dialogue, feeling. They all couldn't be bad. He began another script.

He blinked at page one. Good Lord. Who could this be? He looked at the name on the manuscript, recognizing nothing, and cut to page 20. It seemed immense and powerful and right away, too.

Well, well, he said, kneeling, you a mouthy chap if ye are a poor'n. He poked a finger at it as one might a tomato or a melon. Little woodsy colt, ain't ye? Looks like somebody meant for ye to stay in the woods, . . .

He cut again, and then again. His spine tingled; the hairs at the base of his neck lifted; his breath came short. Rising, he rushed out of his office into the larger cubicle of his boss, the assistant editor.

"Look what I just found," he said, almost in a whisper.

The assistant editor, who was responsible for hiring him (they were at school together), took the manuscript to read. After ten concentrated minutes, he scratched his head, shut his eyes, rocked a few minutes, and then turned to the last page, but looked up before he read it to say: "I think it ends about someone directing the blind." Then he found the last line and read it aloud: "Someone should tell a blind man before setting him out that way."

He looked at his friend and smiled in a worried, fatherly way. "Well, anyway, I'm glad you showed it to me first. I think it was called *Outer Dark*, and the same fellow who wrote it also wrote something about an orchard. Name of McCarthy. Cormac McCarthy."

"But why? Why does a person copy someone else's book? Type the whole damned thing and send it to us?"

"They just do it. No one knows why. You'll probably never see another. Ever hear of Heywood Broun? Wrote a syndicated column. Well, someone used to send his own novels to publishers but signed Broun's name and Broun's address. Broun wrote about it in his column. The guy stopped doing it. There are crazies in every field. You recognized talent. That's good. It has to give you confidence."

"New hope for the two-headed. That's me."

"Don't take it that way. Incidentally, buy the McCarthy novel and read it. I thought it as good a piece of writing as I ever came across. *The New Yorker* gave it a rave but the book was too macabre for some readers. Anyway, make yourself learn something from the incident. Read *Outer Dark*, and think about it. If you bought the book, how would you have promoted it? What would you have done to make it sell?"

The first reader went back to his den, shutting the door tightly. In editorial offices, a shut door means: *I am working.*

With the door shut, he opened one of the "possibles" and wondered when lightning would strike. At least, he would soon be getting book outlines and sample chapters. The afternoon light waned. Rubbing his eyes, he snapped on the desk light. The next manuscript he read had a letter enclosed that said this was a first novel and "wrote itself in seven weeks." There was one character that hooked him right off, but, by page 125, the character was gone from the book. There was a heavy sex scene he thought too physical; following was an eerie dream sequence. It was tingling, but, he asked himself, was it part of the story; what did it add? If he cut it, would the plot suffer? He began to wonder what he should do. The fellow could write. His second book would show up better. Considerable suspense rose up in the next-to-last chapter, and it kept mounting; then, in the last three pages, it resolved itself neatly and well. What on earth was the final chapter for?

There was a knock on the door, and the publisher entered. The first reader stood up.

"Yes, sir?"

"You're here a bit late. I hear you discovered a bit of plagiarism."

"Well, not exactly. I thought it was pretty swell. Jim saw it was a direct copy."

"But you knew it was good."

"I admit to that." The first reader laughed and looked rueful.

"What are you reading this late?"

"It's not much. But the fellow can write. I think his second book might be okay. Look, can I phone him to encourage? I'll phone over the weekend from my home when the rates are down. I'll pay for the call."

The publisher studied the first reader. Was he being put on? *Well, take it for its surface value.* "Ask Jim's judgment. If he agrees, call the author. Be polite. Don't say anything. Let him talk. You listen. Promise nothing. Ask to see the next book, if Jim agrees. Come and see me in a week, and tell me about your call and how you're doing. Our best people started right in your office. Frankly, we need a spring winner. I hope you find it."

The publisher left, and the first reader sat down to read the last chapter of his "find."

The math behind the first reader is as follows:

Starting salary: $7000 to $10,000, depending on the publishing company and its location

Expenses: Office space, typewriter, share of utilities: $1,200 annually

Incidentals: $100 annually

Social Security, pension, unemployment taxes: $650

Total: $10,500 average per year

Cost to locate two manuscripts (in the event two publishable scripts are found during one year): $5,250 each.

If these two manuscripts are published and average a sale of ten thousand copies each, the cost of the first reader is 52 cents per copy.

The first reader's job is a perilous one, and that's where you come in. If he finds nothing today, tomorrow, next week, next month, next season, and the season after next, and the manuscripts come in and the manuscripts go out, there will be a new first reader.

As the sign on the yellowed paper on the wall said, "The first reader know." He know damn well.

What puts the first reader on your side is not sympathy, not justice. Not even a good disposition. The fellow wants to get ahead. If you write well, and he discovers you, whether his firm publishes you or not, he is on his way. And he wants that as much as you want to be published. In the real world in which you and the first reader live, you can trust him to give your work attention.

Today, the traditional relationship of the first reader to the book-publishing industry has changed. The change came about as giant corporations, such as ABC, Mattel, RCA, and Xerox, bought large publishing companies and encouraged them to grow.

And grow they did. Today, one out of every fourteen book publishers issues one hundred or more titles a year. The large ones issue one thousand titles a year.

With this spectacular growth in the number of titles published by the large houses, the very nature of book publishing has changed. Up until the fifties, most of the large houses issued mainly serious general fiction and nonfiction, and fewer than a score published more than one book a week. But, to fill out a list of one hundred, two hundred, four hundred, or even five hundred titles a year, a publisher had to issue books in many fields. This often meant departmentalizing his business into sections devoted to gardening, art, reference, music, crafts, juveniles, religious, and so forth.

Religious books are no longer the province of two dozen firms like Abingdon and Zondervan. The newly merged houses invaded every genre. Today, instead of twenty-four publishers doing the bulk of religious-book publishing, there are 266 houses with religious imprints of their own.

Black history, nursing, anthropology and art were, at one time, the preserve of a handful of publishers who made a specialty of it. No more. Today, a publisher of two hundred titles separates his line into a dozen different departments, and general fiction and general nonfiction are a small part of the whole. This increased the market for book writers, but what did it do to the traditional position of the first reader? It demanded more knowledge of subject matter than most people possessed in order to pass judgment on books of widely ranging subjects. As a result, the job of first reader at many large publishing houses gave way to the genre editor, an editorial employee handling only mysteries, art, juveniles, religion, or the like. The genre editor read and passed judgment on the incoming scripts in his department. This effectively substituted the genre editor, or his assistant, for the first reader at many large houses.

Another reason developed that caused most large houses to discontinue using first readers. As big companies became bigger, their names appeared everywhere: in media book reviews, in TV book programs, in paid advertising, and in publicity stories written well enough to be treated as news. As a result, the general public (there are 100 million more of us now than there were sixty years ago, and more of us can read and write) began sending thousands of book manuscripts to the larger companies.

THE BOOK MARKET

Faced with a flood of semiliterate material, many publishers said: "We won't read unsolicited complete book manuscripts. Our pickings are too lean."

How, then, do you get your offering to the right person at the right publisher, large or small, with reasonable assurance that it will be read and considered for publication? The publishers have laid down the means to explore available unknown talent at less cost to them than by reading complete book manuscripts. The details of this appear in chapter 9.

Of today's 1,350 commercial book publishers, only one hundred are large. How about the other 1,250 publishers? That's a lot of publishers.

The most numerous single group consists of seven hundred small publishers who produce six thousand titles a year or from four to twenty each. The number of small publishers vastly increased in the seventies. We don't know why, but there they are: seven hundred strong—a genuine market for writers.

There is no problem in submitting your complete book manuscript to the small publisher, as all manuscripts go directly to the editor, especially at the houses that issue only four or five titles a year. They have only one editor. There's no other place your manuscript can go.

When a publisher's line widens to twenty or twenty-four titles a year, a procurement program is started for new talent. Solving the procurement problem, that is, getting more publishable manuscripts, is a matter of survival. The smaller publishers are located all around the country, but the literary agents who handle most of the salable work are located in New York or on the West Coast. They shoot for the high dollar, and "an out-of-town twenty-title publisher" rarely gets to see any work from the author whose agent wants a forty-thousand-dollar advance. This pushes the small publisher into a procurement program, and, very soon, manuscripts begin to come in.

At this point, a first reader is added. Of the seven hundred publishers who annually issue four to twenty titles, or perhaps a few more, seventy employ first readers. You may safely assume that an unsolicited, complete book manuscript sent to a small publisher will be read when it is literate and conforms reasonably to the subject matter this publisher is seeking. Just address your work to the editor of the company.

This leaves 550 companies who issue from twenty-five to ninety titles a year. These companies employ most of the four hundred first readers. As book-publishing companies go today, they are not large, although they average a sale of 650,000 books a year and an annual gross income, from books, back list, and rights, of $4 million. From their ranks will come the mergers of this decade as they buy up smaller houses and, in turn, are bought by larger corporations.

Many of the complete book manuscripts they receive go directly to a departmental (genre) editor, either as a result of previous correspondence or because the work comes from a literary agent whose offerings are accepted for reading by this house. However, any house issuing twenty-five to ninety titles a year receives a large number of unsolicited complete manuscripts. These go directly to the first reader. His job, like Raleigh's, is to find something the company will accept and publish at a profit, with enough left over to pay his keep.

4

The Administration Department
Runs the Show

RALEIGH, THE FIRST READER, walks briskly home, in the dusk of an early evening, considering his fortune after being invited by the publisher to come in for a chat the following Monday.

Behind Raleigh, an array of bustling talent produces fifty books a year, and, in the next few chapters, we shall see the whole of the team at work.

You may be thinking: Should I care about the whole team when I deal with one person? Most writers feel this way. The surprise comes when an author's expectations are based on what he thinks *should* happen. To understand reality, we will look at the five departments of a book-publishing house and observe the attitude of each department head. As you understand the attitude of each one, their combined activity takes on a direction you can anticipate, and which, in some cases, can counter to your advantage.

Of the five departments, administration runs the show. Heading it is the publisher, whose main occupation is to survive while towing his company behind him. He does this by seeing the whole picture, a vision obscured from most of his employees.

The publisher holds the hire-and-fire power, and control is vested in him. He passes this control to the other four department heads (editorial, production, rights, sales and publicity) through memos and conferences. The publisher's decision is final, but, up to a certain point, it is subject to rebuttal. Except on high-level matters, the publisher avoids operational details.

37

THE BOOK MARKET

The operational work is done by the four department heads and their staffs. In turning out fifty titles a year, there is a flood of daily decisions to be made. Should the press run of a new book be eight, ten, or fifteen thousand? If the run proves to be high, the unsold copies may have to be remaindered at 30 cents a copy, which is less than the cost of the paper in the book. If a six thousand press run turns out to be low, and another thousand copies could have been sold, it would be costly to go back to press for so few copies, and the sales are lost along with the author's royalties.

Should the high-producing salesman in the Northwest territory have his territory reduced so that he will be forced to call on the smaller accounts that he now skips? Or will he quit if this is done to him?

Which of two dust-jacket designs is best? One is in four colors on white paper; another is in black ink on light-pink paper and costs two thousand dollars less. Which would prove the better buy? Every hour of the day, each department runs on its own steam.

When publishing houses were smaller, the publisher earned his keep by being operational; that is, he was editor-in-chief, or sales manager, or buyer of all printing, and, sometimes, he was all three rolled into one. Today, the publisher of a large house neither edits, sells, nor buys. In fact, of the titles he publishes each year, he has never sat himself down and read fifteen of them all the way through. What does he do all day?

He does much more than he ever did before, but his job is of a different nature. Let's watch him work.

In a large and cheerful room, from which Muzak has been barred, two quilted yellow sofas grace a deep-green rug. Near the center of the room is a large, modern, fruitwood desk, and close by are a half-dozen straight chairs with lemon-yellow cane backs. On the walls are two regional watercolors: one of Cape Cod, one of Sea Island. There are also an amiable nude and a Utrillo. From the wide windows hang pale-green and bright-yellow drapes. One wall is covered with five bookshelves. They hold the publisher's titles for the past five years. A coffee table, in front of one of the sofas, holds a half-dozen magazines and a low brass bowl of calendulas.

On the publisher's desk is a large, flat, black book that lists every title issued by his company over the past five years. Sales for each title are posted weekly for this year's crop, and there is a new entry monthly for the titles of previous years. In the publisher's right-hand desk drawer, an accounting book itemizes the expenses charged to each of the five departments, by month, for this year and the past ten years, as well as the incomes of the sales and rights departments for the same period. Only these two departments have an income, and they have to carry their own expenses plus the expenses of the administrative, production, and editorial departments, which receive no income.

A scratch pad and a water glass full of pencils, along with a wire basket holding incoming mail, are to one side of the publisher's desk. A bulky computer printout, revealing the number of copies of each title on hand and the number of copies on order from the printer, sits to his right on the half-filled desk. A prehistoric fish fossil of rare beauty rests on top of the computer sheets. Suspended from a thin silver wire, close to one of the windows and near the ceiling, floats a dragon kite that moves softly, up and down, like a mobile.

Today, this early Monday morning, the senior editor enters the publisher's office to vent a deep-seated worry and offer a solution.

"We're not getting the good stuff," he says. "For our spring and autumn catalogues, we need more long balls to push up our average sale to twelve thousand. Thank God for the Ames and Hardy books. I expect a fifty thousand sale and a book-club selection for each.

"We're stacked with limited-interest books. They're solid. But they are not going to be popular. We're going to have a hard time moving seven thousand copies each on thirty of our fifty titles." The executive editor looks earnest and worried.

The publisher, facing a crisis in his office, makes it a point to be calm and even-tempered. When he blows up, it is at home. "You say 60 percent of our titles won't sell much over seven thousand copies each this year. That means they will barely break even—maybe even lose one or two thousand dollars each. Do you think half of these will keep selling— say four thousand copies over the next five years?"

"Good God, I hope so!" is the reply of the senior editor. "Yes. Over the next five years, twenty of these limited-interest books should sell another three to four thousand copies each. Easy."

The publisher picks up a scratch pad, and the senior editor is quiet while the publisher writes down numbers. At the worst, he figures, twenty titles will break even, and twenty others should make three to five thousand each. On the ten that will bomb, the company will lose seven thousand dollars each, or seventy thousand dollars. The Ames book that they all hope will sell fifty thousand this year should make that up. And if the Hardy book does as well, and they have one major book-club sale and one major paperback sale, they should end up with a low, six-figure number in the black. *Par*, he thinks, *par*.

The senior editor, clearly seeing his end of the picture, continues to state his case. "We need more popular mass books. I'd like to hire two talent scouts to criss-cross the country. Here's a folder on the cost and the names of two people who can do it."

The publisher agrees to read and consider the idea. They have tried it before. They'll probably try it again. It's a long haul hiring talent scouts, paying their salaries and expenses. The publisher reaches again for his scratch pad. He writes down $28,000 (for salaries of two talent scouts for one year) and then doubles it to $56,000. This larger figure now includes travel expense, office time in going over reports from two talent scouts, plus additional contracted editorial time in reading more manuscripts. Doing it for two years, he thinks, makes it times two, and the figure he writes down is $112,000. He adds $4,000 for the "extras" he left out, and his bottom figure is $116,000. He puts a circle around it and a line under the circle.

If he hired two talent scouts, could he get back that $116,000?

At a profit of one dollar a book, 116,000 books would have to be sold to pay for the talent scouts. But if the profit were $1.50 per book, only 80,000 books need to be sold to break even. That $1.50 profit per book, however, is hinged on a book of 300 pages or less, and a retail price of $9.95 or more. At that rate, if four books are brought in by the two talent scouts, and each one sells 20,000 copies, the venture would be a tie ballgame. Except they would probably have the right of first refusal on the next two or three books their authors wrote.

But, continues the publisher as he thinks the problem out, *who wants to gamble $116,000 to break even? Sure*, he ruminates, *I'll risk $116,000 to make a half-million, before taxes, but I won't risk it to break even— and that's what we'll be doing if we find four books that move twenty thousand each. But what if we find nothing? Or, what if we find losers?* He looks up at the dragon kite turning slowly on its axis in the light ceiling breeze of the air conditioner and wonders how much unhitched talent is out there.

His one experience with talent scouts showed that talented new writers needed considerable coaching, encouragement, and personal conferences. Yes, you can bring them along, but, when an editor's time and supportive costs are one hundred dollars a day, who can put three hundred hours of editorial time into developing a writer and still come out right? As for already-completed manuscripts that need only to be discovered and brought back to the office—the publisher shook his head ever so slightly.

He put down, unread, the folder from the senior editor, then opened it to glance at the cost estimate for two talent scouts for two years. "The cost," wrote the executive editor, "is $78,000 for two people, two years."

He liked Adam, his senior editor. Adam always gave credit to his staff and asked for raises for them first, even before himself, and he rarely turned down a book that then did really well someplace else. *But,* he wondered, *how do you teach those guys numbers?*

Sitting quietly, alone at his desk, the publisher looked like a man bemused with life. He opened his desk drawer and took out the ledger that contained an itemized account of the expenses of each department. He regarded the figures coolly and evenly. This was what he did best. This was what he enjoyed doing. He knows retail book prices are too high. He knows fewer books are being sold. He is not a rebel, nor a revolutionary. He aims to make do with what he has. He picks up a soft lead pencil. This is his scalpel, and, although no blood flows, he both heals and performs surgery each day in his office.

Sensing someone's presence, the publisher looked up. At the doorway stood the first reader.

The publisher waved, and the fat-cheeked boy in jeans bounded in. *He doesn't dress,* thought the publisher.

"Tell me," said the publisher, nodding agreeably, "what have they told you up to now about the book-publishing business?"

The first reader was taken aback. He expected to be asked about himself, and, for that, he was prepared. But not for this. "Well," he said, "Jim—who's helped me most—keeps reminding me in case I forget. I've been told our profit comes from the back list and from the sales of rights."

"You know what these things are?"

"I think so."

THE BOOK MARKET

"Our back-list titles are the ones we've already published that are still in print. We keep a title in print as long as it sells over five hundred copies a year. Back-list titles are profitable to sell, because most of our expenses have been written off. All the fixed costs, like composition, plates, and editorial time, have already been paid for. It costs less to sell these books than it costs to sell our brand-new titles, because we do very little to advertise them."

"How many back-list titles do we sell a year?"

"For today, consider that privileged information. In time, you'll see the figures."

These people come and go, the publisher reminded himself, *and anything you tell them is like putting it on a horn. Yet, if you don't tell them, they sink, because they have no foundation.* "We have a catalogue—a separate catalogue—with all our back-list titles; about 250."

"Gee! If we sell one thousand copies of each, that's a quarter-million books."

The publisher relished the way his first reader put his finger on the button but offered no indication as to whether the figure was correct. Instead, he continued: "Rights' money is paid to us for the use of our author's book by a movie, TV show, paperback, or book club. We and the author share in the rights. Without a few good rights' sales a year, most of us in the business would take a bath."

"Then one of the things we look for in a book is whether or not it has book-club or paperback rights we can sell?"

"Yes. But you can't preguess it. You buy the best book you get to see. Unfortunately, there's not too much good stuff around. Think of these octopus houses that issue four hundred titles a year. That's eight times our speed. What they turn out are run-of-the-mill books, not great— often not even good. How do you think our company makes out, profitwise, on the fifty titles we publish each year?"

"I hear we break even. . . ."

"How do you feel about that?"

"It's better than losing—"

The publisher shook his head.

"Breaking even *is* losing, because it doesn't give you a cash reserve to start something new. Breaking even won't give you inner strength to go on after two disastrous seasons. Any ideas of your own for something new?"

The eyes of the first reader widened, and he breathed deeply. He felt as if he were on a train that was going faster than he was.

"No, not yet."

"Know what annuals and directories are?"

"I think so."

"Look at Bowker. If all Bowker had was *Publishers Weekly*, they'd be up on a stilt nailed to a pole. But they have a flock of annuals and directories. Look, I'll be away next Monday, but I'll be back the Monday after. Get a copy of the Bowker annuals. We have most of them here. No need to buy any. The public library will have any we don't have. I'd be interested in your opinion on each. Why are they properties? What do they have in common?"

The first reader knew he was out of his depth, but his eyes shone. "Are we going to issue an annual?"

"We're publishers. Books are our business. Directories and annuals are books. I have nothing for or against them except that a good annual that builds itself both editorially and in circulation every year is like owning a government bond whose yield is constantly going up."

Inspiration touched the first reader. "You mean like Bowker's *Literary Market Place*. Their price almost always goes up each year. And they carry more advertising. And each year they have a wider frame of contents. . . ."

"Ever hear of *Billboard*?"

"Yes, sir. It's a weekly."

"My dad, Mr. Sam, called it a 'poppa-mamma weekly.'" The publisher smiled. "You see, *Billboard* has had all kinds of offspring. Spinoffs from regular departments in *Billboard*. Some of these became magazines; some are annuals. Magazines do this all the time. Ever hear of *Cartoonist's Market*?"

"No," reluctantly.

"It was a popular department in a writer's magazine. Then a fellow named Dick Rosenthal turned this monthly department into an annual pamphlet of forty pages and got two dollars for it. I doubt if he sold two thousand a year. Well, one year, he dropped the word 'Cartoonist's' from his title and used 'Artist's' instead. Today, his directory, *Artist's Market*, lists all the paying markets for artwork, along with their addresses, what they buy, how much they pay. They list two thousand markets like greeting-card manufacturers, calendar houses, galleries—forty different categories like that.

"But he didn't stop there. He published another directory for craft workers. For sculptors, potters, quilters, tie dyers, people who do découpage—my wife does découpage. She brought home this market guide for craft workers. Must be four hundred pages and sells for over ten dollars, I think. Every magazine publisher in these two fields must be kicking himself. They spent a lifetime overlooking two naturals. I'll bet these two annuals are each going to sell over fifty thousand copies a year. At ten dollars a copy, that's one million dollars. That's the kind of thinking we want here."

"Yes, sir!" The first reader thought he should have come up with a reply that showed some class.

"Think about what I told you. But don't slough off on your first reading work."

"Look!" The publisher pointed to the wall of books. "There's the two hundred fifty books we published in the last five years. And we're asking you to read stuff from which only one in a hundred is as good as these. That's a tough job. And that's what you're paid for. We need you to discover a couple of good sellers written by productive authors. But keep your eyes open and think. People here break their butts to publish fifty new titles a year, and, on most of them, there's darn little continuity. Maybe one in four makes our back list. But on an annual . . ." The publisher's eyes glistened. ". . . What you have is yours. And it's yours every year. The annual never goes out of style, because at the end of the year you have an updated issue all ready to sell. See me in two weeks, and tell me your impressions of the Bowker and *Billboard* annuals." The publisher paused. He thought he had talked too much. "What do you want to be—a first reader all your life?"

"No, sir." The first reader's eyes glazed. "I would like to be a publisher."

A euphoric draft, rising out of nowhere, lifted the first reader out of the publisher's office and set him down in his own. He shut the door and leaned against it. *My God*, he thought, *I'm still here.*

Later that day, in the cool of an early-April evening, the publisher strolled home, taking long, easy strides. He was glad they had finally moved in from Long Island and the two-mile walk morning and evening was a nice change. The several trees in sight were greening up, and the shop windows showed bright dresses in all the pastels of spring.

He passed the Doubleday bookstore. *The bastards,* he thought, *twenty-eight stores, all their own. Twenty-eight stores to push their titles.* Wouldn't it be nice if he had fifteen of his own? He thought about the Walden chain. *Five hundred stores. Wow! If you owned a chain like that, you could push every book you had. There must be ten small book chains around the country.* Could he buy three of them, string them together, and have strong, captive outlets for his own books? Or do it the other way? Sell his company to one of the two great bookstore chains? But why should they buy? What did he have to offer? He sighed. Too few winners was what he had to offer. Ames and Hardy and nothing else.

A boy and girl, arm in arm, passed by, and the boy smiled as he glanced at them. He thought of the first reader. *The poor dumb son-of-a-bitch. Hidden away in a little office, reading crap all day, fighting to find something that sings—hell, fighting to find something literate! And entertaining.* And when he did find something, he would be overly grateful to the author. Forever, probably, if it turned out to be a winner.

Should he take a boy like that and bring him into the administrative department before he got all tangled up in operations? The kid was bright, maybe, but so removed from publishing. He shook his head slowly. They teach dentistry. They teach law. They teach astrophysics, but who teaches anyone to be a book publisher?

He wished he had someone he could talk to in confidence and without reserve. Someone who would listen and hear him out, instead of just listening in order to feed off him. *They're all seconds,* he thinks, and wonders if he is, too. He remembers the day his father sent him to hand-deliver a book to the editor of the *Times Book Review.* He found the right office and stood in the doorway waiting to be asked in. The *Times* editor was working behind a littered desk and engrossed in a piece of copy. He looked up and saw the young man, "We don't need anybody. Sorry." The young man backed out, found a trashcan, and dropped the book in. He replayed the scene in his mind and thought what he might have said.

Approaching a wine store, he slowed his step. Yes, today was Monday, and that was the day his wife often served oysters on the half-shell, with dry champagne, in her sitting room. A bottle of Taitinger in the window turned him around. *No, he thought, that would be a present for me.*

He crossed the street and entered a flower store, the window of which carried a hand-lettered sign: "Fresh Violets." The shop girl picked up a bunch. "The dew's still on them." He noticed a can of mist spray in the flower case and smiled.

"I'll take two bunches," he said. His wife liked things in pairs.

Physically, the administrative department is relatively small, this one employing nine people. Next in rank after the publisher is the executive director of sales and editorial. Then come the comptroller, two secretaries, two bookkeepers, one payroll clerk, and a receptionist.

The executive director of sales and editorial controls these departments and is the liaison between them. He confers with the publisher several times a week, and in every case approves major royalty advances and major sales-promotion budgets. The latter follows in the wake of a large royalty advance. When a publisher pays twenty-five thousand dollars' advance royalty, he needs a sale of twenty thousand copies "to come out." So, once a five-figure advance royalty is paid to the author, the publisher is pushed into extra publicity and advertising for that book.

Before a contract for a book is mailed to the author or to his literary agent, the executive director of the sales and editorial departments sits in conference with the senior editor in charge of the book, along with the sales manager and the publicity chief. Often the executive director accepts the judgment of the senior editor on the editorial value of the book, and the meeting deals mostly with the proposed retail price, press run, and a first-draft marketing and publicity plan.

Sometimes the only person at the meeting who has read the entire manuscript is the senior editor. But they have all seen a *précis* of it, and at the meeting, the senior editor answers questions about the book. "Adam, our last two cookbooks bombed. Why did you buy this one?" Adam explains why he bought it: "There are only two books in print telling how to make hors d'oeuvres. They are both doing well, and each has come out with a revised edition. Our job isn't a cookbook—it's for hors d'oeuvres only."

Duplicate copies of the manuscript are available at the meeting, and, generally, one person will take a copy home to read, because the subject matter interests him or he wants to learn more about the book to help build a better marketing plan.

In the middle of this particular Monday morning, such a meeting is in progress. The publisher sees the group in the conference room and stands by the door, nodding to all and listening. They like him to pay attention.

"This next book," says the senior editor, holding up the manuscript, "is a somewhat erotic modern novel about social values. Three couples, who have never met before and have nothing in common, meet by accident at the zoo, where they are watching a caged chimpanzee painting a canvas. The three couples become socially entangled with one another after the chance meeting."

"How dirty is it?" asks the publicity chief.

"It could be too much for a major book club but not for stores."

"Sounds interesting," says the publisher. "I'd like to hear more about it later." He walks to his office, closes the door, picks up a pencil and a large scratch pad and decides to write down, this Monday, before noon, his immediate business problems. He starts with the figure "1":

1. Would it be better to cut the list to forty and publish only the better books? Which books are the better books?

He doesn't know. Nobody knows. He starts over.

1. Should we use more advertising?

His lifelong belief, taught to him by his father, is that no media advertising can profitably sell copies of a book that isn't moving of its own accord and that when advertising is put behind a book that is already moving nicely, it will push up the sales but not always at a profitable pace. "Word-of-mouth advertising does it," is the motto. At this critical moment, his hunch is to hire the best publicity person he can get.

He walks over to the coffee table and picks up a copy of *Literary Market Place* and starts going through the alphabetical list of entries of each publisher. He is looking to see how many publicity heads have made it to vice-president. That title, he knows, means they are not only good enough for thirty thousand a year but for stock options and status, too. He starts to list the ones who still hold down their operational jobs but are now on the administrative level.

The pages of *LMP* talk to him, and he listens and records the facts. No one who ever ran his publicity department could ever have made it to the administrative level. *That's where we're dragging our feet*, he thinks.

He goes back to his desk and starts to write again:

Which comes first: the kind of books that a publicity person can best publicize, or the publicity person who can do the job better than anyone else?

He underlines the question he just asked and thinks about his situation. He is the one who believes publicity sells books best, but his own publicity head is a second. If they had the number-one publicity person in town, the editorial staff would be alert to a book that would lend itself to being hyped with publicity.

He starts to figure costs. A replacement publicity head who was tops in the city would cost $15,000 a year more in salary, maybe $20,000 more. Add another $10,000 for more travel, more press parties. Maybe an assistant to spin out a flock of publicity releases. He amends his thinking. The right person doesn't send out a flock of duplicate releases. The right person believes in using individual stories, like rifle shots, a dozen times a day. He adds $14,000 for the assistant and puts the figures together. Upwards of $40,000 additional money would have to be spent to do the best possible job. Would that sell 80,000 more books? He doubts it. Could they hype 15 titles and sell 4,000 more of each? That would be 60,000 more books. Selling 60,000 more books would easily be worth the extra $40,000 for a top publicity staff. And well-aimed publicity adds a few thousand dollars to the prices they could ask for rights.

Making up his mind to act, he calls in the executive director to give him the assignment of writing a help-wanted ad for *Publishers Weekly*.

"Let's use a full-page ad," says the executive director, "and give the ad dignity. That way, even if we use a box number, anyone who sees it knows it has to come from a responsible company. We've been behind on publicity for a long time. I like your idea."

"A page costs twelve hundred and fifty bucks," says the publisher.

"I know. And I suggest we run the same thing in the *Times Book Review* this Sunday."

They call in the comptroller to tell him what they are about to do. "We're going to catch it," says the publisher.

The comptroller comes into the office and looks at the dragon kite floating lazily near the ceiling by the window. "I dreamt about that damn thing last night," he says. They tell him the plan. He sits down and looks soberly at the two men before him. "This is a nickel-and-dime business," he says, "and, when you spend a nickel one place, you gotta save a dime someplace else.

"We can close down our floor by nine hundred square feet by making that barn of a reception room smaller and then renting space to an architect or accountant. They don't bother nobody. We can let one secretary go and the payroll clerk. That saves eighteen thousand dollars a year and we bring in six thousand dollars in rent. That puts us twenty-four thousand dollars a year ahead.

"I'm not against the publicity idea. I just want to pay for it first. We sell six hundred thousand books a year right now. If we could save two cents a book by reducing costs, that's twelve thousand dollars saved. Put the two together and we save thirty-six thousand dollars; that's 90 percent of what you need for your new publicity chief."

Each night the comptroller tells his wife: "No one cares about money in that place except me."

The publisher knows that a hard man with a dollar is his best friend and he holds tightly onto his comptroller, but he wishes he had gone to a better school.

"Alvin," he says, "thank you. I am going to think it over."

The comptroller leaves, and the publisher tells the executive director to prepare a full-page ad for *Publishers Weekly*.

That afternoon, the publisher, remembering the words of the comptroller, goes into the office of the production department. "Chuck," he says, "what are the things we could do to save a nickel on every book we print?"

Chuck grins. "There are twenty things you can do to save a nickel a book, and fifty to spend a dime more."

"Review me a few, Chuck."

"As you know, we can use lighter-weight paper. That saves us two ways; first, there's less postage, and, second, the paper costs less. Then we can use a slightly smaller type size to get more words to the page. . . ."

"Well, can you write a rundown of all the things we can do to save a nickel a book, and tell me which you recommend?" The publisher paused, "And all the things we can do to spend a dime more, and which you recommend?"

"I don't mind doing that. Actually it's a good thing to do."
"Thank you, Chuck. Can you get it to me by Friday, please?"

The publisher retires to his office, closes the door, lifts a handful of his most recent titles from the bookshelves and begins to examine the production side of each one critically. In his mind four ideas circle about: (1) Was the comptroller right? Should he first save the forty thousand dollars needed before adding the number-one publicity head to his staff? (2) If he did save 2 cents a book on production, would it cheapen his books to the point where the public would notice it? (3) Either way, if his company were going to grow, didn't they need the best possible person to head up publicity? (4) What to do?

The truth is the publisher had no one but himself to answer the last question.

5

The Editorial Department

THE EDITORIAL DEPARTMENT was getting ready to hold its first-Tuesday-of-the-month meeting, and Adam, the senior editor, with Helen, the executive editor, were bringing in chairs and brewing coffee. A secretary buzzed the operator to hold all calls.

Three other editors strolled in along with Frederix, the director of sales and editorial. His secretary sat at his right to make notes of the meeting. After they were typed and the asides deleted, Frederix sent copies to each editor. Circled in red were new or amended deadlines. In this small shop, each person knew what was on tap, who was late, and who kept his work up. Conference notes were Frederix's method of control. Knowing the schedule of all editorial work, he tried to bring every book along on time. After yesterday's production meeting with Chuck, he was hoping to "gang-up" four books that could be printed and bound as part of the same operation. Although the books would have a physical sameness, he planned to select titles from different fields: religious, science, fiction, and gardening. "Who will ever know?" he asked. In private conversation with Adam, Helen said, "We're being chain-stepped."

Frederix was the hardest-working man in the shop; he was deeply into the operations of all sales and editorial work. It left him, he complained to his wife, with no time to read the books being prepared for publication, no time ever for editing, which he loved, and "damn near no time to think." He was a compulsive worker, always on the job early and never sick. He brought home the manuscripts of all books for which a twenty-thousand-dollars' royalty advance or more was recommended.

Just before the meeting, Jim, the junior editor, approached him.

"Could we ask Raleigh, the first reader, to this meeting? He's been to two of them, and he's working on an idea for something new."

"I never heard him open his mouth," said Frederix. "Bring him in."

Frederix opened the meeting.

"Let's see—our last-month's notes show we have thirty books at work for our winter catalogue, fifteen for next spring, and ten for winter, a year from now. The whole thing is: How much are we off schedule? Who wants to go first?"

One by one, the editors reported on the books to which they had been assigned, and, as they did so, the vagaries of the human condition promptly surfaced. Mrs. Clark, an author who had signed up to do a book with the working title "What Standards Are Your Marriage Based On?" was into a divorce and "couldn't sleep, couldn't think, couldn't write." Her book would have to be postponed. Dr. Waldvogel had second thoughts about doing a book on how liver surgeons wronged both the liver and their patients and returned his advance-royalty check. Mr. Ahlbrant had gone to India to see his guru and hadn't returned his royalty advance but promised to do his novel "soon."

"Only three poop-outs out of forty-five," said Helen. "That's good."

One editor was enthusiastic about a new chapter he had just received and asked permission to read it. "Well," said Adam, "I'd like to hear it, but we've got forty-five books to report on. Could you make a Xerox, and let us all see it instead, please?"

The author of "Oil Substitutes for the Eighties" had secured a fine foreword from Washington's new energy czar. Two books were lifted off the production schedule, because the chapters, as they arrived, needed too much editorial time. "We can't put those hours into any one book. Tell each of these authors we'll let him know more after the work is completed. Ease them off; don't break them off, and maybe the work will improve."

There were no catastrophes, no threats to break contracts, no impending washouts on big books for which heavy advances had been paid.

Two hours had passed, and the chairs of a few editors started to scrape the floor as they began to stretch to get up.

"Just a second," said Frederix. "Anybody know any new writers?"

Six pairs of eyes turned to the first reader. He looked down and shook his head slowly. "I haven't found something yet that I believe in. I keep hoping. . . ."

"Raleigh, have you any ideas for a book we can do?" It was Jim, the junior editor, prompting his friend.

The first reader took a gulp of air and raised his eyes to look at everyone.

"Yeah, I do."

"Good. Speak up."

The first reader felt his stomach freeze.

"I told my idea to Jim. Maybe he'll tell you about it. . . ."

Jim picked it up. "Raleigh and I have been kicking around an idea for an annual."

"An annual?" asked the editorial and sales director. "You mean something we'd do in house?"

"Who would do it?" asked Adam, the senior editor.

"You," said Helen. The laughter subsided, and Jim went on.

"It's a simple idea. The title is 'No Additives,' and the subtitle is 'Four Thousand Nationally Distributed Foods That Contain Nothing Artificial.'"

"Ho!" said Frederix. "Are there really four thousand? How did we find that out?"

"I'll come to that," said Jim. "Chuck set up two pages for me. Both pages deal with bread."

"What do you tell about the breads you select?" asked Helen.

"We give the name of the bread, its weight per loaf, price, ingredients, name of manufacturer, and how to order by writing to one of the manufacturer's national distributors. Our bread category begins with a loaf that contains 100 percent stone-ground whole wheat flour, unbleached wheat flour, raisin syrup, yeast, salt, unprocessed miller's bran, pure butter, soy oil, and wheat germ. No preservatives or artificial colorings added."

"Preservatives like what?"

"BHA, BHT, artificial colors, synthetic leavenings, hydrogenated shortenings, analogue flavors. There are about two thousand additives, artificial colorings, and extenders in use."

"Will you tell how harmful certain additives are?"

"No. Not a word. This is a straight-faced, positive publication. No special pleading. Just the facts, written in an even-tempered way without arguments as to what happens if you eat nitrates, sulphur, or the like."

"How many categories—like bread—will be in your book?"

"Sixty. The categories include crackers, dried fruits, soups, cooking oil. . . ."

"What do you say about crackers?"

"One company lists these ingredients on their box label: whole wheat flour, cracked wheat, safflower oil, sea salt, yeast. Another cracker, however, contains sodium acid, monocalcium phosphate, artificial coloring, and hydrolyzed vegetable protein."

"You wouldn't list that last one? You'd list only those with no additives? Name, price, weight, ingredients, and where to buy it?"

"Right."

"Jim, do you have a budget?" Frederix asked.

"No. I just had these two pages set after Raleigh put them together."

"Where would you sell it?"

"Bookstores, health-food stores, gourmet shops. Paperback rights should bring big-time money. And it's a book-club book, too, I think. At least an alternate selection."

"But," said the senior editor, "no one here has the time or experience to do it in house. Even now, we contract some books out for editing. We'd have to hire a typist, a secretary, and an editor. That's thirty thousand dollars. If you figure ten listings to a page for sixty categories, like bread, crackers, soups, and you have thirty-five hundred listings, you're into a 350-page book. To get thirty-five hundred actual listings, you'll have to mail ten thousand food companies several times. They don't answer form mail any more than we do. That's twenty thousand letters. You'll spend 50 cents a letter by the time the real costs are figured. Add ten thousand to the thirty for the staff, and you're up to forty grand. On a ten-thousand press, that's four dollars a book just for staff and research. Are we crazy?"

The first reader spoke up. "I wasn't thinking in terms of a ten-thousand press but of one hundred thousand. The editorial costs are then only 40 cents a book."

"An initial press of one hundred thousand!" They looked at him.

"This is a multimillion market."

"It just might be," said the senior editor. "But I'll tell you this, we all have our straws in the same ice cream soda. We all experience the same news, the same movies, the same broadcasts, wherever we live. I'll wager that six other publishers are considering this same idea right now. And one of them may be experienced in publishing annuals. For all we know, a book just like this is already on somebody's production sheet."

Raleigh surprised himself and stood up. "Look," he said, "we have a new idea. Why throw it away because someone else in another shop might be thinking about it? We're as good as they are. Let's be the first. May I get together one complete category? You name it."

Helen clapped her hands sharply. "We're not going to dummy up even one category without a cost rundown. I want to see a hard-line budget. And, as for starting off with a one-hundred press, that's foolishness."

"The time for this book," Raleigh said, "is now."

The room was quiet. The simple statement in timing caught them all where they lived.

"It would be two years to get this show on the road," Adam said slowly, "with our lack of experience in annuals. And, if anybody else is on it, they'll be on the streets in maybe nine months and freeze us dead. We have to assume someone else has it." He paused. "It's not a bad idea at all."

"Have you done any market research?" Frederix asked Jim.

"The only market research that matters," said Helen, "is when our travelers take jackets around and ask for orders."

"You're right, of course," said Jim, "but an annual has something special going for it. If we sell only twenty thousand the first year, and during the next ten years we produce a better book each year, we'll be selling two hundred thousand copies a year ten years from today. Have we ever had a title that grew larger each year? All of ours come and go."

"I know a publishing shop isn't a democracy," said Raleigh, "but could we take a vote just to . . ."

"No," said Frederix, a little more sharply than he wanted to. He paused and thought he'd given the first reader a little more line. "Raleigh," he said, "for a minute, let's put 'No Additives' aside. I'm very pleased you came up with an idea. Sometimes these things come in pairs. Do you have anything else in mind?"

The first reader wasn't sure whether he was being put on or not, but he zoomed ahead. "Yes, I have a second idea, and it's a very simple one."

"That's what I was afraid of," said Helen. There was laughter, and Raleigh grinned.

"Do any of you remember *Ginger Man*? My idea is to reissue a book with a strong central character and add thirty full-page photographic illustrations that are both literal and true to the spirit of the book, and, whenever possible, done with the author's cooperation."

"That's three royalties," said Helen. "One for the use of the text, one for the author to help do a shooting script, and one for the photographer."

"What's your market?" asked Frederix.

"Mainly, it's the people who discover the book for themselves and find the photographs attractive, honest, real, intriguing. . . ."

"Pix like that will cost five hundred dollars a day to shoot, plus expenses," said Adam.

Raleigh continued. "I figure maybe one illustration every ten to twenty pages; about thirty full-page illustrations to a book, plus, of course, the full text, and some captions taken right out of the text."

"I disagree," said Adam. "Captions should not repeat something the reader has already read. The caption should be a plus."

"I wonder why no one ever tried this idea before," said Helen.

"Raleigh's just started," said the secretary softly.

"When I was at school," said Layton, the science editor, "*Ginger Man* was as close to me as my skin. I must have read it five times. Last week, at Kroch's, I saw *Ginger Man* on a rack and asked a clerk about it. He said it was alive and well. It made me feel good to know that."

"It's just the kind of book I would want to illustrate with honesty," said Raleigh, "but I don't see how we can. To do *Ginger Man* right means photographing it in Ireland with Irish locale and Irish people. . . ."

"That's two thousand a week for six weeks, plus another two thousand over and above royalty to Donleavy for picture supervision. That puts us in the soup for fourteen, call it fifteen, thousand, above all other costs," said Frederix. "The only way to come out on this is to publish it first in hardcover with our getting 50 percent from the paperback rights to the illustrated edition."

"If we do it," said Adam, "I would not want to dump on the book. Did you see the paperback of *Rose Garden*? They used the full text, and then, in the middle of the book, they inserted about eight pages of stills from the movie. The pictures are small and, to me, add no dimension to make the characters come alive."

"Shooting in Ireland could be fun," added Helen. "I was there three months and I loved it. But you'd want a pickup cast, a great photographer—someone like Joe Monroe, Helen Levitt, Esther Bubley—plenty of time, plus the author himself to help supervise the photographs. The pictures have to be appropriate to the book, but not dated."

"What do you say," asked Jim, "if we all consider this idea, and those of us who want to can come up with books that will lend themselves to photographic illustrations at our next meeting?"

"Okay," said Frederix. "Let's break, and, on the fourteenth, when we meet to consider new books, let me see any comments you people have on these two ideas: the 'No Additive' thing and the photo-illustrated novel."

"I'm hungry," said Adam.

"Hey, just a minute," said Helen. "I've got a list, and I want to give everyone a copy."

"What's this? A menu?"

"Not yet," said Helen. "What I tried to do here was give us some sort of standard to go by when we bring up new fiction on the fourteenth. I did these with Ada. I know all of us in this room live by our tastes. The standards on this list are no substitute for that, but they can help us evaluate a manuscript. Many of these items are familiar to you, but sometimes we forget a few."

"The list is short. Adam, will you read it please?"

The editors, all quick readers, each ran an eye down the page, and several nodded appreciatively.

"Hmm," said Adam, "here they are."

1. Is it dated? Specifically where, how often, and how badly?
2. Where does interest lag? Can it be picked up? How?
3. What's resolved? How important is the resolution to the reader?
4. What's the best thing about this book: style, plot, message, humor, eroticism, cheerful attitude, intellectuality, blueprint to whatever? Does it leave you feeling good? Was reading it

worthwhile, or did you get through it as part of your job? Does it shed any fresh light on the human condition? What is its strong suit?

5. Should it be cut? Where?
6. Does it need adds? Where? Why?
7. How many hours of editing will it take? Who should be assigned to it? Can we strengthen it in some significant way without putting too much time into it?
8. How bad is the title?
9. Seriously, what chapter can we lop off? The first one?
10. Where does the book change your pulse rate? Often? What would you remember about this book six months from now?
11. On a scale of one to ten, how do you rate this book in the field it enters—judged against books published in the past five years?
12. In what ways is this a marginal book for us? That is, can we find something in print and all ready to go—and use it instead?

"That's it," said Adam.

The group broke up, and instantly the phones of several editors started ringing as the calls came through again.

"Well," said Jim, punching Raleigh's forearm, as they walked away, "when you stir things up like that, you'll have one or two people with you and that many more against you. I sure hope you uncover something good in the un-rush mail to show you are doing the job you're paid for."

"Lord, I hope so," said the first reader.

The next afternoon, Frederix walked into the publisher's office. "Want to take a turn around the block? I've got cabin fever." During their stroll, Frederix explained the first reader's two ideas.

"That's something we haven't tried. How do you feel about the projects?" asked the publisher.

By some ancestral osmosis, Frederix felt his survival instinct jostling him. Could it be that the first reader had already spilled his ideas to the publisher, privately?

"Well," he said, "if we put these ideas on the road the same year, we'll be gambling two years' profits."

The publisher smiled. He stopped and put his hands into his pants pockets and pulled out the lining of each. "My father used to say, 'I came into this world with nothing and I'm going out with nothing.'"

"Let's stop at the next bar," said Frederix, "and have a martini. I'll make mine a double."

The task of the editorial department is to seek out, buy, and edit the books that the company publishes. Within the confines of these three tasks, the editorial department has almost, but not quite, all of the authority it needs. In a shop producing fewer than two titles a month, the owner is usually the editor. In a large shop producing two titles a week, or even two titles a day, the chief administrative officer (who may be owner, publisher, or president) cannot even begin to evaluate the books selected by the editors and still do his own work.

One exception does occur when a manuscript is offered at auction and the bidding moves swiftly into six figures, sometimes seven; the head of the company reserves the right of personal approval, not so much in regard to the editorial content of the book, but in relation to the money risked as compared to other ways the same sum might be spent.

How, then, is the editorial department controlled? The control rests in the power of hire-or-fire held by the head of the company. This is rarely used as a threat or a means of domination. If the editors are buying the kinds of books that are selling, they are allowed to run their own course. When their selections fail to sell, the editors are often let go, not because of an intellectual disagreement, but simply because the books they bought haven't moved. To survive, you have to live in the winner's circle.

There is one gauntlet, however, that the editorial department must run. With large companies, there is a vice-president whose authority covers both the sales and editorial departments. This authority includes the right to fix the number of titles published. In addition, the sales manager often wields what amounts to equal power on final selection of books with a narrow market or books saddled with a heavy advance royalty. Aside from that, editors control what is bought.

Work starts in the editorial department around nine in the morning when mail is sorted and delivered to each editor.

Sometimes, a friendly secretary, making sure her boss won't lose some things on his crowded desk, will place a newly arrived manuscript from an important author on the editor's chair. Staffers noticing the empty office and the wrapped manuscript on the editor's chair josh with the secretary to learn what's come in. Editors usually punch no time clocks, the excuse being their reading time at home.

A shop that produces a hundred new titles a year will often employ nine shirtsleeve editors and two executive editors. Their morning editorial mail may include six to fifteen letters per editor from established authors and agents. But the bulk of the mail is of a different sort. Letters from artists seek book-jacket work, and circulars from contract editors ask for part-time employment. Each editor receives several trade periodicals and one or two general magazines along with direct-mail solicitations to buy a useful new reference work or industry newsletter. Often there is an invitation to attend a professional meeting or a political rally or to enroll in a seminar.

In addition, there are responses to the probes each editor sends out in the everlasting search for new manuscripts. No editor trusts to pot luck. Instead, he makes his own luck by ferreting out individuals whose personal experiences seem to make them candidates for doing a book on certain subjects now coming to the public attention.

A dozen times a year, a Xerox of a manuscript arrives with the news that it will be auctioned to the highest bidder and giving the date and latest hour to phone in a bid. If the company is interested, they may phone the agent and ask for additional copies to be delivered at once, so the executive editor can apportion time for two editors to read the script first, then two other editors to read it in case the first two get excited about it. The minimum bid is often big money—$100,000. Sometimes, the agent tries to assemble the publisher, the sales manager, and the executive editor with an offer to make a personal presentation of the book. In this day's mail, the agent writes: "In less than an hour I'll give you the book's logic lines, thesis, reader appeal, market, publicity tie-ins, and six or seven minutes of reading several passages. I invite the three of you to come over, and we'll have a nice desk lunch. No time need be lost, and it will be good to get together."

When a publisher turns out a hundred new titles a year, the editors will usually inspect twenty manuscripts—all of which have been invited into their office in one way or another—for each one that they publish.

This is aside from un-rush books, or, as they are sometimes called, over-the-transom books, that arrive unsolicited. When the company employs a first reader, that's where the un-rush books are delivered.

Among those publishers who employ genre editors, however, the principles of manuscript reading work a little differently. A genre editor is a mystery, romance, juvenile, or other specialist in a particular field, and it is his job not only to buy, edit, and help negotiate a contract with the authors whose work he selects, but, in addition, he is also charged with procurement. It's easier to get the ear of a publishing company with a genre editor heading a division devoted to art, music, and so forth, simply because the genre editor is like the centerfielder in baseball. He has nowhere to hide, and what comes out of the department is his baby. He finds, buys, edits. Therefore, he is more likely to appraise anything coming across his desk, because he is a front-line sergeant, regardless of his title.

Editors who are generalists, passing judgment on any kind of work, or who are first readers, are not nearly so sure about what the company wants to buy as is the genre editor in charge of poetry. It's his territory, and he makes the rules.

The genre system makes mail-sorting easier. Mystery writers send their letters and manuscripts to the genre editor handling mysteries, thus leaving less mail to be sorted that is simply addressed to "The Editor."

Mail that is addressed to no particular person is treated differently from office to office. One procedure is for an experienced editorial secretary, wise to the ways of this particular shop, to open the editorial mail that is not addressed to one individual and sort it for delivery to the most likely editor.

When the company has a policy of reading unsolicited chapter outlines and queries, but will not read unsolicited complete books, the latter are returned unread with an explanatory printed note. An established company issuing a hundred new titles a year will receive from three to fifteen unsolicited complete books a day. When there is no first reader, the employee who handles the sorting of mail may be experienced enough to open each package and determine its editorial nature (*e.g.*, juvenile, art) and mark it for delivery to the editor in charge of that subject.

An editorial workday often includes one impromptu task. For

instance, the executive editor's secretary asks for a one-page report, including an opinion on whether to buy or reject a novel that has been held unduly long when its agent wants an immediate answer before offering it elsewhere.

Usually four hours each day are set aside for pure editing time. Frequently, the editor lunches with an agent who hands him a manuscript that was the subject of the luncheon. At least once a week the editor attends a mini-editorial conference or a sales meeting in which he briefs several members of the sales department on the galley proofs of a new title that the production department handed to him.

When the editor is pushed for time because of the number of manuscripts he receives from the first reader or the response he gets from his own editorial probes, he may ask the executive editor for help. The help comes in the shape of giving part-time employment to contract editors who work at home and do manuscript evaluating. The publisher may have to pay a hundred to three hundred dollars for each job, depending on the length of the manuscript and the kind of editorial assistance requested.

The editor's personal telephone is both a blessing and a pest. When calls become so numerous that the editor can't get his work done, it becomes the secretary's job to answer the phone, find out who is calling and why, so the editor can call back in situations that he believes justify the time. In many cases, the secretary can give an intelligent answer to a writer who wants to know if this particular editor will receive a chapter outline and sample chapters of a book on a given subject.

At night, the editor takes home this week's copy of *Publishers Weekly*, an industry newsletter, or a chapter outline and sample chapter sent to him by an unknown author.

He has time for everything, he tells his wife, except time to think. He wants to think about why he is in the book-publishing business and whether or not he will leave his mark on it. He wants to think about what he really wants to publish, and why this interests him. He loves his work and wakes up each day happy to get to the job and hoping for "something fine" in the mail.

But, he thinks, an editor always works for somebody else. Although he loves publishing, he wonders how much more free he might be as a writer.

6

The Sales and Publicity Departments

BUNNER, the head of the sales department, was having a dinner at home for seven travelers—the men who make their living calling on bookstores. In addition to the travelers, he invited Blockie Schwartz, the new head of the publicity department; Helen, the executive editor; Frederix, the boss of both the sales and editorial departments; and his own chief assistant, Sawyer.

The group had just finished dinner, and brandy was being served in snifters.

"High class, here; it's not like we get in West Texas," said Stu, a traveler.

When the home-office people go on the road, the company pays their expenses. Not so for the travelers. They pay their own expenses and receive an average of 10 percent commission on books they sell to dealers and 5 percent on sales to wholesalers. To tide them over, until their accounts pay up, the travelers receive a weekly draw. The men in the best territories draw $400 a week; the others, $250.

The really large orders come from the wholesalers. Dealers often prefer to order from their nearest wholesaler, instead of ordering directly from the publisher. In this way, the dealer combines orders intended for many different publishers into one single order and receives one shipment and pays with one check. The wholesaler buys his books directly from the publisher at 50 percent off and sells them to the dealer for 25 to 42 percent off, depending on the quantity the dealer orders.

The publisher also sells books directly to the dealer, giving discounts of 25 to 50 percent, depending on the quantity. In a sense, the publisher and the wholesaler compete against each other for orders from the book dealer.

The travelers receive commissions on all orders from their territory, whether they actually call on the account or not and whether the order is a new one or a reorder. Pleasant as this arrangement sounds, all the dinner guests agreed that no one ever got rich as a traveler.

Bernie, a florid, portly, gray-haired man in his late fifties, put it this way: "Every traveler has to support two houses; in my case—three. I got a daughter at Michigan State, my wife and two kids in Scarsdale, and me on the road. My road expenses are never under fifty bucks a day. Thirty grand won't carry us, and that means I gotta sell over three hundred thousand dollars' worth of books a year."

"Shoot," said another traveler, "you got Ingram in your territory. That's a living right there. And you've got two other wholesalers. . . ."

Bernie slammed his fist on the table, rocking three glasses. "Listen, you onion head . . ."

"Onion head?" asked Helen, taking the bait.

"He's green and he stinks," said Bernie. She groaned. "Listen," he continued, "when I started in my territory thirty-eight years ago, all we had . . ." and he rattled off the names of fifteen dealers as though they were the first fifteen letters of the alphabet. "Who's left of that bunch today? Three. That's what." And he named them. "And let me tell you, when Ingram started, I called on Harry Hoffman, and I said to myself, 'There's a man.' So I offered to take his first promotion man with me, on my own beat, and I was the one who introduced him to everybody. I put Ingram into my territory. Who sends candy to all the phone girls on the order desk at Christmas? Me. Who knows their names? Me. Who gets the girls to ask the dealer, after they finish taking down an order, if he needs a book of *ours?* Me. I do that. Those Ingram orders don't flow out of a gate. I work for every one of them."

"Bernie," asked Sawyer, "why is Ingram so popular with dealers?"

"Why? Because they're not like us. They're smart. They care about the dealer. They treat him human. Look, Sawyer, I know, you want to do right, but our home office never listens to me. That airhead, Thelma, on the order desk, and that other one, the blonde, they snap off an order like it's a fresh stringbean. They take orders like they're writing down a classified ad from some housewife who phones in a 'maid wanted' two-liner."

"What should they say?" asked Sawyer, knowing what was coming but feeling it was Bernie's hour.

"Why don't you guys phone in a fake order and listen to your order desk? When I'm in the home office, I tell Thelma and that other one to switch all calls from my territory to me. After I take the order and thank the dealer and show my appreciation, I suggest something else that I know damn well they need. This company would be selling 3 percent more books if we had the right people on the order desk."

"Well, Bernie," said Frederix, "when you retire, that's what you can do. And we'll pay you 50 percent more than they get."

"Listen, big shot," said Bernie, "you could do a lot better than you do now by getting former travelers on your phone desk."

Stu broke in. "You need people on the order desk with light, cheerful voices who know how to be businesslike but can kid around, too. Our order desk has no idea on how to up an order for forty books spread over eight titles to nine titles for forty-two books. That's a 5 percent increase. Do that twenty times a day, and you guys would be doing more than sitting on your tails. . . ."

Bunner gave Helen the eye, and she tried to cut in. But Bernie was off and running. The travelers led an up-and-down, on-the-move life, going from one motel to the next, calling on four, five, and sometimes eight accounts a day, writing up orders at night and swabbing festering mental hurts when they went to bed. When a good traveler like Bernie called on the book dealer and laid down his spring or winter catalogue, the dealer (who had already been shown forty other catalogues that season) had no intention of paging it and writing up an order. Instead he asked: "Well, what do we need?" And the traveler, knowing the store, the dealer, the location, and the kind of trade, wrote up the order. With a few changes, the dealer frequently accepted it. Afterwards, the wise traveler stopped to speak to the clerks, noted the position of the various displays and what was in the window. All the books ordered had to be paid for within ninety days—or better still, thirty—but the dealer could return unsold books within six months if they were in salable condition.

After the travelers had been out on the road for sixteen weeks, and finally trooped back to the home office, they wanted to be stroked, to be asked, "How are things?" and listened to with respect. They had lots of good days on the road and bubbled with stories of success. But, even when they were in a good humor, telling jokes, pointing happily to big sales they made and new accounts they opened, their boiling point was sitting in sight, on the horizon. On the road they were sociable, agreeable, engaging, and generally good fellows. They took the abuse of dealers who were stuck with unsold books. ("What good does it do me to return 'em? They claim they never get 'em, and, when they do, they short me.") Dealers who lost sales because of slow shipments or mixed-up orders saved the whole ball of wax and hit the traveler over the head with it.

"Drop dead," yelled one dealer who had lost a sale of sixty books to his county library, "and stay that way!"

When the travelers walked into the home office, they weren't fighting mad, but, given the right trigger, they gave a good imitation of it.

Although their fuses were short, their angers were shorter. They would swear and stalk away and in a few minutes come back with a funny story. The publisher said, "If you can't love them, you couldn't be in the book business."

Bernie went to the washroom to take a pill for his heart. He returned promptly. "You guys," he shouted at Bunner and Sawyer, "just don't know what's going on. I'll tell you about one dealer—Krohngold— Charlie's News, Sarasota. The best small-town newsstand you'll ever want to see. And beautifully divided into sections: two hundred hardcover books, maybe two thousand paperbacks, and every magazine you ever heard of. This guy, this owner, is open to suggestions. That's why he's good. And he pays on the dot.

"So, why don't he order from us? We give him 40 percent. No, he orders from Ingram and takes a lower discount and I get 5 percent instead of 10 percent. You guys would rather ship a wholesaler three thousand books at 50 percent than ship three hundred small orders at 38 percent. Okay, I see your point. But you've never seen mine.

"Krohngold says to me, 'Look, Bernie, I pay Ingram a hundred bucks a year, and they install this weekly microfiche file that lists thousands of titles and tells me the exact number of each book they have in stock right now. So I phone them my order. The girls on the order desk are cheerful. They ask how you are. They thank you for the order and sound like they mean it. They ask if there's anything special they can do. They thank me for prompt payment. They don't rush-rush, take the order, and hang up. Then they tell me about some new book they think will go in my store and I always order it. So I give them my business. Wouldn't you?'"

"Another thing," interrupted Stu. "When a new bookstore starts up, Ingram sends the new dealer suggested book orders for large, medium, and small stores, and they pay the freight on the first order."

"What do you think we should do?" asked Helen.

"Ah!" said Bernie. "You ask me. Fire those two women. Put someone on the order desk who likes people, who can sell, who gets a kick out of upping an order. Give them some authority. Let them offer a special one percent extra discount, 'because it's Valentine's Day,' or a box of candy for the missus. You gotta be different. On our thirty-dollar picture book, offer one at 50 percent off if they buy three at 40 off. Care about the dealer. . . ."

Harris, one of the travelers, who was bolstering himself with brandy and enjoying the storm, broke in. "If this home office ran a bookstore for just six months, you'd understand what the dealer is up against. His own trade paper, *Publishers Weekly*, sides with who? The dealer? When's the last editorial they ran that said 'Discounts Are Too Low,' or 'Publishers Should Pay the Freight,' or 'Three Percent for Cash Discount in Five Days'? *Publishers Weekly* is what the title says. All the publishers I know are for publishers. They don't break a leg running after the dealer to help him along, give him a hand, cheer him up, do something useful for him. Ingram does everything selfishly, I suppose, to help their own business. Well, let's us be that kind of selfish and think dealer, dealer, instead of publisher, publisher. . . ."

Once more Helen tried to cut it off.

"With our new book, *Fly a Kite*," and she held up a beautiful eight-and-a-half-by-eleven dust jacket, "we're planning to offer two free kites with every five books."

"Are you crazy?" yelled Bernie. "What bookstores sell kites?"

"How will the dealers shelve our kites?" asked Stu. "If they come rolled up, they'll be lost. And they're too big to stick on a shelf."

"That," said Blockie Schwartz, the new publicity man, "is the whole idea." The travelers had been told that Blockie was the number-one publicity man in the business, and this was their first introduction to him.

"I won't sell kites," said Bernie. "I'd be a laughing-stock."

"You're not selling kites," said Blockie, "you're selling service, and that's what it's all about. Now I want each of you travelers to lean back in your chair. . . ."

"Better lean forward," said Bunner, "or someone is going to fall off."

"Use your knowledge of your own territory, and think of the dealers you call on who have skylights in their ceiling or high windows along the walls of the stores, or back entrances with full windows. Now imagine up there, floating in the light coming through the skylight or through a tall window, one of these lovely dragon kites. . . ."

Bunner's wife, on cue, brought a kite into the dining room from the butler's pantry. It hid her from the waist up, and looked light and colorful, yet formidable.

"Does it come disassembled?" asked Stu. "If it does, they'll make us assemble it wherever we go."

"We can get these kites from Thailand. Really beautiful Oriental kites, the real thing, for two dollars, delivered, and the dealer can sell them for seven dollars."

"Sure," said Bernie. "That's the kind of mark-up he'll be yelling for from us."

"This kite you're looking at is the same one pictured on the dust jacket of our book," said Bunner.

"Where do you get the string and the kite-winder?" asked Harris.

"Look," said Blockie, "after you buy a book at Brentano's, you have to find the place to park your behind while you're reading it. All we're doing is supplying a merchandising idea and a beautiful, well-built kite for the dealer to suspend from the ceiling. This is going to sell more copies of *Fly a Kite*. We're printing fifteen thousand."

The doorbell rang, and the publisher entered. Everyone stood up. He greeted all the travelers by name and asked about their families. He asked each about his health and personal well-being. He gave Bunner's wife a white orchid. "Make Bunner take you out to dinner tomorrow night," he told her, "after all the work you've done here." Then he turned to Stu: "That last commission check of yours is your biggest yet. One more like that, and we'll exchange territories."

"Say," said Stu, "whose idea was that about the kite?"

"Alvin's," said the publisher.

"The comptroller? Giving something away? I don't believe it."

"Yes," said the publisher. "Kites fascinate him. He just got interested and won second place in the Novice Kite Flyers event at Southampton."

Blockie sat down at the piano and played, out of nowhere, "Blue Skies," and they all joined in the chorus. The publisher, with urging from Helen, did an imitation of Humphrey Bogart. The whole mood changed, and it was a lively, easy party.

After forty-five minutes, the publisher excused himself and left.

"Now there's a real guy," said Bernie, "a gentleman."

Headed by Frederix and Bunner, the sales department employed four other promotional people. One was responsible for general fiction and the other for the how-to, self-help, and inspirational books. They took turns running the company's booth at regional shows, and both attended the big, national book dealers convention.

Sawyer, the assistant sales manager, toured the wholesalers and chain bookstores and supervised the travelers. As his special preserve, he mothered two or three books each season that he thought needed a good trigger to set them off, and he liked to show what he could do.

Ada, his assistant, wrote circulars and sales letters and prepared two annual catalogues. Of the company's fifty titles a year, half were displayed in a winter catalogue, published just after Labor Day; the others were illustrated in a spring catalogue mailed the first of March. Each catalogue went to thirty-five hundred dealers and five thousand libraries. Printing, mailing, and addressing each catalogue cost $1.20.

Not all fifty books received equal attention in the catalogue itself, or from the travelers or sales department. Books written by authors with a strong following and books receiving an advance of twenty thousand dollars or more came first, followed by books that seemed to have a market well timed with their publication dates. Not all the books that were pushed did well, since no one could predict what the public would like.

Good advance publicity induced some reviewers to unwrap their complimentary copies, and this helped, since major media receive fifty books or more a week and review five to twenty. For specialized books, with a limited market, about thirty review copies were mailed. On "Big Books" (*i.e.*, where the company was stuck with a heavy advance and a large print order), one hundred review copies were shipped out, and one measure of the advance publicity was the number of requests for review copies from smaller newspapers and lesser magazines. When the freebee requests grew beyond 150 copies, Blockie Schwartz, the new publicity director, felt his initial thrust was working, but the number of review copies was cut off somewhere between 100 and 150.

Before the reviews broke, and before the books were printed, the travelers started to sell the company's line to dealers by showing the jackets.

At this point, neither the travelers nor the dealers had read any of the books, nor, in most cases, had the publisher. The only readers, up to publication date, were Helen, Adam, and the "pencil editor" who had edited the book. A set of galley proofs, however, was sent to selected book clubs for perhaps one-fourth of the line. Frederix and Bunner read a one-page *précis* of each book and sampled two dozen pages before a contract was mailed to the author.

It was commonly agreed that no one—dealer, traveler, wholesaler, or publisher—had time to read what was being bought. The dealer, for example, was offered fifty to several hundred books each week by circulars and by travelers. The determining factors governing his purchases were his own instinctive judgment of the titles, the sales appeal of the jackets, the reputations of the publishers, the names of the authors, the subject matter of the books in relation to the times, and the retail prices.

After giving a traveler half an ear for fifteen or twenty minutes, the dealer asked him to write up a suggested order. The dealer checked this against the company's catalogue and, using his own intuition, edited the order.

Bound galleys were sent to the travelers on special books, and advance galleys of all books were available when they showed interest. By "interest," the editor meant one thing; the traveler, another. Sometimes, a traveler noticed the dust jacket of one book catching the fancy of dealers in his territory and began pushing it at every call because it was easier to sell. Happily, he phoned the news to Bunner, who told Helen, and the traveler found bound galleys waiting for him at his next stop.

Having made twelve calls that day, driven two hundred miles and with work still to be done on his order pad, he dutifully read the first chapter and muttered, "What do they think I got time for?"

Of the twenty-five books this company publishes each season, fifteen get a fair shake from the sales department, and five are hyped and punched for all they are worth. The rest are backed with little more than token advertising and twenty or thirty review copies. Some of these die fast and in four months are recalled and pulped. Sometimes one or two of the neglected books pull good reviews from major media. When this happens, everyone in this small office offers to chip in and help the book along. It is as if a slow child from a large family comes home with a gold star for winning the class spelling bee. None of the company's several authors who each season is brushed off, ever understands why, even when he suspects he has been shorted.

I asked a publisher friend how he felt about the neglect of many works by new authors, and here's what he had to say:

In our shop, we have one or two books by new authors each season. Unless they are something special, we don't mount an intense promotional campaign. We do publish co-op newspaper advertising* in the author's home town. We try to place the author on a local TV or radio talk show. Our travelers display the new-author's jacket to dealers, just as they do with our other books, and, of course, it also appears in our catalogue. We send twenty-five to thirty complimentary copies to reviewers and help the author with a mail campaign directed to his acquaintances. We may also use small token advertising in one or two national magazines. If the book is nonfiction and appeals to a special audience, such as nurses or gardeners, we place test advertising in magazines read by this market and also try a direct-mail campaign to five or ten thousand prospects.

In addition, we do co-op newspaper advertising in some other city near where the author lives when we can get the author on a broadcast show there, or if a paper in that city gives the book a strong review. If the

---

* The publisher and the dealer divide the cost of an ad appearing under the sponsorship of the dealer with his name and address.

book moves off the dealer's shelves in either city, and we get reorders proving there is word-of-mouth advertising, we'll go a step further and offer co-op advertising to twenty dealers around the country. But, if the book dies on the shelf, we pull it in 120 days.

Publishing books by new authors is like playing the field in a horse race. Book publishing is a high-risk business, because you never know which of two literate books will sell, or even if either one will sell. There is a certain charm in discovering new talent. We don't have to lay out much of an advance, we get 50 percent of the book-club and paperback rights and first refusal on the author's next two books. Over any five-year period, we usually run into one of these incredible surprises when a new-author book makes it big and pays for the losses of the others for several years. It doesn't happen like clockwork, but, if you fish often enough, you catch dinner.

We fish for books by new authors because we just might find something. But our confidence in our own judgment is not secure enough to make us want to promote new authors in a big way unless there are very special circumstances.

To me, books by new authors are like seeds we scratch into the ground and then let nature take its course. We select the seed; we put it into the ground; we give it a little water, a dab of fertilizer, and not too much else. Some grow; some die. If we boosted each new author's books with a ten-thousand-dollar advertising program, it would add so much additional risk that our new-author program would fold.

In a word, the deal is this: we risk twenty grand bringing out a new author's book in a limited press run. Having done that, we ask the book to show us its mettle before we go further. We want favorable reviews from more than the home-town paper. We want audience response from an author's TV appearance; we want to see the book starting to move of its own accord off the dealer's shelf.

When we get two out of three of the above, we blow the book's horn. Otherwise, we pull back. That's not author neglect; that's simply putting a limit on our original calculated risk. Sure, we could sell ten thousand copies of a first edition of almost any new-author's book, provided we are willing to add on five or six dollars' advertising cost for every book sold. Why do that?

We accept the public's verdict. If a book fails to get reviews, if dealers do not reorder, if the author can't get something moving with a broadcast show, if our publicity department can't spread ink on the book, we accept our loss, recall the book, and give the dealer full credit on unsold copies. That's not author neglect. It's intelligent publishing.

My publisher friend puts together an open-and-shut case showing no author neglect on first books. He risks his "twenty grand" on a limited press run and the author's book either "catches on" or not. If the book moves, the publisher gets behind it and pushes. If, however, the book drops dead, he recalls it and accepts his loss. He isn't mad at the author, and he doesn't expect the author to be mad at him. Both tried an interesting experiment and it didn't work.

When that's the way the ball bounces, we agree the new author hasn't much of a complaint, providing he knows in advance how the game is played and that intense selling will not be done unless his book proves itself by virtue of "its own mettle."

When the promotional and publicity backup given to an author's first book is scant, can the author do anything about it? Yes, indeed. He can cooperate with the publicity department.

Of the 1,350 commercial royalty publishers (issuing from three to twelve hundred titles a year), about fifty have a publicity department capable of performing four vital services: (1) casing book reviewers through personal communications and advance publicity, so they will examine their complimentary copy when it arrives; (2) getting stories about the author and his book into the media so that more people will enter the dealer's store and ask to see a copy; (3) letting the dealer know what the media is saying, so he will place a copy of the book in the window and display it in his store for a few days after a local story breaks; (4) getting the author on TV and radio talk shows in areas where the book has dealer distribution.

These are the main jobs of the publicity director, and about fifty publishers (out of 1,350) have a full-time publicity head, with four or more assistants, plus typing and secretarial help, and a travel budget. Another two hundred publishers have a full-time publicity director with two secretary-assistants, plus one or two typists to get the work out. Then there are another two hundred publishers each of whom has one publicity employee, usually an old and loyal retainer who was a "great second" but could not personally engineer a victory and who now "handles publicity." In that case, there is one typist, no secretary, no travel budget, no travel.

The remaining nine hundred commercial, royalty publishers have one employee whose part-time job is publicity. What actually happens is that Hilda, who takes her turn one day a week at the reception desk, has four jobs. She receives all mail addressed to the Permissions Department and answers, "Yes, no charge," when there is a request to reprint up to five hundred words from one of the company's books. She types the labels for complimentary copies that go to reviewers and is allowed to handle the selection her way, as long as her list is under forty. She writes a "release" on all books, which is included with the review copy. She got started being "our publicity department" when she was asked to write dust-jacket copy, and, because it seemed a shame to waste her time reading a book just to write one piece of copy, she was asked to write a publicity release on the book, too. In this great, inventive country, we have nine hundred Hildas who louse up nine hundred publicity departments.

Hilda, however, is no dumbbell and is not the culprit. In two years of acting as the company's publicity department, no one ever showed her an example of excellence in a release or revealed the standards by which a newspaper departmental editor judges a publicity story, or explained the basis on which a talk-show host selects guests. The older bosses came up through the ranks of administration, accounting, and marketing and rarely knew enough about publicity to establish standards similar to those in their own work areas.

Hilda is your friend. She will welcome the kind of assistance she can approve of in advance, and that costs nothing extra.

At those houses where the publicity director is a talented go-getter who knows his business, and even where the department head makes a publicity break-out for each title and then fulfills only part of it due to being understaffed, any kind of author assistance is welcomed as long as the department head feels that control and approval of each step are clearly vested in him. For instance, if publicity breaks in areas where no books are on sale, the travelers and dealers won't like it one bit.

Do you want to get into the act? If so, what's the first thing you can do?

Start by learning the name of the person who does the publicity. Make a phone call to this person four months before publication date, say you have a few ideas along publicity lines for your forthcoming book, and ask permission to send a short letter on the subject. Don't be explicit or chatty. Ask only that he give a quick glance at your offering of ideas when your letter arrives. When the phone response is, "Yes, glad to see it," explain by letter what you have to offer: "My book, 'Panning for Gold Dust while Living in the Wilderness and Making $400 a Week,' is very much my own child, because I lived the life and did every bit of it myself. This gives me the courage to suggest a review-copy-candidate list that I am assembling and will have ready for you in six weeks. I am also writing an individual release for ten review editors, because I am familiar with their papers." That's the gist of your brief initial communication.

You get to work by picking up the current *Literary Market Place*, at your library. It is one of the seven directories used by publicity people. The section titled "Review Selection and Reference" starts off with seventy book-review services. Most of these won't fit your book at all, but some will be ideal. One of the seventy that would interest juvenile science writers is *Appraisal: Children's Science Books*, which reviews 220 books a year and is published three times a year by the Boston University School of Education. Its circulation is two thousand.

In the same section is a list of twenty book-review syndicates. Some of these are general, like the one distributed by the North American Newspaper Alliance; others are as specialized as the one supplying book news to fifty black newspapers and magazines. The next division in this same section covers 150 columnists and commentators. One of them, Abbey Service, supplies reviews of books on horsemanship, horses, racing, and sports. This is followed by a list of twenty adult-book clubs that, in addition to selecting a book each month for their members, also publish a book-review circular listing other books their subscribers might order. Following this is a list of juvenile-book clubs doing the same thing. Would your book be a candidate for a review in one of these circulars?

Other reference material in *LMP* gives information about the review editors of fifteen hundred newspapers, magazines, broadcast networks, and individual radio and TV stations.

With research, you can hand-pick the best candidates for your book. Can you expect the publicity department to spend fifty hours, at ten dollars an hour, to do the same thing—when they may have two hundred or even one thousand other titles? In some cases, the answer is very definitely yes. In other cases, the answer is no or maybe. That's why you offer to select forty or fifty reviewer candidates and write ten individual releases about your book.

Try the shoe on the other foot.

If you were the head of a publicity department, how do you think you would handle the matter of selecting the right media to review each book? Most publicity people rely on their experience to give them a feel of what to do within the time at their disposal. Your charm is that you know your book better than anyone, and you care more about it. With perspicacity, a little telephoning (you do not front for the company's publicity department; you speak only for yourself), and some research, you can find out some of the things that will help you make the right decisions. Your finger isn't on the trigger. You're simply offering a list of candidates for review copies.

Will your work be appreciated?

What a joy it will be for the publicity people at your publisher's office to give their brains a free ride and coast in on what may be a *fait accompli*. If you fail to connect with reality, you've lost nothing that was in your pocket anyway.

I asked Harold Hansen, who publishes four publicity directories, to suggest other ways that a writer could assist the publicity department. Here's his reply:

For the most part, when it comes to an author's first book, not much immediate demand exists in the marketplace. How do you create that demand? The least costly, most effective way is through publicity. Chances are, your publisher will handle the usual releases to trade magazines read by book dealers and libraries, such as *Book Review*

Digest, Booklist, Choice, Library Journal and *Publishers Weekly* "Forecasts."

And he'll also send out review copies. After that, when it comes to an author's first book, usually the rest is up to you—not in every case, but frequently enough that you want to back up your book.

Here's your game plan.

First, make an appointment to see the publicist at your publisher's office. Acknowledge that you realize he's got his hands full, but tell him that you have very strong feelings about getting publicity for your book. Make a request for a little budget to handle postage and telephone calls. If you get that, later on you can make a pitch for travel expenses.

Assure the publicist that at all times you will keep him informed of what you're up to. Since he is a professional, he is suspicious of amateur efforts. Put him at ease by telling him you'll send him an outline or discuss with him what you're going to do before you do it. Confirm this by letter. Not only will this allow him to make suggestions, but it will also start a relationship that will prove worthwhile not only for your present book, but for ones you've yet to write.

If you get no expense money, face the fact that the dollars you put out to publicize your book will be well spent.

In any publicity effort, the first thing that has to be established is the conviction in your own mind that there are millions of people out there who would be interested in your book. Let me assure you that there are newspaper editors and television and radio broadcasters who want to hear from you. These people have to come up with stories day after day. Each one uses up what amounts to seven books of copy a week! If you can make their jobs easier, they'll be grateful. So don't hesitate to write or phone them.

Sure, you may catch them at a bad time, find them brusque. But let this roll right over you. They're in business, and so are you: pushing a new book you've spent countless days writing.

Let's say the title of your book is *How to Improve Your Tennis.* The subject is national, and the fastest way to get publicity is through newspapers, radio, and TV.

Let's work on print media—newspapers—first.

Get behind your typewriter and write a two-page release. Keep in mind that you're writing for a newspaper, so, in the very first paragraph, spell out why your book is unique. Think what it is you've written that is brand new; put that in your first paragraph, too.

Keep your story simple, and remember it should be helpful to the reader. That's what editors are after. The entire two pages should be devoted to one new concept about improving tennis. Don't talk about yourself or your book, except incidentally. In a four-hundred-word release, the main thing is to offer the reader something he can paste in his hat, something to remember and use. A two-paragraph news story is different. This should give only the facts that make the news.

If possible, a photograph should be included with your release. It would be ideal if it were an illustration from your book and supported the point you were making in your release.

Now you'll need a list of editors to whom you will send your release and photo.

In this case, rather than send it to the sports editors, which seems a natural, let's send it to editors of family pages. Tennis is a family sport, and more space is allotted to features on women's pages than on sports pages.

Where do you get the list? A directory called *Family Page Directory* contains the names of departmental family-page editors at the 533 top dailies in the country. It costs forty-five dollars and is available from Public Relations Plus, Inc. (P.O. Box 327, Washington Depot, CT 06794). They also fill phone orders: (203) 868-0200.

With this directory in hand, check off one paper in each city to which you will send your material. Today, in most cases, there is only one paper in each city. Where there are two or more, pick the afternoon paper. It is more apt to use feature material than a morning publication.

The reason you will mail to only one paper in each city is that this will provide the local editor with an exclusive story in his area. Be sure to mark this on your release in the upper right-hand corner: "Exclusive to you in your city." And under this type: "For Immediate Release."

Before mailing your release to your list of family-page editors, get your publicity department to approve or revise the story and get an approval of the list of towns to receive your releases so that you will be publicizing your book only where it is on sale (not just on order).

So you've written your release and had it duplicated; if you're going to use a photograph, you've had copies made, and you're all set with your list. Address your envelopes—nine by twelve if you're using first class. Use a cardboard if you're sending a photograph.

It would be nice if editors sent you tear sheets.* Some of them do as a courtesy; after all, you did provide them with a good article. Most of them, however, don't have the time for such niceties.

What do you do?

You can ask the publicist at your publisher's office to ask his press-clipping service to look for your article. If your publisher doesn't have such a service, then his sales manager can ask local booksellers to let him know if stories on your book ran in local papers.

Most important of all, if your book starts selling better, you can feel very good about your publicity effort. A six-inch-by-one-column story in a newspaper of fifty thousand circulation, published in an area where your book is on sale at two or more bookstores, may produce six sales of your book. When the people who buy it talk it up to their friends, you can expect the dealers to reorder. Multiply this by a hundred newspapers, and you have the beginning of a groundswell.

For radio and television, the ideal approach is to make yourself available for interviews on local radio and TV stations. Ask your publisher which stations he recommends. Essentially, this means larger cities with wide and viable TV or radio coverage where your book is on sale at three or four, preferably more, large bookstores. This must be verified before you go on the station, or your time will be wasted.

Once that's determined, all you need are directories that will list talk shows and give local contacts for them. *TV Publicity Outlets—Nationwide* covers TV. It's $89.50 for a year's subscription—revised quarterly, which means you get four copies—and is available from Public Relations Plus, Inc. (P.O. Box 327, Washington Depot, CT 06794). Phone: (203) 868-0200.

For radio, there's the *National Radio Publicity Directory*. It's seventy dollars a year and includes a semiannual revision supplement. It's available from Peter Glenn Publications, Ltd. (17 East 48th St., New York, NY 10017). Phone: (212) 688-7940.

When you have these directories in hand, examine the listings for the

---

*Tear sheets are copies of the page on which your article appears, so you can see how much of it was used and how it looks in print.

cities you plan to visit. Rate the programs in each place according to audience size and subject interest. Naturally, a public-affairs program is not going to be interested in improving anyone's tennis game. The most receptive shows usually are those that are on the air five days a week. That means the contact is usually hard pressed to come up with new material and will welcome an author passing through his city.

Work on an exclusive-in-your-city basis, and write to the contact on what you've determined is the best show in a city. Give the contact an outline of what specific items from your book you feel would be good subjects for an interview. Use the material from the release you prepared for newspapers, but don't send an actual copy of the release. Rework the information since you want the contact on the TV show to feel that you're making a special effort where he's concerned. By all means, include a copy of your book. Your publisher might provide you with these at no charge. At most, he should charge you cost. An eight-dollar book usually costs up to $2.50 to print in lots of ten thousand. This does not include administrative or editorial costs.

If your picture on the dust jacket is from twenty years ago, include a current picture. If there is no picture of you on the dust jacket of your book, include a very recent one with the material you send to your TV contact, as it's only natural for the talk-show host to want to know what you look like.

If you have no reply from the contact in a week, telephone him. Check the information in your directory to be certain you don't call when the program is on the air or during the time it's taped if it is pre-recorded.

If you strike out, follow the same approach with the program you've figured is the second best for you. In a city with a one million or more population, when the best TV station has a talk show catering to your subject matter, a sale of one thousand books, as a direct result of a TV appearance, is not out of line when you have ten dealers handling your book.

Use the same approach outlined for radio stations for approaching contacts on TV shows. There's no big need to include a photo of yourself, but do include a copy of your book.

Coordinating a tour that enables you to travel two weeks and be on TV and radio every day—or nearly every day—takes some doing. It can be done and really sells books. Remember, you should make no appearances until your book is available in local stores.

Once you've established dates on radio and TV, be sure to notify the publicist at your publisher's place. He will alert local bookstores to your appearances. Local stores may want to run tie-in ads: "Be sure to watch *The Good Morning Show* next Monday to hear Joe Jones tell you how to improve your tennis game." Or they may want to have an autograph party for you. These take time to arrange, so, again, give as much advance notice as possible of what you're up to. Two weeks on the road can move four thousand books if one town out of three is a big one.

One added thought: if you think you'll have the strength for it—and the time—write or phone local editors on daily newspapers, suggesting a reporter might want to interview you when you're in town. The same editors who ignored your release might be sparked by the fact you're making a local TV appearance.

Now let's suppose you've written something of regional appeal like *New York Nature Spots*. If you work hard and are successful, you can increase the sales of your book without having to get on a plane or train. The subways and busses will do. And, of course, the telephone.

To secure a list of all publicity contacts in metropolitan New York City, you need only one directory: *New York Publicity Outlets*, which covers all media within fifty miles of Columbus Circle. It sells for $47.50, including a semiannual revision supplement. It's available from Public Relations Plus, Inc. (P.O. Box 327, Washington Depot, CT 06794). Phone: (203) 868-0200.

This directory contains all the data you need for daily and weekly newspapers as well as foreign-language and special-interest newspapers, news services, syndicates, and magazines. Radio and TV stations and their talk-show contacts are included.

When dealing with a metropolitan area the size of New York, you adopt one approach for the super papers like the *New York Times*, the *New York Post*, and the New York *Daily News*, and another for the suburban dailies like the *Paterson News* or *Greenwich Times*.

For the former, the personal touch is very important. Read the three Manhattan dailies every day for a week. Be sure to include Sunday editions. Get a feel for their readership, the level at which articles are written.

THE BOOK MARKET

Using *New York Publicity Outlets* as your reference guide, write a letter to the appropriate departmental editor or columnist for your book. For example, the listing of columnists and departmental editors working for the *New York Times* covers four pages in *New York Publicity Outlets*. With a book like *New York's Nature Spots*, you would have to decide among the Metropolitan editor, the author of the column "About New York," the "Weekend" editor, the editor of the "Living" section, and the editor of the "Arts and Leisure" section.

If you read the *Times* for a week, you know your best bet is the author of "About New York." Local nature spots are a natural for him.

A few days after you have written him, call on the telephone, and ask if he has any interest in meeting you. If the answer is no, then I would try the editor of the "Living" section. If you get a no from her, go down the line. When talking to people to whom you've written, if you find they're not interested, ask who they think would be a good person to approach on the paper. If you connect, your book will be brought to the attention of well over one million people who read the *New York Times*.

Don't work with the three Manhattan dailies at the same time. If the *Post* or the *News* should scoop the *Times*, chances are you'll get nowhere with the latter. Of course, if you get no reaction from anyone at the *Times*, then try the *News*. Its circulation is double the *Times*'s, but it doesn't have the book-buying readership of the *Times*.

If you have the time and the inclination, follow the same routine for the suburban dailies. Where there is more than one paper in a town, work with just one on an exclusive basis, of course.

If you don't have the time, simply write a release on your book, and highlight those nature spots near the paper you're writing to. With the suburban papers, make sure the bookstores in their communities have your book on sale. Indicate that you are available for personal interviews and would be more than glad to visit their towns and talk to reporters.

If your budget allows, send a mailing to all the weeklies in the New York metropolitan area. There are close to five hundred and your book has such appeal, it is a natural for them.

Let's pretend you've done the same kind of book on nature spots, but this time it's about Washington, D.C. In that case, there's an ideal publicity directory for you titled *Washington News Media Directory Contacts*, published by Hudson's Directories (2626 Pennsylvania Ave.

7

Rights for Writers

THE EASIEST THING to understand in the entire book-publishing business is the existence of "rights." The principle is simply that a copyright is divisible into as many rights as there are different kinds of buyers. TV rights are different from radio rights; hardcover, from paperback. Each is a separate right that may be sold to a buyer for a particular period of time.

The kinds of rights in a novel are not fixed. With each new age, and its accompanying new technologies, new rights appear. One of the newest is called Computer/Magnetic Tape Rights; another is Microfilm/Microfiche. Their names sound strange, but their meanings are simple. We will describe them when we list sixteen major kinds of rights that authors sell. Depending on your age, you might someday witness a further subdivision of TV rights into "Planet-Earth Rights" and "Solar Space-Colonization Rights." On this earth, however, in Coral Gables, Florida, a new right is being experimented with by fifteen hundred subscribers who receive in their homes, by air waves, a printout of various kinds of information.

It's never easy for a new writer to hold onto all rights, and years ago it was even harder. When pulp-paper writers were selling Western stories to Street & Smith for one cent a word in 1930, they included "all rights" with each story, or another author's work was purchased.

One day, during this period, I published an open letter to Mr. Ralston, who was managing Street & Smith, and asked, as a supplicant would ask a chief, if his company would pay a twenty-five-dollar honorarium to any author whose work was selected for *The Year's Best*

Westerns, The Year's Best Love Stories, and so forth. It never entered my mind to ask Mr. Ralston to renounce his claim to "all rights," but only would he please fling a few pennies to the boys. He did. This chink encouraged other writers to be bolder.

The legal basis for authors to claim all rights to their works, and sell these rights one at a time, had been theirs for many years, but it took a lot of guts to say: "Do business on my terms, or I'll take my work elsewhere." The Authors League of America and several hundred of their members were in the forefront of the battle to peel off and sell one right to one publisher and another right to another publisher. Today, the new writer enjoys the fruits of what someone else did many years ago, and no magazine or book publisher, except in unusual circumstances, prepares a contract that requests "all rights."

The big news is that what was once an occasional source of extra income is now the whole show.

The first big hunk of "new rights" came from motion pictures. Frances Marion, the story editor at MGM, outraged her competitors by paying twenty-five thousand dollars for movie rights of a novel. After that, every author who sold a book tried to reserve all movie rights for himself, while every publisher demanded 50 percent. The pendulum has now swung the other way, and many book contracts for established writers contain a 90-10 deal, with the writers coming off with the lion's share.

The next big source of new money came from radio rights, as novels and magazine stories were made into radio serials, but the overwhelming splurge came from the book clubs. In the last twenty-five years, a number of book publishers have sprouted their own clubs: Macmillan, Prentice-Hall, Doubleday, McGraw-Hill have fifty book clubs among them that they own and operate. Of the 150 book clubs soliciting members today, the largest is the Reader's Digest Book Club with its 2.5 million members, who seem to enjoy keeping up with the reviewers by following a condensed version of the bestsellers. Literary Guild and Book-of-the-Month Club are each in the one-million membership class, with the latter being the largest.

The prize for selection from the top three can run as much as a quarter of a million dollars. The smaller book clubs pay smaller prices, ten thousand dollars and less. The midget book clubs allow themselves to percent of the retail price for each copy sold. When the mass paperback retails for $2.00 the total royalty paid on each copy sold is 12 cents. In this case, the author receives 6 cents for each copy sold, and so does the publisher of the original hardcover edition. On a sale of 100,000 copies, each party receives $3,000.

On most mass-paperback contracts, the royalty rises with the sale. After the first 100,000 or 150,000 copies have been sold, the royalty usually moves up to 8 percent of the retail price. With authors who have a good track record from their previous paperbacks, or whose books seem unusually timely and enjoy great publicity, the royalty has been negotiated to 10 percent. On some contracts, to reduce his risk, the publisher will offer a lower advance (*i.e.*, a lower guarantee against royalties) and, in exchange, offer a higher royalty after a sale of two hundred thousand copies.

When a publisher bids on a mass paperback, his math begins with a butcher-block estimate that a 50 percent sale may be needed to break even, when the paperback costs 40 cents to print and sells for $2.00. In the event only 50 percent of the copies are sold, the publisher has to print two copies to sell one. This increases the *de facto* printing cost of each copy sold from 40 cents to 80 cents. Shipping and packing add 2.5 cents. Six percent royalty on a $2.00 retail price adds 12 cents. Add 5 cents for office overhead per book sold, and last, add 5 cents to pay the "field men," who supervise the distribution of paperbacks at 120,000 newsstands and drugstores. Total cost per copy sold: $1.05.

Large paperback companies employ field crews of thirty, who pick the best spots for each paperback. Small publishers rely on the local wholesaler to do this. This reliance for help has been known to be misplaced, because publishers send wholesalers more paperbacks than drugstores and newsstands have rack space. When the wholesaler's truckdriver drops a load of paperbacks on the drugstore floor in a rope-tied bundle, the store owner plucks off the rack what he thinks are the slow movers to make room for what's new and gives the unsold books to the driver. This short rack life is one reason the average sale of all mass paperbacks hovers at 50 percent of the press run.

The national distributor, the local wholesaler, and the retail outlet take close to half of the retail price, leaving $1.00 to $1.10 for the publisher.

Where is the profit? The answer is to go back to the drawing board.

If you've ever managed a business, you are familiar with the three classic ways the publisher can use to tip the math in his favor.

He can advertise so that sales will climb to 60 or 70 percent of the copies printed; he can increase the retail price to raise his income per book to $1.30; or he can decrease his costs so the book will break even on a 45 percent sale.

Increasing the price sounds simple: how about $2.60 instead of $2.00? Sometimes, when a paperback is price-tested in different parts of the country, this 60 cent price increase will not affect its sale; sometimes it will kill it. Similarly with advertising. Sometimes, dollars spent for advertising are greater than the dollars received from the increased sale.

As a consumer, you are familiar with what happens when manufacturing costs are cut. The paperback you buy uses smaller type (thus requiring fewer pages), thinner paper (cheaper to buy, cheaper to ship), cheaper binding. Each tampers with the product. When the tampering is too great, the public backs off.

Sometimes, an attempt is made to spread the cost of the field men and the home-office overhead over a larger number of paperbacks by publishing twenty additional titles a year with the same field crew and the same home-office staff.

Do these ploys work? How do paperbacks become profitable to publish?

I once had to study 1,080 pages of an agricultural text, *Feeds and Feeding*, and, after wading through all the charts and feed formulas for livestock, I came to the last sentence in the book: "The eye of the farmer fatteneth his ox."

Livestock farmers and publishers might well succeed in each other's business. It is indeed the eye of the individual livestock farmer that triggers the synthesis from which comes feeding and marketing methods that are his very own. The publisher's eye, and I have watched as it roved and settled, is the innocent eye, seeing everything as though for the first time; meanwhile, his mind has been calculating. He manages to survive, because, along with his competitors, he is able to decrease outgo, raise his price, and spread his costs over larger press runs and more titles. It may not be artistic, but it works, and less than that won't run a mass-paperback business.

Today's budget for a mass-paperback publisher who wishes to

distribute three hundred thousand copies each of thirty-six titles is $4.8 million dollars a year for printing and shipping.

The editorial thrust is mass appeal, and the lists bristle with self-help books, sex and violence, astrology, fads of the day, mysteries, and soft-core porno. The mass-paperback publishers are uncritical of success. After Barbara Cartland uncovered a new women's market for mass paperbacks, the same kind of stilted costume romance promptly flowed from half a dozen imitators.

Can liberal-arts-trained editor-managers with a strong literary heritage operate a business of this kind? When a mass paperback is advertised as "flowing with more passion and peril than any other novel that has gone before," some of the editorial help wants out.

Reduction of literary quality in the mass-paperback field has a twofold effect on writers. Fewer Thomas Wolfes will spend four years on a million words. And more and more writers will do what the publishers are doing. They will make their plays for where they believe the money is. And the money is in mass paperbacks.

The raisins in the paperback field are called quality paperbacks and, for the most part, are sold at college and trade bookstores. Many mass-paperback houses work both sides of the street and also publish a line of quality paperbacks. Some firms, however, specialize in them. Quality paperbacks sell for up to six dollars, and, here and there, exceptions add three dollars to the price. Press runs for quality paperbacks are often under twenty thousand. The royalty is 6 to 10 percent of the retail price, and, because the retail price is higher, the author earns more per book than from a mass paperback. However, since the press runs are lower, and the anticipated sale is less, the advance royalty is often five hundred to twenty-five hundred dollars.

The quality paperback is also distributed through outlets that specialize in its subject matter. In the art field, for instance, they are distributed through museum gift shops, art-supply stores, art studios, art schools, galleries, and framing shops. The improving sales of quality paperbacks and their distribution into unusual outlets make them a good prospect for rights sales on literary, cultural, and specialty books.

Here is a rundown of the better-known rights that authors sell.

Hardcover Rights. In conversational usage, hardcover rights means that

93

the publisher will bring out an author's book in cloth-bound, hardcover format and use his best efforts to explore every retail and wholesale avenue for its sale.

Every author's contract is a bit different, not only from author to author, but from book to book. A book contract is more than a fixed royalty for every book sold at wholesale and a fixed royalty for every book sold at retail with an advance paid against the royalty when the contract is signed. Today, with about half the hardcover books barely breaking even, the publisher seeks to share in the subsidiary rights to maintain his financial good health.

The community of astute literary agents, recognizing this need, writes into the author's contract certain specifics that it thinks are what the publisher should mean when he offers to use his "best efforts" to promote the sale of a hardcover. In other words, if the publisher wants to share in subsidiary rights, and in addition wants his share to be substantial, the aggressive literary agent seeks to pin down what the publisher will do to earn it.

Hitherto, the phrase "best efforts" in a book contract meant that the publisher would ship out thirty or forty or even a hundred review copies, and that he would send advance jackets to all his salesmen so they could procure orders in advance of publication, and, following that, the book would be described in his catalogue, and some display advertising would break. After that, the publisher was on his own. If the book failed to catch on, he took his foot off the gas, and the book might be neglected or, as some writers have claimed, abandoned.

What is so earnestly desired from the hardcover publisher is an advance agreement on how many dollars will be spent in magazines, newspapers, and broadcasting, as well as some background as to what will be done in publicity. I saw one contract in which the publisher agreed specifically to use his best efforts to install "up-front flats" * in fifty

---

* "Up-front," in this case, means close to the main entrance of a bookstore. "Flats" refers to a rather wasteful method of gaining attention to a book by stacking four piles, fifteen or twenty copies high. This means utilizing eighty copies, which is a large order for a hardcover. Since hardcovers are sold with return privileges, it is the publisher who really takes the gamble when he offers to push flats into fifty stores. This might require four thousand additional copies. Maybe all will sell; maybe only 20 percent. It is an aggressive, venturesome, and dangerous way to get the bookstore customer to notice a book. In practice, the publisher tries to push flats onto a dealer when a book is selling, and he believes the returns will be light. But when the title is new, and the public's response is unknown, to load fifty bookstores with four thousand copies is like heavily advertising a new product without pretesting.

large metropolitan bookstores. This kind of promotion increases the sale of the book and tends to attract more bidders for additional rights as other publishers, in their normal course of cruising the scene, note these displays. This kind of detail is sometimes squeezed into a book contract because of the publisher's hunger to secure a "decent share" of subsidiary rights.

Mail-Order Rights. The right to issue a book in hardcover format usually includes the right to sell it to bookstores, wholesalers, and every kind of outlet where books are sold, as well as the right to engage in mail-order sales. In some cases, a publisher does not have a mail-order department. If you are selling a book to a trade publisher with little or no mail-order involvement, you might want to investigate offering the mail-order rights to a company with expertise in this area, as well as access to large lists of book buyers with an interest in the subject matter of your book. Some good examples of this would be books about home repair, gardening, photography, crafts, astrology. Why these fields? Because they are replete with magazine publishers who sell books by mail to their subscribers, and have a half-million or more ideal customers for books in their fields.

For example, let's take a photographic book. *Modern Photography*, *Popular Photography*, and *Petersen's Photographic Magazine* sell photographic books by mail. So, if a trade publisher with no mail-order department is buying hardcover rights to your book on photography, you might ask if you could peel off the mail-order rights and sell them to a mail-order publisher who has the qualifications to promote it. Why should the trade publisher be willing to do this? Because you see it from his point of view. You make it attractive by offering him part of the royalty from the mail-order sales. Second, you accept a slightly lower royalty on your mail-order sales to secure a guarantee from the mail-order publisher that all his letters promoting the sale of your book will also carry a notation that the book is available in bookstores. This leaves the trade publisher of your book indebted to you for helping his bookstore sales, and this might mean a better deal from him. Here, the trade publisher, the mail-order publisher, and the author all benefit. This is the attitude to have when negotiating.

Another approach is for the author to sell his book first to a mail-order publisher, offering "mail-order rights only," and then offer "trade hardcover rights only" to a trade publisher* who sells to bookstore outlets. Either one of these is part of a larger segment of rights known as "copublishing rights." As different opportunities surface, the matter of copublishing rights may be further fragmented.

While publishing the *Farm Quarterly*, we produced a hardcover titled *The Good Old Days*. Our initial press run was twenty thousand, and we intended to sell these copies by direct mail, since we dropped 1.5 million circulars into the mails each year to sell books and subscriptions. Harper bought the trade-store rights to *The Good Old Days* and this allowed us to increase the initial press run to twenty-five thousand. As a result, we were able to buy our own twenty thousand books at 15 cents a copy less, because the fixed costs (dust jacket, design, composition, plates) were divided into more copies. I mention this detail because it contains the essence of a symbiotic contract. Harper got a good book without having to edit it or worry about the production. We bought our books more cheaply because the press run was larger, and we received additional income through Harper's royalty check for the five thousand copies they sold.

Book-Club Rights. Generally, the method of submission is for the publisher to send galleys to the book club. Because so much money and prestige are involved, some of the higher-placed individuals at the large book clubs will get a personal call from the publisher, agent, or editor, asking them to read a particular set of galleys. Like going to the well, you can only do this so often.

Condensation Rights. Several magazines use condensations of books and they like to publish these "on the button," that is, close to the book's publication date. Since monthly magazines are made up well in advance (the March issue closes January 1 and goes on sale February 15), the submission is usually via galley proofs. The degree to which the

---

*Although the term "trade publisher" was defined before, some writers find the word "trade," as used here, unrelated to the word as they know it. A trade bookstore is one that deals mainly in hardcover books. A trade editor is one who works with books that are sold mainly to trade bookstores, as compared with an editor who works with mass paperbacks, which are sold mainly to newsstands or drugstores, or an editor who works with books that are sold exclusively by mail. A trade-publisher's list is sold mostly through trade stores.

publication of a condensed version of a book helps its hardcover sales is a gray area. If 70 percent of the book is published, the reader may feel he has had it and doesn't need to buy the hardcover. Also if the book isn't liked by many of the magazine's readers, that can dampen hardcover sales. For these reasons, a condensation can kill hardcover sales. But, if the readers enjoy it and talk it up, the word-of-mouth advertising can cause a book to take off. It's one of the gambles in book publishing.

Commercial Rights. I happened to have been present at a historic meeting at which history was not made. A candy manufacturer, at Tarzana Ranch, in California, where I was visiting Edgar Rice Burroughs, wanted to manufacture a candy bar with a name that in some way simulated Tarzan's victory yodel. I was offered five hundred dollars to come up with a name, and, on the way home, in my roomette, I practiced the Tarzan yodel, trying to break it into pronounceable syllables. A startled conductor, accompanied by a train detective, warily slid the roomette's door open and searched for—I suppose—the body.

The most familiar commercial rights today are in the form of calendars based on an author's characters. "The Star Wars Portfolio" offers "21 magnificent original paintings (suitable for framing), that inspired the movie sets and costumes." There is also *Star Wars Iron-On Transfer Book*—"16 full-color iron-ons designed to decorate T shirts." The publisher of these marvels is Ballantine.

Computer/Magnetic-Tape Rights. Let's say a team of authors has prepared a large, multipaged reference book on every kind of annual and perennial plant. It is so huge and expensive that only libraries can order it. The publisher puts all the data into a computer with organized retrieval possible with the push of the right buttons. He then advertises that the data on the culture of any flower or plant for any given rainfall and temperature zone are available at two dollars per. You send two dollars. The publisher's computer operator presses the right buttons. The computer prints out the data for growing hollyhocks in West Texas, including the available heights, best variety, colors, possible allergies, nutritional values, medical uses, and so forth. A mail clerk sends it off to you, and you tell your friends how complete it is. Another clerk in the publisher's office enters an agreed number of cents on the royalty page of the author, who then benefits by his royalty on that two-dollar sale. Publishers are becoming aware of how to do this and of what kinds of books lend themselves to selling printouts from a data base.

Rights are a two-way street, and magnetic-tape rights, for instance, as separate from computer rights, appear to belong entirely to the publisher.

When the magnetic tape is made, an operator sits before a keyboard, not unlike that of your typewriter, and "retypes" your book. Instead of keys hitting a black ribbon, they punch and encode a tape. When the tape is put through a photographic machine, a series of galley proofs comes out. These are cut into pages. Plates are made of the pages and printed by means of lithography. Sometimes one publisher will sell or lease the complete magnetic tape of a book to another publisher who bought the rights to reprint the book. The author does not share in this sale, which might be for a few hundred dollars. The fact that the second publisher is able to get the hard part of his typesetting done so easily and inexpensively may be of some help in the rights sale for which the magnetic tape was needed.

Microfilm/Microfiche Rights. This is still a new area, and, although the skirmishes over it at this time are small, everyone is aware that somehow, someday, it can be big—maybe. Let's take microfilm. You manage a library and you want to subscribe to two thousand magazines. Some are weeklies, some monthlies, some quarterlies. You want complete coverage. But as the magazines pour in, you run out of space. So you order a microfilm of each page of each issue of the magazine, and it comes to you either in a roll of film (microfilm) or on a three-by-five card (microfiche). The three-by-five card may hold twenty pages *on each side.* You now can store two thousand issues of magazines, covering ten years, in the space of one filing cabinet. It's scary. Right now, authors are paid nothing extra when a library buys the microfilm of a magazine instead of subscribing to the magazine. Great and wonderful as it all appears to be, it's still in the Model T stage, and that's why publishers, authors, and agents do a slow waltz on tiptoe around microfilm and microfiche rights. Xerox has an Ann Arbor subsidiary that is promoting film and fiche magazine subscriptions to libraries but, as far as I know, authors have not yet thought their way into it.

There are barriers between microfilm and fiche and the general public.

When you squint into a lightbox for two hours, looking at blown-up microfilm, your eyes get bleary. Second, to enlarge a fiche to the point where it is readable is expensive and takes time. Third, to put a magnifying glass on a fiche tires the eye quickly. Some librarians are archivists, who love every scrap of reference material in the whole wide world, but they prefer to sit on it quietly and not give the public easy access. To get to it, you have to pass muster. This cuts down on public use.

Paperback Rights. The only thing I have to add is that sometimes an author sells hardcover rights to a publisher who also owns his own paperback division. In this case, the publisher's hardcover contract may specify that he is buying "volume rights," meaning that he has the right to issue both hardcover and paperback editions. The author then receives the full paperback royalty instead of 50 or 75 percent of it. That's very nice. On a sale of one hundred thousand copies of a paperback selling for two dollars, when the royalty is 6 percent, the author will receive six thousand dollars. Otherwise, if his share of the royalty were 50 percent, he would receive three thousand.

When volume rights are sold, however, a date needs to be specified, after which time the paperback rights, if not bought by the publisher's own paperback division, and not sold by the publisher to another reprinter, will revert to the author or his agent for sale to the highest bidder. In the contracts I have seen (and they vary), the original hardcover publisher shares in the paperback royalties when his own paperback division doesn't bring the book out.

When the hardcover publisher buys volume rights, the author may suffer a disadvantage because there is neither an auction nor are submissions made to a dozen reprinters to ask if they are interested. The hardcover publisher's own reprint division simply takes it over. The author may protect himself by naming, in advance, a minimum acceptable advance royalty. This would normally not equal the amount brought at an auction when all the reprinters were having a go at it.

Dramatic Rights. Your nibble for dramatic rights may come from a star who sees a fat part, a producer, a playwright, a director. The author of the book on which a play is based receives a royalty based on the theater's daily gross cash receipts. The amount of the royalty varies with the number of other people who cut their way into the box-office receipts. Is it a musical? Then there are the people who wrote the lyrics and the music as well as the playwright. The highest royalty I've seen paid to the author of a book on which a play is based was "10 percent of the box."

Foreign Rights. Among the more convivial events in the book-publishing industry are the foreign book fairs, where publishers go to buy rights to publish foreign books as well as sell foreign rights to their own properties. Normally, an author will prefer 25 percent of the gross sum paid, rather than this percentage of the net sum. The latter permits expenses in selling to be deducted. When the buyer resides in a country where entry to the publisher's records is difficult to obtain, a flat fee covering foreign or translation rights is often better than an advance based on a royalty arrangement.

Cable-TV Rights. In the immediacy of the eighties, the climactic increase in rights payments to authors is coming from something already with us, but not yet divided into the necessary copyright divisions. The new money is cable TV.

Today, a TV program may be transmitted to a satellite by means of an uplink antenna. The signals descend with equal intensity to all cable systems equipped to receive them, and are then relayed to subscribers. Signals may also come down scrambled to be received by window-ledge converters that permit one household to receive a program that bypasses the cable-TV system.

There are many systems. A few will win out. And, once again, technology is preparing to run faster than the writer's ability to supply material. Outstanding cable-TV shows will cost two dollars and up for one performance with a 30 million audience. Monthly subscriptions to various cable-TV stations will cost from five to twenty-five dollars a month with local, regional, and national audiences; the latter will run into 70 million TV sets tuned into the performance of one sporting event, one informative lecture, or one play based on an author's book. At a cost of a dollar per tuned-in TV set, that's a $7 million (10 percent) royalty. Your TV station will become an electronic magazine rack from which the viewer can select programs suited to his individual taste, whether it be oriented to children, teens, blacks, young marrieds, golden-agers, science students, and so forth. The stern moral is twofold: (1) any right you sell should have precise boundaries; (2) all rights not included in those sold should be retained.

8

The Production Department: Where Manuscripts Come In and Books Go Out

ON THIS PARTICULAR DAY, Chuck, the production manager, is holding a one-man conference, and the one man, Chuck, is getting madder by the minute. The tools of his trade lie before him: a micrometer to measure the thickness of paper, an engraver's magnifying glass, a type-specimen book, a steel ruler with one edge divided into inches and the other into picas, and a telephone pad with a list of suppliers. Next to his desk is a brightly lit narrow tank covered with a sheet of frosted glass on which color transparencies may be laid for better examination.

Behind Chuck's desk, a shelf holds the catalogues and current price sheets of various paper mills. Paper salesmen freely enter Chuck's office, whenever it is unoccupied, to insert new samples and price sheets into loose-leaf binders and drop their old ones into the wastebasket.

Chuck has loosened his collar for comfort as he goes through a thick sheaf of galley proofs that came to him from the editorial department. The galley proofs contain pen corrections on every page; the kind of changes called "author's alterations" or AAs, because they are not typos made by the typesetter but word changes introduced by the author that were not on the original manuscript.

The phone rings. It is the senior editor, Adam.

"Chuck? You wanted me?"

"You bet. Do you know how many AAs are in these galleys? If they make us miss our press date, we have to wait for the merry-go-round to come around again so we can get back on the horse. That's ten days. The sales department wants this book for their L.A. and New York press parties. Do you want to go with a mockup?"

"No. The author phoned yesterday to say everything he wrote looks different in type from the way it looks in the manuscript. When he read the galleys, it was like seeing the work with new eyes. How bad are they—the changes? My secretary brought you the galleys while I was in conference. I'll come right over."

Chuck growled and shook his head. After thirty years as production manager, he still could not understand authors. Why can't they write it right the first time? What was it about words that made them so picky? Chuck makes a red check in the margin of the galley proof where "slim" is changed to "slender" and another check where "lean" becomes "trim." What the hell does it matter?

Adam enters the office. Chuck rises and greets him by repeating Adam's question: "How bad are they? Plenty. Over a thousand lines will have to be reset and sixty galleys reproofed. This author is like a seeing-eye dog for doing the wrong thing. He never makes a change at the end of a paragraph. Not this guy. He's the kind who inserts six words smack into the first line of a long paragraph. This resetting and reproofing sticks you with ten days' delay."

The senior editor waves a hand in greeting and casually picks up the engraver's magnifying glass from Chuck's desk. "Why did you call this thing a 'linen tester' this morning?"

"Because a magnifying glass like this used to be used in textile mills to count the threads in cloth. Goddamnit, this book is going to miss publication date, and there's going to be hell all around. And the costs . . ."

"The author knows he pays for AAs on galleys. But I'd hate to change the dates on those press parties. We pulled that twice this year already."

The senior editor takes the sheaf of galley proofs from the production manager and starts paging through them, engrossed in the task of absorbing not only each change but its effect on the whole book. The production manager takes a long-distance call from a supplier who wants to install a duplicating machine on trial.

"Buy it or lease it," the supplier says. "Test it against the one you have now. Use your own paper, the kind your editors can edit on. What you have now takes a pen like a sponge." The production manager tells him to call back in three days.

"Thanks," says the salesman. "On my own, I'll have it crated up and ready for you the minute you say ship."

Adam starts out of the office. "Chuck," he says, "I'll get back to you before noon."

"It's on your head, Adam. Every hour is that much more delay."

The incident, one of many in the production manager's day, is settled by the senior editor's calling the author, who agrees to allow the senior editor the right to cut down some of the corrections. Adam, wise to the ways of this particular author, had cautioned him to make a Xerox of each corrected galley proof "in case your work is lost in the mail." Now, the editor and author, over an hour-long long-distance call later to be billed to the author, settle on which corrections are to be made and which are to be "stetted."* The production manager voiced the hope that with changes on only twenty galleys out of sixty, the delay would be only two days, which was within the safety period he had allowed.

"I called the bindery for you, Adam, and the cloth is in and they're going to start to make covers and stamp them. The dust jacket goes to press next week. It's going to be close."

Adam grins. "It always is," he says.

Chuck's secretary comes in.

"You wanted me to remind you to set aside three days for the New York reps of printers in Italy, Japan, and West Germany. Here are their names and phone numbers. I called the secretary of your association, the Linen Testers, and they have a library of foreign-printed books. Should I go over and borrow some for you to look over?"

"Hey! That's good. Yes, please do."

The secretary is pleased because she wanted to go shopping uptown, so she says she will bring back the books.

The production manager's assistant wheels in a large bulletin board full of ruled lines, colored thumbtacks, and black headings written with a

---

*The Latin word *"stet,"* as used by copy editors, means, "Let it stand," or "Do not make this correction; use the original version of the copy."

felt-tipped pen. "Chuck, I finished the schedule on the fifteen books in production now. You wanted to check each book against its delivery date and see which ones are bollixed up."

For the next two hours, Chuck and his assistant work two telephones, calling suppliers and checking the progress of the fifteen titles in production.

As the data came in, Chuck dictated the details about each book into a tape recorder—where the snags were on each. Later, his secretary would type up the notes, and the assistant production manager would use the notes to guide his follow-up work for the coming week.

The publisher walked into Chuck's office. "It's such a nice spring day. I had Dave's Deli pack two brown bags. We can pick them up and lunch in the minipark near Madison. This morning, Lila stopped in and left this split of red wine. She said it's the first good day to eat outside. Want to go?"

"That's just what I need," said Chuck.

At lunch the publisher asked Chuck if he could spend the afternoon working up a list of twenty ways to save a nickel a book.

"I went ahead and hired Blockie Schwartz, and then bingo, he brought two people in with him. Alvin's idea is to pay for the whole thing by asking the production department to save a nickel a book." The publisher smiled.

Chuck took a sip of the red wine and nodded. "Yes, I know. You already asked me to do this. So did Alvin. I've been working on your idea for a couple of weeks, and I'll finish it this afternoon and give it to Alvin. He'll probably take it home to read tonight."

"Chuck," said the publisher, "let's walk back the long way. I want to see how many trees have any green on them."

That night, after dinner, the comptroller allowed himself a glass of brandy. Sipping it slowly, he settled easily into his chair. Relaxed, he said to his wife: "I got some homework. I'll do it in the den."

"Don't use your eyes more than an hour," she said.

"Wake me early so we can be together at breakfast."

Alvin found his briefcase and pulled out the suggestions Chuck had prepared on how to save a nickel a book. *There's no better time,* Alvin thought.

"Saving a nickel a book," wrote Chuck, "on every book we print is something we can do. However, we have to think that way long before the manuscript gets to me. We can start by asking the pencil editor* of every accepted book if twenty pages can be cut out of the manuscript. This kind of cutting is possible on most books of eighty thousand words because the cut is only 8 percent. I propose this idea for one book out of every four we publish.

"When the pencil editor cuts twenty pages out of a book manuscript, look what happens:

"We save 7 cents on the cost of the bare paper because:

There are sixteen fewer pages of printed matter.
Two cents is saved on press work because we print sixteen pages fewer.
One cent is saved because there are sixteen fewer pages to be set, and sixteen fewer pages to bind.
Ten cents saved per book.

"If we cut one book out of every four by sixteen pages of printed matter, we save 2.5 cents, average, on every book we print. That's half our total goal of saving a nickel a book.

"There's another thing to be done before I get the manuscript. I'd like our Sales Department to get the discount schedule of twenty publishers who issue 200 books a year or more, twenty publishers who issue 100 to 150 books a year, and forty publishers who issue 40 to 80 titles a year. I would like all of us to hold these discount schedules in our hands, not have someone tell us about them. And they have to be current. The same goes for the return-copy agreements on unsold books from these eighty publishers. By comparison, are we overdiscounting, or are we

---

*The *pencil editor* is the editorial employee who actually edits the book, testing each sentence for clarity, each word for its ability to communicate the intended meaning, each page for cause it gives the reader to turn the page, each chapter for an unbroken logic line that leads from the previous chapter into the following one. When the pencil editor's job is done, he returns to the whole of the manuscript to mark soft spots that can be cut.

overlenient on returns? When Mr. Sam started this business, he gave up 40 percent discounts very fast. It was a new business, and he needed orders. His return policy was simple: if a dealer returns it, give him full credit. Mr. Sam published a book a month. We do a book a week, and we don't have to offer a 40 percent discount so quickly, nor give every dealer full credit on returns, especially if the dealer doesn't pay his bill in sixty days.

"If we make a thorough comparison of what we do and what everybody else does, I think we'll add half of 1 percent gross income to every book we sell. What I'm talking about comes to 2 cents more income per book sold, even if we don't change our present return policy on unsold books."

Alvin fished out his pocket calculator and did some quick figuring. Chuck was right, even after Alvin allowed for the additional money the travelers would be paid when their commissions were based on a gross income of half of 1 percent more. Chuck was a thirty-year man and knew the business. Alvin got up and looked out the apartment-house window to Central Park. In the distance, a thousand lights looked cool and far away. *Would it be best*, Alvin thought, *if the idea on discounts came from one of the travelers, rather than from inside the company?* They were the men who would have to live with it. He continued to read.

"We've now saved an average of 4.5 cents a book. It's time to get into the savings I can effect as production manager. There are a lot of them, but one man can't do it alone. The big thing is standardized format.

"For example, one-third of our books should be the same size, same typography, and be made from the same materials. We can standardize one or two of our books in each of our categories: religion, novels, self-help, and so forth. In that way all our novels wouldn't look alike, because only two would be standardized. Our self-help books wouldn't all look alike, because only five out of fifteen would be standardized."

By standardizing, Chuck means that one-third of the books would have the same:

1. page size	4. binding materials
2. type size	5. back and front boards
3. paper	6. endpapers.

Chuck continued, "Standardizing the six items—making them identical for eighteen books—allows us to negotiate long-term-buying contracts with each supplier and promise minimum-quantity purchases. When I know eighteen of our books will be made of the same materials, I can purchase our printing and binding materials two ways: (a) instead of buying five hundred pounds of endpapers for one book, I can buy five thousand pounds of the same paper at a crack, or (b) if I assure the manufacturer that I will purchase five thousand pounds of endpapers during one year, I can get a slightly better price and still get some variety into our endpapers.

"Why do we try to design each book individually? In truth, it's just a once-over-lightly design job. We don't do it all out. The changes we make on each book are just enough to make it more expensive. But are the designs really *that* different and are they *that* good? How can you design fifty books a year and make them great and separate, with a staff that's still small enough to be economical? We've got our design on an assembly line, and we don't admit it.

"To what extent are our book graphics, aside from dust jackets, responsible for our sales? Let's put fifteen times as much work into one design, and let that be standard for fifteen books. What we have now is a lot of stewing around that costs more than it's worth."

Oh, oh, oh, thought Alvin, *he's stirring up the whole zoo.* Looking at the clock, he hesitated, then dialed Chuck's home.

"Hello."

"Chuck, this is Alvin. I apologize for calling you at home this late at night."

"That's okay. Glad to hear from you."

"Chuck, this report can't go to anyone except the publisher and myself. Are you the one to tell Bunner that his discount schedule is too high? And to tell Helen and Adam their books can be cut? The art department will go wild before anyone settles down enough to realize the new opportunities this report gives them. . . ."

"What do you suggest?"

"Only the publisher can present this. . . ."

"You're right. The art department will feel threatened. So will Helen and Adam. I'll hand the report only to the publisher. Now that I think of it, that's what he asked me to do."

"Good," said Alvin. "Thank you for listening." He hung up the phone and, with a calmer spirit, started again to read the report.

"Look at it this way. We turn out twenty-five books each season, fifty a year. If we standardize nine books a season, we can still have thirty-two of them looking different. The others will have identical physical characteristics, but we can mix them into our general categories (novels, religious, et cetera), so that all the books in one line won't look alike.

"This let's gang print and gang bind. The big saving is in the printing. We change all the plates at one time and have only one press make-ready instead of a separate one for each book. This lets us save 9 cents a book, or, on the average, 3 cents each on all the books we print.

"My next step should have a heading: 'Danger—Beware,' and I'm giving the details because I was asked to. We can lower the quality of materials purchased. We started to creep in this direction ten years ago and have never stopped. Our books have lost some of their class. So have everyone else's. Will the public buck? I don't know. At any rate, here is what could be done: we can go with thinner paper. We buy paper by the pound and if we order paper weighing 10 percent less, we buy it for around 10 cents less on the dollar.

"We can buy job-lot paper when a paper mill has an overrun. There is risk here. If a book sells well and is reprinted, the next edition can't be printed on the same kind of paper, because the job lot we bought has been used up. We may have to pay more for the new paper, but, by that time, we know we are investing in a book that is selling.

"Color work, or other jobs requiring finer surface paper, can be reproduced on matte-finished paper instead of gloss-finished paper.

"Instead of using binder's cloth to cover the front and back ends of the book, we can use paper-based material.

"We can use thin oakboard instead of regular binder's board.

"By using adhesive for hardcover binding instead of sewing, there is a saving, depending on the quantity.

"Instead of varnishing the dust jacket, we can use glossy ink. But, when the white, unprinted part of the dust jacket is exposed to the sun, in the dealer's window, it will tend to oxidize and turn brown.

"Finally, in the matter of saving money, I suggest we announce a company policy to the effect that eighteen books out of fifty will be standardized. The purpose of the announcement is to let the art and graphics departments know what is expected of them. The announce-

110

ment will include the fact that one book each season will have a dust jacket printed in one color, on a colored stock, instead of being printed in four colors on white paper.

"The first group of money-saver ideas in this report will cut our costs per book by 7 cents, the last group will cut costs by an additional 8 cents. That's 15 cents a book or three times the goal. I suggest caution on the last group of ideas. Should the public catch on, we would pick up a label that's hard to lose.

"My final idea is in the opposite direction. A lot of people in this business can walk into six bookstores a day and not see anything, because, to them, everything always looks the same. And they are right. That's my whole point and the point from which I want to make a departure."

Alvin sighed. Here was a nice straight-shooting guy like Chuck that you could always depend on, and now he was marching off into left field. *You can't depend on anybody,* Alvin thought.

"More than three-fourths of all trade books are approximately six by nine inches outside and have a type-page size of five by eight. My proposal is that we think in terms of issuing certain books, maybe two or three a year, in a graphic style that lends itself exclusively to the editorial content of the book.

"Look at *Whole Earth.* It looks like what it is. So do kindergarten books. When we start to design a book, unless it's an art book or a picture book, we automatically think of an overall size of six by nine and a type page of five by eight, with maybe a half-inch one way or the other. Our running heads, type margins, folios, even the typefaces, are very much alike. When a bookstore browser sees two thousand trade books of more or less the same size, he doesn't know where to turn. The immediacy of the editorial difference between them doesn't come across. The dust jackets are different, but the interiors of all the books look alike at five paces.

"I want us to think in terms of issuing certain books in a unique graphic style that is a direct outgrowth from the editorial content of the book. You say, 'My God, that's a completely new design.' Right. Apply this idea only to those books where we can invent a graphic design that uniquely suits one book. We can add a buck or two to the list price because our graphics will make the book stand out."

Here we go, thought Alvin.

"Let's take one example of what I'm talking about. For their book *The Directory of Natural and Health Foods*, the Putnam Company invented a set of graphics born out of the subject matter of the book itself. Now let's compare the invention of graphics that emanate from the editorial ambience of a book to the way we sometimes do it. We say, well, we've used Caslon typeface six times this month, so let's go with Times Roman. We don't invent a complete set of integrated graphics—paper, binding, type face, art, page size—that comes right out of the editorial womb of one book."

Oh, thought Alvin. *That guy will murder us.* For a moment, Alvin's lips parted. Was Chuck throwing the art department a fish? No, this was the real Chuck. *He's serious—good grief*, thought Alvin, *what if we were to publish a book on merry-go-rounds?* Alvin picked up Chuck's report and stared at it solemnly and then continued to read.

"In my office I have a copy of *The Directory of Natural and Health Foods* for you to look at. Note the page size: ten and a half by fourteen inches. If you compress it, it measures three-quarters of an inch thick, but then puffs out to a quarter of an inch thicker, because air filters between the pages when you print on ground-wood paper. Imagine—ground-wood paper for a book that has real style! There are three hundred and twenty pages. The list is $9.95. The front cover is bright, conservative, and directly related to its subject matter. When a dealer buys six copies of a book that size, he has no place to put them except on the counter. The size guarantees display. I think if anyone were to do this on a regular basis, the dealer would rebel, and big jobbers would ask for a larger discount, because they'd have to give a book like this double storage space and double material handling.

"I'm not suggesting we go into a line of ten-and-a-half-by-fourteen books. What I am suggesting is that we explore each one of our fifty titles to see if two or three of them realistically lend themselves to an invention of a complete set of integrated graphics for that one book. Incidentally, in the case of *The Directory of Natural and Health Foods*, the cover paper is lightweight and dog-ears when you handle it frequently. This size book, if bound in paper, needs a heavier stock.

"However, the layout, choice of art, and the way the art is reproduced are a triumph. They use a flock of old-time woodcut illustrations that are strong on nostalgia and reach out to you. And they give all the art plenty of white space. I remember Wilson Hicks at *Life* magazine saying a dozen times a month: 'You can reproduce a good print small, but, when you use a bad print, blow it up to a page.' Well, that's what Putnam did with a lot of seed-catalogue photographs. The whole thing carries like a charm. I'm not talking about the text, only the graphics. A lot of the art is bigger than life size. It's an object lesson on how to get by with ordinary photographs and end up with a great publication.

"The cost per thousand of press impressions on this kind of book is less, because it can be printed very fast on a newspaper-type press.

"Last year we rejected a book on roller coasters: big-time thrill rides at amusement parks. There's a fan association of people who love these rides, and the book we rejected was written by the nation's number-one fan. Anyway, this might be the kind of book that lends itself to the invention of a complete set of integrated graphics."

Alvin put Chuck's report into his briefcase and started to sort out the ideas he had read, wondering which would be risky, which would be efficient. He'd call a few comptrollers at the big chain bookstore operations and find out if books with special graphics sold well. He undressed quietly and retired for the night.

In the bed next to his, his wife heard him lie down and after a few moments, said softly, "Alvin?"

His regular breathing was the answer.

She turned quietly in her bed, tucked her pillow under her stomach. He was a good man, she thought, and she should let him sleep.

9

How to Select the Right Publisher and Be Assured of a Prompt Reading

WHICH PUBLISHER should be your first target? Who can resist the pleasure of saying, "Oh, did I tell you? Today, I packed my new book off to Random House?"

Do you want your book going to the publisher who issues the most titles a year or to the publishing house owned by a multinational corporation—like Gulf and Western or ITT? They should be able to pay their bills, at least, wouldn't you think?

How are you going to decide, with 1,350 active royalty publishers, which one to choose? Here is a brief summary of what to look for in choosing your publisher.

1. You want, first of all, to review the ones who already have books in the same field as your own. Unless you've hit upon a wide-awake, hungry young publishing house, and have some kind of personal connection with them, your best bet is to choose from the publishers who are currently in your field.

2. If you find publishers with a clear interest in your field, which should be your first target? The one with four hundred titles? Or would you prefer a smaller house issuing perhaps thirty titles annually? Should you approach a house with one or two books in your field but which has

a total annual line of only a dozen books? There's an argument for and against each choice, and you should weigh these against your prejudices.

When a large company with four hundred titles a year offers you a book contract, your work represents one-quarter of 1 percent of their potential gross income from the sale of new titles. That makes you a tiny frog in a very large pond. In addition, any publisher who is large enough to issue four hundred titles probably has thirty well-established authors to whom a large advance has been pledged. The books of these authors may outgross all the others, when you include the revenue from rights and trade sales. This can reduce your impact on the company from a quarter of 1 percent to perhaps an eighth of 1 percent of their total gross income.

If you market your book to a house that issues only twenty-five titles a year, you may represent 2 percent of their gross new business for the year, even if yours is a first book. Relatively, this makes you sixteen times more important to the publisher. Worlds have turned on less.

If all that mattered were the above figures, it would be simple to choose, but there are intangibles. Although books do get lost in a publishing house issuing two or three titles a day, yours may find a lover who urges its attention on sales and publicity people as only an inner-circle friend can do. Without such a supporter, a book may fade away at a large house. Should your book catch on, a large house knows what to do with it and has the risk capital, the expertise, and a whole wide world of distribution at its disposal. The smaller house may be smaller because that's the way they want it, or their size may reflect their lack of publishing skills, a lack of energy, or a lack of willingness to risk money. If you are considering a publishing house that issues fewer than a dozen titles a year, you can expect considerably less distribution, fewer travelers, and in the latter's place there may be commission salesmen who represent numerous small houses, not just your publisher alone. This places the commission salesmen under control of their own marketing company rather than the individual sales manager of any one publisher whom they represent. Bunner can't phone Bernie, Stu, and the rest and say: "We're close to a major rights sale, and we have to make the *New York Times* bestseller list with the Jason book. Give it everything you've got on every call. We'll pay double commission on all Jason sales the next three weeks. Go, fella, go."

But there are always compensations. The smaller house shows a more sanguine side of itself to newcomers and less established authors, because the smaller house doesn't get its choice of everything good that's being offered. When a literary agent auctions off "the season's coming blockbuster," and the floor bid is one hundred thousand dollars, the small publisher has no stomach for the risk. If the book bombs, the first man to lose his salary for that year—and maybe his shirt, too—is you-know-who.

The reality of the situation is that the publisher with only two dozen titles to his credit each year rarely gets an opportunity to make the gamble even if he wanted to. The feisty literary agents who handle famous names don't think in terms of shooting off a letter to Minnesota, Kansas, Georgia, where some of the small publishers dwell, in areas known as "the country." They would rather deal with heavy-money people within a cab ride from their office. This makes the small publisher more dependent on his own devices, and he relies a bit more on the un-rush mail.

In the area of quality paperbacks, however, the small publisher has beaten the giants hands down, when you compare the number of such titles they have on the *New York Times* weekly bestseller list to the number of quality paperbacks issued by major Eastern houses. If yours is a quality paperback, rather than a hardcover, take a long close look at the *New York Times* weekly bestseller list of quality paperbacks for any six-month period, and note the small houses whose names appear four or five times in that period. It's a curious edge that the smaller houses have developed. If your book is best suited to a quality-paperback publication, the suggestion from here is to do your homework and go to the smaller publishers who are outshining their big competitors. For the week I am looking at, out of fifteen quality paperbacks on the *Times* list, I find four titles issued by Meadowbrook, Running Press, Ten Speed Press, and Workman.

Can you risk offering your hardcover book to a royalty house that publishes only half a dozen titles a year? One reason they are worth considering is that, if one of them issues six titles a year, and yours is one of the six, you are suddenly 16 percent of their potential gross for the coming year. You'd think they simply have to get behind your book. That's what you'd think, and you'd be right, but some of the small houses are fumblers, while others are the great growth companies of the future. If you are thinking of submitting to a tiny house, you might consult *Literary Market Place* for the last five years and see how the personnel of this house reads each year. Is it always changing, always the same? Has their number of titles increased or decreased? And, most of all, you want to examine their catalogues for the last three years. Do they actually issue one? Are some of their so-called new titles actually back-list titles?

Should you go to this trouble to find out a few hard facts about Jones and Jones, who state they issue six titles a year? If your book took you two years to write, and if you believe in it half as much as an expectant mother believes in what is taking her only nine months to produce, you won't regret the two or three hours of time and several phone calls to get some data on which to base a judgment. Chapter 29 of this book lists the addresses of headquarters offices of the larger chain bookstores. You might make a phone call or two and learn whether this particular publisher sells any of its titles in lots of five hundred at a crack to the chain you are calling. Will they tell you this? Possibly. It depends on how you state your case. Better to spend a few hours for research and a ten-dollar bill for telephone calls than to find your book mired in mud.

What's the easiest way to choose a publisher?

Stick a pin through a page of book-publisher listings, and go with the one your pin finds. It's called the dart theory, and some senators have held that it outperforms mutual funds.

Here's how to select one dozen publishers who currently publish material in the field of your book. What we can't tell you is which of the dozen is best for you and best for your book. To answer that, you have to rely on your own taste, your luck. At the worst, once you have selected one dozen publishers who are currently issuing titles in the field of your book, you could put their names in a hat and pull one out. The method is not artistic, but, if you selected the dozen with care, the odds would be with you.

The reference material that will assist your selection of one dozen publishers is available from three books, and your main branch library has each. Start with *Publishers' Trade List Annual*. It contains the catalogues of most commercial royalty publishers whose titles fill the shelves of trade bookstores. Study the catalogues until you find a dozen publishers who appear to publish books in the field about which you have written.

Do your research in easy stages: an hour or two a day for three days will do it handsomely. If your book is tied to an esoteric subject matter, ask the librarian to show you the card file of books on similar material, and copy down the names of the publishers. If those publishers are not in the current *Publishers' Trade List Annual*, write for their catalogues.

After assembling a list of one dozen publishers that you believe issue books in your field, read their editorial requirements in the current *Writer's Market*. This may help you decide which are the better candidates for you.

Now for the last piece of research. Look up your dozen publishers in *Literary Market Place*. The information about each publisher will include the number of titles published annually, along with their address and phone number, and some data on the company's personnel.

You are now well along on your marketing program. All that remains is to decide on the person to whom you should send your book at the publishing house of your choice, and whether you should send the entire manuscript, an outline plus two or three chapters, or just a query letter.

Arrange your list of publishers in a sequence that appeals to you. Starting with the first four, look up each one in *Literary Market Place*. Does the publisher's listing include the name of an editor assigned to handle works such as you have written? Perhaps your book is a juvenile, and the publisher's listing includes the name of his juvenile editor. Phone this editor person-to-person, and state that you have completed a juvenile book for children aged six to nine and wish to know whether the editor would prefer to see the complete manuscript or a chapter outline and several chapters. If you can't get to the editor, ask for the assistant juvenile editor. If this fails, leave your number and ask for a collect return call. If the person who speaks with you is less than courteous, or if the editor's secretary gives you a hard time, you have eleven others on your list. Here's how the conversation might go when all is well:

"Good morning, Essex."
"This is a paid long-distance call from Portland, Oregon, and my name is Carl Johnson. I have just completed a three-hundred-fifty-page

science-fiction novel, and I want to verify that the person to send it to at Essex is John Freedman. May I speak to Mr. Freedman or his secretary, please?"

"Just a minute, please."

"Mr. Freedman's office."

"This is a paid long-distance call from Portland, Oregon, and my name is Carl Johnson. I have just completed a three-hundred-fifty-page science-fiction novel, and I want to verify that the editor to send it to at Essex is John Freedman. Is that right?"

"Well, yes, Mr. Freedman does edit s.f., but I'm his assistant and I read the slush—I beg your pardon—all the unsolicited books. My name is Estelle Brooks. Send it to me, please."

"Thank you. I'll mail it today. How's the weather there?"

"Terrible."

"Jump in your time machine and come to Portland. It's spring and holding. . . ."

By making two or three calls like this, you will get a reasonably firm commitment that a specific individual at one publishing house of your choice will read your manuscript. When you ship off the script, address it to that particular person, enclose a note of thanks, and refer briefly to the phone conversation. Because of your letter, your work will go directly to the editor whom you address. This unassuming trifle lifts your work out of the unsolicited class if the company has a ban on reading such material.

In some instances, a publisher's listing in *Literary Market Place* will not include the name of any editor whose job tallies with the subject matter of your book. An example of this would be Alfred A. Knopf, where the editors are generalists; none is a genre editor devoted only to mystery, romance, history, and so forth.

In this case, place a station-to-station call to the company, and ask for the editorial department. The person who answers may be a recently hired employee who does not know the workings of the staff or may be someone who just walked by and heard the phone ring. You're taking a normal marketing risk, and you want to take it with good spirit. You ask for the name of the editor to whom your particular kind of work should be submitted and whether you should send the complete manuscript or several chapters and outline. If you get the name of a particular person, place a person-to-person call to this individual and verify what you were told.

"I was speaking to Mrs. Hillard, and she said, if I wanted to submit a manuscript on fifteenth-century Indian culture in America, I should send it to you. My purpose in calling is to verify if this is correct." At Knopf, you might be told to send your material to Robert Gottlieb, Editor-in-Chief, or Ashbel Green, Senior Editor, either of whom will disperse it to the right editor for evaluating.

I would advise against sending a manuscript, or even an outline and several chapters, without having made some contact and verified its correctness. If the verification is okay, send a brief note stating that your material was shipped today and enclose a five-dollar check covering its packing and return.

Why not just address the work to the company's editor-in-chief and ship it off? What could be simpler and more direct? Well, it may be simple and direct, but some book publishers return unsolicited work unread, and to get his work back with a printed card to that effect can throw an author into a state of free fall. It's not worth the emotional knock to chance it.

Although some publishers, with justifiable reason on their part, do return unsolicited work unread, there is a human loophole. A genre editor in the mystery department has a more tolerant attitude, because his is the responsibility of finding mysteries that people will buy and recommend to their friends. On this, his livelihood depends.

If you reach him at the right time, he will be willing to say: "Sure, send it on. Address it to me." And he will take it home because it's his choice to do so. But if the publisher dumps ten unsolicited mysteries from the general public on the editor's desk each day and tells him to take them home to read, the editor will rebel. Such is the nature of the animal.

You may wonder what good it does to have the editor's name on the manuscript when you don't know him, he doesn't know you, and your accompanying letter is brief and to the point.

Some editors have been at their desks for ten or more years and are so accustomed to seeing their own name on letters and envelopes that they take it for granted. A few editors are new and enjoy recognition. But many editors have been in the business for a while and have traveled the country as talent scouts, attended literary parties and asked numerous people to keep them in mind. Therefore, any script addressed to them could be from someone whom, at one time or another, they invited to "send something to our shop. I want to be first to read it." The more elaborate your name, *e.g.*, Lefabe Orleans Maximilian, the less likely they are to think they know you. Tricky pen names are extra baggage. The more familiar your name—Carl Haven, Jenny Edwards—the more likely it is to have a familiar ring.

Getting a fix on the name of a particular editor does two things for you: (1) it establishes that this department is alive and well; (2) it gives the editor no immediate cause not to look at your script. If you have to lug a dozen scripts home each week, any excuse to bypass one of them can turn a faint yes into a prompt no.

What if you have only an idea for a book and wish to approach an editor? This is a chancy beginning for a new writer. A professional writer with an established following will sometimes use a "query letter" under these circumstances. A query letter should be short—no more than a page, and it should describe the book. Ask if the publisher wishes to see the book when completed, or, better still, if he would like to see an outline of it, or an outline and several chapters. Enclose a stamped, self-addressed envelope for reply.

If you are a new writer, all the publisher knows about you is from your one-page letter. You almost have to show some evidence of your literary style as you reveal the idea of your book. If there is a show of wit or irony, the flash of a bright phrase; if your book idea flowers on the logic of its presentation; if function is favored, and the perfect little adjective is occasionally fitted into place, your query letter performs as it should.

A naked query letter (no outline, no sample chapter) isn't suited to the unpublished writer, because it leaves the editor too much in the dark. You can alleviate this by enclosing a chapter outline. You could also offer to make some adjustments to editorial suggestions sent in response to your outline.

Can you pull this same marketing approach if your book is already completed, by writing a chapter outline of it and enclosing three chapters? In reaching for this coup, you might outfox yourself. You can try it, of course, but what do you do if the editor says your outline is too close to something already on their next year's list, and they want the emphasis turned in another direction and your manuscript revised? Would you be willing to do the book over? If you do decide to take that risk, and you are receptive to ideas that change your emphasis, then you might submit a new outline and several altered chapters and ask for an advance of two or three thousand dollars to go ahead with the book. Even if your complete book, or your query, or your outline is turned down by two or three publishers, please do not be discouraged. Put your book to the test at least eight times before you go back to the drawing board. A book outline and several chapters have a special chemistry of their own. They will appeal to some editors and not to others. The reason for the appeal may not be in the basic quality of what you are offering but in the human nature of the buyer. Ever walk into a fruit-and-vegetable store and come out emptyhanded? Yet next week you could go into the same store and come out loaded. It depends on what you need and how you feel, doesn't it? Editors are much the same. And with a half-dozen manuscript decisions to be made on Friday, and a big week of editorial conferences coming up, he may just try to clean off his desk by sending back a lot of material.

It's indeed a business in which the fortunate are favored but, with 1,350 active, earnest publishers, there is every good marketing chance for a manuscript that's better than halfway decent.

Now is the time to answer a question of logistics. Should you submit your original copy or a duplicate? Should you use multiple submissions, in which you send a Xerox copy to many publishers at the same time? Answer to the first question: Hold your original. Submit a duplicate. But a poor-quality duplicate won't do. You require Xerox or IBM quality. Answer to the second question: State in your letter that this is not a multiple submission. Most publishers do not favor multiple submission, because it makes them schedule the reading of your work promptly, and this they may not be able to do. Sometimes a multiple submission may be kissed off for this reason and returned. "We can't get to this for ten weeks. Better just return it." It's an open decision, and it's your decision. A multiple submission of a complete manuscript forces the publisher's hand, and it's the better part of valor not to jab when you're at the starting gate.

THE BOOK MARKET

ON THE OUTSIDE

Stick to simple, clean, neat packaging. Use correct postage. Insure your package if you want. Use an office-supply-store label for addressing. Avoid art or frills.

ON THE INSIDE

It takes months, sometimes years of work, to complete a book. Spend the extra money, and have it typed on an electric typewriter with a disposable ribbon or its equivalent. This insures a clean black copy even from a so-so copying machine. Make three copies. This costs about twenty-four dollars each for a three-hundred-page book. Don't bind them. With three copies you won't have to get the job retyped in case of loss. And you have a copy available if you want to revise it. Use eight-and-a-half-by-eleven, white, twenty-pound, bond paper. Leave an inch-and-a-quarter margin on all four sides. Your name goes on page one with your address in the upper right-hand corner. A covering letter should be typewritten and short; one full page is usually longer than you want. The manuscript speaks for you.

Avoid underscoring and putting words or phrases in caps except under the most unusual circumstances. If your typewriter has a "ball" that lets you employ italic typewriter type or some other typefaces, don't use them. Minor and occasional corrections in black or blue ink on a page, after it has been "typed for good," are okay. Instructions to the printer are not the author's domain. Have someone who can spell, punctuate, and check the grammar go over your whole manuscript before you ship it out. Any paragraph with a series of long sentences is, normally, not as good as a paragraph that is broken up with shorter sentences. A simple, declarative sentence remains God's rarest gift to man.

Almost nothing will kill off a good manuscript. You are a writer, and you are justified in believing in yourself.

10

The Literary Agent

EVERYONE SEEMS TO AGREE that a great agent is a writer's best friend, but the actual reasons for this are rarely given. Here's what the agent can do for you.

If your book manuscript, in his opinion, is not readily marketable, he will say so to protect the two of you. The agent lives by his reputation for submitting only the kind of work that has a reasonably good chance of breaking even at worst and is a good bet to be profitable. He refuses to submit material that's thin, trite, or close to what was offered, recently published, and did not sell well.

Why not ship the scripts out anyway, and let them make their rounds? The publisher makes the investment. Let him be the judge. Making a Xerox copy of a book manuscript and sending it to thirty publishers can't cost more than forty dollars for each one, and that includes UPS delivery. What's twelve hundred dollars these days? Or the agent can send Xerox copies to ten publishers and spend only four hundred dollars. In fact, he can really be chintzy and make three copies and ship them out for $120.

Truthfully, it's not the cost that creates a problem with duplicate copies. What's at stake is the tacit agreement between agent and book publisher. The latter reads all submissions from any well-known, respected literary agent as part of his normal operating expense. When the agent sends the publisher a string of thirty so-so books within a year's time and each is turned down with nary a request for any of the agent's clients to make certain changes and resubmit—everyone loses. When only one of the agent's books is read and rejected by a wide range of publishers, he drops down but a step. But when the agent ships out thirty different books and doesn't get one bite, he hasn't dropped back a step; he's been dumped. Now, his books may be returned the same day, unread. "We're not reading this kind of material at this time," says the one-line note when the agent opens the package.

The agent's screening doesn't mean the work has to be great or even very good. But it cannot be poor or barely fair. It has to be more than literate, and of sufficient length to command the price needed in its own competitive market.

You know that one half-gallon of milk delivered to your kitchen door by the local dairy costs around $1.25. However, if plain water were substituted, the price would still be 80 cents. By the same token, although it costs around two dollars each to publish ten thousand copies of a three-hundred-page hardcover book with a four-color dust jacket, it would still cost $1.60 to do the same thing with a hundred fewer pages.

The binding, the dust-jacket artwork and plates, the sales and administrative costs, the advertising, promotion and publicity—all cost the same regardless of the hundred-page differential. Yet, to the book-buying public, the two-hundred-page book looks like less value.

What does this have to do with the price of fish?

If you have written a novella that will run 160 to 200 printed pages, and it's purely regional and not universal enough to attract a national market, or if its literary quality is closer to "just fair" than "fairly good," the hardcover retail price will still have to be at least nine dollars, and that's far too high to make it competitive with a fatter book that, on a literary level, might be a notch or two better. So the agent might screen this book out.

But what if the novella is first class?

Now that's a completely different story. Quality sells. But true quality is absent from most editorial submissions. The "in-house" vernacular phrase for this is "We buy the least worst." It's not said bitterly or cynically. It's just a statement of what's so. Do you disagree? Aside from your own work, how do you feel about the general level of what you read—especially if you read two or three books a month?

From the publisher's point of view, an exclusive line of quality books means so few titles a year (maybe ten, perhaps only eight) that there's not enough volume to employ his own salesmen to call on the trade. It takes almost fifty titles a year to support twelve travelers, and this pushes the publisher into volume that reduces the average literary quality. His editorial policy now becomes a search for a manuscript that he can sell for more than it costs him to manufacture, and in quantities of at least fifteen thousand copies for each one he buys.

It all sounds, at one and the same time, so sweetly reasonable and so distressingly maddening. Don't they think about quality, message, ideals, social values? Yes, sometimes they do. Much more so than almost any other kind of manufacturer. But in the main, high literary quality doesn't surface often, and the publisher contents himself with seeking manuscripts that live in the present, are easily read, and will have some kind of hold on a sizeable market. It is this attitude that leads the publisher to the literary agent. Here is a person, the publisher feels, who understands his position.

So we see that the first thing the literary agent does for the writer is the same thing he does for himself: He maintains a good reputation by screening material. When books come in that the agent feels should not be marketed, he is human enough to want to question his own judgment. Often he has an assistant or employs a manuscript evaluator as a check against his own editorial feelings. As a last resort, he may have lunch with an editor friend.

"Harry, I got trouble."

"Again with Peters? What'd he do this time?"

"No, it's Jason. His last two books were okay. You did one, and we had a book club and a TV adaptation, and we made the *Times* list for all of four weeks in tenth spot. I just got his new book. . . ."

"It's bum?"

"I think so."

"What do I have to do?"

"It's in my briefcase. Will you take it home to look over? Give it an hour. It's not an official submission. I need another judgment. Will you help me?"

"Sure. Okay."

Two days later, the agent gets the manuscript back with a one-line note: "You were right."

The agent returns the script to the author, adding to his own comments the brief fact that he had shown the book to Harry—and it drew a fast no. This makes the agent out to be something less than God, and there is hope the author will not take it too hard.

That's the first main job of the agent: to know what the publishers are buying and to protect both the author and himself by submitting only what appears to have some kind of reasonable chance of acceptance. Writing is a lonesome job, and having a comfortable relationship with an agent allows long days of doubt to dissolve in the warmth of encouragement and reassurance.

An agent can be especially helpful when a publisher reads your manuscript and wants to buy it. The agent will almost certainly get a better deal than you can get for yourself. For a case history, let's watch an agent sell a quality paperback to a publisher.

Quality paperbacks (also called trade paperbacks) are entirely different from mass paperbacks. The former are priced much higher ($3.95 to $8.95) and sold through trade bookstores and specialty outlets suited to their particular subject matter. They are printed on better paper and bound securely. Editorially, their subject matter has less to do with romance and adventure, soft-core porno, Westerns, mystery, and crime. Verse, essays, even novellas appear, as well as considerable nonfiction. They are a little cheaper to produce than a hardcover. It's not the paperback binding that is cheaper—the savings here is only 30 cents a book. The real saving, especially on short-run quality paperbacks (press runs under ten thousand), comes from the absence of a dust jacket with its demand for artwork, plates, and four-color printing and varnishing.

But there's something else the quality paperback has going for it. Everyone knows hardcovers have gone up in price, and the general belief is that this constantly rising increase (twelve dollars is almost normal) is what has caused a cutback in their overall sale. There's a lot more experimental work in quality paperbacks, and their physical quality (paper, binding, printing) has not yet been grossly cut as is the case with mass paperbacks, some book-club editions, and some trade hardcovers. Editorially, you might say, the quality paperbacks belong more to the inquiring readers who patronize trade bookstores than to the general public.

On this day, a literary agent, having submitted a manuscript of a proposed quality paperback to a publisher, receives a letter saying that a contract is forthcoming and the terms will include a royalty of 10 percent of all the income the publisher receives. The agent promptly tears up the letter and throws the pieces into his wastebasket, then retrieves and tapes them together and calls the publisher for an appointment.

The agent is upset, because the royalty is based on what the publisher receives for each copy sold, instead of being based, as is the custom with hardcover books, on the retail price. The proposed terms cut his client's royalty by 22.5 cents for each book sold.

Want to check out that 22.5 cents? When a trade paperback sells for $5.00, and the dealer buys it at 40 percent off, the publisher receives $3.00 for each copy sold. The author receives 30 cents when his contract provides him with 10 percent of the publisher's gross income from the sale of the book. However, when wholesalers and large chain stores place large orders, they buy a five-dollar book for $2.50. The publisher then pays the author 25 cents (10 percent of $2.50).

The way the publisher sees it is that, if half the copies are sold through wholesalers and large chain stores, and the other half through trade stores, the author's average royalty will be 27.5 cents per book sold. If, however, the publisher pays the author a royalty of 10 percent based on the list price of $5.00, the author receives 50 cents per book sold. The difference of 22.5 cents per book in favor of this publisher is worth fighting for, and that is the publisher's intention.

The literary agent, having lived his professional life in the hardcover field, where the royalty the author receives is based on the list price, isn't about to accept royalty terms based on the money the publisher receives from dealers or wholesalers. Let's watch the agent and publisher as they meet to work out their differences.

The literary agent takes a slow deep breath and asks for 10 percent of the list price, or 50 cents a book, when the retail price is $5.00. He asks for an identical royalty on books bought by wholesalers or chain stores, plus a raise in the royalty to 12 percent (60 cents a book) when the sales pass thirty thousand, plus an advance of five-thousand dollars.

The two parties seem far apart.

In even tones, the agent explains the nature of his requests and in five minutes rests his case. The publisher answers, speaking not unpleasantly and hoping he has control of the situation.

"Abe, you know we don't pay royalty on the list for trade paperbacks. It's not in it. It costs the same to publish a trade paperback as a hardcover, except for the binding, which is maybe 25 cents cheaper. But trade paperbacks sell for $3.00 less a copy, and we collect $1.80 less on every book the dealer buys." The publisher spreads his hands and leans back in his chair. "You know all that, Abe. Nothing's new to you. You know we sell the wholesalers and chains at 50 percent off. They'll buy half the print order on this book, and, when we collect $2.50 and give you 25 cents royalty, all we have left is $2.25 to pay for editorial, design, printing, advertising, and publicity, and we eat the returns. If we had a shot at making 40 cents a book, I'd pay you 50 cents royalty. But we're lucky to come out with a 20 cent profit per book, and even then it's a risk. No chance on our paying a 10 percent royalty on the list. Why do you start off like that?"

The publisher loosens his tie and rings his secretary. "Can you hold my calls for ten minutes?"

"Mac, let me ask you a question. . . ."

"Ask all you want. We can't pay anybody 60 cents on a five-dollar trade paperback."

"Do your travelers get 6 percent commission on trade paperback sales to bookstores?"

"They get a draw against their commission. We give 'em better than 6 percent in territories where the men have big mileage between calls."

"Do your travelers get 6 percent on orders from wholesalers?"

"Abe, they get plenty. Believe me. Plenty. Four out of our fourteen salesmen don't earn their draw."

"Mac, what do you plan to pay on sales over thirty thousand?"

"Same thing; 10 percent of what we get."

"Want to make that 15 percent?"

"I'll go 15 percent of what we collect on all sales over forty thousand and give you a two-thousand-dollar advance."

"Mac, I got you the wrong morning. Let me call you back in three days and tell me if you can do a five-thousand-dollar advance and go to 10 percent of the list and 12.5 percent at forty thousand."

"Who else you offering this to?"

And so it goes, 'round and 'round, jab and parry, stall and run, demand and plead, offer a carrot and throw a fish. The agent does it with the ease of a major-league outfielder running a ball back full speed, reaching up his glove and hauling it in just short of the wall. The author, negotiating his own contract, with two years' work at stake, is under greater stress and can either cave in or become unreasonably stubborn.

In the above conversation, did you notice when the publisher walked into a trap laid by the agent who asked, "Do your travelers get 6 percent commission on trade-paperback sales to bookstores?" The publisher, not sensing where the conversation was going, said he paid his salesmen more than that when the travelers' calls were wide apart. The agent came right back, asking how much commission the publisher paid to his travelers who called on wholesalers, and the publisher, now seeing where he was being led, slipped away and simply said, "Plenty."

The point here is that both men knew that six wholesalers and four chain stores buy half the total sales of many trade paperbacks. In other words, ten calls result in half the business. The travelers who make these calls often receive a reduced commission per book because the orders are so much larger. Thus, although the wholesaler and chain store do buy at 50 percent off, the publisher fares as well, or better, than when a dealer buys at 40 percent off, because of the reduced cost of selling, and because most wholesalers pay better than most dealers.* Abe was letting Mac know he knew what was going on, but he was careful not to paint him into a corner.

Did the agent get 10 percent of the list?

Actually, no. But he did get a $3,500 advance and a flat royalty of 7 percent of the list price on all books sold (35 cents royalty on a five-dollar book) and a 9 percent royalty (45 cents on sales over 25,000). No one lost. Up until the last moment, the publisher held out for paying the author reduced royalty on "all books sold at 50 percent off." In the case of this particular book, that clause would cover orders from the National Association of College Stores, which was interested in the book for their 2,400 members. In the trade-off, Mac dropped his demand for reduced royalty on sales to wholesalers, and Abe accepted a lower royalty and a lower advance than his original demand.

What are the financial results of having an agent?

See it this way: If you are your own agent, and you earn one dollar, you keep the whole dollar. If you have a good agent, you will usually

---

* Because book publishers routinely ask the author to accept less royalty on sales at 50 percent off, this subject is discussed again in the next chapter, "The Book Contract."

earn 30 percent more, or $1.30, instead of a dollar, because the agent's publishing knowledge improves his bargaining ability. On the $1.30 you earn, the agent receives 10 percent, or 13 cents. You receive $1.17. You end up with 17 cents more on each dollar your book earns, because your agent provides you with better terms.

Okay, you say, if agents are so helpful, I want one. Where do I find mine?

It's perfectly true that most established literary agents (the ones who make practically all their money from commissions) will return un-solicited manuscripts from writers they do not know. Once the agent offers to read what the general public sends in, his office may receive several hundred scripts a month that cost fifteen dollars each to review, and, out of the lot, the agent will be fortunate to sell one every three months.

The established agent shuts his door not from prejudice but from a need to earn a living. Yet, at night, in bed, alone with his thoughts, he counts not sheep but writers. Herb and Jack and Bill haven't written a book for three years, and maybe they never will. Jane just had a baby, and so did Irv's wife—chances are those two would be more concerned with diapers than manuscripts for the next three months. Soon the agent is down to his famous five—the tight little stable that keeps him going. Oh, for another five like that!

Where are they? Where can he find them? The bad ones can't write; the good ones won't. How does an enterprising agent find talent? The agent turns and twists and tries to think about something else.

The next morning, opening his mail, he finds a letter: neat, brief, well typed, plus a two-page outline of a book. The letter asks if he would care to see a few finished chapters. The first two pages of chapter 1 are enclosed.

"Hmmpf," says the agent. "I might as well read it."

Fortunate timing, a really good outline, a sparkling first two pages, and what do you know—the agent calls the writer by phone and, casually enough, says: "Sure, I'll read a few chapters."

Yes, it's a back-alley way to get an agent and occasionally it has worked. If you try it, one affirmative response out of twelve would be good. No response out of fifteen might mean something sour with the outline or with the first two pages enclosed.

Where do you get a list of agents? In the current *Literary Market Place* a boldface asterisk appears before the listing of each agent who is a member of the Society of Authors' Representatives (101 Park Ave., New York City, NY 10017), or the Independent Literary Agents Association (P.O. Box 5257, FDR Station, New York, NY 10022). These agents have agreed to abide by certain standards. Usually, this means no reading fee is charged and, except for the sale of manuscripts at 10 percent commission, no other literary services are offered for which a fee is charged. *Literary Market Place* gives a few morsels of data about each agent that may be helpful in deciding to which one you might send material. Enclose a stamped, self-addressed envelope if you want your material returned. You have no guarantee anyone will answer, nor is the agent obligated to return your material, but, if you catch him on the right hour, and your enclosures are first class, you just might have a deal. This idea suits unpublished-book outlines and is not for articles, stories, verse, columns, or complete book manuscripts.

Is there another way to latch on to a literary agent? Let's say you are marketing your own book by sending your outline and a couple of chapters to the proper genre editor. If the editor likes the outline and writes you to say he'd like to see the entire book, phone him and ask if he would care to consider suggesting an agent. Don't ask the editor to name two agents pronto with their addresses and phone numbers. Just ask whether the editor, in a week or two, might come up with the name of an agent who would be willing to work with you. This gives the editor the time, if he wants to bother, to call the agent and ask if it's all right to do this.

What if the editor rejects your outline but offers some pleasant and encouraging remarks? In this case, you might do the same thing.

Why should the editor bother? Why should he give you the benefit of his inside information and take a chance that trouble won't ensue with him in the middle?

There are several human-factor reasons. First, editors are congenial people and like to help writers. They live by good will as well as by the size of their advances and the speed with which their royalty agreements reach 15 percent of the list. Second, when an editor recommends a writer to an agent and the writer is any good, the editor has done the agent a business favor and expects some mileage out of it. Not fifty bucks for Christmas or a lunch at a good restaurant, but a manuscript by a writer whose book the editor's company can sell. If you're good, therefore, you won't be the first writer he has helped.

If you are unknown and simultaneously mail Xerox copies of your book to ten publishers, with a note to each explaining what you are doing, you will usually be rebuffed by having your work returned unread. How come the agents can make simultaneous submissions?

Book publishers haven't gotten used to receiving multiple submissions of a manuscript. They dislike the whole idea, and very much so. It puts a gun to their heads and says, "Speak up or you lose." Simultaneous submission attempts to force a prompt report and a prompt offer when it has always been easier and more convenient to stall.

In days gone by, a publisher read only the original typed copy. If he received a carbon copy, he snorted. What was he supposed to do; bid against somebody else? This is a club, Buster. Simultaneous submission was a sin. If you did it, at best, you got a lecture; at worst, you were scorned and the book came back, same day, express collect.

But the ease and clarity with which Xerox copies can be made and the promptness with which a half-dozen agents started doing this with their very best work, put an end to publishers' demanding (and getting) the right to see a book manuscript exclusively and to hold onto it in silence, often for months or, in the case of new writers—for just as long as they pleased.

They held on not because they were studying the manuscript, or engaging in spirited editorial debate over its merits, but just because it was easier to hold it than to read it, make a report, and do something about it. In the twenties, thirties, and forties, it was not news when a publisher held onto a book for one year. All the writer could do was pretend that the publisher was seriously involved with it and finally, regretfully, had to let it go. "They held mine fifteen months, and then I got it back. Boy, I sure wish I knew what they said about it." What they usually said was, "Go tell Sam to get this stuff out of here this weekend, even if he has to work all Sunday."

The Xerox copy stopped that cold. If a publisher doesn't reply in what the author considers a reasonable time, like three months, the author can send a registered letter, return receipt requested, and say he is taking the book out of the publisher's hands and resubmitting it elsewhere.

Previously, this meant retyping the whole darn thing, as no one would read a carbon copy. On that fine edge, the book publishers made monkeys out of new writers who fed them their books.

Today, it's another story.

By the auction method, publisher is pitted against publisher, and the price of many books goes beyond what they are worth in terms of the sales they eventually earn. The question is: can the new writer pull off the same deal? Can he write to ten publishers and say: "Here's my newest. Are you interested? If so, let me have your offer by this coming Thursday, the fourteenth." The answer to the question is no. Only the recognized, respected agent can pull this stick-up act. An editor may return a simultaneous submission sent directly by an author with a summary note. That kind of note isn't so easy to palm off on an agent. He just might have something good coming up two weeks from now, and here you are insulting the guy.

When a new writer sends a batch of Xerox copies to a list of publishers, and a handful happen to answer, the writer quickly finds out he is better at writing than juggling. If you have ever fished from a sailboat with two lines in the sea, you know what can happen when a snook and a kingfish hit at the same time the wind starts to blow. Multiply that times two, and there's bedlam.

The main reason the new writer cannot hold his own auction or submit Xerox copies simultaneously is that, on the average, the new writer's work doesn't merit the senior editor's preempting the editorial time of an associate and telling him to stop what he is doing to get on with this Xerox copy today. The agent gets away with it, or, to be perfectly honest about it, *certain* agents get away with it, because they have a reputation for doing this only with their better work.

So we end up with one more reason for wanting a first-class literary agent. He can market your book simultaneously when he feels it has the merit to justify the demand for immediate reading and a prompt editorial conference, and on important works he can hold an auction.

With these six reasons for seeking a first-class literary agent, you are naturally wondering if there is a "catch 22." Yes, and it's a stinker, too. The literary agent who operates without charging a reading fee, who makes his money only from commissions, and who does not advertise, has no ready means of contacting new writers. Further, it is his habit to dodge them, because he can't sell enough of their work on a 10 percent commission basis to justify advertising, reading, making a report, and then trying to sell it. You want him; he needs you. But he doesn't want you along with all other new writers. So he backs away. That's the catch 22.

We have already listed several ways of getting to the agent who makes his money on commissions only. There is another way, and it is just as tenuous. But what of it? No actor, singer, boxer, or musician gets an agent by falling out of bed on a Sunday morning.

There are seven specialized professional-writers' associations, and leading writers in these fields have made great personal contributions, over and above membership dues. The addresses of these associations often change when a new secretary or president is elected, and the time required to receive a reply from a letter varies from one day to forty. Here are the seven sisters:

American Medical Writers Association
5272 River Rd., Suite 290
Bethesda, MD 20016

Science Fiction Writers of America
68 Countryside Apts.
Hackettstown, NJ 07840

Mystery Writers of America
105 East 19th St.
New York, NY 10003

Society of American Travel Writers
1120 Connecticut Avenue, N.W., Suite 940
Wash., DC 20036

National Association of Science Writers
Box 294
Greenlawn, NY 11740

Society of Children's Book Writers
Box 296
Los Angeles, CA 90066

Western Writers of America
Route 1, Box 35H
Victor, MT 59875

If your material is within the editorial range of these associations (mystery, science fiction, juvenile, and so forth), here is a possible way to get a line on the agent you may want. Assume you are unknown, have talent, and are able to produce copy in sufficient volume to make it profitable for an agent to work for you in one of the above seven fields.

Your first step is to write a letter to the association of your choice and ask if they have a recent newsletter or two and you could have a copy. Enclose two dollars. Read the newsletter carefully to find out whether association members do the kind of literary work that parallels your own.

Then write the association again and ask if they will help you get in touch with one or two producing writers in your area who are members. The association will not release names and addresses of their members, but they will forward mail. So all you want is the names (not the addresses) of several members within a three-hundred-mile radius of your area, to whom you may write in care of the association.

Will the secretary bother with you?

Let's look at it this way. Every mystery writer, every Western writer, every well-known writer who is a member of one of these associations was once unknown. Tomorrow's members of these associations are unknown today. Would you want to be the association secretary who cavalierly gave the back of his hand to John MacDonald thirty years ago? Any association secretary knows that 10 percent of their members drop out each year, and they have to have replacements. So ordinary courtesy, and usually a little more on top of that, is the order of the day.

If the secretary's reply is affirmative, and you receive the name of a producing author in your area, familiarize yourself with the author's work as a matter of professional courtesy. Tell the author your position: you are writing mystery fiction, for instance, and want an agent. May you call in person, or phone, and discuss this? Enclose a stamped, self-addressed envelope. You might get an answer. I never met a writer who forgot the poignancy of being a nobody. Perhaps he will look at your work and recommend an agent.

Employing these ideas takes persistence and a certain amount of nerve and pluck, and it can cost some out-of-pocket money. I would say that, if ten new practicing writers who have written twenty thousand words or more each, during the past five years, were to try two of the methods suggested, five would get what they wanted. So, depending on how you view statistics, Aron the Greek says you have one chance in two. Your own wit and intelligence supply the percentage you have going for you.

How about the agent who advertises? Should you patronize his services? There have been excellent agents in this field. The new literary agent, like the new writer, starts on the level best suited to his beginning.

A literary agent who advertises almost always does one of two specific things to pay his bills and make a profit: (1) charges a reading fee, or (2) offers manuscript criticism or revision suggestions for a fee. This is in addition to selling scripts for his clients on a commission basis.

THE BOOK MARKET

Should you try first to get a commission agent, or should you first go to a literary agent who advertises with the understanding in your own mind that you will be offered literary services and be expected to pay for them? It depends, really, on one thing. No one can predict the quality or integrity of the agent of your choice or what's in the stars the day he reports on your script. Every writer, every juggler, every stock-market forecaster has good days and bad days, and I am not, of course, referring to the "stars" as the cause, but to the variety of personal complications and multiple decisions that have to be made. Much depends on where you stand this very day as an artist, as a writer of merit. I firmly believe that every writer of merit can make his own breaks and that you should try any practical idea to reach a literary agent who happens to appeal to you.

11

The Book Contract

THE WORLD EXPECTS the author of a book to be lucid, even entertaining, but the book-contract writer exhibits a glum, flat, convoluted style that would bring instant rejection from an editor. Merely to read a book contract, word for word, at a single sitting, is a pain in the neck. Why should this be so?

A contract should have the same meaning for both parties; otherwise, it becomes troublesome if a difference of interpretation arises after it is signed. Some authors have felt the unrepentant legal language in a book contract weighs them down, and a few free spirits have amended their contracts with appropriate questions.

One author, eyeing a sentence that seemed to inject a full-blown new character, ". . . The Party of the First Part meeting Adverse Judgment," wrote over the last two words, "Who He?"

Model book contracts written for the benefit of writers by their own associations also employ legal language and are no breeze to read. There may be no other way.

All book contracts address the same problems: Who will get how much, and who is responsible when something goes wrong? They share the same subheads: Translation Rights, Delivery of Work, and Out-of-Print Provisions, but their terms vary from publisher to publisher, and often from author to author. In spite of this difference, it is not unusual for an author whose book has been accepted to receive a letter saying: "We are enclosing our standard contract."

There is no standard contract.

The variations depend on the size of the market for the book, the author's track record, the retail price of the book and its cost of manufacture, advance nibbles from paperback houses, and the negotiating ability of the author or his agent.

Is it possible for an author to negotiate a simple contract with a book publisher and hold up his own end? If there were a simple contract, the answer would probably be yes. But contracts that serve both parties have to take into consideration many of the following points:

1. The territory to which the author grants rights to the publisher.
2. The author's guarantee that the book is his own and does not, as the lawyers say, infringe on any copyright currently in force.
3. The author's guarantee of delivery date of the manuscript. Suppose you agree to June 1, and you deliver October 1. Did you break the contract?
4. What happens if the author delivers the manuscript, and it is accepted and set in type, and the author receives galley proofs and immediately becomes very sad about the whole thing and makes many changes? Who pays for this?
5. Will the author receive an advance? When, and how much? In consideration of the advance, does the author incur any responsibilities? "Why no. I just took the money."
6. What royalties will be paid and on what are they to be based? The retail price? The dealer's price? The wholesaler's price?
7. Will the author grant the publisher first refusal on his next book? How about the next two? Will you make it three? At the same terms? When is a first-refusal clause binding?
8. Will the author be allowed to examine the publisher's records?
9. Does the publisher own all or part of the reprint and book-club rights, and, if so, how much?
10. How about rights not mentioned in the contract? Who owns them?
11. If the publisher goes bankrupt or simply sells his business, who owns the book contract?
12. If the sales of the book drop to under fifty copies a year for two straight years, or if the book goes out of print, does the publisher still control the book?
13. If the two parties can't agree on what they signed, how will the matter be arbitrated?

There's more to a book contract than these thirteen points, but they do cover 80 percent of most contracts' terms.

Now we return to our original question.

Can a new writer, with no experience in contracts, fend with a publisher who sends him a "standard contract"—usually five or six pages long, printed in small type, and with a covering letter that seems to suggest there is really nothing much to do except to sign and return it? A few publishers take advantage of inexperienced writers who cross their paths, but most of them are not all that bad: They are satisfied with the lion's share. If some terms in the contract are onerous, they expect to give a little. This, in spite of the fact that the publisher knows the new author is fearful of getting his manuscript back and having to start the marketing process all over again.

There are three ways to stave off the possibility of a really bad contract. By far the best is to have a literary agent who has negotiated several hundred such contracts in the last fifteen years. That's almost the only way to be an equal party to a book contract. However, many agents won't fool with a new author, because the commission earned on the sale of a first book is usually too low to justify his time. When a book sells seven thousand copies at eight dollars each, the author receives around six thousand dollars royalty. The agent earns 10 percent, or six hundred dollars. Because the agent must read so many books by new authors to find one that is salable, he often backs away. An exception may occur when the spadework of finding the new author is done for the agent by someone else; that is, the author is recommended to the agent by an editor or by one of the agent's clients.

Is there a second choice?

Yes. An attorney. Vance Packard is one of many authors who employ an attorney. He writes me: "I am really dumb about contracts. I take my lawyer's word everything is all right."

If you live in New Orleans, or Cedar Rapids, the chances are excellent that your town has some fine attorneys, people who merge industries or sell and lease shopping malls. But of attorneys who have current knowledge of book contracts, there may be few. Having an attorney without this experience might be like going to an experienced, successful, book-contract attorney and asking him to put a new stock into registration through the Securities Exchange Commission. Even then, a good attorney with no book-contract experience is better than no

141

attorney, although it is not an ideal situation.

Can you handle the matter yourself?

Normally, not too well.

I hope, in this book, that I come off as an optimist who believes that a little talent and a lot of persevering hard work make a success of any author. But I am not optimist enough to feel that an inexperienced author can challenge a book publisher when the latter is buying and the former is selling.

So what is the author to do? Roll over and play dead?

No. The author can fight back guardedly. And not think of himself as a giant-killer.

If you meet the entrance requirements of the Authors Guild, a section of the Authors League of America, you have a floor to stand on. New authors can join as associate (nonvoting) members, when they have a contract offer from an established publisher. Being an associate member gives the author access to recommended forms of trade-book contracts and to surveys of royalties currently being paid by publishers. So, if you have a contract in hand, that's really the thing to do.*

Following are the bottom-line conditions you should accept on the thirteen points mentioned before.

(1) *The size of the territory to which the author grants rights to the publisher:* Years ago, before authors had much clout, many book contracts started off by saying that the publisher would be satisfied with exclusive world rights in all languages. That's neat, simple, complete. Today, the author has narrowed this down to granting the publisher the exclusive right to publish the author's work in the English language in book form in this country and its possessions and in Canada. When the author has an established agent, it is often possible for the author to retain rights to the British edition and to foreign-language editions. These rights are then separately placed by the agent.

If, however, the author does not have the bargaining power of an experienced agent and has no way of placing British and foreign-language publishing rights—and if the publisher does not want too large a share of the income (like 50 percent)—the author may wisely decide to

---

* Sample book contracts are also available, and the sources appear later in this chapter.

grant the right to sell British and foreign-publication rights to the publisher. In this case, these rights should revert to the author if the publisher does not place them within a reasonable time, say eighteen months. For selling translation rights, a fair share is 25 percent of the gross amount paid, and any commission or expenses the publisher pays his foreign agent should not be deducted from the gross amount.

(2) *Who owns the paperback and book-club rights:* The author owns them by right of original creation. But the publisher wants a share. You know his argument: first-time books, by relatively unknown authors, are often money-losers. The publisher says he must have a cut into all main subsidiary rights, or he can't bring out works by new writers. The argument is more than half-true. Writers are usually offered 50 to 90 percent of the money paid by TV and the movies. For paperback rights, the "first-book" writer usually receives 50 percent of the amount paid, the other 50 percent going to the publisher. The author's 50 percent should be paid on the gross amount, not the net. The "net" amount is subject to expenses incurred in selling the rights and is difficult to argue after the fact.

What if your publisher owns a number of book clubs? Request a right to approve an in-house sale, and ask, in advance, a 10 percent royalty based on the amount paid by the book-club subscriber for your book. An offer of 5 percent is a poor man's lunch.

The receipt of a "standard publisher's contract" and the big buzz it creates in the home has a lulling effect on new writers, who feel that, since this is their first book and probably not their best one, the rights aren't going to be worth much, so why make a fuss. No one knows how much your rights will be worth or who will want them. The publisher doesn't know. You don't know. Sometimes, even the eventual buyer doesn't know until someone rubs his nose in it. Hang on to every right you can. Your rock-bottom settlement figure, as a new writer, is 50 percent for any right.

The wisest thing, if you can pull it off, is to grant your publisher book rights, plus a 50 percent share of book-club and paperback rights, and retain for yourself all other rights, such as TV, movie, microfilm, sound-reproducing and commercial uses.

But what if you have no agent to sell these rights? Then, after granting the publisher half of the book-club and paperback rights, offer him a 20 percent fee to sell the above-named five rights (TV, movie, and so forth) with its being your privilege to revoke this in two years for rights not sold.

When granting any right, it is wise to limit the length of time the publisher has to exercise it. An example would be for the author to take back paperback rights unless the sale is consummated within one year.

(3) *The author's guarantee that the book is his own, and infringes on no copyright currently in force:* This means if you use a short quote or a long one, the responsibility is yours to get permission from the copyright owner. Often included in this section of the contract is a clause that may make the author responsible for damages suffered by the publisher from lawsuits, such as libel, invasion of privacy, violation of oaths of secrecy, obscenity, defamation of character, and so forth. This is a broad responsibility. Lawyers' fees, out-of-court settlements, and damages awarded by the court can bankrupt an author.

A publisher issuing several hundred books a year may spread his risk by setting aside for that purpose a five-hundred-dollar reserve per book. This an author cannot do. A large publisher can also buy reasonable insurance against some of these risks; a single author cannot.

I asked Gay Talese for any comments in this area and he replied:

You've marked a difficult task for your new project; and there is no doubt that for writers the language of the contract is confusing, and often disturbing when trouble arises between writer/publisher or between a reader (via legal action) with the publisher/writer. In my experience with three publishers (Harper & Row; McGraw-Hill; World Publishers) I have had no great trouble . . . and I hope this continues with my present publishers, Doubleday & Co.

If I have any suggestions that you might pursue in your queries to other writers . . . I might direct you to the problem of legal expenses: most contracts put the writer on notice that he will have to pay half of the legal expenses if anybody sues for libel, invasion of privacy, or whatever. I know Tommy Thompson and Neil Sheenan had trouble in recent years. . . . Though the cases against them were not won by the petitioners, the writers, as defendants, incurred expenses and time consumed . . . when in fact the lawyers for the publishers should have been the only ones involved, in my opinion. Just as newspapers and magazines have full-time attorneys who handle all cases, I think the publishers should rely on their own attorneys to protect (and financially cover) the writer's problems . . . unless, of course, the writer is just sloppy and is totally to blame. The nuisance suit, however, is a real fact of modern-day writing; and it is to this that I direct your attention.

Some out-of-court settlements are a shakedown. The suits are without merit and yet can cost the publisher a loss of time, energy, and legal services. This is an assumed risk and part of being in the publishing business. The author should bear no part of legal fees or out-of-court settlements and limit personal damages to 30 percent of the payments received over a given number of years that the contract is in force, not for the "life of the contract." The damages should refer only to those awarded and upheld by the court.

Some authors, to their sorrow, may already know of other risks in the business. Truth, for instance, is usually a defense against civil libel. In the matter of criminal libel, proof of malice counts most, and truth is of small defense.

What if the author does a nonfiction book and polishes off a well-known banker? Before publication, however, he shows the publisher his entire file and says that's his total proof. The publisher decides to go ahead. In civil libel, who's responsible financially? It depends, in part, on the book contract. If a criminal-libel suit is brought, and malice is proved, everyone who had a hand in the case shares some of the guilt, and this can include even the copyreader and the dealer.

(4) *Author's guarantee of delivery date:* When you guarantee a delivery date, you are expected to keep it. If you fail, there are penalties, and they will be enforced if it is in the publisher's interest to do so. What are these penalties? Sometimes the contract is declared void, and any advance you have received must be returned. Other times, the author is allowed a leeway of three months beyond the delivery date, and, then, if the book

is not delivered, the contract may be declared null and void. Sometimes, the author does not have to forfeit his advance, and, in this case, the publisher may want something for his consideration. Perhaps the book is less than half-completed. In this case, the incomplete book belongs to the publisher, who may complete it but not use the author's name. There are variations; none is standard. In the main, when you accept an advance before writing the book and agree to a delivery date, expect to keep it, or suffer some kind of loss.

Sometimes, the delivery date is contingent on two innocent words. In the phrase "delivery of the completed book manuscript, satisfactory to the publisher on May 1, 1982," the innocent words are "completed" and "satisfactory." Did you agree to furnish an index and a foreword and to secure permission for quoted material? Were these items included in the definition of the "complete" manuscript? It is best to have a line in the contract allowing the author another three months to complete the job before the advance is returned.

What if you complete the manuscript on time, but the publisher says it is not "satisfactory" to him? In such a case, the author should keep the advance and the publisher should be allowed to reject the manuscript.

Let's say you keep your part of the bargain and deliver a manuscript on time, and the publisher says it is satisfactory. Is there a corollary to which the publisher must respond? Yes. The contract should state that he will publish your book within a given time, say one year, after delivery of the complete manuscript.

(5) *What royalties will be paid?* The royalties vary.

A mass paperback, sold mainly through newsstands and priced at around 30 percent of the retail price of the cloth-bound book, pays a gross royalty of approximately 6 percent of the retail price to be divided between the author and publisher. Thus, a $2.50 paperback pays the author 7.5 cents for each copy sold. Better-known authors are granted the right to approve a paperback sale before it is consummated, and their royalties often increase after the first ten thousand dollars is paid.

The royalty for "quality paperbacks," meaning those sold mostly through bookstores, and retailing for about 60 percent of the retail price of the cloth-bound book, varies from 10 percent of the publisher's gross receipts of the sales to 10 percent of the retail price. This is quite a difference. The variance in royalty may depend upon the risk the publisher is taking. Is the author well known to trade-bookstore readers? Is the subject of the book currently selling well? Are there special problems in distribution and manufacture? Does the author have an agent? Who else is bidding for the book?

Cloth-bound books carry a royalty that rises in steps as the sales increase and is based on the retail price of the book. A new author may be offered a 10 percent royalty on the first 7,500 sales, 12.5 percent on the next 7,500, and 15 percent after that. Thus the royalty on a ten-dollar book would be a dollar a copy on the first 7,500 copies sold, $1.25 on the next 7,500, and $1.50 after that. If the 10 percent royalty on the list price carries all the way to 10,000 copies before it is increased, it should be argued. As opposed to new writers, well-known writers earn a 12.5 to 15 percent royalty, starting with the sale of the first copy.

When books fail to sell, and the publisher pulps them, the author receives nothing for books destroyed. When the books are returned by bookstores and the sale for the book is dead, the publisher may find himself holding 4,000 copies of a novel priced at $8.00 and not salable at that price. Such books are frequently sold at 10 or 15 cents on the dollar to "remainder houses" who resell them for perhaps 25 cents on the dollar to trade bookstores that have "remainder tables."

The publisher's receipts for remainder sales do not cover his print costs. Sometimes, the author receives 10 percent of the total cash the publisher receives from remainder sales; sometimes all sales at 70 percent, or more, off the list price bear no royalty for the author. It's best to get *something* on remainder sales; then you know what happened.

When a retail book dealer buys your book, what part of the list price does the publisher receive? If your book retails for $8.00, and the publisher gives a 40 percent discount to a bookstore, he collects $4.80 per book. On library sales, the publisher collects from $6.40 to $7.20, depending on the quantity ordered. When a bookstore orders only a few copies, perhaps under five, the discount is 25 percent to 33 percent and the publisher collects $5.30 to $6.00 per book. Perhaps the average trade-store discount is 36 percent which pays the publisher $5.12 on an eight-dollar book.

The wholesaler, however, receives a 50 percent discount, and so do the large bookstore chains that frequently order in lots of several thousand. These big orders are usually not for one book, but for many different titles. It is a trade practice for the wholesalers and big chains to "group" their orders until they have enough different titles to justify an order that earns them a 50 percent discount. To the publisher, this means several things. First, when a single customer orders a thousand books, he need fill only one order. That's less paperwork and less labor in shipping and billing. Second, the credit rating of the wholesaler and the big chain is better than the average trade store. Third, the big single order is less of a physical problem, the traveler making one call instead of thirty to sell a thousand books. The selling cost is less, too, because the travelers who call on the chains and the wholesalers earn a smaller commission on very large orders.

Nevertheless, the publisher writes a clause into all book contracts reducing the royalty paid to authors on sales where the buyer earns a discount of 50 percent or more. The argument is that the publisher receives less money and, therefore, should pay out less money in royalty. The first part is true, but the lower sales cost and better credit more than make up for the higher discount.

I always preferred a wholesaler order of a thousand books at 50 percent off rather than thirty orders totaling a thousand books at discounts ranging from 33 percent to 44 percent. Given the single order for a thousand books, you can fill it, ship it, bill it, collect your money, and go after a reorder more easily and with less labor.

Yet, in most book contracts I have seen, the publisher requests a reduction in the royalty paid to authors when books are sold at 50 percent off list. I don't think a new writer can eliminate this entirely from a book contract, but, when tables are supplied in the contract for royalty reduction due to the larger discounts, he can recognize an unfairness and request a change.

Let's look at the math.

This is very important, because wholesalers and large bookstore chains are responsible for over half the sale of many trade books.

When an eight-dollar book is sold at 36 percent off, the publisher receives $5.12. When the same book is sold at 50 percent off, the publisher receives $4.00, or 22 percent less. Yet the publisher may offer the writer a royalty on that same book of 60 cents instead of $1.20, or 50 percent less. This, in spite of the fact that the book sold at 50 percent off is cheaper to ship, cheaper to sell, and easier to collect.

If your seventh-grade math is still sound, and you spot this, you have a decent argument to amend the publisher's request for a reduced royalty, at least on the scale asked.

There is one disadvantage in large orders from book jobbers. The publisher never gets to know the name and address of the dealer who buys the book. By that token, he loses some control over his retail outlets, and his personal touch with his own business eases off.

(6) *Will the author grant the publisher first refusal on forthcoming books?* If yours is a first book, you owe the publisher something for his consideration of you. Yes, he should have first refusal of your next book, possibly of your next two. The terms should not remain the same as the first. For your second and third books, you deserve better terms in the contract on items such as advance, royalty, and a guaranteed amount of dollar advertising the publisher will perform. If you granted a 50 percent participation to the publisher in book-club rights, you should reach for 55 percent on all over your share of the first ten thousand dollars. If your advance is under five thousand dollars on your first book, ask for that sum on your second. If you are undecided about what to do, but you still want a connection with this same publisher, you can give an option for your next two books "on terms to be mutually agreed upon." The seven words in quotation marks are *an agreement to agree*, and, if there is no agreement, the option lapses. The phrase does maintain a degree of amiable relationship, but puts no iron clamp on the author.

(7) *Will the author be allowed to examine the publisher's records?* The author, or his agent, should be permitted to examine the publisher's records, should doubt occur as to the correctness of payments. While publishers can be frugal when it comes to writing book contracts, they do not generally cheat. I have never heard of a publisher that fudged on his royalty payments. I am sure that at some time some publisher must have done so, been caught, and the matter hushed up, but the chances of this happening to anyone over a ten-year period are slight.

(8) *In the event of bankruptcy, who owns your contract?* Bankruptcy is rare, but a clause should provide that the contract reverts to the author in

such a situation. When a publishing company is sold, part of the sale price is based on the book contracts in the publisher's safe and the strength of the publisher's back list. Without either, it would be hard to sell a publishing company, unless perhaps it owned a printing plant and were bought for that reason. If you request a clause that returns your contract to you, in the event the publisher sells out, you take away an asset from the publisher, and you can expect, in turn, to be asked to give something up elsewhere in the contract.

(9) *Should the sales drop off to the point where there is little or no activity, or the book goes out of print, who now owns the brown cow?* The reason contracts are a pain in the neck is that they must be precise to mean anything. What is "little or no activity"? If the contract says: "Should the author's royalty statement for a total of four consecutive periods, each covering six months, fail to produce revenue demonstrating hardcover sales in excess of an average of fifty sales per period, and not including remainder sales, sales of sheets, or unbound collated books, the book contract becomes void unless rights leased by the publisher produce an average revenue of five hundred dollars for the author for each of these four periods." This illustrates Mathieu's Law: The more deadly the language, the more precise.

(10) *What if the book is simply O.P. (out of print)?* In that case, you want a clause allowing the book to revert to you when it is out of print for a given period, say one year, during which time orders cannot be filled.

(11) *If the author makes changes after the type is set, who pays?* The publisher usually sends galleys to the author for proofreading, and, when this occurs, the publisher has usually made a sad mistake, as most authors are terrible proofreaders. More often, the galleys have already been proofread and are then sent to the author "to be proofed," so that if typos do go through, the author gets the idea that he is responsible since he has agreed to proofread the galleys.

However, the literary muse is so constructed that once a book is written, and time passes, and the author rereads it on a cold, marrowless day, he starts to feel sick. To repair his feelings, he starts to change copy, and this can get expensive.

150

To put the hat on the author, most contracts provide that such changes (as apart from pure typo corrections) are to be charged to the author, once they exceed 5 or sometimes 10 percent of the total typography bill. The 10 percent figure is a reasonable one. This means if the typography costs two thousand dollars, the author may make corrections other than typos, up to two hundred dollars, and, after that, he pays the bill.

(12) *How about rights not specifically mentioned in the contract?* The author should grant the publisher book rights, dealing with book publication, and a clause in the contract should state that all other rights belong to the author. With new inventions, new rights appear. The computer, television, radio, and the tape recorder, when put together in new combinations, create the new rights of the next decade. Don't sign them away.

(13) *If a rumpus breaks out after the contract is signed, and the two parties cannot agree, then what?* A clause should be included in the contract providing for arbitration under the rules of the American Arbitration Society.

What do other writers do about hiring agents or attorneys? The Authors Guild Book Contract Committee regularly surveys the contracts of its members. In the last report I read (Number 7), out of 326 authors reporting, 227 were represented by an agent or attorney, leaving 30 percent handling their own contracts. So, the weight of the evidence is to secure one of the two to assist you.

If an agent or an attorney is so important, why don't all authors use them? Because people are not the same. Some authors are unwilling to pay an agent 10 percent of their literary income or to pay an attorney for his time. Some authors are permanently distrustful; some live in communities where attorneys with book experience are not available; and some may have had a disastrous experience with an agent. A number of writers have very good personal relations with their publishers and don't feel the need of interposing the services of anyone else.

This informal discussion of points normally included in a full-blown book contract may help to prepare the writer who first sits down to examine the actual animal itself. If you've never seen such a contract or listened to its special language, it can be overwhelming. The choice of innocent words like "net," "gross," "complete," or "satisfactory" can greatly alter the meaning as far as the author is concerned.

When should you first read a "full-dress" book contract? Preferably, not the morning of the same day you receive it for real. If you have seen several before that day of mixed emotions, you are ahead.

The Authors Guild section of The Authors League of America (234 West 44th St., New York, NY 10036) has a membership requirement of one book published within the past seven years, or publication of three articles or stories in national magazines within the past eighteen months. You help yourself and others by joining. Their sample contract is for members only. As mentioned earlier, a new author can join The Authors Guild as an associate (nonvoting member) when he or she has a contract from an established publisher. As a member, the new author will then have access to the guild's recommended form of trade-book contracts and other confidential published data useful to writers.

Model book contracts may be secured from the Society of Authors' Representatives (40 East 49th St., New York, NY 10017). Enclose $1.25 in stamps and a Number-10, stamped, self-addressed envelope.

If your book is in the science-fiction genre, you may write to the Science Fiction Writers Association (68 Countryside Apt., Hacketts-town, NJ 07840) and state whether you want a paperback or a hardcover sample book contract. The price is $1.25 for each. Enclose a Number-10 stamped return envelope. As befits full-fledged science-fiction writers, their book contracts are in an outer orbit.

Peter Pautz, executive secretary of the Science Fiction Writers Association, writes:

> I am very happy to see someone caring about agent-less new writers! As to the SFWA's model paperback and hardcover contracts, to our knowledge no one has ever signed a contract such as these (or is likely to), but we believe they do exemplify an advance stage of author-publisher cooperation.

Peter L. Skolnick, one of the founders of The Independent Literary Agents Association, says his group has not prepared a model book contract, "although this is a project we may very well undertake in the foreseeable future." He added: "We do make a membership list available to writers in search of an agent." When you first approach an agent, a query letter should be sent, not a manuscript.

12

The Phenomenon of the Local Book

A BOOK WRITER has to start his career somewhere and a good place to begin is close to home: writing the local book. About one hundred local books are published each year, and most of them are profitable to publisher and author alike. How do you get your idea? That's what this chapter is all about.

To recognize an idea for a local book is easy, so let's discover one right away and, at the same time, name the kind of entrepreneur who might be very happy to bring it out.

Many of our cities and towns are located on rivers and have century-old records of community growth brought about by ready transport to and from the nearby waters. Each one of the nation's major rivers, the Mississippi, Ohio, Missouri, Colorado, Rio Grande, and their tributaries, easily contain the material for fifty local books.

What would such a book be about?

Let's examine the editorial side first, because it is from your selection of subject matter that the search for a publisher receives its direction. A good way to begin is to tell the story of how rivers were an entryway, and how goods and animals flowed into the local wharves, giving people a reason for congregating in this particular place. The first few chapters of such a local book can reveal how this river (or it could just as well be a great, wide lake) contributed to the city's growth, culture, residential habits, sports, industries, and leisure activities. Many rivers have a bad local name among older residents because the banks were tracked by smokey railroad engines and sprawling industrial growth whose wastes were dumped into the moving waters, killing the fish and making swimming a messy affair. Today, as chemical-waste controls take effect, young people are rediscovering riverbanks. Government dams sustain the waters at a higher level by holding them in pool stage. Sediment drops to the bottom, the current lessens, and the waters start to clear.

Federal funds bring wide green parks to what used to be riverside dumping grounds, and urban redevelopers find the riverbanks an attractive site for stadiums, residential towers and showboats.

A river book, updated every three years, can be a welcome new source of advertising for marinas, waterfront restaurants, boat rentals, riverview high-rise apartments, party boats, passenger steamboats, and scenic hilltops that offer a breathtaking site for residential development. Such a book is like the river itself; it goes on forever, with updated editions as new river activity springs into life.

Who would be interested in publishing such a book?

Think in these terms: Who could use it to further his own interests? Let's say your city has one major employer and that firm has some difficulty in bringing people to your town because it isn't New Orleans or St. Louis. Perhaps the quality of life in your town is not known and appreciated by the country at large. Wives balk when husbands say they got an offer "for fifteen grand more to move to Worthington." Money alone won't dislodge talent. The very names of some cities sound like prison sentences to some people. And that can scare off the talent a growing company needs.

Three times a week, the *Wall Street Journal* publishes a double-page spread of advertisements for executive help at annual salaries of thirty to one hundred and fifty thousand dollars. Fewer than one-third of these advertisements are from companies located in cities of one million or more population, and at least that many are from towns of under one hundred thousand. Will a book about the local river make an employer's offer more interesting? In itself, it won't make the difference, but it could be one of many small things that sway the balance. That's exactly why a large local employer, having troubles filling important jobs with highly talented people, might risk fifteen thousand dollars publishing such a book, especially if it was a good job editorially and enjoyed some sort of advertising support. Fact is, the fifteen-thousand-dollar gamble might well turn into a fifteen-thousand-dollar profit. What would the sponsoring company do with the book? It would mail fifty copies to the "head-hunters" it hires to secure top management help and also mail copies to selected prospects of its own choice. The rest of the copies could be offered for sale locally.

If you owned a company grossing a quarter of a billion dollars a year, and it was suffering for lack of a president, a chief engineer, or a creative accountant (the kind who knows how to set up nontaxable reserves), a gamble of fifteen thousand dollars to publish a book might make the company's location a bit more attractive to the whole family of the person you are gunning for.

Who else might want to publish a river book? Who are the interested parties behind riverfront development in your town? Will such a book help them? If so, the cost of bringing it out is modest in relation to the gains they seek. That's the way to see it. Find the entrepreneur who needs this kind of editorial assistance, and, if his personal goals are substantial, the cost of producing such a book is not a major factor.

To protect yourself, you want to work on an honest book, not one that goes out of its way to promote a chain of marinas or some other commercial venture that may want you to say things that are opposed to your own good sense of truthful reporting. Once a writer gets a reputation for being just a P.R. person, it's hard to change.

A friend of mine, Ben Klein, has been publishing a book about the Ohio River for many years. Ben is a successful printer and does his river book as a hobby. I asked whether anyone offered to sponsor his book. "Yes," he said. "A local newspaper originally sponsored it and sold copies through the newspaper. When I expanded my river book to include a much larger territory than my home city, the local newspaper dropped me."

I asked Ben if he could dig up a couple of sponsors if he really wanted them.

"I can think of two who might want my book. There's an oil company within a hundred miles of me with a gross into the hundreds of millions. They own tug- and towboats and barges. Most of the people who run this company live in a river town that's under one hundred thousand population. They might sponsor this book just to get their company's name on it as a P.R. job, if it fulfilled their ideas of progressive river outlook.

"Another possible sponsor is a big multi-interest company just fifty miles up river. They own barges, tug- and towboats, and passenger boats. They're river people and they want to support river interest."

What does "river interest" mean? A writer who investigates a river that flows through industrial areas will notice that the economy of shipping bulk commodities (like coal, grain, or fuel) has changed. Barges are now a most efficient way to ship. Large barge companies—and there are hundreds of them along the rivers—are doing well and expanding their interests into barge parking lots, marinas, passenger steamers, tug, and riverbank, hilltop home developments.

Ben Klein's ideas of sponsors for a river book are good ones. Almost every river city has several large companies of this kind, to whom you might show a dummy with three chapters already laid out, including photostats of pictures pasted in and, perhaps, the heads and subheads laid in by using "stick-on" letters. By including words of copy to go with the three sample chapters, plus a chapter outline of the balance of the book, you clearly show what you are offering.

There are more to river towns than a dozen famous cities. Smaller rivers, like the Red, Platte, Delaware, and Suwanee have cities, towns, and industrialists, whose deep feelings for the river come from living and working alongside it. If you live alongside a river, a local book is probably waiting to be written. Incidentally, when you sell your river book to a publisher, you should reserve for yourself the right to sell one-time publication rights to your local newspaper.

Quite a different idea in local books comes from Lois Rosenthal, who calls hers *Living Better in Cincinnati*.

What proved remarkable about Lois's work is the reliability of her research and the way in which she parlayed her idea into additional successful books that were related to her first one.

Lois started by collecting data from several hundred local retail establishments that offered interesting, good-quality merchandise, usually for less money than available at other stores. For instance, one item reported an annual auction of used costumes offered by the local opera company. Another item was supplied by a magazine printer. He had the core ends of rolls of paper, thirty inches wide, weighing up to twenty-five pounds, and available at 15 cents a pound. "Preschoolers can draw murals and not run out of paper, and it won't cost their parents a fortune to keep them happy on a rainy day."

Other items include: A women's apparel store with "salesmen's samples on the racks; in back were designer names." A graduate of Cordon Bleu "teaches only up to three people at a time because everyone learns while cooking: $12 per lesson. Evening classes and Saturday classes for children." And there's this one: "If you see a performance of the Contemporary Dance Theater Group and get inspired (which is easy to do), you can learn to dance from the people who inspired you, as the members of the company do the teaching." In her preface, the author says: "What could be better than finding just what you've been looking for at a place you never heard of and at a price you can afford? You'll find entertainment, relaxation at what-am-I-doing-here kinds of places that are inexpensive or free or incredibly beautiful or just plain zany. I call it Living Better."

Of the various local directory-type books that both preceded and followed *Living Better in Cincinnati*, a few failed right away. They were short on style and coverage. Others kept going and grew in stature. Several expanded their coverage into nearby towns. Because Lois's book sold so well locally, she was offered a job writing a weekly column for her home-city newspaper in which she could continue the central idea of her book. Meanwhile, the publisher who brought out her first book asked her to write a second one titled *Living* Even *Better in Cincinnati*, and, a year or so later, suggested she shorten the title to *Living Better* and go national. She did. Then lightning struck. Book-of-the-Month Club selected *Living Better* as *pro bono publico*, a book "for the public good," and mailed it as a bonus to its subscribers. As many authors have discovered, when you get something good going, it continues to crackle. The last note on Lois's *Living Better* idea, but probably not the final one, is that she has now completed a tri-state edition.

An event in my own home became an item in one of Lois Rosenthal's weekly newspaper columns. My wife collects original nineteenth-century prints and magazine covers from around 1880 to 1910 and decided to have a five-day sale of old magazine covers. She mailed a letter to that effect to about two hundred people. Lois received one and came to investigate. She wrote up my wife's magazine covers. We live in one of those rambling, old-fashioned homes, but it wasn't nearly large enough to contain the people who came each day for five days. Most of our callers had followed previous recommendations reported by Lois and had great faith in her judgment. I suppose that's the essence of her *Living Better* series. The reports are based on personal interviews, the facts are straight, and people trust her taste.

Would you like to do a local *Living Better* book, similar to those on the market in other cities? If so, you should first determine whether your city already has a book of this kind. Two are probably one too many. If your research reveals that one or two were previously published, try to get copies and find out what happened. Examine them critically. Would you have bought one?

If no book of this kind is being published in your city, you might look at some of the other current titles * and see if the idea still appeals to you after closer examination. None of the books Lois wrote contained advertising, and the publisher's income was the result of bookstore, newsstand and mail-order sales. If yours is a local book, and your city has a population of around two hundred thousand, this limits the sale to somewhere between three and four thousand copies, even if you include nearby, outlying villages. With this kind of low, four-figure sale, your publisher has to work inside a stringent kind of box. If your book is large (three hundred pages, six by nine inches) the printing costs will be too great to support a small sale, unless the retail price of the book is close to ten dollars. That's steep for this kind of book. If the book is physically thin (130 pages, five by eight inches) its very size may prohibit a retail price over four dollars, or four-fifty, especially if it is a paperback. So, a lot of thought has to go into the graphics of the book to give it the class to outweigh its relatively small size. The splendid thing about a book of this nature is that it can be issued annually and, as suggested above, may lead to greener pastures.

If you have ever pecked your way through five hundred pages of double-spaced typing to get down the facts that you researched, you know the agony of writing one clean sentence that rings true when you

---

* *Detroit Guide*, by Martin Fischoff; *The Seattle Guidebook*, by Merle E. Dowd; *The Portland Guidebook*, by Merle E. Dowd; *Factory Outlet Stores in the Carolinas*, by Diana Pegram; *Kids and Kansas City*, by Bonnie and Debbie Gillespie (a list of places to take kids); *A Greenville Album*, by Thomas A. Williams, who knocked on doors in his town and looked over old photograph albums and came up with a photographic tour of Greenville from yesteryear; *An Irreverent Guide to Washington State*, by Jim Faber. F & W Publishing Company (9933 Alliance Rd., Cincinnati, OH 45242) may have copies left of either the first or second edition of *Living Better in Cincinnati*. Write first to see if any copies are left. The price is $6.00.

read it two months afterwards. It is just as agonizing to do the damned research as to write it up. For that reason, any kind of book idea that lets you dip into someone else's source material is a nice gift. This thought leads into a local book that is easier to do when your newspaper has a column on where to fish, hunt, camp. There is a real market for this kind of book, especially when it is reissued and kept up to date. Books like this are rewarding to advertisers of vacation homes, lakeside recreations, fishing camps, boat rentals, and the whole kit and kaboodle of supplies needed for outdoor camping, fishing, hunting.

Perhaps fifty daily newspapers carry daily or weekly outdoor columns, and, if you live in a community that supports such a column, it will give you starter ammunition. You can lay out a map of fishing, camping, and hunting grounds within a three-hour drive of your home base and covered during the past year by your local newspaper's outdoors column. This will give you somewhere between two and three hundred places where you can start to do your own research.

Naturally, what the columnist writes is his own copyrighted affair, but the actual leads are public information, and you can use all the locations, as well as adding additional ones, in your investigations. If your local paper has *no* such column, then you might be able to make an arrangement for yourself, a sort of Lois Rosenthal-backwards kind of deal. Go to the newspaper and offer to write an outdoor column, and show them four or five samples. Writing four or five samples isn't cheap to do. It takes research, travel, and interviews. Then you want to mail a copy of each writeup to the owner of the site you covered, and ask for comments and corrections. When you travel this route, you walk with God and fear no editor. If the newspaper hires you, your expenses for your future columns are then paid, and you'll have something extra going for you, too. The something extra is the right to make a book of your updated columns at year's end, and, if the newspaper wants to be the publisher of your book, that's fine. If you enjoy the outdoors, this can be a very good way to enter book writing.

At your library, you can examine a few newspapers that have outdoor columns to test the pitch. These include the *New York Times, Detroit Free Press, Miami Herald, Washington Post, Cincinnati Post, San Diego Union, Minneapolis Star Tribune,* and *Milwaukee Journal.* Jimmie Robinson, who does the outdoors column for the *Star Tribune,* is one of the columnists who turned his work into a book. Dave Roberts, one of the more popular survivors of this profession, now works for the *Cincinnati Post*. If you want to do a column for your local paper, or, if you want to do an outdoor book, and would like to pretest it, you might send Dave three sample columns, or three sample chapters, and ask what his fee might be for a critical review. He knows the trade, having started in 1922. Another way to pretest your outdoors copy is to mail samples to an outdoors columnist whose work you like. Outdoors writers are constantly traveling from one fishing or hunting spot to another and may not answer mail promptly. Some may back away from doing any kind of critical review. "Hell, I write!" one of them told me. "I'm not going to pick at another man's copy." You may have to try two or three to get one affirmative response. Keep plugging and have confidence. The point is that the market is there for a forthright outdoors book that is kept up to date, is written by a person who understands the subject from personal experience, and who gets back to both the readers and the subjects interviewed to retain a oneness with his audience.

The number of women who fish the streams, lakes, and coastal waterways keeps growing. Not all the outdoor writers are aware of this. A new column, or new book in this field, can pick up an audience of its own by recognizing women who enjoy the outdoors and are competent with rod, line and tent.

Three local books are popular with authors and readers alike. They deal with gardening, cooking, and eating out. The gardening books explain where to buy plants, seeds, shrubs, and garden supplies locally and give the various kinds of plants (using the common and Latin names) that grow best locally, along with problems, culture, and uses. Certain regions are plagued with unholy blights, such as the ubiquitous black spot in roses, especially present in humid climates when the rose receives under seven hours of full sun a day. The best local treatment is offered, along with advice on where to obtain plants with more resistance to this fungus. The varieties of tomatoes that bear early and those that are late are given, and similar data for peas, lettuce, and other vegetables.

The cookbooks often have a regional or local tone and sometimes an ethnic flavor, when the market for that is large enough.

The eating-out local books cover all the restaurants that serve good-to-excellent fare including the occasional plain-Jane, family-owned restaurant that still provides good food, moderate portions, and dinners at four and five dollars.

I have heard about, but not seen, a local book that describes special services available to householders such as house-sitters, nurses and nurses' aides, tutors, rug cleaners, handymen who specialize in cement walks, carpentry, or chimney work in their suburbs, and so forth.

And, finally, here's an original idea for a local book that may appeal to some writers who have a fondness for produce of all kinds and enjoy the sophistication of selecting what's best in the market. People who hybridize fruit and vegetable plants are doubtless motivated by the requirements of large growers rather than by the hopes of consumers who buy and take a bite. Have you noticed the new kind of tomato in the bins of produce stores? It is on the dark pink side, rather than red, yet firm, smooth, often unblemished. When you take it home, you find it has the taste of a rubber ball. This hybrid came about because picking tomatoes by hand became expensive, and the growers wanted a tomato that could withstand a mechanical picker. They got it. So did we. How can you spot this freak in disguise before paying 40 cents for one?

Ever notice carrot tops before you buy the bunch? When the green growth coming right out of the carrot is black and sooty and rather unappetizing to look at, it means the carrots are old and have a stale taste.

When ruby red grapefuits are just in from Texas, they are not sweet. Why? At what season are they more edible? How do you tell when a honeydew melon is ripe, as compared to the casaba with its bright yellow rind and sweet white flesh?

Some bananas ripen into golden yellow; others turn a dull, yellowish tan and never really taste good. Why? How do you spot this before you buy the banana and take it home, waiting hopefully for it to turn a bright yellow?

The heads of broccoli grow on thick and relatively heavy stalks. Sometimes the heads have been whittled down, and you can see where a knife has pared off one-third or more of the green, flowering heads. This increases the cost of the broccoli head because the stalk has not been pared. Why was the head pared? Is the remaining part just as tasty?

Apples from the State of Washington are the reddest, firmest, nicest-looking fruit you would ever want to see. Why do some taste unripe, as though they were picked too soon? What did the hybridizer do? What varieties of apples are tasty when you buy them? Are they keepers, too?

One of the reasons it is hard to know which produce is best is because the grading system uses words and symbols that are clear to U.S.D.A. inspectors but confuse the consumer. Codes like "No. 1," "Grade A," "Fancy," "Grade AA," and "Excellent" all sound like a means to identify first-class produce. The code names chosen vary from one kind of fruit and vegetable to another, and none of them bears the kind of name that lets you know which ones are second rate, when, in fact, that should be the intent of the identifying code.

Where can a writer find out how to judge produce and when is the season for each? You'd think any produce man would know. Often he knows as little about produce as a typesetter knows about type design. Ask a typesetter: What is the virtue of Bodoni? He will look at you blankly. Ask a produce man to explain the difference between thin- and thick-skinned grapefruit, the reason for the difference, whether to avoid one or choose one, and why. Not infrequently, the answers are doubletalk.

The owners of some produce stands go early to market four or five days a week and buy their ware at the trucks or as it comes into the warehouses. Here you will find a few learned men whose experience in produce is bountiful and who may speak to you out of their wisdom.

Are there advantages at the big chain stores' produce departments over the small independent stores? Are there disadvantages? What are they?

In your town do they have any farmers' markets? Are they really farmers' markets to which local farmers bring their own fresh produce? Or are they second-rate, picked-over goods that didn't sell when fresh and found their home at a farmers' market that is no more nor less than a low-level produce stand?

Do local farmers offer city people the chance to pick berries and fruits in season? If so, give their rates.

Tree-ripened peaches, pears, and plums are hard to come by. The riper they are, naturally, the more they spoil and suffer damage in shipping. Can tree-ripened fruit be obtained? Where and for how much?

Since the seasons bring new crops, a local produce book may best serve its readers when issued twice a year. A town with a three hundred thousand metropolitan population might support a twice-yearly sale of five thousand local books on produce. Is there a sponsor for such a book?

Since such a book might have to sell for two or three dollars, your publisher may require some kind of supplementary sponsoring. Can you find a way to do this and still not debilitate the editorial approach?

Perhaps a vitamin manufacturer might be the "supplement" you need and offer particular vitamins, in certain seasons, to take the place of the fresh produce that is missing or too expensive.

It's fun to float like a butterfly, sting like a bee, create like a writer, and think like a publisher. A nice combination.

13

The University Presses

SCATTERED LIKE A WEB through the fifty states are eighty small publishing houses known to the book trade as university presses. They produce two thousand new titles each year and represent a market that gives work to editors and authors alike.

Although these presses have much in common, their wide range of titles looks like a crazy quilt of subject matter.

Witness these university-press titles: *The Twice Born: A Study of a Community of High Caste Hindus, Cocktail Party Cookbook and Guide, Three Years in Mississippi* (the last by James Meredith), *Cricket in a Thorn Tree: Helen Susman and the Progressive Party in South Africa, Travel Accounts of Indiana and Adjacent States, 1679–1961, Chinese-Soviet Relationships, 1945–1970, History of the Organ in the United States.*

A handful of titles selected from all the university presses? Not quite. The above selections are from Indiana University Press at Bloomington.

How does this curious mixture of subject matter come about? Each press director explains his choices differently, but a common factor does exist.

In the academe, college teachers are expected to publicize their expertise (politics, sociology, and so forth) and create an identity for themselves through magazine articles and books. When large numbers of instructors at one college do this abundantly, it becomes easier to attract superior students and secure more funds either from the state legislatures or alumni. The teacher who accumulates a wide audience among either his peers or the lay public can expect better pay and more favorable treatment. Do you want to be stuck in a closet of an office with a noisy air conditioner? That's easy. Just remain unknown.

The graffiti in the ivy reads "Publish or Perish." But the commercial book-publishing houses expect to sell enough copies of their books to make a profit, while most books written by college professors are intended for a limited audience. This means that the professor, in order to publish, has to choose a popular subject and attract a wide, general audience or find a subsidized press. That's how university presses were born.

The books of the first university presses were often *Festschriften*: honors lectures delivered by distinguished professors or dissertations by graduate students. Not only did they not sell, they were hardly read beyond the author's circle. Historically, this was the modest origin of the older presses.

Once a university press is started, the problems arriving with it are common to all. The local teachers can't write, and the director turns out to be unknowing about the book-publishing business. The books become dead storage.

The first change is usually to get a new director, and this often means bringing in the head of the college news bureau or the head of the English department. A director of this stripe is rarely experienced in circularizing libraries and college bookstores and is inclined to believe that a straightforward announcement of a new book is really all that should be necessary.

Sometimes, however, the new director brings a special charm to the job. Sitting down to read a manuscript, regardless of its subject matter, he asks that the author be clear, logical, and readable. This, of course, is the beginning of editorial wisdom and immediately puts the new director in conflict with the locals, who expect automatic publication from their own university press.

Many directors had to come and go before it was recognized that a press needs two people: an editor who is able to attract writing talent and a publisher who knows how to work the book market and has the salesmanship and intellectuality to get the necessary subsidy from the administration.

Once this kind of editor-publisher team was put together, it moved away from its historic purpose: to permit the local teachers to publish. It moved away, because talent is so scarce and spread so thinly about the globe that an editor-publisher team, to justify the existence of a quality book-publishing organization, has to buy the best writing talent it can find, regardless of the location or profession of the author. You can sense the scenario in a minute, but in real life it took sixty years of backing and filling before the university presses became professional with high literary as well as scholarly standards. Since 1940, the progress has accelerated.

As this literary progress spread, first to one university press, then to another, the editor-director team quickly built up a power structure inside the establishment of the university and, in almost every instance, won its case: Publish what you like, regardless of who the author is, where he teaches, or even if he does not teach.

The purpose of the university press shifted from being a vehicle for the locals to gain publication to making a name for the university through its press.

To you, the author, this is a very good thing. What counts is scholarship, readability, clarity, logic, and originality.

Here's how John Gallman, director of the Indiana University Press, says it:

> We are an international publisher. Our authors are not only residents of Indiana, they are residents of the world. We would like people to think of us as an important publisher of serious nonfiction and translations. We import books from British publishers, arrange for translations from quite a few languages, and seek manuscripts of merit, from sources all over the world. Following is a list of our main subject matter: Literary Criticism (especially theory and U.S.), Translations (especially from Russian and Chinese), Film, History (Politics and International Relations), Public Policy, Environment and Ecology, African Studies, Music, Women's Studies, Folklore and Anthropology, Linguistics, Semiotics, Philosophy, State and Regional Studies.

Because most university-press books sell only several thousand copies, the author usually receives no advance at all or a very modest one, and the royalty is normally under four thousand dollars. Mr. Gallman says: "At Indiana, we pay royalty on the basis of the list price and the royalty is negotiable. It goes up to 15 percent, based on the type of book and the amount of the sale; it might also be 5 percent, based on the same reasons. The average sale is around two thousand copies when you eliminate our top best-selling titles. We do not use fiction. Our main work is to publish scholarship."

Indiana also issues books with broad reader interest: *On the Take*, by William J. Chambliss, is a detailed look at Seattle. The author painstakingly shows how the local crime network is connected to national business and political interests. *Private Lives of Public Servants*, by Kenneth Lasson, is a perceptive study of six civil servants: their daily work, their attitudes, and their lives. One of Indiana's popular regional books is *A Home in the Woods*, taken from the diary of Oliver Johnson, 1820–1830. He farmed near Indianapolis: "jist one great big woods for miles and miles in most every direction."

How does Indiana University Press sell its books?

> We have our own salesmen in the Midwest [says John Gallman], where our travelers represent several other university presses. Elsewhere, we use commissioned salespeople. We spend about five thousand dollars a year for general media advertising and also use scholarly journals for specialized books. We have thirty-seven employees and gross $1.5 million a year and expect this to rise to $2 million next year.

Other letters from editors and directors appear in this chapter to give the reader some touch with the intimate human side, because that's what editors and publishers and books are all about. The chapter concludes with names and addresses of about seventy university presses.

If this gives you less than you need to go on, there's an editorial resource called the *Directory of the Association of University Presses* (One Park Ave., New York, NY 10016). It is eight and a half by eleven inches in size, 124 pages, spiral bound and sells for $5.00, postpaid. Each of the seventy American university presses that is a member of the association uses a full page to describe its activities.

The directory offers no data on royalty arrangements with authors, although, from the following letters and interviews, you can piece together a pretty fair picture of what to expect.

Susan E. Kelpe is managing editor of University of Missouri Press, at

Columbia. They publish twenty-five titles a year. Miss Kelpe writes:

> I do feel that working for a small publishing house, one that
> has grown tremendously in the seven years that I have worked
> here, is quite satisfying in many ways. One has the opportunity
> to participate in all facets of the publishing process. I feel that I
> have some stake in each book that we produce, including a
> responsibility for the mistakes that so often occur. While that can
> be frustrating at times, in no way can any people on our staff feel
> that they are not in a position to make a visible contribution, in
> either a positive or negative way. Everyone must be an asset or
> the whole operation must pull the dead weight that results. In a
> day and age of large corporations and vast university campuses,
> being in such a position is an unusual opportunity.
>
> We have large lists in the subject areas of literary criticism and
> history, especially nineteenth- and twentieth-century American
> history, and other scholarly areas. We also have an active poetry
> award (five hundred dollars for the author) and a short-fiction
> program designed for authors of first books. Payment for this is
> 10 percent royalty of our receipts. Authors should request the
> rules for our Break-Through program.

If you have an idea for a nonfiction book with broad-based reader
interest, preferably one dealing with the Missouri region, write for the
Current Books and Selected Backlist catalogue of this press, and see if
your manuscript or chapter outline is in their ballpark. Then send a
query.

One recent Missouri book, *Hurry Home Wednesday*, by Loren Reid,
tells about growing up in a small Missouri town from 1905 to 1921. The
town described is Gilman, where young Reid grew up and observed the
town, first as a schoolboy, and later as a reporter. He also set type and
sold advertisements. He describes the town's railroad, moving pictures,
early automobiles, the impact of World War I, the perils of the eighth
grade, and certain amusing and tragic events reported in his father's
newspaper. *Hurry Home Wednesday* may offer another author the idea
of doing a documentary historical narrative about a small town in his
own region for a university press located there.

Missouri's every-other-year Break-Through program selects three books. Usually, two are poetry, and one is fiction. The books are 120 to 160 printed pages. The Break-Through poetry books are not anthologies. One poet to a book. The Missouri press prefers not to have one long poem occupying most of the book.

The short-fiction Break-Through books are either a collection of short stories or a novella, because they are trying to keep the book under 160 pages. "It takes a valiant effort," says Miss Kelpe, "to discover quality short fiction by new writers. By 'new writer,' we mean someone who has not yet published fiction in book form but usually has had some kind of fiction publication in the 'little magazines,' or the small presses."

One of the recent Break-Through fiction titles is *The Van Gogh Field and Other Stories*, by William Kittredge (144 pages, $9.00). Mr. Kittredge, who is from Montana, says his short fiction "revolves about the relationship between love and isolation, the empty landscape and human solace. I am most centrally concerned with the interaction between what is real and what seems to be real and the ways in which one becomes the other. I am fascinated by the ways we make up our lives and invent ourselves."

Virginia Faulkner is editor-in-chief of the University of Nebraska Press, at Lincoln. She writes:

> Our list is by no means limited to scholarly or supplementary texts, nor are we primarily interested in the work of authors of this region—although of course we are always happy to publish worthy books by members of the faculty of our parent institution.
>
> We do not publish original fiction, original poetry, or *Festschriften*. We ask that authors who are interested in placing their manuscripts with us first write a letter of inquiry describing their proposals (aim and scope, intended audience, extent in typescript pages) and their qualifications to undertake the work; we also ask that they provide a curriculum vitae. Manuscripts should not be sent unless solicited by the editorial committee.

The University of Nebraska Press catalogue of current books is attractive, well illustrated, and has enough white space for easy reading. *Mountain Passages*, by Jeremy Bernstein, is so well written it can make an editor weep. Bernstein sees mountain-climbing as the most adventurous and one of the most dangerous of enterprises; his feeling that climbing is both absurd and marvelous imparts a special flavor.

There's a cheerful bit of Americana, *A Lady's Experience in the Wild West in 1883*, by an Englishwoman, Rose Pender, who made the grand tour of the Old West.

One Day on a Beetle Rock, a paperback, by Sally Carrighar, is a lovely thing. The time is a day in June, in Sequoia National Park, high tide of the animal year. The characters are a weasel, a Sierra grouse, a chickadee, a black bear, a lizard, a coyote, a deer mouse, a stellar jay, and a mule deer. The day begins with the weasel's furious predawn hunt and closes with the tiny song of the deer mouse.

If I were shooting for a book in the general region adjacent to Nebraska, I would plan a comprehensive popular book on the large federal, state and county parks as well as the outdoor recreation available: boating, backpacking, climbing, fishing, hunting, hiking, camping, salt- and sweetwater canoeing, semiclosed nature reserves, and lake sports. There are a half-dozen university presses in this area. Then I would try to find a foundation that would feed and house me for a year while I researched and wrote the book. A receptive affirmation of the idea from one of the presses would help secure the grant.

A different slant on this idea is *The Great Lakes Guidebook*, by George Cantor (paperback, $5.95), published by the University of Michigan Press. Here, the emphasis is not so much on recreational facilities as it is on regional coverage for the tourist (the spectacular skyline of Detroit, the serenity of out-of-the-way villages). In short, it is a travel guide complete with essays on history, suggested walks, and scenic drives. Between these two approaches, writers may create an adaptation of their own. If the University of Nebraska Press interests you, write for their large, attractive, current catalogue, and then send a query letter when you develop something that you feel appeals specifically to them.

One of the demurrers on the popular recreational guides comes from Susan Foard, editor of University of Virginia Press. Miss Foard says:

> It would be hard to get a book such as this through our Press Board, since we serve scholarship mostly. Our criteria is "does it serve the scholar?" Another criterion is "does it serve any avant-garde interest?"
>
> We might shy away from a recreational guide in our region

because the book would find a mainline publisher since it would serve not only the residents of Virginia but also a multitude of travelers who come into our state for its beauty, its open spaces, and its historical sites. Since the market is there, we would leave this book to the trade publisher.

We are not turned off because a book will be popular. But we want more than that. My advice to a free-lance writer is to start with something you have lived with; like, say, you have been watching hawks and from this experience write a book on hawks in eastern America. A book such as this should communicate the knowledge the expert gained.

John G. Ryden, editor-in-chief of the University of Chicago Press, answers our inquiry about the standards they apply in deciding whether or not to publish a book.

Most of our books are scholarly. That is, they are intended for a narrow group of specialists in a field. We expect the scholarship to be sound, the work to be of significance. It should be well organized, succinct, and clear. Most of all we expect it to be original. We publish in addition a select list of books each year intended for a broader audience, either one that cuts across a variety of disciplines, or one that might be vaguely defined as that of the informed general reader. For these, we would expect the same qualities listed above, plus a vital, but difficult to define, intrinsic appeal. Of course they must also be highly readable.

You ask what other university presses continue to "earn my special respect"? Princeton, California, Harvard (recently) and Yale (sometimes) come most quickly to mind. Johns Hopkins is very solid. There are also some that specialize. Oklahoma, with its fine list in frontier and American Indian studies, is one; LSU, with its excellent history program, particularly the *History of the South* series, is another.

Of course there is no American press like the University of Chicago. We publish more books; we sell more books. (I can document this.) And I think we do the best books and we've got the reviews and awards to prove it. In 1978 we won both the National Book Award and the Pulitzer

Prize. We are also the largest and most important publisher of scholarly journals.

Oh, yes, there are Oxford and Cambridge to be reckoned with. They are superb. But remember, I said we are the best American press. And besides, they had a head start.

Mr. Ryden offers this suggestion to writers with the competence to write for one of the university presses:

> Give your book idea to a university press through a query letter or, maybe, by going there in person, your appointment in hand. If they like the idea, ask if they want an outline and two or three sample chapters. If they say yes—work it up. When they see your material, and tell you to go ahead, then perhaps you can interest one of the foundations in financing your time while you write the book. There has been a failure on the part of the foundations to perceive the workings of the university press. The foundation is often willing to give an author a grant to do research for a book, or even to write it, but they don't want to soil their hands with the business of publication. They assume all publishing is at a profit.

Mr. Ryden's idea is worth capturing and feeding. If you are a free-lance writer, interested in the contemporary scene, and writing a book with broadly based reader interest, you might locate a small foundation in the same geographical area where a university press has shown an interest in your work. In such an instance, a letter from the press encouraging you to proceed and offering a cordial reading of the final work is a tolerable recommendation for a grant.

At Chicago, the royalty is based on the net received by the press (not the list price that appears on the dust jacket), and the payment is usually 10 percent on the first twenty-five hundred sold and 12.5 percent on the next twenty-five hundred.

Several recent Chicago books appeal to large numbers of readers. In *A Place on the Corner*, by Elija Anderson, the author lived out for three

175

years at Jelly's, a street-corner bar and liquor store, in a low-income black neighborhood on Chicago's South Side. In his book you see how the patrons divide their social strata: the regulars who are employed and involved in a stable family group, the wineheads, and the toughs. There are scenes of sentiment, human caring, fighting, and bittersweet humor. In the loosely organized social system at Jelly's, every customer can be "somebody." For this reason, most of them return to the place on the corner.

Two others are *Our Amish Neighbors*, by William I. Schreiber, and *Growing Up American*, by Alan Peshkin.

Luther Wilson, editor of the publishing division of the University of Oklahoma, writes:

> Our list is not limited to scholarly books. We publish a fairly large number of general trade titles, such as the recent *Maya Ruins of Mexico in Color*, by William Ferguson and John Q. Royce, which was a Book-of-the-Month Club selection, and *In Search of Butch Cassidy*, by Larry Pointer. Our list is concentrated primarily in four areas: American Indians, Western History and Americana, Mesoamerican archeology (including a number of popular guidebooks), and Greek and Roman classics.
>
> Our authors come from as far away as South Africa (F.W. von Mellenthin's *Panzer Battles* and *German Generals*), and as near as Norman. Our best-selling Western titles, *The Gunfighter* and *They Called Him Wild Bill*, were written by a British author, Joe Rosa.
>
> We publish a number of series, the most prestigious and, coincidentally, most successful of which is our *Civilization of the American Indian Series* with 150 titles in print.
>
> We do not consider unsolicited manuscripts. We prefer a letter of inquiry outlining the author's project. If interested, we will request the manuscript for review.
>
> I have been an editor for a commercial publisher (Harper & Row), and for two university presses (Cambridge and University of Oklahoma). I by far prefer the university press. It is a perfect place for an intellectual voyeur.

Along with most other university-press editors, Mr. Wilson reports to

176

the provost, who in this case is the dean of the graduate school.

Mr. Wilson mentions that, in his experience, the salaries of editors-in-chief at the larger presses range from twenty-five thousand to thirty-five thousand dollars. This salary drops down gradually at the smaller presses with fewer employees and titles.

Oklahoma's royalty is based on the gross income received from a particular book. The amount of royalty varies with the size of the market and any unusual investment in making up the book—adding twenty-four color plates, for instance.

Oklahoma produces forty-five new titles a year, employs forty people and grosses $1.5 million a year. They look to break even and do receive, when needed, a subsidy that can run into "high five figures," but, they say, they "cannot pull this every year."

Mr. Wilson, an engaging, experienced editor, has an open editorial mind on any book with a broad-based reader interest that contributes to the culture and knowledge of the people in Oklahoma's general geographic region.

Their eight-and-a-half-by-eleven-inch, thirty-six-page catalogue is a handsome, well-illustrated, two-color job. Here is the subject matter of three books of broad-based reader interest.

The dispatches written by Charles Fletcher Lummis about the Apache War in 1886 while the U.S. Army pursued Geronimo. Lumis was a reporter for the *Los Angeles Times*.

A busy person's guide to indoor gardening—two hundred selected plants. Editorially, the book is hung on two simple secrets to success with houseplants: Choose the right plants for your home condition; give each plant the very best conditions your home can offer.

A book on travels in North America, 1822–24. A translation of the original German text, profusely illustrated. It is volume 63 in Oklahoma's *American Exploration and Travel Series*.

Editorial opinion among the university presses allows room for considerable variety in a book, even those with a popular base. One vision of this appears in the editorial outlook offered by John H. Langley, director of the Regents Press of Kansas University. He writes:

Ours is a regional press with some pretty serious competition: Oklahoma, Nebraska, and Missouri are cases in point, and I do not mean their football teams. We are constantly searching for and thinking about the sort of books our press should develop to better serve our community.

We did find that there is a strong interest in the "environmental" type of book. Grace Muilenburg and Ada Swineford's great book on stone fence posts showed us the way toward other possible texts on the Kansas environment.

What other types of books could be done on the Kansas environment? One of the largest wildlife refuges in the Middle West is at Cheyenne Bottoms, right in the center of the state. This is a station for birds on the "fly-way" between Mexico and Canada. A very interesting book, with appeal to bird lovers and naturalists, could be done on Cheyenne Bottoms. The Texas A & M Press published a very successful book on Texas ranches. Why not one on Kansas ranches?

Some of the Kansas "outposts" have been done to death . . . Dodge City, for instance, but others have not been touched. A good example is Hays, Kansas, the location of Fort Hays, and a rough and ready outpost if there ever was one.

For our press, as with any other, some manuscripts are more logical submissions than others. For instance, we are publishing a book on poisonous plants of the Great Plains and also doing a weed manual, but we would never consider a textbook on botany. We simply do not have the machinery to sell a textbook.

Looking at our own state, how can the free-lancer find good book subjects? Start at the beginning: the peculiar conception, birth, and demography. Kansas contributes many possible subjects.

Kansas was a great place for movements. Carrie Nation was raised in Kansas and she started her great crusade against the Demon Rum from here. Why not an interesting book with lots of pictures on Carrie's early days in Kansas?

On April 18, 1894, the First Kansas Colored Infantry participated in the battle of Poison Springs. In this battle, 117 black men were killed, many after they had surrendered or had been wounded. There is a good book about this regiment if someone wanted to do it.

The *esprit* of university-press people is shown in a response from Mrs. Gwen Duffey of the University of North Carolina Press:

We were primarily a regional press in the early days (founded fifty-six years ago), but broadened our list over the years, with emphasis most recently on history, social sciences, and literature. Two recent titles could be classified as regional—the McKinney (on Appalachia) and the Albright (Moravians in Winston-Salem, North Carolina).

Before we publish a book, several authorities in the particular field are asked to read the manuscript and submit written comments. An evaluation of the manuscript from the editorial point of view is made by the press, and suggestions are made concerning organization, use of language and punctuation, and the proper treatment of footnotes and bibliography. The result is the product of several hands and minds as opposed to a work of fiction, which is purely the author's.

I find working with a university press most satisfying. Commercial houses are concerned primarily with making money (for themselves and their authors), but the university press is concerned with the dissemination of knowledge. We are a nonprofit corporation and are subsidized in order to make ends meet. If, by chance, some of our titles sell well and make a profit *(Wild Flowers of North Carolina, Hiroshima Diary, Bridge to the Sun*—the last also being made into a movie), we put that profit into the publication of a book that needs to be made available to scholars but that we know will have only a limited sale, mostly to libraries.

At our press, the first printing (fifteen hundred to two thousand) usually loses money, and it is only after the sale of the first printing that royalties are paid. Working for a university press is, therefore, less commercial, even more idealistic, than other types of publishing, and we can honestly take pride in our contribution to learning while not being preoccupied with making money. We are associated with an academic

THE BOOK MARKET

community where there are thinking and caring people (at least the majority of them are).

You ask about anecdotes. . . . I could tell you about the baby mockingbird in the water cooler, the editor who ironed a large batch of galleys after dropping them outside on a rainy day, and index copy that came in with the entry "Jesus. *See* Christ," but I fear that this may not be the sort of thing you had in mind.

Evalin F. Douglas, managing editor of the University of Kentucky Press, offers these comments:

Our list falls into two categories: scholarly and regional. Our scholarly list is strongest in American literature and history, especially of the Ohio Valley and the South. We have a strong Romance Language series. We also publish in biological sciences, sociology, geography, and occasionally in other fields. The physical sciences are out of our orbit. We don't publish fiction (except out-of-print classics in certain series) or poetry.

The Kentucky catalogue bristles with books of broad-based reader interest, one of the most remarkable being *We Be Here When the Morning Comes*. The book is a verbal portrait in words of a community and its people at a particular instant in their lives. The people live along the Clover Fork of the Cumberland River, and the time is the coal strike in 1973–74. A foreword by Robert Coles says:

There is a substantial body of "literature" devoted to the people of Eastern Kentucky and West Virginia. Not all of these articles and books are worth much. Many of them, for decades, have stressed the ignorance, the backwardness, the deficits and limitations of the region's people—those "hillbillies" whom the rest of America left behind decades ago. As for coal miners, their only distinction is that they are employed hillbillies, in contrast to those who distill liquor illegally, who speak, at best, a quaint English, and who come forth occasionally with "interesting" arts and crafts as examples of their "folk culture."

How convenient for the rest of us, including those who own and run the region's coal mines. If the people of Clover Fork, Kentucky, some of whom we meet and get to know in this important and powerful book, could be portrayed convincingly as seriously retarded culturally, as not very smart, as provincial and even as a little odd, then who is to worry about the way the rich and influential corporations treat them? Aren't they lucky just to have jobs?

. . . I hope many social scientists, among others, will read this wonderfully strong, passionate, candid, and, yes, scholarly book— scholarly in the sense that the people who speak in it know whereof they speak (about themselves) and do so with intelligence, perception, thoughtfulness. They are short on theory, no doubt about it. . . . I only wish some of us in the social sciences, some of us who call ourselves sociologists or political scientists or psychiatrists, would be as blunt and as plain spoken. . . .

Is there a market for books similar to *We Be Here When the Morning Comes*, or Indiana's *On the Take* at the university presses?

One of the University of Kentucky catalogues is devoted exclusively to their popular line and is called "Kentucky Books." It may lead some writers into considering a query to a university press in their own regions about a broad-based book.

Scott A. Johnson began work with the University Press of Michigan in 1970 after receiving his M.B.A. Mr. Johnson writes:

Probably the best and most recent example of our publishing profile, outside of the scholarly or text areas, would be our recent publication of *The Great Lakes Guidebook* [mentioned on an earlier page]. Another book that is thoroughly scholarly in its content, but nevertheless has a very wide lay audience, is *The Mushroom Hunter's Field Guide*, by Alexander Smith. *The Mushroom Hunter's Field Guide*, revised in 1963, has sold well over a hundred thousand copies, primarily to a bookstore audience.

181

THE BOOK MARKET

The University of Michigan Press pays the author 8 to 15 percent of the gross money received from the sale of cloth-bound books. Paperbacks pay the author 5 to 6 percent. For books of very limited sale, the story is no advance and no royalty. Such books represent an investment on the part of the press in scholarship. When a popular book moves into a large sale, the profits usually go into publishing more scholarly books or into reducing the subsidy the press requires.

The University of Michigan Press attempts to break even. The sale runs to four thousand copies on the scholarly books with a wide audience and one thousand, and sometimes less, on highly specialized titles.

They issue fifteen to twenty books a year and report to the dean of the graduate school, the financial vice-president of the university, and the president. Mr. Johnson estimates the salary of the press directors in the range of thirty thousand to thirty-five thousand dollars a year: "lower at the small presses, higher, to the mid-forties, with the larger, older ones."

Elizabeth Dulany, managing editor, answered some questions about the fiction program of the University of Illinois Press. In 1973, this press began publishing four books of short stories a year. Each book is a collection from one writer. Generally, mainline book publishers back away from short-story collections as the public seems averse to buying them. To support the short-fiction writer, Illinois publishes these collections in both paper and cloth, the list prices being around $3.50 and $7.50. No advance is paid. The press run of the paper edition is 1,500 to 2,000, and the cloth edition is 750 to 1,000. Royalty is 10 percent on the first 5,000 sold. The authors chip in with their time to help publicize their books locally by appearing at bookstores, getting invited to be guests on talk shows, and wriggling their way into some ink from the columnists. To submit a collection of stories, write a query first, telling something about yourself and the nature of your material.

The University of Illinois Press publishes forty-five to fifty titles a year, and about a dozen have a broad reader base: *Morning Chores* is about the good old days in farming; *The Factory Girls* is a collection of writings on life and struggles in the New England factories in 1840, written by the "girls" themselves, who, in their own words, tell the story of the first trade unions of women workers in this country.

An oral story, told by four different Cuban women, reveals the life in

182

Cuba today as lived by four women with different stations in life. The Illinois catalogue that I saw offers titles with an attractive and inviting human quality.

On balance, the university presses offer authors an interesting but not always profitable market. From their point of view, they are more than fair in financial treatment to authors, because most of the presses require an annual subsidy from the university.

The director of a large university press receives twenty-five thousand to forty thousand dollars; the editor-in-chief is paid fifteen thousand dollars and up. That's for one year of work. The author often works one full year, sometimes more, to complete either a scholarly book or one with a broader reader base. For this, he receives, on the average, no cash advance and a total royalty of one thousand dollars.

Should this imbalance be corrected? Is labor worth its hire?

There are several ways this might be done. Just as the man who sweeps the floors is paid a realistic wage for his efforts, and the sweeper's honest wage is included in the subsidy advanced to the university press by its mother college, so, too, the author might well be offered some kind of base payment. Two thousand dollars' guaranteed base payment would be better than what is now provided, on the average. This could push the annual subsidy too high for a university press that is publishing twenty-five titles a year—it might run it up forty thousand dollars.

The additional cash paid to authors need not come entirely out of an increased subsidy. Several marketing ideas could produce additional revenue. One is used by the University of Kentucky Press, and perhaps one-third of the other presses have titles to do it. For Kentucky, it is simply a matter of producing a separate catalogue describing titles that deal with their home state. The one I have before me contains twenty-four pages in full color and lists seventy-five titles. Some are current; others were published previously. Some titles are *The Kentucky Thoroughbred, The Kentucky Harness Horse, Audubon—His Kentucky Years.* The catalogue is mailed to University of Kentucky alumni. Several presses do the same thing, and I believe the idea could work for several more presses.

Presses like Ohio, Chicago, or Princeton have small interest in their home states, their domain being world scholarship, yet, one book in fifteen has a broad reader base. In this case, the separate catalogue I suggest would include titles issued over the past five years and having a broad reader appeal. Three members of my family and a number of friends are graduates of the University of Chicago, and I showed them the current catalogue, which has eight books with this kind of broad base. I asked if, as alumni, they would be interested in receiving a Chicago catalogue describing forty books of this kind. They said yes. I reported this fact to the energetic editor-in-chief at the Chicago press, John D. Ryden, and he thought well enough of the idea to pass it on to his market director. Alumni of schools like Chicago are a bountiful group of literate book buyers.

Before me are catalogues from Harvard, Illinois, Miami, Kansas, Pennsylvania, Texas (at Austin), and Virginia. They sparkle with lively books. How many alumni of these fine schools receive such a catalogue regularly?

In the Southwest and the Great Plains, there are many university presses. Could they supply regional retail bookstores with a cooperative rack of thirty titles that had a broad reader base, and changed titles every four months?

Mr. Kopenhoever, of the University of Tennessee Press, implemented two ideas to sell more books. The first, called *Books for the Tennessee Library*, is a catalogue mailed to libraries in that state. Second, Mr. Kopenhoever is working with his editorial department in developing and selling a series of paperback books for a broad reader audience in Tennessee. Two of these books are *Tennessee Strings*, which covers the history of country music in Tennessee, and *Visions of Utopia*, which describes the birth and fall of three small communes, 1825–94. Mr. Kopenhoever plans to produce a catalogue of these broad-based paperbacks for the alumni and may test large lists of book buyers when a geographical breakdown of Tennessee buyers is available. While working for Kentucky, this same gentleman used the inside back cover of the alumni magazine and several other university publications for nine Kentucky books, and he sold a gross retail value of twenty thousand dollars in one year. The books were offered at 20 percent off the list price.

There is, however, one special difference between most of the authors of scholarly books and the personnel on the payroll. Sue Kelpe, managing editor of the University of Missouri Press, puts it this way:

"Scholars do not submit manuscripts to university presses with the idea of making any royalties. In the academic world, it is necessary to publish to gain promotion, tenure, better positions at other universities. The important thing is to publish and for your book to be favorably received."

If you are the marketing manager of a university press, you can't beat the rap when your editor-in-chief selects a translation of a fifth-century work that describes the infusion of Christianity into Armenia, price, fifty dollars. Go sell that to the alumni.

Not all university-press books, however, are scholarly. Free-lance writers produce some of the titles too, and it is for these people we speak.

The university presses have come a long way. Their catalogues are like so many gems, and their directors and editors are people of good will and professional backgrounds.

When submitting work to the university presses, the best procedure is one that serves both parties.

1. *Book ideas:* Usually set forth in two or three pages. Write for the catalogue of presses in your general area, and examine other university-press catalogues at your library. For a further overview of the presses, order a copy of the directory published by the Association of University Presses (price and address given earlier). Select one press to which you will send your book idea and your qualifications, enclosing a stamped, self-addressed return envelope.
2. *Book outline plus sample chapters:* Following the above method, include the outline and several "ready-to-go" sample chapters. Ask whether the editor wishes to see the complete manuscript.
3. *Complete book manuscript:* It is generally unwise to submit this without being invited. After selecting the press you believe is best suited for your book, it is best to submit either your book idea or a chapter outline and several chapters.

The names and addresses of many of the better-known presses follow:

Brigham Young University Press
209 University Press Building
Provo, UT 84602
Acquisitions Editor: Louise G. Hanson

Georgia State University,
College of Business Administration
Public Service Division
University Plaza
Atlanta, GA 30303

THE BOOK MARKET

Brown University Press
Alumnae Hall, 194 Meeting St.
Providence, RI 02912
Director: Grant Dugdale

Bucknell University Press
Lewisburg, PA 17837
Director: Mills F. Edgerton, Jr.

Cambridge University Press
32 E. 57th St.
New York, NY 10022
Editorial Director: Walter Lippincott, Jr.

The Catholic University of
  America Press
620 Michigan Ave. N.E.
Washington, DC 20064

Colorado Associated University Press
1424 15th St., Box 480
Boulder, CO 80309
Editor: Frederick R. Rinhart

Columbia University Press
562 W. 113th St.
New York, NY 10025
Editor-in-Chief: John D. Moore

Cornell University Press
124 Roberts Pl.
Ithaca, NY 14850
Roger E. McCarthy

Duke University Press
Box 6697, College Sta.
Durham, NC 27708
Director and Editor: Ashbel G. Brice

Duquesne University Press
101 Administration Bldg.
Pittsburgh, PA 15219
Fir. and Rts. and Perm.: John Dowds

Fairleigh Dickinson University Press
285 Madison Ave.
Madison, NJ 07940
Editor: Harry Keyishian

Fordham University Press
University Box L
Bronx, NY 10458
Editor: H. George Fletcher

Guild of Tutors Press of International College
1019 Gayley Ave. Suite 105
Los Angeles, CA 90024

Harvard University Press
79 Garden St.
Cambridge, MA 02138
Editor-in-Chief: Maud Wilcox

Howard University Press
2935 Upton St. N.W.
Washington, DC 20008
Senior Editor: Cheryl C. Hobson

Indiana University Press
Tenth and Morton Sts.
Bloomington, IN 47405
Managing Editor: Natalie Wrubel

Inter-American University Press
Box 3255,
San Juan, PR 00936
Director and Editor: John Zebrowski

Iowa State University Press
Ames, IA 50010
Managing Editor: Rowena Hames Malone

The Johns Hopkins University Press
Baltimore, MD 21218
Editorial Director: Anders Richter

Kent State University Press
Kent, OH 44242
Editor: Martha Gibbons

Louisiana State University Press
Baton Rouge, LA 70803
Executive Editor: Beverly Jarrett

Loyola University Press
3441 N. Ashland Ave.
Chicago, IL 60657
Director: Rev. Vincent C. Horrigan

The M.I.T. Press
28 Carleton St.
Cambridge, MA 02142
Director: Frank Urbanowski

Memphis State University Press
Memphis, TN 38152
Associate Editor: Nancy Hurley

186

Museum of New Mexico Press
Box 2087
Santa Fe, NM 87503
Editor: Richard Polese

Naval Institute Press
Annapolis, MD 21402
Senior Editor: Frank Uhlig, Jr.

Northern Illinois University Press
DeKalb, IL 60115
Manuscript Editor: David P. Etter

Northwestern University Press
1735 Benson Ave.
Box 1093X
Evanston, IL 60201
Business Manager: W. Michael Nelis

Ohio University Press
Scott Quadrangle
Athens, OH 45701
Managing Editor: Holly Panich

Oregon State University Press
101 Waldo Hall
Corvallis, OR 97331
Managing Editor: Jeffrey Grass

Oxford University Press
200 Madison Ave.
New York, NY 10016
President: Byron S. Hollinshead

The Pennsylvania State University Press
215 Wagner Bldg.
University Park, PA 16802
Editorial Director: John M. Pickering

The Popular Press
Bowling Green University
Bowling Green, OH 43403
Editor: Ray B. Browne

Princeton University Press
Princeton, NJ 09540
Director: Herbert S. Bailey, Jr.

Purdue University Press
South Campus Courts-D
West Lafayette, IN 47907

The Regents Press of Kansas
366 Watson Library
Lawrence, KS 66045
Director: John H. Langley

Rutgers University Press
30 College Ave.
New Brunswick, NJ 08903
Senior Editor: Marlie P. Wasserman

Southern Illinois University Press
Box 3697
Carbondale, IL 62901
Chief Editor: Joyce Atwood

Southern Methodist University Press
Dallas, TX 75275
Editor: Margaret L. Hartley

Stanford University Press
Stanford, CA 94305
Editor: J. G. Bell

Syracuse University Press
101 E. Water St.
Syracuse, NY 13210
Director: Mrs. Arpena Mesrobian

Teachers College Press
Columbia University
1234 Amsterdam Ave.
New York, NY 10027
Senior Editor: Mary L. Allison

Temple University Press
Broad and Oxford Sts.
Philadelphia, PA 19122
Editor-in-Chief: Kenneth L. Arnold

Texas A & M University Press
Drawer C
College Station, TX 77843
Editor: Margaret Ingram

Texas Christian University Press
Box 30783
Fort Worth, TX 76129
Director: James Newcomer

University of Alabama Press
Box 2877
University, AL 35486
Editor: Francis P. Squibb

187

THE BOOK MARKET

The University of Arizona Press
Box 3398
Tucson, AZ 85722
Director: Marshall Townsend

University of California Press
2223 Fulton St.
Berkeley, CA 94720
Director: James H. Clark

University of Chicago Press
5801 Ellis Ave.
Chicago, IL 60637
Editor-in-Chief: James L. Romig

University of Delaware Press
326 Hullihen Hall
Newark, DE 19711
Director: James Merrill

University of Georgia Press
Athens, GA 30602
General Editor: Robert Buffington

University of Illinois Press
54 E. Gregory Dr.
Box 5081, Sta. A
Champaign, IL 61820
Managing Editor: Elizabeth G. Dulany

University of Iowa Press
Graphic Services Bldg.
Iowa City, IA 52242
Editor: Art Pflughaupt

University of Massachusetts Press
Box 429
Amherst, MA 01002
Director: Leone Stein

The University of Michigan Press
930 Greene St., Box 1104
Ann Arbor, MI 48106
Editors: Mary C. Erwin, Carol Mitchell

University of Minnesota Press
2037 University Ave. S.E.
Minneapolis, MN 55455
Senior Editor: William A. Wood

University of Missouri Press
107 Swallow Hall
Columbia, MO 65211
Director: Edward D. King

University of Nevada Press
Reno, NV 89557
Director: Robert Laxalt

University of New Mexico Press
Albuquerque, NM 87131
Managing Editor: Elizabeth C. Hadas

University of North Carolina Press
Box 2288
Chapel Hill, NC 27514
Director: Matthew N. Hodgson

University of Notre Dame Press
Notre Dame, IN 46556
Director: James R. Langford

University of Oklahoma Press
1005 Asp Ave.
Norman, OK 73019
Editor: Luther Wilson, Jr.

University of Pennsylvania Press
3933 Walnut St.
Philadelphia, PA 19104
Editor: John McGuigan

University of Pittsburgh Press
127 N. Bellefield Ave.
Pittsburgh, PA 15260
Editor: Louise Craft

University of Puerto Rico Press
Box X, UPR Sta.
Rio Piedras, PR 00931
Editor: Juan Martinez Capo

University of South Carolina Press
Columbia, SC 29208
Director: Robert T. King

University of Tennessee Press
293 Communications Bldg.
Knoxville, TN 37916
Director: Carol Orr

University of Texas Press
Box 7819 University Sta.
Austin, TX 78712
Director: John H. Kyle

University of the Trees Press
Box 644
Boulder Creek, CA 95006

University of Utah Press
Salt Lake City, UT 84112
General Editors: Margaret Lee, Paula
 Roberts

University of Washington Press
Seattle, WA 98105
Editor-in-Chief: Naomi B. Pascal

University of Wisconsin Press
114 N. Murray St.
Madison, WI 53715
Editor-in-Chief: Elizabeth Steinberg

The University Press of Hawaii
2840 Kolowalu St.
Honolulu, HI 96822
Editors: Elizabeth Bushnell, Stuart Kiang

The University Press of Kentucky
Lexington, KY 40506
Director: Kenneth Cherry

University Press of Mississippi
3825 Ridgewood Rd.
Jackson, MS 39211

University Press of New England
Box 979
Hanover, NH 03755
Director: Thomas L. McFarland

The University Press of Virginia
Box 3608, University Sta.
Charlottesville, VA 22903

University Press of Washington D.C.
University Press Bldg.
Dellbrook Campus
Riverton, VA 22651

University Presses of Florida
15 N.W. 15 St.
Gainesville, FL 32603
Director: Phillip L. Martin

Utah State University Press
UMC 05
Logan, UT 84322
Chairman of Book Selection Committee:
 T.Y. Booth

Vanderbilt University Press
2505 West End Ave.
Nashville, TN 37203
Director: John W. Poindexter

Wayne State University Press
The Leonard N. Simons Bldg.
5959 Woodward Ave.
Detroit, MI 48202
Director: Bernard M. Goldman

Wesleyan University Press
55 High St.
Middletown, CT 06457
Editor: Joan Bothell

Yale University Press
302 Temple St.
New Haven, CT 06511
Editor-in-Chief: Edward Tripp

14

The Small Presses

IN 1965, the first directory of small-press publishers appeared (40 pages, $1.00). Three hundred publishers were listed. At that time, it was estimated that ninety thousand people read the works of writers who appeared in the small presses. Today, the same directory is still being published. Now, there are 480 pages, 4,000 listings, and the directory itself sells for $10.95. The people who buy the books and magazines published by these presses are now estimated at 1.5 million, a 1,500 percent increase in fifteen years.

How did this increase come about, and what manner of person owns a small press?

An anthropologist, Robert Briffault, once said, "In the beginning, there was the name." And from a name much can be surmised. As an example of this, Gertrude Stein pointed to the words "real estate" to indicate deep-seated meanings within a word. If truth lives in this observation, a comparison of the company names of small-press book publishers with an equal number of mainline book publishers might tell us something.

What do you make of these columns of names?

The Blue Horse	*Bobbs-Merrill*
Dragon's Dream	*Doubleday*
Second Coming Press	*Prentice-Hall*
Shameless Hussy	*Harper & Row*
Wild Horses and The Potted Plant	*McGraw-Hill*
Shankpainter	*Houghton Mifflin*

THE BOOK MARKET

Voyeur	*Little, Brown & Co.*
Rockbottom	*Macmillan*
Delirium	*Simon & Schuster*
Cat's Pajamas	*Alfred A. Knopf*

In the right-hand column are the names of men who, years ago, gave identities to their businesses by virtue of using their own names. The small-press book publishers in the left-hand column are, like the name at the top of the list, a horse of another color. Why the whimsy, irony, and sly bit of poking fun in the names of these small presses? The small-press publisher doesn't expect to make a living out of his venture, and, perhaps, he wants to be the first to tell you this through his choice of a name.

The name he gives his small press is also a reaching out for compatibility with authors and readers whose tastes are similar to his own. Does it sound flaky? Actually, their editorial attitude is similar to that of the commercial book publishers who set up shop sixty or a hundred years ago. That's how it was with Holt, Knopf, Liveright, Harper. All they wanted was to locate readers who agreed with their tastes. It worked then, and it's starting to work all over again.

What are today's small-press book publishers like?

Close to 95 percent of them are able to operate only by holding down a nine-to-five "outside" job. They contribute their savings and often part of their bread-and-butter money to their love: small-press publishing.

To writers interested in selling their books to a small press, this chapter offers information in the following order:

1. Letters from owners of small presses, indicating the kinds of people who control them.
2. Some of the things small presses have in common.
3. How to select the press that will have an interest in what you write.
4. Pretesting your small-press book prior to offering it to a publisher.
5. A selected list of small-press book publishers with their addresses.

We'll begin with three letters that reflect the human condition of the small-press owner. Here's the first.

Carol Denison is the one-woman operator of Calliopea Press (Missoula, MT 59801). Her recent volume, *Color Poems* (nine-and-a-half-by-thirteen inches, loose-leaf, twenty-five dollars), was partly funded by the National Endowment for the Arts and is illustrated in color, and here's what she has to say:

I completed the courses for my Masters in Printing Technology in 1976, in Rochester, and came to the mountains of Montana for fresh air and a place to print. My interest in the liberal arts has expanded as I meet writers and read poetry and fiction. In addition to being a small-press publisher of poetry, fiction, and some nonfiction, I attempt to produce beautiful books.

The large publishing houses put tight restrictions on publishing policies: Publish only what will sell, and produce it as inexpensively as possible.

Calliopea Press publishes a book because I like it, and I lavish as much time and money on the production as I possibly can. The writer comes to the press, and we sit down and discuss the format and design over tea, and, often, the writer helps crank the press. This process gives a personal pride to the work that cannot be achieved any other way.

I receive a continual flow of manuscripts from writers and poets. The approach I am most responsive to is an author's sending me a personal letter with a few samples of work. Whole manuscripts are cumbersome to handle, and some are far too long for me to publish. I attempt to answer each inquiry to the press and request an entire manuscript if I like the sample I receive.

If I were a writer presenting a book idea to my press, I believe I would try to visit the press, if at all possible, and make personal contact and discuss my work and the press's capabilities. If a visit were not possible, I would surely phone the press prior to sending the manuscript.

Calliopea's newest publication is *Color Poems*, by Siv Cedering Fox. This was a very magical book to produce. I wrote to Siv because I loved her published poetry *(Mother Is* and *The Juggler,* particularly) and wanted to print some of her work. I explained the idea of making a portfolio and using colored papers and colored inks, and asked if she would like to participate in such a project. Within three days, I received

193

a favorable reply and a manuscript entitled "Color Poems," which was complete and waiting for the right publisher and format. Siv asked her friends to illustrate it, and I struggled with the design and printing. Siv came to help with the printing of the final pages, and collation of the book. We held a well-attended reading and publication party here in Missoula. A very fulfilling experience.

Cat's Pajamas Press (527 Lyman Ave., Oak Park, IL) is owned and operated by John Jacob, now in his twelfth year of small-press publishing:

I am most willing to work with writers who stand by their work, who put in time on what they do, who are not involved in twelve different projects all at once, who are experimenting in their work, who write interesting short prose or very unusual poetry. I have published one book of criticism, but it was short and with experimental titles—by Tom Montag of *Margins* fame. I haven't done how-to books and would not unless someone offered me a technical book on running. (I am a running enthusiast and have appreciated some of the technical pamphlets put out by the publishers of *Runner's World*.)

My prime offer to writers is publication. I do not "train" writers. I discover writers who publish and write things I am sympathetic with; I work with people who are changing their style, and who can send me many manuscripts before I accept something, but I think it is more encouragement than training that I offer. Once I find a writer I like, I never tell him what to do.

When grants come through, authors may get small payments. I pay illustrators and cover designers cash, and they get a few copies of the publication. Authors receive a minimum of 10 percent of the press run free, sometimes 20–25 percent. After that, they get a 50 percent discount. I promote and publicize as funds permit and encourage writers to sell their own books and furnish extra copies for that purpose. Authors keep all money from such sales. Eric Felderman, at Yale, and John Oliver Simon, in Berkeley, have done well with books I've published via that route, and now Bernie Bener, in Virginia, and Derek Pell, in New

194

York, are doing the same. Four of my books have been picked up by distributors in the past two years. I have standing orders from libraries and bookstores, and other consignment orders as I drum them up. But it's hard, and no author I publish will make much money publishing with me.

It's taken me ten years to get the network I've established with the press, and some years things have been slow. Reviews from the American Library Association have helped sales or the illusion of sales. It's a constant uphill fight.

Right now all editors, publishers, and writers have choices. They can write good material, or they can write stuff that will sell and appeal to the mass mind. Sometimes it is the same thing but rarely. But they have that choice.

A free-lance writer should submit to this press by (1) sending the whole manuscript, or (2) several chapters and an outline, or (3) just a query letter. Please enclose stamps for return.

What I like most about being a small-press book publisher is the absolute freedom of doing what I want. I don't feel responsible for the ignorance of the American public, nor do I level blame at the fact that very few read my books. I accept it, work as much as I can to change it, and leave it at that.

Bruce Thompson owns and operates Walnut Press (P.O. Box 17210, Fountain Hills, Arizona):

I retired from farm management, agricultural consulting and food research a few years ago, and entered small-press publishing, with the entire business to learn.

This year I probably will publish three children's books, possibly a reprint of *Black Walnut for Profit*, perhaps a reprint of *Animal Husbandry*, maybe a new *Handbook of North American Nut Trees*, and my newest, *Syrup Trees*.

I would be darned pleased to publish and promote any writer who has something to say within the fields in which I have some competency,

195

such as agriculture, aquaculture, forestry, and history. I can't see any point in joining the crowd just because some idea might be popular. I would be pleased to help an author in any way that I could, if he really had, in my opinion, something to say that needed saying. So much for me.

Writers ask me about the Arizona Authors Catalogue, which describes seventy-six titles by Arizona authors. Boye DeMente got the Arizona Authors Association going, and it now has 270 members. Something will come from it. DeMente had a background in publishing eight or nine guidebooks and credibility in our area. He was helped by Maureen Jones-Ryan, who had contacts at radio and TV stations. Between them and a couple of gals, they announced on TV and radio, *over and over*, that an Arizona Authors Association was being formed and that anyone interested should contact DeMente. About sixty people did in short order, and he put out a newsletter, listing the Arizona authors whose works had been published.

Maureen did a beautiful job of interviewing some of the authors on public TV. Membership grew to 125. Another newsletter followed, then a seminar and more radio and TV. On faith, each author put in twenty dollars for listing his own book in a prospective catalogue. Time passed, membership grew, and we printed and mailed fifteen thousand copies of a respectable catalogue, using volunteer help. We mailed the catalogue to lists of schools and bookstores. Nine days later, our first batch of orders arrived.

As you know, all good things have a tendency to grow. We shortly will need a well-paid secretary and then a publisher with more venture capital than I can personally command to publish new books of our members. I know where some salable manuscripts are and how to get them published now, but I don't have the one hundred thousand dollar venture capital needed, but I'd love to try it.

Almost all the seventy-six titles listed in the Arizona Authors Catalogue are self-published books or the works of small presses. There is no reason it cannot be repeated elsewhere.

Have Carol, John, and Bruce helped you understand their own attitudes? Each is different, yet there is a similar theme. Of the four thousand small-press publishers, 325 produce books. The others publish magazines.

The small-press book publisher really is small. He may issue one title a year or one every other year. Rarely will he issue ten titles. A three-title-a-year publisher is an active one.

Press runs are low: Three hundred is not unusually scant, and two thousand is high. Most books are issued with paper covers; perhaps one-fifth appear in cloth. The staff of a small-press book publisher is often one person. Perhaps thirty have a full-time staff of more than three. Most have no telephone listing under the names of their presses and use a post-office box number rather than a street address.

Gross income rarely reaches twenty thousand dollars a year, and three thousand is above average. The owner works for a living at almost any kind of job you can imagine to subsidize his press. The editorial categories are perhaps 40 percent poetry, 30 percent nonfiction, 15 percent novels, and the balance a mixture of graphics, surrealism, literary criticism, and experimental prose. The payment made to authors varies from nothing, to payment in books, to 10 percent of the gross cash received by the publisher.

So much for material common denominators. The intellectual and emotional ones are there, too. We can pick some of these up from direct quotes. Here's Curt Johnson, publisher of December Press:

> If a large publisher came along and subsidized December Press, I'd start January Press. Big presses are concerned with big black bottom lines; small presses like to think they are guardians of "literature." I like the freedom of being a small-press publisher with only myself to please. I also like the friendships I've made, though I must add that it has been my discovery, and a disillusioning one, to be sure, that all authors are egotistical, selfish, and weak in many ways (but strong in the ways that count, the good ones).
>
> Everything being equal, you publish an unknown to a known writer any day. If it is almost good enough, but not quite, you publish it. It spurs the author on to keep going.

A last quote from Bernie Kamoroff indicates the sanguine, spirited attitude of the small-press publisher:

THE BOOK MARKET

There's always room between the cracks for the little person, in any field, including book publishing. The more the big corporations head toward the big-sellers-only books, the bigger the cracks get. Small presses treat writers, I find, fairly and honestly. If I were a writer trying to sell a book to my own press, Bell Springs, I would simply submit it. Period. Nothing to it. The publisher either likes it or doesn't.

While amiable communications like these give an inkling of the kind of market offered to free-lance writers, they tell us nothing about why the small presses increased in number by 1,500 percent or why their readership grew from ninety thousand to 1.5 million since the mid-sixties.

Several events did occur, almost at the same time. The first one came from the outside in. The small-press publisher, himself, was not the cause of it through scurrying about seeking new talent. No latter-day Joyce, Lawrence, or Hemingway appeared under a small-press publisher's imprint (or anyone else's) in this period.

The big push came from a new development in printing. There used to be no way to print even one copy of a book and still get out from under the burden of spending two thousand dollars alone for typesetting and page make-up cost. This put a real damper on the number of titles a small-press publisher could issue in any one year and limited the number of people who had the cash to be small-press publishers.

Today, through the use of cold type, photo negatives, and offset printing, the small-press publisher with only twenty-five hundred dollars to work with can produce a modest-sized book, such as a novella, by doing some of his own production work and by being willing to accept slightly lower-than-normal commercial-printing standards.

Small-press publishing is now financially easier to get into as a hobby, or even as a career for creative, venturesome couples.

What else, besides the functional fact that it is cheaper/easier to own and operate a small press, caused the 1,500 percent increase?

According to the small-press people themselves, the real reason for their growth is the public's gradual perception that the mainline book publisher is not a publisher at all but a market tester. When a book sells well, he imitates it, and so do his peers. There is less concern about values: literary, social, cultural, spiritual.

198

Once the publisher has been led into an overwhelming advance to the author and printed fifty thousand copies or more, there is no easy turning back. The book is hyped, and the more susceptible people are led by the nose into buying it.

Some of these people don't even know they have been taken; others buy a book, read it a little, throw it away, and don't care, but a segment of the public does care. They haven't got their backs up. They aren't even mad. They are just experimenting at bookstores buying a few titles here and there from small-press publishers. It doesn't take too many people to turn small publishers with an average press run of five hundred into publishers who have started to set new sales records. But not all small publishers have the same attitude toward sales. They like them; fact is, they *love* them, as long as the sales don't interfere with the even tenor of their days or jiggle their policies. If the small publisher's print shop is in the basement, and the publisher already works at a nine-to-five job, it might be three months before a jobber's order for one thousand bound books can be turned out and much longer if the jobber orders five hundred each of three titles. What interests the small publisher is the book, not the sales—not even the reviews. His faith is in the book, the author, and in himself.

Meanwhile, change is coming.

When a small segment of the public started to shop the lists of the small publisher at bookstores, this move, slight though it was in terms of national sales, was not lost by the mainline publishers. They don't miss much. And the same is true of the big chain bookstores and the big jobbers. Let's take them one at a time and see what is happening; you can put your own mind to work to guess the outcome.

Among the big book publishers who noticed the slight jump in sales on the part of a few small-press book publishers were Random House and Viking. What did they do? What would you expect them to do? They reached out to put a finger on the pulse of the industry, if small-press book publishing can be called an industry. As publishers, they did the direct, sensible thing by entering into an agreement with five small-press book publishers to distribute their books. Little or no mention was made of helping select titles, publishing more titles, or subsidizing the press so that press runs could be increased, printing quality could be improved, and authors could be developed, perhaps with help from the home office. Are such steps in the wings? Are other mainline book publishers,

THE BOOK MARKET

like Viking and Random, going to follow and offer to distribute books for small-press book publishers whose perspicacity they like? Will this elevate the quality of writing in the same way that the major-league baseball teams helped their own cause and gave the public a much better ballgame by subsidizing the minor-league teams and providing a talent pool? Vocally at least, the small-press publishers are against being subsidized, against being a minor-league counterpart.

Even if the Viking Press and Random House experiments fail (*i.e.*, the books they distribute for the small-press publishers fail to make a profit), someone else is sure to take it up with a different twist. And, of course, if it succeeds, other publishers will scan the list of small publishers to try and duplicate the feat. If a few mainline book publishers develop or locate the kind of talent that appeals to both the masses and the literati, you will soon find thirty or forty of the small book publishers with mainline book publisher connections and a somewhat different kind of publishing orientation.

Is this good or bad?

It is neither. It is simply change.

As hard evidence that this is not a casual effort by two publishers, Viking and Random, a jobber has entered the picture. The jobber, Ingram Book Company, Nashville, Tennessee, is the nation's largest book distributor to stores, libraries, book chains. Ingram published, for the first time ever, a book catalogue titled *Best of the Independent Presses*, with a four-color cover, fifty-six pages, and an illustrated description of 228 titles. It was followed by an equally high-quality catalogue for the autumn season of the same year.

Susanna DePalma, the department's manager, advises: "We ordered a minimum of three hundred copies of each title listed in our catalogue, although all the publishers couldn't supply that many books at once. We distributed ten thousand copies of our catalogue and, at the end of thirty days, received orders for an average of two hundred copies for each title we had in stock."

That's a sale of almost fifty thousand copies by one jobber in thirty days. In the small-press field the impact of that is like the name of one of the small presses, "The Second Coming." You can assume, in the competitive publishing world, that all the other jobbers quickly knew what was going on. Sure, Ingram had the jump, but others could

200

observe the event without the pain and expense of being the leader in this move. The Ingram catalogue has continued to come out twice a year.

Ingram, however, didn't list just any kind of title in its catalogue.

They included only the titles they thought would sell and might enjoy a very special and loyal audience of their own. Their original request to small-press book publishers asked for titles in this area: Energy/Ecology, Do-It-Yourself, Eastern Thought, Poetry, Women, Alternative Life-styles, Regional Subjects, Drugs, the Occult, and Vegetarian Cooking. If they were guessing right, would this cause the small-press publisher, in some instances, to try to duplicate the kind of title Ingram wants? Ho! And what have we here?

And what if other jobbers duplicate Ingram's feat and select the same range of subject matter?

Meanwhile, how did Viking and Random fare in their own distribution of small-press books? Random House is owned by the Newhouse newspaper chain, and Richard H. Liebermann is Random's vice-president in charge of trade sales. What did he have to say? "We're not interested in seeing more titles unless one of them is a truly outstanding book or promises a steady sale."

Another voice and a shade of difference here.

These are the three reasons why I believe the small-press book-publishing field is now subject to change:

(a) A segment of the public, turned off by some of the commercial publishing output, has started to shop in bookstores looking for something different. A few of these people have located products of the small-press book publisher and found them acceptable reading.

(b) Two commercial mainline publishers promptly sensed what was going on and started to sample the field. Whether they persevere or not, it is likely that several other publishers will do the same thing. In the end, a certain amount of better distribution, or even subsidy, may become available to certain small-press publishers.

(c) Ingram Book Company, a leading book jobber, has distributed a catalogue of small-press titles to the nation's bookstores and large libraries. It is not unlikely that other jobbers of their relative size will follow, thus making large distribution easier and, at the same time, setting a somewhat rough but discernable pattern of the kinds of titles currently desired by the jobbers.

There is one more reason the small-press field has grown. This is the National Endowment for the Arts, which pays a direct cash subsidy to numerous presses, conducts seminars where typesetting, printing, binding, and paper selection can be discussed, and provides funds nationally (when matched in part by the individual states) for local offices whose purpose is to bring writers and small presses together.

The curious thing is that for probably the only time in the history of government bureaus, this bureau does not interfere. Its guest list for seminars, its membership list in its various suborganizations, and its subsidy money is passed out largely on the basis of publishing logistics rather than on editorial content. That is, a small-press publisher who issues what most university people would call passably good literature, but does so on an irregular basis, keeps no records, and is dilatory with correspondence, or one that is newly established, won't get a nickel. The thing that NEA encourages is independent publication, with a press run that goes at least into several hundred, has some sort of established periodicity, and, in some sort of reasonable and general way, is related to literature and the arts.

The NEA doesn't favor any one side of the literary street. On one occasion, their grants were *equally divided* among 134 small presses: $930.23 each. This included Backwash, Bad Breath, Fag Rag, Juice, Nausea, Stroker, and Yellow Brick Road.

However else you feel about government intervention, from gas regulation to million-acre wildlife preserves, you will be happy to realize we actually have one federal bureau that is honestly trying to foster a free press for the little people without acting like Big Daddy or carrying a big stick.

If you would like to be published by one of the 325 small-book presses—which one is for you?

1. Begin with a copy of *International Directory of Little Magazines and Small Presses* (P.O. Box 1056, Paradise, CA 95969, paperback, $10.95, edited by Len Fulton and Ellen Ferber). Before ordering a copy, prowl through a current edition at your library to see if you feel your work will merit the attention of publishers in this field. Most of the four

thousand presses listed are publishers of magazines, not books. However, 325 of the presses do publish books, and this directory lists them all with their names, addresses, phone numbers, and editorial requirements. The publishers at the end of this chapter are only 97 in number, because we have eliminated the ones that do not publish regularly or want unsolicited material, or are not devoted mainly to the publisher's own writings. Our list is imperfect and will change with time. The suggestions that follow offer ways of making this list specifically useful to yourself.

2. Start with the first publisher (Abraxas) and look it up in the *Directory*. This is easy, because the list is alphabetical. If the description of this publisher's editorial requirements makes him appear like a good market prospect for you, check his name, and go on to the next one. By the time you have completed looking up the publishers at the end of this chapter, you will have between ten and twenty prospects.

3. What if your book treats an esoteric subject: the qualities of human nature in the rugged, food-sparse environment of the Hadzas in the Yaida Valley of East Africa, or, more esoteric, a documentation of the devices whereby our federal government authorizes itself to print paper money to pay its bills? A neat method is available for authors with this kind of rare subject matter. *Small Press Record of Books in Print* (Box 100, Paradise, CA 95969) is stocked at most libraries because of its usefulness in ordering small-press books. One section in this annual, called the "Subject Directory," lists the various categories under which small-press books have been published. For example, here is the list of categories under the letter "A":

African Literature, Africa, African Studies
Anarchist
Anthropology, Archaeology
Antiques
Architecture
Arts
Asia, Indochina, China
Aviation

Under each category are the names of authors and titles of small-press books. If your book falls into one of these categories, then simply write down the authors whose books are akin to your own. You may find a half-dozen. Under the first category, "African Literature, Africa, African Studies," you will find listings such as these:

Ake, Claude, *Revolutionary Pressures in Africa*
Bangs, Richard, *African River Safaris*
Barnett, Don, *With the Guerrillas in Angola*

Now turn to the main section of *Small Press Record of Books in Print*, and look up the name of the author. In the instance of the first title above, you will find:

Ake, Claude, *Revolutionary Pressures in Africa*. Zed Press 1978. 5½ × 8½. 144 pages. $13.00. Revolution against capitalism in the era which the African continent is entering. This book explains why the violent era is occurring and what forms it will take. A political book about the future of Africa.

Let's say this description of the book (condensed here) relates to your viewpoint in the book you have written about Africa. You now know the name of the publisher, Zed Press. Where is Zed's address?

You pick up *International Directory of Little Magazines and Small Presses* and look up Zed Press. Here you find that Zed Press publishes in England, and the address is given plus this description: "A socialist, mail order publisher of books on revolution and imperialism in the Third World. Our aim is to provoke thought and reflect current debates in 5 main areas: Africa, Middle East, Asia, Women in Third World, and Imperialism." The United States address is given, as well as other useful data for writers interested in this publisher.

Using this three-step research method just described, writers can locate precise markets for unusual books among the small-press book publishers.

4. Up till now, your research has been done outside the immediate orbit of the publisher. At this point, you reach out and touch him. You do this by writing a brief note to each of the publishers you selected as being a good market prospect, asking for a current catalogue. Enclose a

stamp. About half will reply. Why so few? Their catalogues may be out of print, their filing system might be imperfect, or your letter might have been mislaid. It happens in the best of places and sometimes at the same rate.

When you receive your catalogues, study each one and see which publisher might have a logical interest in what you have done and also which publisher appeals most to you. What do you do if the best candidate doesn't answer your request for a catalogue? I would simply phone and say I had asked for a catalogue but not received it. (Use station-to-station rates on the weekend.) This voice contact gives you an additional feel for the field.

5. If you have written a novel, how can you tell whether or not your general style and quality of writing is in the "ballpark" of what passes for good small-press fiction? Your library will have a book that answers this for you: *The Pushcart Prize: Best of the Small Presses* (issued annually by Pushcart Press, P.O. Box 845, Yonkers, NY 10711). In reading this book, you will discover that some of the magazines in this field publish excerpts of novels, and this will offer a new source of markets for you.

If you've written a novel or a well-researched nonfiction book, you've surely put a year or more into it. A week's more research to find the best possible market is the prudent way to protect your investment.

If the material in the *Pushcart Prize* isn't to your taste, there is an alternative: *The Small Press Review* (Box 100, Paradise, CA 95969) sponsors a book club with a half-dozen monthly selections. You might order a few of these to sample the writing in the field. This publication also lists new small presses—up to thirty in each issue—and three or four of these publish books. A sample copy of *The Small Press Review* is one dollar.

6. At this point you may wish you had access to some kind of critical feedback from small-press book reviewers so that you can see the field from another point of view. This kind of thing is available from several lively magazines that specialize in reviewing small publishers' books. *Northeast Rising Sun* (Box 303, Cherry Valley, NY 13320) is a good example. One dollar brings a sample copy. The name of a publisher whose book is reviewed and is in the same field as your own might supply you with a good marketing lead.

7. A final source for information leads into the ubiquitous activities of

205

the National Endowment for the Arts. They help fund several organizations that have their own organ. One of these is *Coda: Poets and Writers Newsletter* (201 West 54th St., New York, NY 10019). A single copy is $1.50. They also publish *Dispatch*, same address, 25 cents a copy. *Dispatch* carries job openings for writers and some market notes for book authors. In addition, they will tell you if a local affiliate of the NEA is in your area. There are several hundred such local offices around the country, and each has its own program involving fiction writers and poets. All are co-funded by the local states' arts programs and the NEA. Visiting one of these local offices may be useful if for no other reason than seeing their own library of small-press books.

Another organization is Western Independent Publishers (P.O. Box 31249, San Francisco, CA 94131). This is the new name of the West Coast branch of COSMEP (Committee of Small Magazine Editors and Publishers). One dollar will bring you their latest newsletter. This publication is for small-press publishers. Reaching out to learn about their problems will clue you in as to what to expect. There are also announcements of new presses and news of changes in some of the older ones as they respond to the times and to the attitudes of their owners.

If you've followed the above six steps right down the line and done your homework, you've become a literary agent—of your very own book. In the professional sense of the word, you are now ready to market.

One good way that saves time and expense is to send a naked query letter first. Describe what you have to offer in two or three paragraphs, and ask if the publisher would like to see an outline and two or three sample chapters. Give the length (number of words) of your book, and enclose a stamped self-addressed envelope. You might try this naked query letter to three publishers at a time and allow two weeks for answers. What if all three reply, or even two? Normally, one will be more encouraging than another. Select the one you think is best for you, and send off what the publisher requests. Allow thirty days for a reply. If there is no reply in thirty days, then send a copy of your material to the next publisher who said he would be interested. What if both want to skip your offer of an outline and ask to see your complete book? Select one. *You* are doing the marketing, and you make the selection. Your book goes to one publisher at a time. You do not make multiple submissions of your book.

A variation of the naked query letter is to enclose a two-page outline and possibly two sample chapters, and ask if the publisher would like to see the whole book. Try this with your three best candidates, and enclose a stamped, self-addressed envelope.

The final way is to send the entire book forthwith, preceded by neither query letter, nor outline, nor sample chapters. Send your book to one publisher at a time, and do not submit it to the second publisher until you have received it back from the first one. Make a Xerox copy, as manuscripts do get lost. The disadvantage of sending the entire book without any kind of invitation is that you might run into a great deal of time loss. Some small-press book publishers have taken the position of Igor Greenspan of Angst, in Seattle, who writes: "We are kept quite busy with our current stock of writers matched against the number of titles we issue a year. We have found that unsolicited manuscripts are, in general, a nonproductive task for an understaffed small press such as Angst."

The list at the end of this article attempts to exclude this kind of restricted market. In addition, we have eliminated all but two small-press co-ops as well as all presses that are quite new, or publish irregularly, or specialize in the work of the owner. No doubt, some good markets are not included, and that is one reason why you might want to use the research ideas suggested here to augment your own choices.

Should a book you are ready to market to a small-press publisher be editorially pretested? Hardly anyone does. What kind of competition are you up against? Of the established two thousand writers who manage to sell two books or more every six years to a mainline publisher, less than 2 percent send a book to a small-press publisher. And literary agents almost never ship a book to a small press because their "take" of 10 percent of the author's receipts would be too small. Perhaps twenty books find their way to the small presses from agents during the course of one year, and these are often books of verse written by selling authors to whom the agent owes a lagniappe.

With this competition knocked out, why spend the time and money learning what someone else has to say, when you've already worked on your book as hard as you know how, and any kind of really serious criticism might require revising the whole thing?

Let's see it from the other side. Here's what Henry Wheelright, publisher of Stone Wall Press, at Boston, has to say:

THE BOOK MARKET

I have just returned from a most pleasant trip to London for the book fair and back into the maelstrom. We are planning four titles (two for the spring, two for the fall). Average press run: five thousand, perfect bound.

For the free-lance writer—we are something special because we generally stick to fairly pragmatic outdoor themes. We *have* to be specialized *and* something special to survive in the land of Publishing Giants, and we expect this of our writers, free lance or otherwise. Fresh, original, well-written text with good accompanying art or photos. The rehash crowd need not apply. There is no substitute for good literature, and this is the bottom line.

Editorially pretesting a small-press book has become especially useful, since mainline publishers are waiting in the wings to offer distribution to small presses—this, in spite of the fact that few writers do pretest.

The four thousand small-press publishers are almost the only group that supports freedom of the press for love and then picks up the check. In this group there are doubtless some irresponsible editors, and semiliterates with a printing press. That leaves 90 percent, perhaps thirty-six hundred men and women, who work as hard as anyone we know to keep our free press free and practice what our Constitution preaches. You deserve to let your spirit lift a little as you pass your eye over the market for books that these good people represent.

Before me is a three-inch stack of letters, and I selected one at random. Reading it carefully allows me to think John Cage's idea of chance selection has its points. This is from Allan Kornblum, publisher, of the Toothpaste Press:

I am primarily a poetry publisher.

I can print 2,000 copies of a poetry book, and sell a few hundred copies a year until the book sells out, 5–10 years later. A major publisher would lose money on storage, but it's no problem for me to keep the books in my attic. Thus I can keep a young writer in print.

This past weekend, I went to the COSMEP mid-winter board meeting in Austin, and discussed ways to improve the organization. We're planning a micro-fiche catalogue with ordering information, making small-press books as easy to order as Random House.

Now I sit in my office, 6:30 P.M., eggplant warming in the oven, whiskey and grapefruit juice joining magic with a few ice cubes in my glass. My wife is making salad, and Annabel is wheeling around in her little walker while Woody Guthrie sings songs for children in the background.

You ask me to update my last letter to you and I wish I had adopted the habit I have finally acquired—that of keeping carbons of my letters. In the past, whenever I resolved to make such carbons on a regular basis, my 60s' past started to resound in my ears, something about spontaneity, and suddenly carbons seemed too calculating, and besides, too much trouble. Finally, I discovered that actually the opposite was the case, *not* keeping carbons was more trouble, people would write mentioning my previous letter and I wasn't always sure what they were talking about.

For myself and many of my friends, one barrier to be overcome was the acceptance of the fact that publishing is a business. I now use a contract, I have an "Author Information Questionnaire," use an eighteen-column ledger to help me see where the money went, and where it's coming from.

A belief in the writing is still the impetus for my work, for the hours I put into the make-ready and inking of each sheet that goes into my books, for the hours of hand folding, and collating, for the endless letters, for stuffing ads, packing orders, doing the billing and paying the bills. But by learning the simple principles of business organization, I'm able to move through many of the tedious aspects of publishing more quickly and efficiently.

Primarily I solicit work from authors I respect, whose work I am familiar with. Occasionally I accept an unsolicited ms. When I decide to publish, I send the author my contract and author information questionnaire. If I like most of the book, but have qualms about a work, or parts of a work, I will mention these qualms in my letter, along with words to the effect that this will be their book and they make the final decision. When it becomes necessary to delete 1 poem or add 7 blank pages to get the last poem in, I suggest the deletion, but allow the writer to make the choice if a poem needs to be deleted. I will not, on the other hand, add the 7 blank pages.

I give my authors a modest advance against future royalties. I report once a year. Royalties are 10% of the list price of the books as they sell. Authors get 20 copies besides, and a 50% discount on additional books.

THE BOOK MARKET

We send out 50 initial review copies, and usually another 15–20 copies in samples and publicity. Our usual run is about 1,000 copies and the run takes about 4–5 years to sell out. We do not remainder our books. If an author suddenly catches on 4 years after a book has been printed, we're ready to sell copies with as few as 50 left in a carton in our storage area. We publish approximately 5 titles per year, and put out a catalogue of our books every 12–18 months. We have attended ALA's annual convention for several years and will be attending our first ABA convention this summer.

There is no doubt that our 4 grants from the National Endowment for the Arts have helped keep us on our feet.

The majority of our business is done through direct mail. The mailing list has been built by attendance at book fairs. I have heard such small press fairs bad-mouthed recently. But frequently those people show up in a T-shirt, sit with head in hand looking discouraged, then go out for a beer after three hours. I believe that one can stand up and say hello to people as they pass at a book fair, without having "sold out." Supposedly my authors have done their best to make their words communicate. As publisher it is my responsibility to carry on the process not only as designer and printer, but also as salesman, otherwise the author is communicating to the corrugated cardboard cartons in my attic.

A LIST OF SMALL-PRESS PUBLISHERS *

Following are 102 of the several hundred small-press book publishers. Prior to submitting work, please review the six suggested steps for selecting the small-press publisher best suited to you and your work.

Abraxas
Warren Woessner
2322 Rugby Row
Madison, WI 53705

Ata Books
Dorothy Bryant
1920 Stuart St.
Berkeley, CA 94703

---

* A few small-press publishers are co-ops, and two of these, Alice James Books and Downtown Poets Cooperative, appear in our market list. Writers who reside outside their geographic area can seldom submit books for publication, simply because they cannot participate in the actual handwork of publishing. If you live near either of these co-ops and are a producing poet, both of these co-ops are worth visiting.

Academy Press, Ltd.
Anita and Jordan Miller
360 N. Michigan
Chicago, IL 60601

Acrobat Books, Publishers
Tony Cohan
213 S. Arden Blvd.
Los Angeles, CA 90004

Akwesasne Notes
Sotsisowah, Editor
Mohawk Nation
Rooseveltown, NY 13683

Aldebaran Review
John Oliver Simon
2209 California
Berkeley, CA 94703

Algol Press
Andrew Porter
P.O. Box 4175
New York, NY 10017

Alice James Books *
Cooperative
138 Mount Auburn St.
Cambridge, MA 02138

The Alley Press
Paul Feroe
1764 Gilpin St.
Denver, CO 80218

American-Canadian Publishers
Arthur Goodson
Drawer 2078
Portales, NM 88130

Apple-wood Press
Philip Zuckerman
Box 2870
Cambridge, MA 02139

Assembling, Assembling Press
Richard Kostelanetz, Co-compiler
141 Wooster St.
New York, NY 10012

Autumn Press, Inc.
Nahum Stiskin
7 Littell Road
Brookline, MA 02146

Bell Springs Publishing Co.
Bernard Kamoroff
Box 322
Laytonville, CA 95454

Bern Porter Books
Bern Porter
22 Salmond Rd.
Belfast, MA 04915

Black Box Magazine, Watershed Intermedia
Alan Austin
PO Box 4174
Washington, DC 20015

Black Sparrow Press
P.O. Box 3993
Santa Barbara, CA 93105

Blue Horse
Jacqueline T. Bradley
P.O. Box 6061
Augusta, GA 30906

The Blue Oak Press
D. A. Carpenter
2555 Newcastle Rd.
Newcastle, CA 95658

Blue Wind Press (Dynamite Books;
    Overdrive Books)
George Mattingly
P.O. Box 7175
Berkeley, CA 94707

Brasch & Brasch Publishers, Inc.
Walter M. Brasch, Ph.D., Editor
220A West "B" St.
Ontario, CA 91762

Calliopea Press
Carol Denison
1001 South 4th West
Missoula, MT 59801

THE BOOK MARKET

Capra Press
Noel Young
631 State St.
Santa Barbara, CA 93101

Carousel Press
Carole Terwilliger Meyers
P.O. Box 6061
Albany, CA 94706

Carpenter Press
Bob Fox
Route 4
Pomeroy, OH 45769

Cat's Pajamas Press
John Jacob
527 Lyman
Oak Park, IL 60304

Chandler & Sharp Publishers, Inc.
Jonathan Sharp, Howard Chandler
11A Commercial Blvd.
Novato, CA 94947

Charles River Books, Inc.
Jane Cooper Williams
59 Commercial Wharf
Boston, MA 02110

Cheshire Books
Michael Riordan
121 Stanford Ave.
Menlo Park, CA 94025

Chronicle Books/Prism Editions
Richard Schuettge
870 Market St., Suite 915
San Francisco, CA 94102

City Lights Books
Lawrence Ferlinghetti
261 Columbus Ave.
San Francisco, CA 94133

Copley Books
7779 Ivanhoe Ave.
P.O. Box 957
La Jolla, CA 92038

Creative Arts Book Company
Barry Gifford
833 Bancroft Way
Berkeley, CA 94710

The Crossing Press
John and Elaine Gill
R.D. 3
Trumansburg, NY 14886

Curbstone Press
Alexander Taylor
321 Jackson St.
Willimantic, CT 06226

Daughter Publishing Co.
Parke Bowman
P.O. Box 4299
Houston, TX 77042

Dawn Horse Press
Daniel Bonder
Star Route 2
Middletown, CA 95461

Dawn Valley Press
Nancy E. James
Box 58
New Wilmington, PA 16142

December Press
Curt Johnson
4343 North Clarendon
Chicago, IL 60613

Diana Press, Inc.
Coletta Reid
4400 Market St.
Oakland, CA 94608

Downtown Poets Co-op *
David and Phyllis Gershator
G.P.O. Box 1720
Brooklyn, NY 11202

Dustbooks
Len Fulton
Box 100
Paradise, CA 95969

The Ecco Press
Daniel Halpern
1 West 30th St.
New York, NY 10001

ETC Publications
Richard W. Hostrop
P.O. Drawer 1627-A
Palm Springs, CA 92262

Fiction Collective
English Department
Brooklyn College
Brooklyn, NY 11210

The Figures
Laura Chester
2016 Cedar
Berkeley, CA 94709

Full Court Press
Christopher Weills
Box 4520
Berkeley, CA 94704

The Future Press
Richard Kostelanetz
P.O. Box 73
Canal St.
New York, NY 10013

Halty Ferguson Publishing Co.
William and Raquel Ferguson
376 Harvard St.
Cambridge, MA 02138

Hanging Loose Press
Robert Hershon
231 Wyckoff St.
Brooklyn, NY 11217

Hellcoal Press
Ann Dunnington
Box SAO
Brown University
Providence, RI 12912

Holmgangers Press
Gary and Jeane Elder
7200 Collier Canyon Road
c/o Several
Livermore, CA 94550

Holy Cow! Press
James Perlman
P.O. Box 618
Minneapolis, MN 55400

Icarus Press
Margaret Diorio
P.O. Box 8
Baltimore, MD 21139

Iris Press
Patricia Wilcox
27 Chestnut St.
Binghamton, NY 13905

John Muir Press
Barbara and Ken Luboff
P.O. Box 613
Santa Fe, NM 87501

Lame Johnny Press, Associates
L. M. Hasselstrom
Box 66
Hermosa, SD 57744

Lawrence Hill & Company, Publishers, Inc.
Lawrence Hill
24 Burr Farms Rd.
Westport, CT 06880

Moon Books
Anne Kent Rush
P.O. Box 9223
Berkeley, CA 94709

Mudhorn Press
Sasha Newborn
209 W. De la Guerra
Santa Barbara, CA 93101

Naturegraph Publishers, Inc.
Sevrin Housen
P.O. Box 1075
Happy Camp, CA 96039

New Rivers Press, Inc.
C. W. Truesdale
P.O. Box 578,
Cathedral Sta.
New York, NY 10025

THE BOOK MARKET

The New South Company
Nancy Stone
4480 Park Newport
Newport Beach, CA 92660

Northwest Matrix
Charlotte Mills
1628 E. 19th
Eugene, OR 97403

O O L P (Out of London Press)
Luigi Ballerini
12 W. 17th St.
New York, NY 10011

Padre Productions
Lachlan P. MacDonald
P.O. Box 1275
San Luis Obispo, CA 93406

Panache Books
David Lenson
P.O. Box 77
Sunderland, MA 01375

Parachuting Publications
Dan Poynter
P.O. Box 4232-Q
Santa Barbara, CA 93103

Penmen Press
Michael McCurdy
Old Sudbury Road
Lincoln, MA 01773

Porter Sargent Publishers, Inc.
11 Beacon St.
Boston, MA 02108

Press Pacifica
Jane and Richard Pultz
P.O. Box 47
Kailua, HI 96734

Pushcart Press
Bill Henderson
P.O. Box 845
Yonkers, NY 10701

Rara Avis
Jacqueline De Angelis
1400 Macbeth St.
Los Angeles, CA 90026

Red Clay Books
Charleen Swansea
6366 Sharon Hills Rd.
Charlotte, NC 28210

Red Dust, Inc.
Joanna Gunderson
P.O. Box 630
Gracie Station
New York, NY 10028

Reed, Cannon and Johnson
Ishmael Reed, Steve Cannon,
   Joe Johnson
2140 Shattuck #311
Berkeley, CA 94704

Release Press
Larry Zirlin
200 Carroll St.
Brooklyn, NY 11231

Rook Press, Inc.
Ernest and Cis Stefanik
P.O. Box 144
Ruffsdale, PA 15679

Ross-Erikson Publishers, Inc.
Robert Walton Brown
1825 Grand Ave.
Santa Barbara, CA 93101

Running Press
Lawrence Teacher
38 South 19th St.
Philadelphia, PA 19103

Sagarin Press
Roy H. Sagarin
Box 21
Sand Lake, NY 12153

Saint Andrews Press
Ron Bayes
St. Andrews College
Laurinburg, NC 28352

Seagull Press
Carolyn Bennett
1736 E. 53rd St.
Brooklyn, NY 11234

214

Seven Woods Press
George Koppelman
P.O. Box 32
Village Station
New York, NY 10014

Slow Loris Press
Anthony and Patricia Petrosky
923 Highview St.
Pittsburgh, PA 15206

The Smith, The Generalist Assn., Inc.
Harry Smith
5 Beekman St.
New York, NY 10038

SmokeRoot
Rick Robbins
Department of English
University of Montana
Missoula, MT 59812

The Spirit That Moves Us, Inc.
Morty Sklar
P.O. Box 1585
Iowa City, IA 52240

Stone Wall Press, Inc.
Henry C. Wheelwright
5 Byron St.
Boston, MA 02108

The Swallow Press, Inc.
Durrett Wagner
811 W. Junior Terrace
Chicago, IL 60613

Swamp Press
Jo Mish
300 Main St.
Oneonta, NY 13820

Telephone Books
Maureen Owen
Box 672
Old Chelsea Sta.
New York, NY 10011

Ten Speed Press
Philip Wood
P.O. Box 7123
Berkeley, CA 94707

Thorp Springs Press
Paul Foreman
2311-C Woolsey
Berkeley, CA 94705

The Toothpaste Press
Allan and Cinda Kornblum
Box 546
West Branch, IA 52358

Treacle Press
Bruce R. McPherson
437 Springtown Rd.
New Paltz, NY 12561

Turkey Press
Harry Reese
6746 Sueno Rd.
Goleta, CA 93017

Unity Press
Doug Davis
113 New St.
Santa Cruz, CA 95060

University of the Trees Press
Christopher Hills
P.O. Box 644
Boulder Creek, CA 95006

Van Dyk Publications
Adrian C. Van Dyk, Jr.
2440 Old Sonoma Rd., No. 8
Napa, CA 94558

Vanguard Books
Ashley Bullitt
P.O. Box 3566
Chicago, IL 60654

Vermont Crossroads Press, Inc.
Constance C. Montgomery
Box 30
Waitsfield, VT 05673

Walnut Press
Bruce Thompson
P.O. Box 17210
Fountain Hills, AZ 85268

215

THE BOOK MARKET

West End Press
John Crawford
Box 697
Cambridge, MA 02139

The Workingman's Press
Barry Gifford
c/o Serendipity Books
1636 Ocean View Ave.
Kensington, CA 94707

Yardbird Publishing Co.
Box 216
Fairmount Station
El Cerrito, CA 94530

Z
Kenward Elmslie
Poets Corner
Calais, VT 05648

15

The Subsidy Publisher

THERE IS YET another way to get your book published. You pay for it yourself. Using this method, the author may hire individual contractors to design the book, set the type, and print and bind the job. The author does the recordkeeping, selling, and promotion. This is called self-publication, and is covered in great detail later on in the book. Another way of paying for your own book is to hire a subsidy house to do the publishing for you.

About twenty firms engage in subsidy publishing, and three of these, Dorrance, Exposition, and Vantage, publish 70 percent of all subsidized books. The total number issued a year is about fifteen hundred.

Occasionally, a mainline book publisher engages in subsidy publishing. Usually, this occurs when a corporation, a religious group, or a government bureau (in one case, the CIA) wants a particular point of view expressed in book form from a source other than itself, and it involves a commercial book publisher by offering a subsidy. Perhaps fifteen such titles appear a year.

Occasionally, a motion-picture producer will offer an unpublished book manuscript at a modest royalty, provided the publisher will guarantee an initial twenty-five-thousand press run, and spend one dollar to advertise the book for every copy printed; meanwhile the motion-picture producer guarantees to publicize the book in "previews of coming attractions" that precede the movie.

While publishing *The Farm Quarterly*, I had one experience in which subsidy took a different form. Two professors of agriculture wrote a book about grain farming. Their manuscript had forty color illustrations. This meant a thirty-thousand-dollar initial investment to print only eight thousand copies, and I demurred. The authors offered to buy four thousand copies at five dollars each and use them as texts in their own classes and the classes of their colleagues, who had already seen the manuscript and agreed to adopt it. This subsidy cut our gamble, and we went ahead. Surprisingly, translation rights were bought by the Italian government, which distributed the book to large grain farmers in Italy.

Then, the late Jack Garst, the cattle feeder from Iowa who entertained Khruschev at his farm in Coon Rapids, became interested in the book and sent copies abroad. A modest worldwide sale developed. By the end of ten years, forty thousand copies had been sold, twenty thousand at five dollars each for use in class and twenty thousand to our readers at ten dollars each.

These different kinds of payment to publishers illustrate that a subsidy can take many forms. Compared to self-publication, subsidy publishing is a no-fuss, no-muss method but, like anything else in this world, it suits some people and not others. Normally, there are lots of reasons for going ahead and having a subsidy publisher produce your book, but there is one excellent reason against it. The reason against subsidy publishing arises when an author enters into it with the need to make a profit.

You personally might succeed in making a profit. Some writers do. Not many.

Why is this so?

The impersonal statistics that tilt the odds against an author's making a profit on a subsidy-published book consist of the degree of readability of each book and the size of its market.

These same two measuring sticks sit on the commercial book publisher's editorial conference table while a book is being considered for purchase. That's why he is a commercial book publisher and not something else. He wants a book that most people can read easily and that will find a large, general market. Do you blame him for that?

In an earlier chapter, we saw that university-press books start off life with a press run of two thousand or less. Because they have no value? Their press runs are held down to the restricted nature of their market. I saw one University of Virginia book that analyzed, sentence by sentence, the handwritten, first-draft version of *Ulysses*, by James Joyce. It was written for a roomful of Joycian scholars. The price was $42.50, and the press run, under one thousand. Subsidy from the State of Virginia was the only way this study could be published and, by the trickle-down system, the scholarship of this work will flow into undergraduate English-literature classes three to five years hence.

I wish that when I studied *Ulysses* my instructor had had the benefit of this book, by Dr. Phillip F. Herring, so that some of his theories could have been passed on to me. When it comes to restricted readership, however, Dr. Herring doesn't have it all to himself. Here are fifteen titles of subsidy books:

> History of Elizabeth City State University
>
> The Body Image in Gender Orientation
> Disturbances
>
> Dysfunctionalism in Afrikan Education
>
> The Life and Times of Aurelius
> Lyman Voorhis
>
> Idaho Springs: Saratoga of the Rockies
>
> Visiting Cards of Prima Donnas
>
> Mr. Lincoln's Many-Faceted Minister
> and Entrepreneur Extraordinary:
> Henry Shelton Sanford
>
> Aspects of Freemasonry in Modern Mexico
>
> Papuan Belief and Ritual
>
> The Statutes at Large of Pennsylvania in the
> Time of William Penn
>
> The True Story of the Siege of
> Kumamoto Castle
>
> Social Thought of Lu Hsun, 1881–1936
>
> Late Glacial Chronology
>
> Agriculture in Sierra Leone
>
> Soviet Democracy—Principles and Practices

The titles suggest that most of these could be books of worth, yet would you like to be the sales manager assigned to unload three thousand copies of any title in the above list? This is the point at which the subsidy publisher enters the picture.

He enters because the commercial book publisher, in instances such as these, says, "No, thanks." For the writer, this "no" narrows down the choice of publication. Because subsidy publishing suits certain writers but not others, let's see who might be likely candidates and who might not. We offer twelve examples.

1. A widow, in comfortable circumstances, is left an unpublished manuscript by her husband. The manuscript may relate to his profession or be an account of the life of his parents and grandparents; it may be a book of verse or a scientific or political treatise. It remains his offering. When published, the book is in the nature of a memorial and provides the widow with the satisfaction of not having left a task undone.

2. A teacher, in order to establish his personal contribution in his own field of learning, wishes to publish. The teacher sees this as an investment in future advancement, and the IRS agrees. The book sets forth his personal thinking, his research, and his original conclusions. He does not have to borrow to publish, and, although this will reduce his savings, he believes his income as a teacher will be enhanced.

3. A businessman who owns 51 percent of a profitable corporation is not averse to generating some takeover bids. With this in mind, he writes a book that has been on his mind for some years. It relates the early beginnings, growth, development, and future of his corporation. He intends to send a copy to the chairman of the board of the Fortune 500 companies, card enclosed.

4. A retired worker, with fifty years of good, hard work behind him, and a comfortable pile of capital, as evidence of prudent living, decides he knows a thing or two and wants to detail it. His subject is the overabundance of federal bureaus, with examples. He has never contributed to charity except for an annual ten-dollar gift to the Red Cross, and this book seems to him like his personal contribution to his times. His wife thinks he must know something because he reads a lot and is usually quiet.

5. A poet has thoroughly enjoyed writing verse all her life. She doesn't know anyone to talk to about her poetry. She would just love to have a tastefully designed, small book of her poetry published and distributed to college teachers of poetry, creative-writing teachers, book reviewers, well-known poets whose names and addresses she has noted in Who's Who, and the poetry associations that abound in many states and whose

names and addresses she has just learned are available. The writer can afford the venture, and she feels: "It will give me, for the very first time, some kind of feedback on whether the poetry I write touches other human beings the way it does me."

6. A nurse worked for many years with natives in the interior of an underdeveloped country. Now retired, and on a comfortable pension, with the regular savings of a lifetime invested in annuities, she has second thoughts about her life's work. Painstakingly, she writes her experiences and illustrates them with snapshots from her forty-year-old picture album. She wants this material published so that it can be sent to all bureaus engaged in this kind of work, which she feels needs reassessing.

7. A small school has a fifty-year birthday celebration, and the president wishes to publish a book about the meaning of this school to three generations of students.

8. A famous musician employs an assistant who is a cross between a valet, porter, masseur, and secretary, and on occasion lends him out to other musicians on tour. The valet talks little, makes notes, and has an innocent eye for all he sees. Upon his demise, the valet leaves a small legacy to his girl friend, now in her sixties. She wishes to preserve the memory of her lover and have his notebooks published. The names of the famous people impress her more than how the performers looked to the valet.

9. A successful dentist in this life, but a historian in any other, is an enthusiastic member of a small national fraternal organization and writes its history.

10. The Chamber of Commerce of a town that is a county seat seeks to attract tourists and gathers together writings about all the town's good points. They decide to publish this information as a book and send it to travel agents throughout the country.

11. An older, unpublished novelist, rebuffed by the eight commercial publishers who have seen his manuscript, puts his novel aside with an unhappy sigh. Three years later, he comes upon it. Rereading it as though for the first time, he makes some corrections, revisions, and cuts, and, in his joy in this work, decides to have it published, which he can afford to do.

12. A story writer (by hobby) and a successful computer programmer

by trade has a dozen stories published in the small-press magazines. Three book publishers who saw the stories when they were offered as a collection of short stories sent them back without comment. The programmer decides that he will program his own life and publish his collection of short stories.

The common denominator of these writers is that each could readily afford the gamble even if his financial return were small. They shared another common denominator. Not one wrote to his publisher nailing down the particulars of what was important to him and asking if the contract covered it.

The poet (number 5) should have written:

> . . . it is my impression that our contract, which I am ready to sign, covers all costs of design, printing and binding, as well as the costs of procuring the necessary lists of teachers, reviewers, big-name poets and poetry clubs, and sending each a postpaid copy of my book, plus a letter asking for a response. I expect to pay only the figure mentioned in our contract as total payment for this.

Since this was the main reason the poet was entering into a subsidy agreement, she should have confirmed precisely what she expected before signing her contract and sending her check.

Why didn't she do it?

Because the matter was so close to her, she assumed the publisher understood what she wanted and agreed. The responsibility of the publisher to perform this obligation was not agreed to in correspondence, nor did the promise appear in the contract.

Had the poet sent the letter suggested above, she would have been asked to reread her contract, which specifically excluded this character of work without payment for time and materials.

In addition to the poet, the writers described in items 3, 6, and 10 should have spelled out what they believed to be essential items of their agreement prior to signing their contracts and sending payment.

None of these writers did this. Had they done so, each would have learned that the publicity and promotion that the subsidy publisher would perform was specified in the contract, and in no case did this

222

include, for example, what the nurse wanted: "compiling a list of eight hundred bureaus engaged in supplying nurses to underdeveloped countries and the heads of government in the countries of each, as well as the minister of government in charge of that bureau."

Can this kind of misunderstanding be prevented?

Very simply.

First, read your contract. Second, employ an attorney (for a fee of about two hundred dollars), and inquire specifically whether certain features that are important to you are included. Third, double-check the matter by spelling out the features that are important to you, and ask your publisher if these are covered in your contract the way you want them to be covered.

Normally, no commercial publisher does the work requested in the instance of the nurse or the poet to publicize a limited-press-run book, unless the author authorizes the publisher to divert royalties for that purpose or pays separately for it.

Then why should the subsidy publisher be asked to do it?

Because, in the author's mind, this is the main reason the author is paying to have the book published. Sometimes, when the contract speaks of "publicity" or "promotion," the author defines these words to mean what the author wants, not what the publisher intends.

If, in your own experience, the main premise of a subsidy publication hangs upon a book's being distributed to a large group of people, this needs to be spelled out precisely in the contract before you sign it and before payment is made. You want to know who prepares the list; who prints, stuffs, seals, and stamps the letters; who pays for the books; who pays the postage of the books themselves. A mailing of one thousand books and letters can easily exceed three thousand dollars. Does the contract detail who pays? If it doesn't, the subject is closed.

Although the twelve writers described above are justifiable candidates for subsidy publishing, there are various terms to investigate in a subsidy contract, just as in a contract to lease a car or employ a builder to erect a house. We'll take these up, but, first, let's look at the authors who, it seems to me, should not proceed into subsidy publication.

1. Kurt spent a lifetime as a grocery clerk. He is an Alsatian, and so is his wife. They are of modest means but frugal, solvent, and tidy. Their joy is their basement. Here all their foodstuffs that can be canned, jarred,

frozen, or preserved for the next two years are stored. Kurt went through the eighth grade, but, after his early retirement, because of a heart problem, he started to spend one day a week at the library. His reading choices span a wealth of subjects, and, although he isn't always sure about what he has read, he certainly has advanced himself, his wife believes. "Don't read too much, Kurt," she says, "or you'll be ashamed of me."

Kurt is working in longhand preparing a book on what, as a grocery clerk, he has learned about people. He has learned a lot. His lack of formal educational background doesn't allow him to distinguish between ideas that are trite in themselves or expressed tritely, and ideas that, if not highly original, are at least freshly phrased. Kurt wants to have his book published and sell it to grocery clerks everywhere. "They'll all do their jobs better," he says. "Actually the store manager should pay for my book and let the clerks read it on store time." He adds, with a grin, "That would be the day." For Kurt to use his four-thousand-dollar Certificate of Deposit to have his book published would reduce his retirement income by a dollar a day for the rest of his life, but, as Kurt says: "We'll turn the furnace down lower."

2. Ethel is a kindergarten teacher with a physical handicap and at this time is unable to save any money and has no emergency fund. Her father loves her dearly and will lend her anything she needs. Ethel makes up stories that she reads to her classes, and she wants to publish a book of them and sell the book to kindergarten classes in every state. "Once the teacher reads the first three stories to her class, the children will demand that she buy the book for all of them," says Ethel.

3. Before Mr. and Mrs. Chernov came here from Russia in 1950, they lived a life of terror, hunger, hard work, struggle. They now lease a mom-and-pop Seven-Eleven convenience food store in the Russian section of Brooklyn. They make a go of it by not having to pay retail for the things they take home and by carefully managing their funds. Over the years, in Russian, they have written the story of their struggle, and they want all Americans to read it so they "won't be pushed into the grave."

"I'll pay myself to have it published in a good book," says Mr. Chernov.

4. Bessie is a poet. Everyone who knows her admits this because her

couplets rhyme. Bessie is a night cleaner at an office building, and, although she earns much more than she ever thought she would, her savings account is a little over four and a half thousand dollars, and she is fifty-two. Bessie wants to publish a book of her couplets and leave one copy on every desk in the building. She makes the full round of the forty-two floors every six months, as her boss believes every night cleaner should be rotated regularly. Bessie gets around every six months and wants to surprise the workers in the building, whom she never sees, floor by floor. Bessie says: "They'll all buy copies for their friends. How many night cleaners are poets?"

5. Alec wrote a novel. One. And he sent it everywhere, beginning with Ace Books and going all the way to Avon Books. He stopped at Ballantine. "It's a put-up job," he says. "My book isn't all that bad." Alec has a wife from whom he is divorced, two children, and alimony on which he is enough in arrears to be just this side of getting a subpoena. He is determined to have his book published, by himself, if necessary, and send it to his former wife. "Then she'll know," says Alec.

Two common denominators have star-crossed the above five writers. None can afford the experience, should it fail to repay even 50 percent of their investment, and none thought of editorially pretesting their work.

We questioned each on the idea of editorially pretesting and the probability of financial loss. Here's Bessie, the poet:

"How do you know what I need, what I want, and what will happen? The people who work in my building will be surprised when they find my book on their desk. Boy, will they! I'm going to wrap each one in fresh tissue and tie it with a dark-blue ribbon. Here's my new one:

"Sleep all day, Clean all night,
What you say?
I'm out of sight!
Yes sir,
But not uptight.

"I'll sell two, maybe three copies to lots of people. I ask you—how many poets clean offices and give everybody who works there a book of their poetry?"

My wife listened to Bessie and read her verses. "You can't win," she said to me, "and maybe you shouldn't."

THE BOOK MARKET

There is a basic difference between a subsidy publisher, such as Bessie might go to, and a trade publisher. The latter publishes your book and pays you a royalty of around 80 cents for each book that retails at eight dollars. Having invested your time in writing, you invest nothing more. The trade publisher assumes the financial risk, and, with a sale of eight thousand copies, he "makes out." Should the book sell fewer copies, he would lose money. Therefore, his critical judgment works in high gear on every book he accepts. Even then, he may lose money on *half* the titles he issues. He lives in the hope of a few of his books being bestsellers, and others selling paperback and book-club rights. He also has steady back-list sales from one of every six titles he publishes.

The subsidy publisher, however, issues your book only if you pay him. He plans to make a profit, or at least break even, whether or not your book sells one hundred copies. He isn't "turned off" by a book with a restricted market, and his critical judgment operates in a lower gear. Even then, subsidy books differ today from what they were two or three generations ago. Today, more are well researched, with better writing, and graced with current awareness.

With twenty subsidy publishers in the field, the contract terms offered writers vary, and for that reason we have prepared a checklist for authors to submit to a subsidy publisher before signing a contract. A hedged answer to any of the following questions means for you to beware— because you may be about to buy something, the terms of which are ambiguous. God's rarest gift to man is a simple declarative sentence, and that's the kind of response you want to the following questions.

1. What will be the retail price of my book?

The answer to this should be a simple figure, like ten dollars. On receiving this information, you, the author, should estimate in your own mind whether your book is worth ten dollars, if that is the retail price. Visit your bookstore, and examine books in the same field and price bracket as your book. Check the number of pages they contain, the size, the weight, the "feel." How will your book compare, pricewise, with the market? Will the contents of your book stand up to a ten-dollar bill? This is something you have to answer—but at least, in thinking about it clearly beforehand, you are better off than in never giving it a thought until suddenly you realize the book is priced out of the market.

226

2. What will the book look like?

Ask the publisher for a dummy. He should supply it free. This will let you hold in your hands, in your home, and at your leisure, a sample of what your book will feel and look like physically (size, weight, paper). A dummy appears slightly thicker than the printed sample because it has more air between the pages, since it was not machine folded and bound. Your dummy will not be 100 percent like the finished product, but, within a small and reasonable limitation, your book should be what the dummy is. A dummy shows you, in advance, what the eventual reader will see.

3. Will there be a dust jacket, and, if so, in how many colors?

A simple question. Likewise, the answer should be simple: "Yes, two colors." What if the answer is "No," or "Yes, one color"? In either event, you know the answer before you have ordered. By looking around a bookstore, you can see for yourself how many books, in the same general field as your book, have dust jackets comparable to yours. The cost of a dust jacket is one of a hundred different costs in producing a book. By your paying for this cost, your book "looks more like a bookstore book"; by omitting it, you save money and alter the product.

4. How many copies of my book will be printed by publication date?
Again, a simple numeral should be the answer.

5. How many copies are being printed, folded, bound, and delivered on publication date?

Again, the answer should be a simple numeral, but perhaps different from above. In the trade, a book is usually printed in flat sheets called press sheets. Some copies are bound on publication date, while the remainder are held in press sheets until there is sufficient demand to justify binding them. You want to know how many copies are being bound for publication day and how many are being held in press sheets.

6. Who owns the press sheets?

The contract may clearly specify that the publisher owns all unsold press sheets. A direct question and a direct answer are your best bet.

7. Who owns the bound copies that are not sold?
The answer should be either "you" or "the publisher."

8. How many bound copies will be furnished to the author as part of the contract, with no additional payment?

The answer should be a simple numeral, plus "freight paid" or "f.o.b."

9. Is there a storage fee for holding unsold books or flat sheets beyond a given time?

No one gives free storage space indefinitely. A publisher pays for it and has to pass this cost on. You want to know when this charge starts and how much it is.

10. What is the minimum number of direct-mail pieces exclusively advertising your book the subsidy publisher will place into the U.S. mails to sell your book? When will they be mailed?

The answer may be five hundred, one thousand, five thousand or none, but all the answer need contain is a figure and a date. Then you know beforehand, which is the point of this checklist.

What if a contract says: "We will consider various means of promotion—including newspaper and magazine advertising, TV and radio advertising, direct mail, and we will invite suggestions from the author. The publisher will decide what forms to use and what expenditures to make."

The above sentence is an offer to consider promotion—not a promise to perform it.

11. What are some other books this publisher has issued?

Ask the publisher if he will send you three typical books for ten dollars. It's worth your ten dollars since you are considering spending five hundred to one thousand times that. Would books such as these satisfy you? Only you can answer that. Show them to a friend. Do they look like "bookstore books"? Settle this in your own mind before you go ahead. Many books issued by subsidy publishers are beautifully designed. Some are indifferently designed.

It costs five to ten dollars to set the type and make a negative of one single page of a book. If your book has two hundred pages, the publisher needs to pay over one thousand dollars to his printer merely to set the type and make the negatives. Editing, paper, binding, presswork, and plates add from one to several thousand dollars more, for even one thousand printed copies. There are as many different kinds of quality in book manufacturing as there are in shoes or dresses. If you want the cheapest price, then you need to accept less quality.

I do not know of a printer capable of producing attractive, quality work who could produce two thousand copies of a 300-page book, binding five hundred and leaving fifteen hundred in press sheets for less than $2.00 per book. To this cost would have to be added all costs of editing, advertising, publicity, and sales. In other words, you get the quality of editing, printing, promotion, and advertising that you pay for. The subsidy publisher normally does not pay part of these costs, as a financial risk of his own, in order to sell more books and thus take in more money through mail-order or bookstore sales. If you desire a high-quality book, plus advertising, plus promotion, you are the one who pays for it and who hires a professional to perform this task. This is what subsidy publishing means. Nothing is thrown in "for free"; although it may be included in the contract price. You have a right to know in full what you are buying.

12. How many lines of paid advertising exclusively devoted to my book will appear in large city newspapers and national magazines?

The answer should be two simple numerals, one for newspapers and one for magazines. A "line" equals one-fourteenth of an inch. When a publisher speaks of a "fourteen-line ad" he means an ad that is one column wide and one inch deep. Since the subsidy publisher is, for all intents and purposes, a professional publicity man, salesman, promoter, and printer, whom you have hired to serve you, it follows that, if you want advertising to appear, the cost of it need be reflected in the price you agree to pay.

13. What are the names of nearby bookstores that sell books issued by this subsidy publisher?

Let's admit the other fellow is a statistic, not you. A fair sampling of titles of subsidy-published books appears earlier in this chapter. Are such books hard to sell? To appreciate this, ask your publisher for the names of nearby bookstores that currently handle some of his titles at retail. You will learn whether locally or within a few hours' drive of your home such stores exist. Out of one thousand authors whose titles are issued by subsidy publishers, fewer than ten ever go to a bookstore and ask: "How many titles of this publisher do you sell?" But, a year after the author has

229

THE BOOK MARKET

had a book issued by a subsidy publisher and enjoyed a national sale of only fifty books, he will then enter six bookstores to ask what he should have asked a year ago. Our point: Ask beforehand. Don't blame the bookstore owner if he doesn't buy from the subsidy publisher.

The bookstore dealer doesn't care too much who publishes a book. Neither does a retail customer. Let's watch a retail customer enter a bookstore and start to browse about in an aimless way, then, from the midst of the juvenile department, say to a clerk: "My aunt is having a birthday. I need a book on découpage. Do you have any?"

The customer buys by subject matter or by the name of the author. Almost never does the customer say: "What's new from Bobbs-Merrill?" or "Did anything come in this week from Random House?"

Ask yourself: Will a customer ask for my book by subject matter? If not, and if your name is not known, how does the customer get to the book? Ever hear someone go to a bookstore and ask: "I want a book on how to make and sell private-brand peanut butter. Do you have it?" No, it's not a joke. Although the peanut-butter book is not a trade book, it is a very valuable book to a limited audience. It could be sold by mail to food-processing companies. It could be sold to large peanut-mill and jobber combines, such as the one President Carter owned, or as a giveaway to food-processing companies to attract larger orders for peanuts from them. It's a forty-dollar book and worth it. But a bookstore dealer would not be likely to stock it.

The point: if your book deals with a subject of wide general interest, the retail-bookstore customer may ask to see what books the store owner has on that particular subject, just as the customer did who wanted to buy a découpage book. However, if your book has a limited sales potential, even though it might be just as worthy as the peanut-butter book, the bookstores might not handle it.

What kind of book does the bookstore owner want? He doesn't particularly care who wrote it, or what it's about, or who published it, as long as people come in and ask for it, and he can sell one or two copies a month, perhaps more. Since he regularly sells thirty to three hundred books a day, he must replace the ones that are sold or he must go out of business. He *wants* to buy books.

But books with a restricted market are best sold other ways: for instance, by direct mail to specialized lists, or through specialty stores.

(Art-museum shops, gun stores, delicatessens, antique shops, farm-implement stores, photographic dealers, and greenhouses are some of the sales outlets for books I published.) Sometimes a book might be offered as a premium through a co-op, or as a giveaway by an association.

If my book were of wide general interest, I would want to know whether bookstores in my area (not just two or three, but twenty) stock titles published by the subsidy publisher with whom I am considering doing business. If, however, my book has a severely limiting title, the above would have no bearing, as the potential bookstore sales would be small.

Pretend for a moment that Charles Darwin never existed and that his theory of evolution were unborn. How many bookstores would buy a volume titled *Theories in Regard to the Difference in Shell Markings on Tortoises Found in the Galapagos Islands?*

Publishing titles with market restrictions is a service that the subsidy publisher performs.

14. How many commission salesmen does the subsidy publisher have on the road selling for him and other publishers?

The answer should be a simple numeral. Many trade publishers successfully use commission salesmen who work for several publishers.

15. How many subsidized titles has the publisher issued in the past year?

The answer should be a simple numeral.

16. Of the titles issued under subsidy in the last twelve months (some subsidy publishers also issue a royalty line), how many sold over five hundred copies?

Again, the answer should be a simple numeral.

17. On what date is my book promised for delivery?

The answer should be a date.

18. What penalty will the publisher pay me in the event the book is delivered forty-five working days after this date, provided no adverse act of God is involved (strikes, flood), and provided I, the author, have lived up to my agreement?

A penalty of 1 percent on the total price for each late weekday of delivery is reasonable.

231

19. How many copies of my book, as included in my contract, will be sent for review to critics, and may I have the list of the critics?

The answer should be a simple numeral, plus a yes or no.

20. How many copies of my book, as included in my contract, will be sent to libraries, book chains, large bookstores, and book wholesalers as a sample to induce quantity orders; and on what dates?

The answer should be, in each case, simply a numeral and a date.

21. Does any part of my contract, or any answer to this checklist, include the words "up to"?

The answer should be yes or no. If your publisher offers to send "up to fifty copies for review," and the publisher sends five copies for review, he has fulfilled his contract. The purpose of this question is to single out any clause where the words "up to" might appear so you may reconsider it.

22. Have I hired a lawyer to look over my contract?

If you have been consulted by friends, as a contract expert, when they sign contracts of one thousand dollars or more, then you have good reason to feel you can judge your own contract. A lawyer will charge from fifty dollars to two hundred dollars to advise you on your contract. Even a businessman who enters into contracts every month in the year often asks a lawyer for advice—and then makes up his own mind on what to do.

Probably, we've left out some questions. But, if the above twenty-two are answered, you will know more than beforehand.

The author should own all rights, and his royalty should be in excess of trade royalty, which is between 10 and 15 percent. The subsidy publisher, in the event he acts as the author's agent to sell various literary rights, should receive a fee of no less than 10 percent. Trade publishers ask for 50 percent of paperback and book-club rights, and usually get it from authors of a first or second novel.

In one respect, the trade publisher and the subsidy publisher are the same: Neither gives unstinted editorial time. Both pay the same general wage scale, which, in New York, Boston, and Philadelphia areas, is fifteen to twenty-two thousand dollars for a "shirt-sleeve pencil editor," and eight to twelve thousand for an editorial secretary. When you add the proportionate administrative and overhead costs that ride on the backs of an editor and an editorial secretary, you are looking at three thousand dollars a month editorial time.

When an editor is given a firm work schedule of twelve books a year, the human condition is such that he soon yearns for a respite: seminars, conferences, travel, long lunches with literary agents or authors to help procure new talent, or the necessity of reading incoming mail, even the other fellow's mail, to keep from "getting one-eyed." An unending assembly-line schedule of one book a month is a severe one, and pretty soon this dwindles to ten or eleven a year.

Talented and productive editors, like writers of similar ability, are rare. When a publisher issues two hundred titles a year, and this is not unusual, he requires twenty shirt-sleeve pencil editors who can each turn out ten books a year. It is difficult to find and keep competent, producing editors in this quantity.

The tendency, therefore, on the part of all publishers is to reduce the amount of editorial time allowed to each book, whenever possible.

What does all this have to do with the author who is considering subsidy publishing? The subsidy publisher is faced with the same pay scale as the trade publisher in paying editors and secretaries and the same costs for office overhead and administration. Like the trade publisher, he cannot add the overall cost of one editor for four weeks without adding several thousand dollars to the cost of producing a book. The subsidy publisher does add enough to take care of copyediting (spelling, punctuation, grammar, consistency in style in matters such as quotation marks, italics, and the like). But he can't do a revise or a rewrite or send an editor to visit a writer to rework a half-dozen chapters.

The meaning of this to an author of a subsidized book, or any other kind of book, now becomes clear. By editorially pretesting a book in which you are investing a great deal, you are more likely to produce the best book that can be published under your name. Nothing else should be your goal.

What if there were no subsidy publishers? Without any form of subsidy publishing, we would lock in every author whose work is currently unacceptable to trade publishers. In the past, this has included almost every form of literary and ideological creation from *The Communist Manifesto* to Upton Sinclair's *Jungle* as well as every point in between.

PART II
Self-Publication

16

Self-Publication—Who Needs It?

WHEN AN AUTHOR PRINTS, sells and publicizes his own book, the operation is called self-publication. Around thirty years ago, the content of a self-published book was predictable. It was a religious, educational, or scientific treatise with a limited market. A sale of six hundred copies was good. Reviews of self-published poetry and novels rarely surfaced in the columns of newspapers and magazines.

Today, self-publication is a respectable endeavor, because the quality of the work has improved, and the public generally has come to understand the need that motivates the author to self-publish.

I published my own book [says Susie N. Baltomeyer] for one reason. Enlightenment. I wanted the world to be enlightened about me.

I am what our New Orleans masters a century ago called an octoroon. One afternoon in an art museum I saw a painting of a young girl dressed in a white satin blouse, her wrists cuffed in irons. This painting could have been myself reincarnated. Right then I wanted people to know who I was, what I could do, and how I did it. I walked over and kissed that painting.

My book, *An Octoroon in Nepal,* is a true life experience I had several years ago with a yak herder and trader high up in the snow country of the Himalayas. He dressed in the skins of his own animals and was larcenous, loving, fierce, full of pride, and very much his own man. He walked into the valleys barefoot and up into the high snows in sandals. From him, I learned to chant

237

and to meditate. He beat me, and I left him. It was all so sad, so wonderful, and so forever gone.

Why did I self-publish *An Octoroon in Nepal?* Because the experience was mine alone, and I knew myself better afterward. In Nepal, I came to grips with my own human condition, and this is what made me want to enlighten people about myself.

Deep in our hearts and minds are universal feelings, and, sometimes, when we reveal these, the public responds. Self-publication has become a respectable way to do this, and for some writers the process is a profitable one. From them I learned that some of the things I once believed to be certain now appear to have a loose footing. I thought it self-evident that to succeed in book publishing you needed experience in the graphic arts and in marketing.

Then I began to meet some of the people who self-published and made a howling success out of it. They entered the field with no publishing knowledge or printing experience and with little money. But they did have an enormous supply of motivation, a great capacity for work. Yet, up to the moment of self-publication, they were unknown beyond their own backyards.

The euphoric glow given off by people who self-publish and make large sums of money is unrelated to the dollars they bank. If the gain in dollars were all they had to show for it, their success would be shallow. Their success is one of enlightenment. They enlighten their families, their friends, their communities, and, best of all, themselves, with their accomplishments and vitality.

The authors who self-publish and make little or no money, or who lose a few hundred dollars, all appear pleased with their personal venture. The ones to whom your heart can go out are the many hundreds of authors who lose their cash reserves, who stumble and fall each step of the way, and whose books receive no attention from anyone that the author regards as important. One of these is Iron John, as his steel-mill friends call him. Unexpectedly, Iron John came upon the details of a "sweetheart" contract between his employer and his union, and, as a result, he self-published a long, rambling, bitter discourse about it. "They're the same," he told me, "union leaders, bosses. They want us for what we can do for them, the bastards. Blackballed my book. That's why nobody bought it."

Iron John's book is source material for scholars, rather than a book for the general public. Written in anguish, it reads with great difficulty.

Three thousand miles away from Iron John in the little northern California mountain town of Laytonville, where jobs are scarce and opportunities limited, a public accountant found semiretirement boring. As a result, he proceeded to self-publish a book explaining *How to Be a Small-Time Operator and Stay Out of Trouble.* To date, Bernard Kamoroff's book has grossed three hundred thousand dollars. Each year the sales increase as the author continues to mail review copies to lesser-known periodicals and hauls in a stream of nice reviews that lead to more orders.

The words "self-publisher" really fit Madge Reinhardt, as her book is printed in her basement on a second-hand A.B. Dick machine and hand sewn and bound in the living room. Cardboard slabs from cereal boxes, contributed by her neighbors, supply the binder's boards to which cloth is applied with Elmer's glue. The quality of writing in Madge's novel, *You've Got to Ride the Subway,* attracted me, as did the story itself: A young woman cannot shake off an emotional attachment for a girl she knew at college. She decides to confront this by visiting her friend and trying to discover her true self. I tried to give the sales a push. Was the lady prepared to accept an order for six hundred copies for a jobber friend of mine?

Nope.

"I print and bind eight copies a week," she said. "Fifteen if I have to. My husband helps me finish each book; he puts weights on top of newly bound copies to press them. And that's the way I want to do it."

Who needs self-publication?

This unique publishing process fulfills the needs of an individual who wants to enlighten others about personal experiences and ideas and gain recognition while doing it. I can't think of a more human venture.

17

The Self-Published Author:
The Lover Who Cares

IF YOU ARE TEMPTED to consider self-publication, would you want to compare your reasons with those of authors who have done it?

"I printed my own book because I wanted to make a profit." Is that one of your reasons? If so, it's a good one. Self-publication, however, turns out to be a great deal more than simply printing your book. Usually, when you have only a single book it costs more to sell one copy than to print it. And the actual selling takes considerable personal time. When profit is your only motive, it may not be strong enough to justify the money and energy involved. It takes a combination of a certain kind of person and a certain kind of book to turn self-publication into a happy event.

My research indicates that ninety authors out of every hundred lose money when they self-publish. This is not to say they regret it, nor that they wouldn't do it again. But it suggests that the profit motive alone doesn't supply the author with enough sustenance to generate the emotional support he may need.

Ten authors out of every hundred make a profit. Five of these make under two thousand dollars; four authors double their money, and one makes it big. Chapter 21 gives case histories of authors with no publishing background who were able to sell close to, or over, one hundred thousand copies of their self-published books. Why, then, didn't the regular royalty publisher offer these same authors a contract when they submitted their books to them?

THE BOOK MARKET

Many self-published books are never seen by the first reader at a royalty publishing house. The author decides to go it alone because he wants to savor the whole experience. In other cases, authors chose the risk of self-publication rather than run the gauntlet of what appears to them as an unfriendly attitude toward unsolicited manuscripts.

There is, however, an important reason why books of this kind may do well when privately published but fall flat when issued by the usual large-publisher methods.

The self-published book of modest editorial quality and limited sales appeal, whose unknown author puts originality and persistence into sales, will outsell the same book issued by a mainline publisher. In the latter case, the author's book will appear in the publisher's spring catalogue and then be dumped if the sales are slow and the book doesn't move off the dealer's shelf on its own merits. The book is dumped because the publisher believes his costs to turn the book around and make it sell will be greater than the rewards.

To give any book a hard sell requires ten hours a week of the sales-promotion manager's time and costs ten thousand dollars for fifty-two weeks. An in-house charge of this weight will sink any mainline book that garners only a modest sale (five thousand copies). Listen and you can hear the publisher: "Hey! How come we card ten thousand dollars in in-house costs for a book that ends up with a five-thousand sale? Who is responsible for this? I want an answer."

And he deserves it because someone who was in control wasn't thinking like a publisher.

The reality of the situation is that a book by a new author "of modest editorial quality and limited sales appeal" is not supposed to receive this kind of attention. The mainline publishing thinking is that the real risk was in actually producing this kind of book in the first place, and now it has to show its colors before anything much is done. Such a book receives token advertising in a few specialized publications catering to its editorial content, and not much else. If the reviews are so-so and the book sells only five hundred copies in three months, it's dumped. This means it may be recalled and shredded, or else remaindered at 10 cents on the dollar. By using several four-inch-by-one-column ads in national magazines, plus similar ads in ten Sunday newspapers, that five-hundred

The Self-Published Author

sale could have been upped to four thousand by the end of the year. But it would have been accomplished at a loss to the publisher.

Let's shift to Scene Two.

In the littered, cozy den of the self-publishing author of the same book, all is different. Now, the author is the publisher, and it's his book! This month he received orders from two jobbers: Ingram ordered fifty, Baker & Taylor, thirty; plus orders from three chains, twelve from Brentano, six from Doubleday, and twelve from Kroch. Dalton and Walden are yet to be heard from. Oh, boy, what are *they* going to do?

The author figures to ship 150 copies this very month and unload his entire press run of two thousand by the end of the year. Excited and very much alive, he thinks ahead to next year when he should be sold out! Will he order another two thousand, or play it safe and order just fifteen hundred? The sweetness of it all!

The exuberant self-published author gives lovingly of his personal time. Often a spouse helps out. They don't keep track of their time, and they relish the work. Of the self-published books that break even or make a few hundred or a few thousand dollars, almost all are in this delicate fix: There is no charge for the hours put in nor for the abundance of love that flows from the energy nozzle they turn on their book. Their book crawls forward, never stopping and always responding to the personal kind of effort behind it. The mainline publisher can't afford to give this kind of attention to a book of modest editorial quality and limited sales appeal. That's the whole story.

While I was working with Charlie Oviatt, a McGraw-Hill science editor, he told me: "One person in the sales department has to love your book, or it's gone." With publishers issuing fifty, one hundred, two hundred, and six hundred individual titles per year, few sales executives have the time to punch hard at one particular book unless the company is stuck with a big advance or a guaranteed advertising expense of thirty or forty thousand dollars.

The saving grace that separates a royalty book from a self-published book is that the latter has a lover who cares. This is the one fine edge that the self-publisher has going for him. And if he's a salesman and his book is even moderately good, he's in. If he can't sell, and his book is wooden or dated, the end comes quickly.

THE BOOK MARKET

Following are reports from four self-published authors. The first author, Walter Hammerstein, wrote one of those happy "naturals." Here he is, talking into my recorder:

I know more about raising home-garden tomatoes in our state than anybody I see at state fairs. My tomatoes are better, earlier, and later than anyone's. And there are more of them. The fruit is firm and tasty and keeps. It's not just one thing you have to do, like watering, or even twenty, like cultivating or knowing which suckers to nip. It's when and how.

For ten months, beginning with the time my seeds went into the cold frame, and ending in November with canning, I told my tape machine what I did each day. I transcribed it all on five-by-seven cards and separated the cards into categories like preparing the ground, testing the soil. I wrote my book from my cards—and then put it aside for two months and revised it. I showed it to people who never grew a tomato in their lives. When something wasn't clear to them, I made changes. I paid a horticulture professor one hundred dollars to read my one-hundred-page book. He wrote down nine questions and said I should answer them in my book.

I showed chapters to growers of state-fair-prize tomatoes, and they helped out with their own experiences.

With my book, tomato plants, and a yard, you got tomatoes.

I got bids on my book from four printers. The one I picked charged me 75 cents a copy for six thousand copies. I pick up and pay for one thousand books at a time, but I had to agree to pay for all the books within three years, plus half-a-cent-a-month-per-book storage charge for the ones I don't pick up.

The first prospects I called on were nearby nurseries who sold tomato plants. They are so busy in April and May that anything that saves them time is a moneymaker, and I explained how my book would answer the same questions they get every hour of the day during these two months. I gave them 95 cents' profit on every copy they sold at $2.95. When they bought and paid for six books, I was willing to leave twelve more that they could pay for when they ordered more copies. You wouldn't believe how many nurseries sell a dozen books each and every weekend in spring.

I visited hardware stores in my neighborhood and made a small wire bookrack that holds six copies of my tomato book and attaches easily to the store's own rack of seed packages. In April and May I am like a milkman—running back and forth keeping the racks supplied.

I mailed review copies to the garden editors of all the daily newspapers, country weeklies, and community papers in our growing area—an eighty-mile radius. I include a two-page chapter outline and a Xerox of two reviews from newspapers. If the garden editor is busy, this makes writing a review easier. All I ask is that they give my name and address and the price of the book when they print the review.

I don't know a day when somebody doesn't send me $2.95 in the mail for my tomato book. It took me three months to call on the nearby nurseries and hardware stores and send out review copies. Then, I started to make personal calls on book retailers and nurseries beyond our county. Thinking up sales ideas for your own book is like weed seeds; when they get going, they multiply.

The newest places I discovered to sell my book were neighborhood lumber and millwork companies who cut and sell wooden tomato stakes to oblige gardeners in their communities. I find their credit is better than bookstores.

Naturally, the person who does the buying isn't always there. In that case, I leave copies of reviews, a copy of the front cover of my book and copies of letters from gardeners who bought my book and liked it, and a wholesale-order blank. Then, when I get home, I follow up on my call with a sales letter. Unlike most salesmen, I am a writer. I keep a card file on every store that is a likely customer, and I send them a sales letter and order blank in February and another in March. One of the techniques of selling, I found out, is to let the other fellow do some of it for you. With this in mind, and a great deal of bird-dogging, I compiled a list of garden catalogues that sell books along with seeds. A few of these catalogues now offer my book. They demand a 50 percent discount, but they buy more, and their credit is good.

Tomorrow, I leave to spend a week on the road. At each town, I have enough stops to reduce my gas costs per call. I know my first edition of *The Beautiful Tomato* will sell out, and I expect it to go on forever.

THE BOOK MARKET

Would a royalty publisher push my book the way I do? Hell, no, they couldn't afford to hire a person to put that much time into it. What I got is me, not just my book.

Why did I go into self-publishing? To make money. I love growing fine tomatoes and winning prizes, but, after all those blue ribbons, I wanted to make money, too. My wife laughs and says: "Walt, you just wanted to be appreciated."

Some self-published authors have a float. For them, there's tea and cake and music for all. Here's Adele Adamson:

My work is poetry. It's more than my hobby; it's my love. Sometimes I write twelve lines in the morning and tear them up in the afternoon and write twelve more. Only a real writer knows that can be a day's work. I have two hundred completed poems and I think about forty are good or close to good.

For our twenty-fifth wedding anniversary, my husband gave me nine hundred dollars to print seven hundred booklets of my poetry. We had a catered party and fifty guests, and each one received an autographed copy. And I gave thirty copies to people in my neighborhood: my dressmaker, the junior-high-school librarian who helped our daughter so much, and neighbors like that. My husband said, "Adele, you put a price of two dollars on these books; let's get it."

I was so surprised, because I thought the books were a present. The fun began when my husband, who owns a franchised car wash, tried to think about ways to sell an eighty-page book of poetry, paperbound, with seven blank pages. The blank pages are opposite some of the full-page poems.

My poems are about our Earth, the good view of life that comes when you open your eyes and live in the presence of the bounty that Nature gives you.

We started off by sending one hundred review copies of my book to newspapers around the country and fifty copies to big libraries. We had some pleasant letters, three reviews, and no orders.

Then I wrote to the state legislator from our district and sent him a copy of *My Bed Is Green* and asked how I could get in touch with poets in our state. It turns out that in our state, and just about every state, there are dozens of poetry associations and clubs. The Department of Education, at the State House, is the place where you get this list. It's free.

I wrote the secretary of each poetry association and poetry club and explained how I came to write *My Bed Is Green* and enclosed a complimentary book and a copy of my three reviews. The reviews aren't so great, but there I am with my name in type as the author of a new book of poetry. I enclosed a stamped, self-addressed envelope and asked for the names of the club's members and their addresses. About one out of six replied and gave me his club's membership list. I sent each poet a letter describing my work and an order blank. In my letter I thought of myself as though I were writing to a fellow-poet who was a friend and asked about the recent work this poet had written and described my own book. Almost every poet who ordered my book sent me some verses, and I answered every letter.

I received eighty-one orders for each one thousand letters I mailed to poets, but the problem was I didn't have enough names to mail.

We have three local bookstores, and they agreed to place my book in the window for one week. I bought a small ad and paid for it myself and described the book and where it could be bought. One store sold four copies; one sold two, and one didn't sell any.

Then the local TV station news editor called me up, and I went on TV and read two of my poems. The bookstores sold four more copies, and I was excited. I called our local radio station, and they put me on to read one poem, but they didn't say where my book could be bought and didn't give the price. But a greeting-card manufacturer heard the poem on the radio, and he phoned me and bought greeting-card rights to that poem and paid me thirty-five dollars. I didn't know whether to die from joy right then and there or hit the road and start calling on every radio station in the country. My husband restrained me.

A week after the radio broadcast, I got a letter from an antique dealer, about fifty miles away. He said: "I want this poem to print and frame for tourists." I charged him the price of ten books: twenty dollars. My sales crept up until now I have 192 copies left.

I am so delighted with my twenty-fifth-silver-wedding-anniversary gift, and I love my husband so much more because he worked with me on something personal that was important to me.

How about the man for all seasons, the lifelong-unpublished novelist? An author, below, by the name of Howie (Gem) Bluestone relates his experiences in the self-publication of a love story:

In fiction, you make your own world, and my world became the characters of my novel. To be alone at the typewriter and master of what I do delights me.

My novel studies the difference in relationships between a man and his wife and the same man and his mistress. The mistress, Melissa, is a strawberry blonde all the way. Her mind both puzzles and intrigues him. She moves from job to job and yet doesn't need the money. The jobs seem of little significance: doing secretarial work, showing new sparkle jewelry to boutiques, selling fancy shopping bags to department stores. Once or twice a year, she gently takes leave and spins off on a trip: sunning at "Trop" or climbing the Whites in New Hampshire.

One day her lover asks what she is going to do with the rest of her life besides grow old. "Before ten years are up," she says, "I'm going to love and be loved. You can be sure." His incoming breath feels cold at the back of his throat and he looks forsaken. He heard her wrong, she says. "To love and be loved is all I ask for now and the next ten years. That's what I meant." She slides long slender fingers down the bridge of his nose, over his lips. Her fingers part as they cross his mouth and come together again on his chin. She rubs his upper lip and smiles into his eyes. He melts, warily.

What is going on inside her? Just rootlessness and that's all? She holds him tight and brushes her hair against his cheek. The long strawberry-blond hair always manages to rouse him. As a lover, she is faultless. To him, never boring.

At home he doesn't tend his wife's mind, and, in dismay and loneliness, she builds a world of her own beyond his knowing. In the end, he finds why his mistress is what she is and moves at long last into his wife's body and mind.

I feel my novel will help all men and women find more love and peace with their spouses.

Why am I into self-publishing? I had to answer that question. And I asked it of myself many times. My chief reason is that this is a very private novel. It reveals the inner nature of my chief characters, and I cared for them so much I wanted to control the whole thing. But there was something else. I didn't believe I could bear to receive one rejection after another—maybe a dozen over two years! And I couldn't see this thing bottled up, and me waiting, and the novel iced up on a typed page. It was the most real thing in my life, and so I went ahead with it.

Before printing my book, I looked up "Marriage Counselors" in the yellow pages of the phone book and went to see two. I asked if they would read my book and tell me if my probing of the human mind was rational and if my resolution of the conflict was true to my main characters: two women and one man. I offered two hundred dollars to each, and this was accepted. Both counselors read my novel, and each obliged with what I asked. They also gave me some conference time. Because more women buy novels than men, or so I was told, I selected women marriage counselors. Their points of view put me on a slightly different tack, and I made a number of changes to show the lover's frustration by his own actions rather than to tell about it.

I found that I could read my book any time of the day or night, and it never bored me, and I kept praying and wondering what other people would think. The time had come to find out.

So I answered all the classified ads in the *New York Times Book Review* from printers who printed books for authors. From the replies I picked one with the second lowest price and sent an $850 down payment to get my book started. The printer, it turned out, was just a printer. Everything else was up to me.

Many months later, after I thought I would *never* hold my book in my hands, a strange truck came into the apron of our driveway. Two men got out and began opening up the rear end. They put a large well-wrapped skid on the tailgate, and an automatic lift carried it down. I walked outside to see what was going on, and one of the men said to me, "Where do you want these skids?—we got two." Each skid was larger than any door in our home and bound with steel straps. My printer was the shipper. I gaped, and struggled to think what to do. My wife and I unpacked the skids. Fortunately, the books were wrapped in kraft paper, five to a lot. We carried them, somewhat wildly, into our home and tried to figure out where to put them.

Three thousand books overwhelm a small private home, and I was the one who had been complaining that my wife's shell collection was all over half of the living room.

Why didn't I think about any of this beforehand? I suppose I was waiting for someone to put a coin in my slot by making physical delivery of my books. I should have had labels typed for review copies and a sales campaign already blocked out. But I held off—waiting to hold a printed, published copy of my own book in my hands. It was really neat. Slow to arrive, but good. "It looks like a book should," was my wife's first comment.

For the three thousand bound books, I paid my printer fifty-eight hundred dollars. This sum also paid for an additional two thousand press sheets that were unbound. To have these bound would cost a dollar each additionally, plus delivery charges. If I didn't order them within two years, there would be a storage charge.

I priced my book at $8.50 a copy, and it's a professional job of 280 pages. Here's how the math looked to me on that first day of delivery:

Projected Income

Revenue from 1,000 books to be given away or sent to reviewers	$ 00.00
Revenue from 1,000 books sold direct at $8.50 each	8,500.00
Revenue from 3,000 books to dealers at $4.00	12,000.00
	$20,500.00

Printing Expenses

First 3,000 books	$5,800.00
Next 2,000 books at $1.00 each	2,000.00
Cost of 5,000 books	$7,800.00

The first day's math held promise. It gave me $12,700 expense money to sell 4,000 books or about $3.00 a book. Fortunately, I didn't have to pay for my time, and my wife worked right beside me. If my out-of-pocket sales and advertising cost averaged under $3.00 a book, I would show a profit.

I started off by getting a list of marriage counselors and mailed four hundred of them copies of my book. I enclosed comments from the two marriage counselors who had read my manuscript in the rough and their comments after they read the completed book. I wondered if it occurred to either one of them that I would follow their suggestions and then go ahead and publish. I think not. They were sort of surprised by the experience.

I sent four hundred review copies to newspapers and magazines and eighty copies to radio and TV stations with book programs. I sent sixty copies to prominent clergymen and asked for a quote and mailed individual letters and copies to twenty-four columnists.

In three months, I had some ammunition and was ready to sell. I bundled up all the comments, reviews, notices, and a few mentions from the columnists and had these multilithed. I bound them, by hand, into an eight-and-a-half-by-eleven manila file folder and began sending thirty of these a week, with a personal letter—as personal as I could make it—to bookstores and bookstore chains, along with an order blank and a dust jacket, but no free copies. The stores don't read them anyway, I found. Each time, I asked for an order.

I mailed only thirty of these folders a week, because I didn't have the energy to send more. I did the assembling, stamping, folding, sealing, and running back and forth to the post office. My wife typed the letters. When sending a folder to the cloth-bound-book buyer at the home office of a chain store, I phoned station-to-station first, to get the name of the buyer. There are about forty chains, and they account for almost half the bookstores.

I couldn't sell one book wholesaler. One wrote back and said they never ordered from a one-book publisher. Another returned my letter and said, if their customers ordered my book, they would order from me. One wholesaler wrote on the front of my letter that he returned: "Do not write us further." Three days later I got an unsigned order from them for twenty-five books, which convinced me that, in a big company, you should deal with the sergeants. Let moguls deal with moguls. I am a

251

one-book publisher, and I deal with the sergeants. When I find out who the cloth-bound fiction buyer is at a big chain, I ask for the buyer's secretary and ask *her* counsel. Like everything else, this works some of the time.

I always had a fertile, daydreaming mind. Now I have a productive, practical mind. Every week I mail out some kind of new campaign to some new list I scratch together. No less than one order a week arrives from a book dealer, and they come from all over the country. One woman wrote from the Madrid airport, enclosing a check for $8.50 and saying she wanted the book by the time she came home. I answer every order personally and enclose an extra order blank. I expect to sell out in three years.

Would a publisher have put into my book the kind of effort I am putting into it? If I had to pay for my wife's time, and my own time, at the minimum wage, plus rent, and light, the whole thing would be a bust. Between my wife and myself, we put almost one hour of time into each order. The publisher would pay three dollars just for that—my entire allotted sales cost per book—and I don't pay one cent. Besides, I love it. It's been the greatest and I do not regret one minute of it.

On my next book, though, I am going to try the royalty route and show the editors some of the reviews and fan letters from my customers from my first book. What people do for you, without asking anything for it, is the happy surprise.

The next report comes from a well-traveled lady who fell in love with folklore:

Almost every year after World War II, my husband was invited to go abroad and explain x-ray diagnostics. We went directly into the interior of underdeveloped countries and stayed at provincial health centers. We traveled almost everywhere in the Orient, to all of Africa south of the Sahara, and the four coastal countries of South America alongside the Pacific.

One time, after finishing a week of diagnosing x-ray films of all the local tumors, my husband and I took a vacation in Bolivia, and it was there, in Sucre, thirty years ago, that I started collecting folk tales and primitive drawings that illustrate them.

Later, Dr. Jean Marie Matin, in what used to be the Belgian Congo, at Stanleyville, asked me what my folk tales revealed about the human condition, and whether what was revealed was universal. The question lit me up and gave my work a new dimension. It seemed more important.

Everywhere we went, when there was time, I hired an interpreter and pushed fifteen or twenty miles farther into the interior beyond where my husband was needed for his work—beyond, for instance, an outpost of civilization like Kynam, just outside of Tananarive, in Madagascar. Twenty miles beyond places like that takes you into the bush, the *veldt*, the dry washes, the high barren, Godforsaken hill country that pock every "third-world" country I know. With an interpreter, I dug out folk stories that had been handed down, and I tried to find local native art that illustrated them and showed the spirit and feeling of the people.

My main interest turned from being just a collector of all this art and folklore to finding the thread that connects us all. This motif never left my thoughts. Then, suddenly, my husband had a stroke and passed away. After a year, I turned to my book for solace. All told, I had gathered seventy-two separate folk tales and forty-one primitive works of art.

When no royalty publisher wanted the book, I decided to publish it myself in memory of my husband.

The book came off the press looking like an imitation of what I had thought I was buying. I didn't realize that, when a large, colorful drawing, with all greens, purples, and yellows, is reduced to four by three inches and reproduced in black and white, it no longer gives the viewer an emotional or artistic bounce. And, when you had a two-inch fragment of a sandstone engraving from perhaps five hundred years ago that showed how a primitive artist regarded a pregnant girl-child, and you reproduced it in the same size, you ended up with a blob.

Recently, I saw how this should have been done in *The Roots of Civilization*, by Alexander Marshack, published by McGraw-Hill. This book has an illustration of a female head, carved in ivory seventeen thousand years ago. In its original size it was fifty millimeters, but in this book, it is eight and a half by eleven inches! And the blacks in the reproduction are truly black and the whites are white, while, in my book, the pictures look mushy. My printer simply didn't know how.

Since then, I learned that the negatives of my illustrations were shot without filters; a yellow filter, for instance, holds back the yellow but strengthens the blues. My husband could have told them. In my text, I tried faithfully to retell each folklore story as the interpreter had given it to me. Native storytellers are like primitive musicians—they repeat and repeat and often remain in the same key. My documentary folk tales might please a scholar but it wasn't the everyday reading Aunt Jane buys at her mall bookstore. That thought came to me from a book reviewer of an Arkansas newspaper, who lived in the bush country of Peru during the Peace Corps movement. "Before a bright fire on a cool equatorial evening," he wrote, "when your belly is full and you are half-dozing and there is nothing else to do, these folk tales are the only game in town. But to read through endless repetitions of the same phrasings of the same scene is too much. Some of the good country music you hear on radio came right from hill people in Arkansas, but it's been edited and honed down. The author relates her folk tales to the human condition, but she pummels her points."

Ouch!

I sold only a few copies, but I did send gift copies to societies my husband belonged to and some of the stations where he read tumor films. I made a portfolio of the letters of appreciation that I received, and, one time, I carried this to my husband's graveside and read some of it to myself. I didn't cry, but I found more in the letters than I had seen before. I wish I had spent more time thinking about my reader. You have to come to terms with what the public likes and not work from inside a cupboard. I should have shown my work to some editors or book reviewers and allowed a dialogue to develop between them and myself. To do this had never occurred to me.

Do these reports help you frame the questions to ask yourself before going into self-publication?

Let's look again at the central question.

Why are you considering self-publication?

To help you organize your own reply, the next chapter asks six questions only you can answer. Money will print your book. The mind, the heart, and a helpmate can sell it.

18

How Do I Get Started?

IF YOU CAN MANAGE an unvarnished *yes* to the next six questions, you may be the right person to consider self-publication. Before asking the questions, we will briefly discuss costs.

For the self-publisher, after the manuscript itself is completed, there are two remaining costs: printing and selling the book. Of the two, the larger is the sales cost as shown by these figures:

Cost of printing one book	$2.00
Cost of selling one book	3.00
Cost of printing and selling one book	$5.00

In this case, the author spent one and a half times the cost of printing one book to sell one book. Is this normal? How about friends and acquaintances? Wouldn't a telephone call do the job or a postcard? Yes, a single card or call will often sell a book to a friend.

After you sell the first two hundred copies and start to reach out to people who never heard of you or your book, the sales cost per book starts to mount. However, when the reader feels your book speaks directly to him and loves it for what it is, he starts to beat a drum that is stronger, cheaper, and more productive than paid advertising. How do you get the reader to feel this way about your book? The most practical method is to spare nothing to make it as splendid as you know how. Doing this reduces your major expense: the cost of selling.

THE BOOK MARKET

In considering whether you can afford self-publication, the interesting thing is that you have many choices. You can publish in many styles and at different prices. Your investment, for instance, on an illustrated hundred-page book, five by seven inches in size, can be under nine hundred dollars on a token edition of five hundred copies. An edition of this kind is set in typewriter script, multilithed on a small office press, and bound in a soft cover with wire staples. Such a book "doesn't look like a bookstore book," but token editions serve a very practical purpose and are discussed in a later chapter. What if you require a quality job of bookmaking? You can produce two thousand copies of a six-and-a-half-by-nine-and-a-half cloth-bound book of 350 pages with a well-designed type page and a colored dust jacket for eight thousand dollars. Both kinds of books serve a purpose. Between them are many varieties in size, quality, cost.

Although a person of modest means can afford some kind of self-publication, the dollars involved are not all that matter. There's the attachment some people have for their dollars. One person with one hundred thousand dollars in a savings account may lose four thousand dollars in a self-publication venture and spend the rest of his life regretting the loss of one dollar a day in income every time he goes to the store to shop. "See that hunk of cheese? That's what I can't buy today because of that book!" Another person with barely ten thousand dollars in liquid assets can lose half of it with equanimity and look back on the experience as a good one. So the answer to the question of whether you can afford the gamble depends not only on how many dollars you have, but on your emotional and intellectual drive to publish as weighed against your ability to absorb a loss if that becomes necessary.

I have received several hundred letters from authors who failed to make a profit in either self-publication or subsidy publication, and the sustaining factor that lifts the author over the dollar loss is the need to publish. When this need is absent, and the only reason for self-publication is the profit motive, you have to ask yourself whether you want to go into a business where the rate of success is ten out of one hundred, and where some of the people who show even a small profit consider themselves successful.

The main needs in life were once believed to be food and shelter. After the advent of Freud, sex drive was included, along with the *id*.

Robert Audrey, in 1960, said a new factor came ahead of everything: territory. We are still learning which of our needs comes first. An author's need to publish can be overwhelming, and its denial can be punishing.

Can you dig into your real self to ask these six questions and come up with the answers?

1. Are you able to explain your private reasons for self-publication in a few simple, declarative sentences? Don't be ashamed of your answer. Don't be proud of it, don't criticize it. Just be honest. These are your reasons. You should know what they are.

2. Have you the time—time away from your family, job, sports, leisure, social and intellectual interests—to devote eight to twelve hours a week for two years into selling your book?

If you have a spouse, live-in friend, or partner to match your hours, your chances of success are that much greater. Sometimes the burden of typing thirty individual sales letters at a crack can be too much for a writer who hunts and pecks and makes typos. A congenial helper who can type (without pay) is a built-in bonanza.

Selling, for the self-published author, begins with creating ideas. As the idea is implemented, the work proceeds into the detail of putting materials together, making phone calls to get the name of the right person when a sales letter is going to an important buyer, typing the letters and envelopes, licking the stamps, and taking the job to the post office. Most of your selling work is not cracking out snappy ideas. It is steadfast perseverance at office detail. To do it well, you need the time, energy, the motivation, and, best of all, you need to feel the pleasure of accomplishment every time you place a sales job in the mails, or make a sales call by phone or in person.

3. Do you persevere once you start something?

4. Are you willing to submit your manuscript, before it goes to the printer, to the best and most objective minds you can reach who will comment on your work?

Your editorial goal is excellence. If your work is nonfiction, you want to know whether your conclusions are original, your research sound, and your text lucid.

If your work is fiction, you want to know whether you indeed have a beginning, a middle, and an end, and, if not, whether the lack of any of these will leave readers unfulfilled. You want to know if you left out a "must scene," a confrontation the reader wants. You want to know if your story moves forward in a logical line that the reader can follow. And, finally, you want to know if the reader is hell bent on turning the pages.

If your work is poetry, you might want to know if your rhymes are true, your meter constant, your ideas original, and your phrases fresh.

You don't have to accept all the comments you receive from others, but you may be ahead by learning what they are. A manuscript kept under cover until the day of publication is overprotected.

5. *Can you write clear, reasonably correct English that other people find fresh and readable? Have you some recent evidence of this?*

6. *Can you afford self-publication?*

To succeed as a self-publisher, you almost have to come up with a *yes* to each question. If you can give that answer, with no fingers crossed, your chances of success are no longer ten out of one hundred, but the opposite, ninety out of one hundred. And you will have earned it.

19

The First Step

WHEN YOU TYPE *"finis"* on the last page of your book manuscript, and decide to go ahead and self-publish, your gamble is half over. The other half—the publishing part—is still to come. Fortunately, the kind of advice open to you, at this point, is better than that available to the author who intends to sell his work to a mainline publisher.

The royalty author may seek advice from experts in the field of his book along the lines suggested in the chapter about tilting the odds in your favor. The self-publisher, however, has the best of all fields of advice open to him: editors of mainline publishing houses. It's unethical to offer a fee to an editor who is a prospective buyer for an advance opinion. But with the self-publisher, there is no conflict of interest, since he is publishing the book himself.

Being both new and amateur, he is noncompetitive, even attractive, to a mainline editor who normally regards this kind of activity as something more daring than he might do himself.

How does the self-publisher get his book pretested by an editor of a mainline publishing house?

You may have some devilish thoughts that, since you are now a self-publisher, what you do is your own business and you certainly don't have to bother with editorial pretesting. It's quite the opposite. By deciding to self-publish, you have doubled your gamble: first you invest your time and money in writing the book, and then you make a second investment of time and money in publishing. You simply can't afford a shot in the dark.

How do you locate the editor of your choice?

THE BOOK MARKET

Let's say your book is a piece of genre fiction: mystery, romance, science fiction, Western, Barbara Cartland type; or maybe it's a novel for young people or a juvenile. What if you have written a Western novel? Consult some of the publisher's catalogues at your library and see which ones have a full line of original Westerns. This would indicate the publisher employs a full-time Western editor. Also, look over the paperback Westerns at a large newsstand, and notice the names of the original hardcover publishers. There are other sources of information. *Literary Market Place* and *Writer's Market* will occasionally name the genre editors of book-publishing companies. Glancing through six copies of *Publishers Weekly* will supply additional leads.

This should give you eight names of publishers who appear to have a full Western line. To which should you go? That is the question you cannot answer, and so you have to proceed by blind luck and assume the editor of Western fiction at any mainline publishing house knows the business. This is a fair assumption.

Pick one publisher.

Phone the publishing company and ask for the editorial department, and then ask for the name of their Western editor. Now send the editor a letter along these lines:

Dear —— :

I'm about to take a gamble and want to know if you would care to do a job for me for which I offer two hundred dollars in advance. What I want to buy is your opinion of my 60,000-word Western novel. I intend to self-publish my book and, since I have already invested considerable time in writing it, I am seeking a professional opinion that will tell me whether my novel has merit before I spend a lot of money for art, printing, binding, etc.

My manuscript is titled "Shoot Out," and the opening three pages are attached along with a two-page chapter outline.

Last month, I submitted the novel to two Americana authorities to check the accuracy of background, color and location. A Xerox of their replies is attached. I have since corrected the parts checked in red.

May I have permission to send you my novel for your criticism and evaluation? My check for two hundred dollars will accompany the manuscript, and I agree in advance to accept what you send me as payment in full.

I hope you will agree to assist me and advise the address where I may send the work. Many thanks.

Sincerely yours,

————————————

P.S. If you are busy at this time and cannot take on this job, and care to suggest a competent, currently experienced editor in the field of Western novels, I shall be appreciative.

What kind of answer will you get?

Out of three such tries, you are almost certain to get one acceptance. You want to pretest your novel with two editors before going ahead into self-publication. Any editor, even the very best, can make a mistake. The ablest editor I know, and the person I would elect to pretest my own novel, flubbed the biggest-selling novel that ever hit his office. How could this happen? It happens to all of us. Neither the novel, nor any useful purpose would be served by naming the editor, or the author, who was in the same philosophical ballpark as Norman Rockwell; also my editor friend was intellectually removed and, probably, a little against Rockwell, because of his own cultural background. I have no other explanation.

Test with two editors, but not two at the same time. Work with one, then the other.

Don't attempt to induce the editor you query into some special relationship of kin, culture or the like. Play it straight up.

If yours is a nonfiction book rather than a novel, you will want to submit some chapters, if not the entire book, to people in its field who can advise you on accuracy, practicality, and originality. But such people are not editors. They are technicians. After making the corrections you receive from these specialists, you now want to approach an editor of a mainline publishing house who works in the field of your nonfiction manuscript.

The letter you send can be of the same general structure as the suggested sample letter to the Western editor. And the price you offer will be the same.

The other large group of people that can offer you good advice are book reviewers writing for major newspapers and national magazines. Select a reviewer whose point of view is somewhat similar to your own.

263

THE BOOK MARKET

The letter you will send could resemble the sample suggested for the Western editor. The book reviewer, however, is your second choice, because he is less accustomed to working directly with a writer.

Should you ask advice of someone you know locally as to whether you should risk self-publication? The answer is definitely *yes* if you are able to get to a self-publisher who has produced a book that sold over five thousand copies, or to an individual who has both editorial and sales experience in mainline publishing. A successful businessman in real estate, parking lots, or the like has little background for judging your book or knowing how to sell it. He also may not understand your special relationship to the book. That relationship is a hard thing to pin down with a pure "P & L" pencil.

A local book reviewer may try to discourage you from self-publishing. An editor may do the same. Statistically they are right. But, in your case, if you do editorial pretesting with competent objective people, and find affirmative answers to your editorial content, you are strongly ahead of the average.

Publishing today is a specialized business, and many editors have never been trained to do a detailed five-page market study on one book, let alone on twenty. Most editors have never written a dozen direct-mail campaigns to trade dealers, nor have they called on jobbers and made a sale. Editors know the editing business. Rarely are they marketers. Similarly, most marketers have little editorial experience and are not capable of taking a fairly good writer who has done a so-so book and working with the writer, as a pencil editor, to make a better book.

Accept marketing advice from a book marketer, and editing advice from an editor. Be leery of those who profess knowledge of both areas unless you know their track records. A good businessman may very well help you in record-keeping, accounting, pricing, or estimating expenses, but that does not mean he knows who buys books, or why, or from whom.

Sometimes, the person who can help you the most may be practically unknown, like Alex Dworden, author of *How to Repair an Electric Razor*. Alex showed me a letter he mailed to pretest his book. His book idea is a no-miss proposition because it is so functional, and Alex has such a sweet way of selling it.

Here's the letter he addressed to the "Manager, Repair Department

264

and Customer Service" at the home office of eight electric-razor manufacturers:

Dear ——:

I have completed a short manuscript titled "How to Repair an Electric Razor" and am coming to you for advice. The work consists of eighty pages and there are two hundred words to the page. The book is divided into eight chapters and a chapter outline is enclosed.

I own a small appliance-repair shop and plan to offer this booklet to customers who do not wish to pay my minimum rate of $9.95 for electric-razor repair.

I would appreciate permission to send you several chapters and will circle in red pencil a total of twelve short sections that contain one to three paragraphs each. With the manuscript, I will enclose my check for twenty-five dollars in exchange for your comments on the twelve passages checked.

All I want to know is whether the material checked is factually accurate, in your judgment. If it is not, would you indicate on the manuscript, or enclose a letter telling what is needed to make the material acceptable. The manuscript will be a Xerox copy so that you can write on it.

By pretesting my manuscript with an authority such as yourself, I hope to give my readers a more useful book. Many of my customers are handy with small tools. I also sell repair parts for razors.

I agree to accept whatever comments you send me as full value for the twenty-five-dollar check. Enclosed is a stamped, self-addressed envelope, and I look forward to hearing from you.

Sincerely yours,

———————————

The thing that charmed me about Alex was his attitude after I expressed the hope he could uncover a way to sell his book at more places than his own shop. He said:

As you say, that's the hole in the cheese. I can't sell enough books at my own shop to make it pay. At the most, three or four books a week is all I do. It's still a fun thing to have around, and I am proud of it. I framed the six replies I got from the big electric-razor people and have them displayed in my shop. I think these letters give me razor-repair power.

But not sales for my book.

So I began asking the manufacturers' reps who call on me for the names and addresses of other shops that sell new electric razors, repair old ones, and carry a large stock of spare parts on major razors. Like I do.

I visited each store owner and offered him my book, with his name on it as publisher. I said they didn't have to use my name as the author of the book, but they could if they wanted to. I really didn't care. As it turned out, they all said for me to keep my name on the title page as author, but naturally, they wanted their own names, addresses, and phone numbers in big type as publisher, which suited me. For this purpose I use a paste-on decal, and I sell the book to them in lots of one hundred at $1.50 each.

I told each one frankly that every time he sells a book, he makes at least another two-to-five-dollar gross in selling spare parts to the customer who buys the book.

I think Alex will sell *How to Repair an Electric Razor* as long as he lives, especially if he keeps it up to date when important changes in razor design are made.

You could think of *The Alex Book*, as a Des Moines columnist fondly referred to it, as the ideal model of a self-published book. "Ideal" because the author knew the subject, knew where to go to check his facts, and had a handle on sales. The closer you are to this kind of cozy position, the less your risk.

The whole risk drops by more than half when you pretest your book editorially to learn how it stacks up with editors or book reviewers, if you have written fiction, or with technical experts as well as editors and book reviewers, if you are doing nonfiction.

You may be wondering how the royalty publishers handle a manuscript when the first reader loves it, the associate editor says, "Well, maybe," and the senior editor says, "It just might catch on, but if I had to hang for it this minute, I'd say no."

The sales manager is asked and says: "If it's not a long ball, let's forget it. We've got too many ifs on the list already."

The publisher intervenes. "Let's get some oxygen into our brains and ask somebody else."

What now?

The answer is contract editing. An outside person is employed to evaluate a manuscript or to edit it for a flat fee.

I located some of these people and their names and addresses follow. You will find about three hundred more listed in *LMP* under the heading of "Consulting and Editorial Services" and "Free Lance Editorial Services." Which one is best for you? It's impossible to answer that categorically, but you can make an honest pass at it.

Write some of the individuals of your choice and enclose a two-page chapter outline and one complete ready-to-go chapter.

If you consult *LMP* for additional leads, you will see that many of these three hundred individuals specialize in copy editing and indexing, which is not what we are talking about in this particular instance. You want an editorial evaluation of your book. The correction of grammar, spelling, and punctuation is necessary, but an editorial evaluation should precede it.

You might say something like this:

Dear ——:

I am considering purchasing an objective editorial opinion on my manuscript, "A Tree House Is a Necessity" and am enclosing a two-page chapter outline and chapter 1. Would you care to tell me your charge for an editorial opinion and give me your background for this kind of work, please?

Some of the things I would like to know are:

My book runs eighty thousand words. I would expect to pay your fee in advance and accept what you send me as value received. Could you indicate what might be the nature of your response, to any degree that you wish, based on my enclosed material or on previous work you have done? This will give me some basis for knowing the quality of your work, although I would not wish to be billed for this sample.

I do realize that showing me editorial evaluations you did for other publishers violates a professional confidence. On my part, if possible, I would like to have some idea of what to expect.

Thank you very much,

The above supplies a possible approach.

Here are some of the people who do this kind of work and a few words about each from their correspondence with me.

Miss M.J. Abadie
403 East 70th St.
New York, NY 10021
(212) YU 8-5960

Yes, I do manuscript analysis and advise on both royalty and self-publication. Along with an analysis, I sometimes include a sample of how I would handle a rewrite as part of the fee. My fee is usually $300 for a book length of 300–400 pages.

I can handle fiction and nonfiction. Fiction, any subject as long as it is adult. I do not do sci-fi, poetry, or plays. Non-fiction, any subject that is not heavily scientific. I do not do textbooks.

I have experience with major trade publishers (Pantheon Books, Dutton, Dell, Norton, to name a few) and with university presses on serious subjects. I was for ten years associated with the Bollingen Series.

I also am a book designer and a graphic artist.

One of the books Miss Abadie helped design (published by Princeton University Press) is The Mythic Image. *The New Yorker called it "... extraordinarily handsome and thoroughly illustrated."*

Elaine Andrews
225 West 12th St.
New York, NY 10011
(212) 675-5185

I do professional evaluations of manuscripts. My field is both adult and juvenile nonfiction. I specialize in the humanities, with emphasis on history. I do not do fiction at all.

I have worked in the social sciences in the secondary education divisions of two major publishers and in the juvenile trade division, and am presently the editor of a historical, scholarly journal. I am also the author of a nonfiction juvenile book published by the education division of Macmillan.

Arthur Orrmont
Editorial Director
Author Aid Associates
340 East 52nd St.
New York, NY 10022
(212) PL 8-4213

We work with all kinds of material, fiction and non-, adult and juvenile, including poetry collections, except cookbooks, texts and the technical. Our specialty is bringing the problem book up to publishing standards. I am ex-editorial department head, Farrar, Straus; senior editor, Popular Library; and executive director, Fawcett Books. I have also published fifteen books of my own, best known of which is *Last Train Over Rostov Bridge*.

Marjorie M. Bitker
2330 East Back Bay
Milwaukee, WI 53202
(414) 276-5462

I am competent to evaluate most kinds of fiction with the exception of Westerns and Science Fiction, which are out of my range! Ditto juveniles. But everything else I think I can cope with and provide a practical appraisal.

In regard to nonfiction, I can handle autobiography, biography, short informal essays (such as the collection by Jessica Mitford on muckraking), music manuscripts and literary criticism. No poetry, please. The kind of poetry I like is seldom written nowadays!

For the last twenty-two years, I have been a free-lance book reviewer and contributor of various kinds of articles to the *Milwaukee Journal*. Last year, Random House brought out a new edition of an earlier novel of mine, *Love in a Dry Season*.

Vincent Buranelli
27 Cold Soil Rd.
Lawrenceville, NJ 08648
(609) 896-2180

The books we handle are nonfiction, nontechnical (*e.g.*, no math or music). Our work includes books on travel, history, biography, philosophy, reference, textbooks and encyclopedia articles.

Mrs. Glenn Clairmonte
8109 Third St.
Downey, CA 90241

During the years 1952–59, I prepared for publication more than 500 book mss. for 56 publishers in New York City, and then returned to my beloved California. Since then I have continued to work at $10 an hour (rewrite, proofing, etc.). I no longer do indexing. I wrote a biography on John Sutter published by Nelson and another on Calamity Jane published by Swallow Press. I have also written for the *New York Times* and for their Sunday *Book Review*. Every novel that passes through my hands is judged on plot and characterization and authenticity, as well as for the reader's entertainment and satisfaction. I do not handle math or science.

Frances G. Conn
8320 Woodhaven Blvd.
Bethesda, MD 20034
(301) 365-5080

We prefer to work with biography and textbook material,

particularly in education and the social sciences. I have been doing this kind of work for more than twenty years in addition to writing and editing.

Ivan R. Dee
1036 Judson
Evanston, IL 60202
(312) 869-5498

I sometimes help authors evaluate manuscripts for book publication and prefer to work with serious nonfiction, especially history, politics, sociology, contemporary affairs, and the like. My major experience was as editor-in-chief of Quadrangle Books for eleven years. I have also worked with the *Chicago Tribune* book review section; Field Newspapers Syndicate; as editor of a city magazine; and with the American Library Association.

Martha G. Ellis
P.O. Box 1427
Sequim, WA 98382

Yes, I do evaluate manuscripts, both for individuals and for publishers. After eighteen years of salaried work, I recently turned to full-time freelancing. I have edited over a dozen books for Prentice-Hall, Allyn and Bacon. My particular expertise is in the natural sciences and environmental studies. I do not feel qualified to evaluate fiction.

20

The Token Edition

IS THERE AN INEXPENSIVE route to self-publication? Yes, and it's called the token edition. This provides a faster, cheaper way to get into print and receive some immediate public reaction.

The token edition gets its name from the fact that it has the ring of the real edition but not all of its substance. For instance, it is generally bound in paper and may be smaller in size than the usual six-by-nine-inch cloth-bound trade edition. The cover is often printed in only one color. Sometimes, the author leaves out some material to reduce the total number of pages. The press run is low—two hundred to seven hundred copies—and the composition is often done on an IBM typewriter. Complete cost: seven hundred to twelve hundred dollars for five hundred copies of a five-by-seven-inch book of sixty-four to eighty pages, paperbound.

The press run is only large enough to get a reaction from influential people whom you believe would be attracted to your book once they had a copy in their hands. At the same time, the token edition lends itself to local testing at the retail bookstore level and to library display.

Sometimes, the token edition can be displayed away from home if the writer belongs to a trade or professional association and takes it to conventions. At these meetings, there are always people "looking for an item," and you might make a marriage. The charm of the token edition is that it doesn't oblige you to buy several thousand books and make a commitment to place twenty to one hundred promotion pieces into the mails every week, for the next year. For some self-publishers, this gives substance to each day's existence, and this is especially so when you are working with your own property. Not all writers feel up to a long program of publicity and selling. For them, the token edition has four prime advantages:

1. The investment is smaller, perhaps 75 percent less.
2. There is less pressure on the author. It's almost like tossing a paper airplane into an updraft, just to see what happens, compared to racing a plane down a runway and lifting up a large cargo on your first flight.
3. Sometimes an author can be so frustrated in an attempt to get a hearing that any way to serve the human need for fulfillment is good. The token edition can do this.
4. If the token edition happens to attract few buyers, there's no need to berate yourself over having made a public show, because none was made.

The token edition has disadvantages, too. Here they are:

1. Because the edition is inexpensive, it will present a modest appearance—modest in weight, thickness, binding, illustration, and use of color. Despite this, it need never look tacky. One sure way to provide for good looks is to employ a graphic artist to help you design the book. The rate varies from five to twenty dollars an hour. What you want, primarily, is a sample page of straight type and a sample page showing how a chapter begins. Do you have running heads and folios? Where should they be placed on the page? *Running heads* are the few words above the top of the type page that repeat the title of the book or the title of the chapter. Someone has to decide where to place these words and what size type to use. *Folios* are simply the page numbers. Unless centered, they need to be placed separately for a left-hand page and a right-hand page. How large should your overall page be? And, inside that page, how large should the page of type be? Graphic design is a bundle of such small decisions. Put together, they give a book its style.

To give the printer control of the graphics may work to your disadvantage, unless you have seen and approved of the printer's samples and can point out what you like and why. The samples you seek are the printer's own design, not samples of the printer's work in following the design of a graphic artist.

274

Similarly, if you employ a graphic artist, ask for samples of the artist's work beforehand. Explain your vision of what your book should look like. How do you want to make the reader feel? Point out what you like in the artist's samples and why. You don't just go to a printer and hand over seven hundred dollars and walk home with a token edition. The planning can be a disadvantage if you don't recognize it in advance and make yourself part of it.

2. Sometimes, you may have to leave out material to cut costs.

3. A token edition's short press run increases the cost per copy. Let's pretend the cost of setting the type and making negatives and plates for a hundred-page book comes to five hundred dollars. This does not include paper, printing, binding. If you print only fifty books, the typesetting, negatives, and plates cost ten dollars *per book*. The reason for this outsize figure is that the fixed costs (in this case, five hundred dollars) are spread over a very small press run (fifty). Naturally, you are going to print more than fifty books, but the relative smallness of your press run determines the eventual cost to you of each book.

What is the impact of this?

Let's say the complete cost of the token edition is $800, and 200 books are printed. Thus, the cost per book is $4.00. Sometimes, the modest appearance of a token edition precludes selling it for $8.00 which is the least you would have to charge for a book in order to make a profit when the printer receives $4.00 per book. Three reasons you need a large mark-up are (1) the discount you give on copies sold through dealers, (2) your sales cost, and (3) each copy you give away is one less copy you can sell.

A token edition is not to be seen as a profit-making venture in its own right. Its justification is to get immediate public reaction and to attract a publisher to take it on. The undertaking is an investigative expense.

Because your money and energy are involved, you want to settle in your own mind why you are publishing a token edition, what you hope to get out of it, and what steps you intend to take after receipt of your copies. After writing this down, examine it critically a week or so later. Your token edition can become a lever that opens your door into situations you cannot enter by making a personal call or mailing a manuscript copy of your book. Following are true accounts of three authors who published successful token editions.

The first author, a dissident Russian, arrived in New York City with a novel under his arm. He spoke imperfect English, but his novel was written in beautiful, fluent Russian. The book was translated, but, for two years, no publisher made an offer.

The second author, a native American in Oakland, California, loaded his bike onto a plane and flew with it to New Orleans. Arriving there, he began a leisurely adventure following the banks of the Mississippi River northward a thousand miles or more toward its source. He kept a diary.

The third author, living with her family in St. Paul, wrote a novel about a young woman who experienced a strong affection for another woman while at college. Years later, she wanted to meet this woman again to learn if the attraction had cooled or if the relationship still claimed her and perhaps was to contribute to her lifestyle. Several publishers showed interest; none offered a contract.

THE TOKEN EDITION OF VICTOR MURAVIN

In Victor Muravin's novel, a Russian seaman named Vikenty Angarov is framed for a crime he did not commit and serves a long and bitter sentence in Siberia. His punishment over, he returns to his work as a sailor and finds a new life when, suddenly, along with thousands of others, he is hauled back to Siberia because of Stalin's fear of reprisal from men he has unreasonably punished. During his second exile, Vikenty finds himself in a sub-Arctic gold-mining camp. During a blizzard he escapes and, after horrendous adventures, is cared for by some Lapps. After Stalin's death he is pardoned and returns to the sea.

That's the bare bones of the novel. It is a gripping tale with a surprising love interest.

The author is a man with a mission. He wants Americans to know what he knows.

By a turn of circumstance, I became his friend and read his novel, which I thought was superb. One day he asked me for a list of book dealers and jobbers in the New York area, and I sent these to him.

Soon after, he published a token edition. It was regular book size, six by nine inches, 482 pages, and lithographed from pages that had been produced by an electric typewriter. The book was "perfectbound," that is, it opened flat so that it could be read easily. The copy I received carried no price tag.

Victor gave copies to some of his dissident Russian friends and one of them asked a New York woman, Lillian Zelig, who had encouraged a number of Russian artists, to read it. On receiving Victor's token edition, she invited Alvin Garfin, publisher of Newsweek Books, to come to her home and look over her "find." Surprising things happen to token editions. One person reads it, loves it, and starts to push the book—not for any commercial reason, but simply because the book enters that reader's mind and heart.

Was Alvin Garfin a prospective publisher for Victor Muravin's work? Newsweek Books are promoted in *Newsweek* magazine and sold through the newsstands that sell *Newsweek*.

By coincidence, however, on the evening Mrs. Zelig gave Garfin the Muravin novel, he was thinking in terms of issuing some trade books. He took the token edition home to read and entered trade publishing with Victor's book as one of his first titles. *The Diary of Vikenty Angarov* appeared in a well-made, beautiful edition. The reviews were abundant, glowing. The *Washington Post* called it "a record of the price the Russian people paid in wasted lives for 'the triumph of socialism,'" allowing the author's friends to feel the purpose of the book was made clear. The *New Yorker* called Muravin "a strong writer in the middle register, with a calm, camera-eye aplomb that is shatteringly effective." *Publishers Weekly* said the author showed "a compassionate and evocative talent." "Up in Boston," Mr. Garfin told me, "we did have one negative review. The paper said that the Angarov book was a real lemon."

"What did Victor say?"

"I told him about it, and he appeared pleased. In Russia, a lemon is a delicacy. . . ."

Would Victor Muravin's novel have been published, had his token edition never appeared? It's hard to say. The original manuscript gathered a lot of admirers. New York's Russian newspaper published one chapter. Pushcart Press included a section in its annual prize anthology of works of new writers. But up to the appearance of the token edition, no one offered a contract. Sometimes, a token edition has a vigorous life of its own because people like to discover things on their own.

"IF MY TOKEN EDITION SELLS OUT, I CAN ALWAYS PRINT MORE"

Bil Paul is the self-publisher of *Crossing the U.S.A. the Short Way: Bicycling Along the Mississippi River Route*. It has maps, road descriptions, and the author's experiences en route.

This is Bil's fourth bike book. The first three were printed for fun and given away to friends. A few copies were placed on city busses for people to read free. This time, Bil felt he could take the leap into publishing a book by printing a token edition and selling the copies.

The things that make it a "token edition" are its number of pages, sixty-four; its overall size, five by seven inches; press run, six hundred; the elimination of thirty pages of available copy and illustrations to keep the book within sixty-four pages; and holding the front cover to one color. It's a delightful book in every way, and, by making a token edition out of it, Bil could test it in the marketplace without too much cost to himself. The test has been favorable, and Bil may issue a larger edition.

Here's Bil:

You ask: How was the type set for the Mississippi bike book? Simple. On the very typewriter I'm using at this moment. I set the typewriter on "stencil" so that I'm not using the ribbon, and, making sure that the type is very clean and makes uniform impressions, I type *through* an intense carbon paper onto regular typing paper. This is similar to the IBM typing system, where the carbon ribbon is used only one time and makes a clean, sharp, black impression. The disadvantages of my system are that one has to learn to type without seeing the characters popping out in front on paper (because you're typing onto the dark surface of the carbon paper) and one has to type virtually error free (because errors can't be corrected by erasure or correction fluid). But I found this method a beautiful way to go, because there is little expense.

After I typed this material and pasted it into my page layouts, the actual size of each page was reduced at the printers by 30 percent. This made the typing look even sharper and cleaner.

Before shipping the pages off to the printer, I cut out and pasted the typed copy and the halftone prints (Veloxes) onto my layout pages. I produced the halftones in my darkroom by making positive halftone prints directly from 35 millimeter negatives. I placed a special halftone screen about a quarter-inch above high-contrast photographic paper under the enlarger, and then proceeded almost as though I were making a normal print.

278

I used rub-on type for the title on the front cover and for the large inside lettering. The number of type styles available in instant rub-on lettering is incredible.

Some of the captions under the photos are in script. I did it with a goose-quill pen—very simple. I like to introduce a note of something informal—not by machine. Also, it's fun! Doing my own typesetting, artwork and pasteup of the pages saved me three or four dollars a page for each of the sixty-four pages.

The bike book was the first book I've had printed by Braun-Brumfield in Ann Arbor, Michigan. They have a local rep in San Francisco. I sent Braun-Brumfield pasted-up page flats—they did everything else from negative-making to printing and binding. I paid them just over five hundred dollars for 620 books. That makes my cost about 80 cents per book, for the Braun-Brumfield part of the process. They took six weeks for the job. Not being able to communicate face to face can make for confusions and delays. An example with this book was that some of their people may not have dealt with a book that used high-contrast photos to be reproduced as line copy (not halftones).

I think printers who specialize in small press runs keep costs low by combining many small-run books like mine in one operation—and by standardizing on only several kinds of paper.

Self-publishers interested in finding an economical book printer might go to a bookstore that has a shelf of offbeat books. On finding a small-press book with a satisfactory quality in its printing and binding, write to the press and ask where the book was printed or for any other advice you need. Small-press people are a close-knit group and helpful.

My first thought was not to use a heavy paper cover on the bike book. Then I changed my mind when I found that it wouldn't raise costs much, that it would help protect the inside of the book, and that stores would be more willing to sell it. For the front cover I tried to produce something attractive that explained quickly what the book was about.

The size of the book was selected from one of Braun-Brumfield's standard sizes (five by seven). Incidentally, a printer can't add or subtract one, two, three, four, or five pages from the book. He usually works in increments of sixteen pages—sometimes eight—so your book has to be something like sixty-four, eighty, or ninety-six pages—a number divisible by sixteen. It's important to emphasize to self-publishers not to go ahead with designing a book until they've found a printer and can work out the size, number of pages, binding, and mechanical details beforehand.

My retail price is $3.50. I didn't sit down with a calculator in the late evening hours agonizing over price. I selected it from a combination of gut feeling (comparing my price with other comparable books) and realizing that I might be selling some of the books to wholesalers for a 50 percent discount. I also had to give myself latitude for sales and advertising costs.

If I sell every book I will make a profit and pay for my bike trip. The killer is that publishing so few books makes the cost per book rather high. Postage for mailing books and the price of mailers also make costs jump. My token edition is similar to a market test.

I hope a regular royalty publisher will buy it. Recently I sent out a test mailing of brochures to about fifty midwest bike shops (I got the addresses from my downtown public-library collection of telephone-book yellow-page sections from big cities). Reaction to that mailing was very good, and I went on to mail to another eighty shops. I received orders from 7 percent of the total mailing—considered an excellent return.

Interestingly, I'm getting a fair amount of orders from my having listed the book with Bowker and their International Standard Book Number system (ISBN). They put it on their vertical-file index, listing my book as a pamphlet. Public and school libraries from the Midwest have been ordering from this listing. I have also placed my book with some bike-book distributors (who themselves sell directly to the public). One has reordered, making me happy.

It should be emphasized that one should go the full route by listing with Bowker and getting an ISBN number (it's free) and getting a copyright and Library of Congress catalogue card number. My library orders as a result of the Bowker listing were really unexpected. I should say also that, if I had to do it again, I'd perfect-bind my book, because then it would be listed as a book proper and not as a pamphlet.

I've had poor luck trying to get reviews. In La Crosse, Wisconsin, where my bike trip ended, the *La Crosse Tribune* reviewed the book but didn't say how people could order it. The national bicycling magazines didn't give me a review even though I advertised with them. Maybe they still will. One can put only so much energy into requesting reviews.

In the largest-selling bike magazine, *Bicycling*, I ran a display ad and a classified ad later. I came close, but I didn't sell enough through them to pay for the ads. The number-two magazine, *Bike World*, has lower rates, and, through them, I made a profit with classified ads. My book is selling mainly in the upper Midwest states and in Louisiana, so national ads aren't too practical. That's why I'm trying the bike-store route. I don't like to sell face to face to people but I love the mail-order route. At this point I've sold half of my books and given away forty.

You asked if any woman noticed the sentence in my book that next time I'd like a companion. Not yet.

It's gratifying to realize that some cyclists will be bicycling the Mississippi this summer because of my book. I got my first feedback letter from a person who was following my route.

I'm hoping one of the major bike manufacturers will take the book on and distribute it, because it contributes to bicycle touring. A token edition gets to the attention of these manufacturers better than a manuscript with loose photographs.

The book has been a rewarding experience. All of us self-publishers feel as if we have children when we finish and distribute our books.

To order a copy of Bil Paul's book, the address is P.O. Box 5530, San Francisco, CA 94101. The price is $3.50.

NOT MONEY, BUT COURAGE

Madge Reinhardt's first novel, *You've Got to Ride the Subway*, sheds light on the human condition, and, since that was the author's goal, it looks like a worthwhile undertaking. It took courage on Madge's part to write this novel, because there are always people who wonder out loud how autobiographical a book might be.

Chris, who is the protagonist of *You've Got to Ride the Subway*, is a small-town Minnesota woman with a husband and several children. A pull toward other women stirs within her. Chris's feelings are not especially sexual. More to the point, she feels that a woman has a charisma that many men lack. It isn't the possibility of the sex act with the other women that attracts Chris but the femaleness and the body chemistry.

THE BOOK MARKET

There are some scenes in a lesbian bar that are revealing of Chris and, by the same token, of all of us. I haven't read much better copy. The novel ends, partly unresolved and without a sunset. Chris returns home, hauling her problems with her, but more relaxed and mature because of her family's understanding and her own honesty.

Madge Reinhardt, like Chris, is her own woman, and her first novel is as much a part of her as her own body. If a large publisher wanted to bring out *You've Got to Ride the Subway*, I suspect Madge would smile pleasantly and say, "No, thanks." But then, you never know. She might accept so she could give more time to her next book!

Here's Madge herself telling how she goes about the day-to-day work of being a self-publisher.

I grind out my own books in my basement on a hand-cranked A.B. Dick mimeograph. I use a good grade paper—A.B. Dick's best vellum, because my operation, using my own labor, is so cheap that I can afford the best paper of its kind. *Subway* is done on "India Color," a tinted, opaque paper that doesn't allow printing on the other side to show through. That's the main problem with cheap mimeograph paper. I am able to print four pages on one sheet. Then I fold each sheet, and put six sheets (twenty-four pages) together to make one signature. To hold the signatures together, I sew them by hand. I collect enough signatures to make one book and put them into a "press," fold-side down, and leave them overnight to press together. Next morning, I turn them so the folds are on top and glue them together with Elmer's glue, and I glue a strip of heavy cloth to the spine.

For my cloth-bound copies (using wallpaper glue or rubber cement) I cement several sheets of soapbox or cereal-box board together and then glue a blue-denim cloth over the boards. I cement in tan endpapers with rubber cement. After the books are printed and bound, I carry them to our family room, where my husband sets up some weights to hold the books together tightly for a day or two. Each time I get an order for twenty-five copies, it's the millennium.

Bit by bit, I'm finding my own particular audience. This is no operation where books are placed in bookstores throughout the country simultaneously and then withdrawn in four months and pulped if they aren't selling. This is a gradual discovery of an audience—the opposite of the necessary method of operation of a commercial publisher.

My distribution is through building up a direct-mail list and through reviews, and through listings in such standard places as Bowker's bibliographics *(Books in Print,* and so forth), *Small Press Record of Books,* Elliott Shore's *Task Force on Alternatives in Print,* at Temple University in Philadelphia, *Publishers Weekly, Weekly Record,* and *Wilson's Cumulative Index.* And I have publicized through mailings to church workers of my denomination and to a mailing list of gay organizations, which I rented from Resources (Box 134, Harvard Square, Cambridge, MA 02138). Resources has all kinds of lists, incidentally.

My book is displayed on the COSMEP* van and at book fairs, such as the New York City and San Francisco October fairs, and the November BooksWest Fair in L.A., and an annual fair in St. Paul sponsored by five small private colleges in the Twin Cities. I am also a member of Western Independent Publishers (San Francisco) and sell some copies through their catalogue and warehouse.

The national magazine *Ms.* (paid circulation 514,000) wrote for a review copy of *Subway.* Ingram phoned me for a copy, but I didn't send it. If they ordered one thousand books, it would snow us in. Selling eight books a week keeps me afloat.

My experience with the establishment press was as follows: I rewrote a book-length manuscript for an editor in a major house, and they kept the manuscript for nine months—sufficient time, if I recall correctly, to give birth to an entire baby. The pregnant period was spiced with encouraging letters from the editor: "We like it," "We're keeping it for more readings," and so forth. When, after nine months, I asked for a decision, the manuscript was returned. I consulted a literary agent, who told me the book was too "literary." ("People aren't reading literary stuff anymore.") He also informed me that the book didn't shoot for a definite mass audience because it had a little religious searching in it and a little sex in it, and never should those twain meet in any way that might offend religious people or bore sophisticates with existential issues. The

---

*Several small-press publishers' organizations, including COSMEP, have merged into Western Independent Publishers (P.O. Box 31249, San Francisco, CA 94131).

point, he stated, was that religious people don't believe in sex, and sexed-up people don't believe in God.

Some of us could have gotten accepted if we'd said something different from what we meant to say. Commercialism seems to need either a salable name or else a distinct category that has instant mass appeal. This leaves little room for experimentation or even for prophecy. We independents are free to publish junk, but we're also free to experiment in a way that may rise above the things that are commercially published by the conglomerates, who are not always literary in their basic motivation.

Is there a precedent in history for self-publishing? Well, here are a few people who self-published at least some of their work: Walt Whitman, Upton Sinclair, Edgar Allan Poe, Mark Twain, Lord Byron, Virginia Woolf, Carl Sandburg, Ezra Pound, D.H. Lawrence, Edgar Rice Burroughs, Anaïs Nin, Rod McKuen, Eugene O'Neill, Zane Grey, Rudyard Kipling, George Bernard Shaw, Theodore Dreiser, and T.S. Eliot. Well-known, self-published work includes *Leaves of Grass, The Rubaiyat, Huckleberry Finn, Lady Chatterley's Lover,* and *Robert's Rules of Order.* James Joyce's *Ulysses* was published at the expense of a friend of Joyce's, and Joyce helped in distributing, packaging, and mailing the books.

The small-publisher tradition is one that I'm willing to follow.

Madge Reinhardt's print job of her first novel is just what she describes—a home-made product by an ingenious woman. Although I have never met Madge, she won our love and respect for her publishing attitude and for the contents of *You've Got to Ride the Subway.* The book may be ordered from the author's Back Row Press (1803 Venus Ave., St. Paul, MN 55112). The cloth-bound edition is $8.95; the paperback, $5.50.

If a token edition is such a good idea, and you go ahead and publish one, what do you do with your copies when your printer loads you down with three hundred of them? Dazed, but game, you hand over $850 and start to drive home . . . very carefully.

Here are some things you might do with the books.

1. Send complimentary copies to review editors of all the newspapers in your area, and to regional and national magazines whose book-review

columns include reviews of subject matter similar to yours.

2. If you would like a grant, offer your book as evidence, in a grant proposal, to allow you to do more of the same thing. Any city library has copies of *National Directory of Grants and Aid to Individuals in the Arts,* or *National Directory of Arts Support by Private Foundations.*

3. Now is the time to find out if book dealers will sell your token edition. Show it to them and put the question yourself. Offer 40 percent discount off the list price. Put a list price on the front cover.

4. If your book has special outlets, as Bil Paul's bike book does, make a few personal calls, and, when you understand the best pitch to make, try a mailing to fifty such special outlets.

5. If you think a royalty publisher might want to take it on, look into *Literary Market Place* and *Writer's Market,* using the current editions. A morning's work may supply you with more than a dozen leads.

6. Mail a dozen copies to well-placed people in the field of your book and ask for their comments. Study your replies; then try another two dozen copies with perhaps some changes in your accompanying letter. Now you have testimonials.

7. Draw up a list of interested people who you think might buy a copy. Can you locate fifty, a hundred, two hundred? Send each a letter with an order blank, circular, and a return envelope, and enclose a few quotes from your testimonials.

8. A pause for a short ego trip. (You earned it.) Send complimentary copies to some hard-bitten locals along with a personal letter.

9. Would any trade paper be interested in your book? Can you locate the particular person at that trade paper who might do the write-up about your book and address your copy to that individual? Try to put the lead in his hand. With the right lead, it's already easy for a journalist to do a story.

10. There is a passel of publicity news stories in almost any token edition. First, there is the suburban paper. Consider the local editor's point of view. How many of his readers published a book that day? You're news. Send a suggested news story with your book. You can't expect the reporter who may be given your book to spend several hours reading it. Make it easy for him.

11. How many people, places, and activities mentioned in your book will benefit from what you published? Are there publications with columns or departments that have enough interest in this to mention the

connection between your book and their own field of interest?

12. The last idea concerns luck. You want to make your own. The main idea of a token edition, if you want a regular publisher to take it on, is to place your book in the hands of people who will help you because they believe in your book. What if Victor Muravin's token edition had never reached Lillian Zelig or Alvin Garfin of Newsweek Books? Victor's faith would have been undimmed. He would have kept on placing his book in the pathway of people who had reason to know that what he said was worth the coinage. Alvin said jokingly that the book had a cast of thousands. It attracted a score of friends in high places, but there were ten times that many more who would have worked for the book, had they seen the token edition. For instance, I felt that it would make a great motion picture and made a few phone calls to help it get a reading.

Bil Paul's book, if placed near the right watering hole, will attract a bicycle manufacturer, or a large regional bike jobber, or the owner of a chain of bike stores, or a mail-order-catalogue company that specializes in bike supplies. Then it will give Bil the jackpot he deserves for a straight-shooting book that makes anyone feel good just to read it.

Madge's novel could light up the late-late TV hour and attract a 10 million audience for a credit-company sponsor that wants to specialize in credit cards for women.

Now take your own book. If it's first class, and you've made it as good as you know how, create your own luck by making it available to the kind of person who has influence and will find your work a natural outgrowth of his (or her) own intellectuality.

21

Three Case Histories

THE SUNSHINE BOOKS

Beverly Nye had never written a book nor been in any part of the publishing business. Encouraged by a friend, she wrote her first book. It took six months. As of this moment, it has sold 117,000 copies.

The idea for the book came from Elaine Cannon, feature writer for the *Salt Lake Tribune*. She suggested using the mimeographed notes Beverly prepared for her homemaking classes as a basis for a book. "You're missing the boat," Elaine told her friend. "Your material is much too good to go to waste."

I'm not a literary person [said Beverly Nye] and I wasn't sure what to do next. I wrote up some of my notes and showed this to a book publisher in Salt Lake City, who suggested I finish the book, have it printed, and sell it to my classes.

While I was writing the book, my husband was transferred to Cleveland, and so I finished my book there and took the manuscript to a printer and asked if he could print it. He said yes, and I signed a contract to buy fifteen hundred copies of a paperback book, five by eight, 106 pages, for three thousand dollars. I didn't read the contract too carefully, I was just glad to get under way. That's how I became a self-publisher. At the time, the term was unfamiliar to me, as were most terms in book publishing.

THE BOOK MARKET

Just before my book was published, I bought a thirty-day Greyhound bus ticket and prepared to board the bus with my teenage daughter. My idea was to visit five cities where I had lived and was familiar with Mormon church groups and home-extension classes. I thought I would give homemaking demonstrations, offer recipes, tips, and suggestions for homemaking, and then sell my book. The title was A *Family Raised on Sunshine*, the price, $4.95. The books were supposed to go on the bus with us, but they weren't ready, so we set out anyway, and the books caught up with us in Kansas City. I remember ripping open a big case and taking out my first book. There seemed to be an awful lot of them. I had the feeling that they would be growing moss in my cellar when I was ninety-two.

To bring an audience together for my homemaking lecture, I published a one-column-by-five-inch ad in the local paper of each city we visited and printed handbills, which the church people and the home-extension people passed out to their friends. A modest fee was charged to attend the lecture, and I was allowed to keep what was left after paying for the rental of a hall. After my lecture, I offered my books to the ladies, and usually more than half the people there bought copies.

Twenty years' experience with homemaking classes was behind me, but I had never sold my own book or any other book, and it was an exhilarating experience.

By the time my Greyhound pass expired and my daughter and I were on the way home, our fifteen hundred books were almost sold, and I dared myself to order five thousand more.

Back home in Cleveland, my son suggested that I try to get on a television show and demonstrate homemaking ideas and mention my book. We took turns calling the stations in Cleveland, telling about the book and what I had been doing and asking if I could appear on a show. Most everyone said no. Finally, one station, WEWS, whose popular program *Morning Exchange* was the one I most wanted to be on, said, "Well, all right, we'll give you seven minutes at the end of the show." I went on for the full seven minutes, demonstrated some homemaking ideas, and offered free recipes, tips, and ideas to anyone who wrote in.

Within a week, WEWS received five thousand inquiries. They phoned and said, "Come back any time you like." Shortly after, my husband was transferred to Cincinnati, but I still return to WEWS and do talk shows on homemaking.

There's one little thing Beverly left out when she first told me her story. The oversight had to do with the action she took *before* going on WEWS. Ray Nye, Beverly's husband, supervises a group of insurance salesmen for the Reliance Insurance Company, and I suspect Beverly must have picked up by osmosis exactly how to sell. Whether it had all come from dinner-table conversations about what some insurance salesman should have done but didn't, and what her husband told him to do next time, is something no one but a marriage counselor would ever find out. In any event, Beverly did the right thing before going on WEWS.

She went through the yellow pages of the Cleveland telephone directory and located a category headed "Book Dealers—Retail." Writing down the name of each on a card, she divided them into geographical location and proceeded to call on the stores, phoning ahead to get the names of the buyers. Beverly explained she was going to be on the WEWS program *Morning Exchange* for seven minutes and showed the buyer a copy of her book. Her son accompanied her on the first few calls and then began making some by himself, while Beverly, striking out alone, took a stack of calls too. Together, they cased the town.

"No one bought a lot of books," she says. "Three here, six there, once in a while twelve. They all warned us the books would be returned if they didn't sell, but, all in all, more than half the bookstores in the city had some copies before I went on WEWS."

And it was a good thing.

The day after Beverly hit the air waves, the ladies in Cleveland, Ohio, who wanted to be Beverly's kind of homemaker hit the bookstores. The Walden store on the West Side sold a thousand books. The manager said: "For a week, one customer out of four bought A *Family Raised on Sunshine*." Did that cause the other Walden stores around the country to jump in and order? Not at all. The home office looked on their Cleveland experience as a local matter. No one was asking for A *Family*

THE BOOK MARKET

Raised on Sunshine in Oakland, or Fort Worth, or in three hundred other cities. Who was Beverly Nye? A local homemaker raised up from obscurity by a TV program. If Beverly were to appear on another TV station, with a good spot on a popular program, the chain bookstores in that city would be sure to order. Till then, see you later.

None of this bothered Beverly. A well-composed, religious person, with few materialistic itches, she kept her faith up as sales quieted down. Mr. Nye was transferred again, his fifth move in fifteen years, and the family moved to Cincinnati. After buying a home and settling down, Beverly called on the bishop of the Mormon church, a gentleman named Wallace, who had come to F & W Publishing Company as a market manager from Procter and Gamble, the soap, coffee, and diaper people. During her conversation with Mr. Wallace, Beverly showed him a copy of her book, saying modestly that she had printed it herself and might be needing more copies, having now sold twelve thousand. "Budge" Wallace heard her out, and, being new on the job, but sensing that *Sunshine* was a publishing property, he asked Richard Rosenthal, president of F & W, to look at *Sunshine* and asked Mrs. Nye to relate her experience. Richard, to his credit, remained standing, although his eyes, the story goes, blinked. A contract was offered. Mrs. Nye signed, and one year later the book, now in its eighth edition, had sold 117,000 copies, and was headed toward a half-million.

As is true of many books accepted by any publisher, this particular one did not find instant approval from the entire staff. One staffer found some recipes rather heavy on cream, butter, sugar. Another wondered whether religious overtones surfaced and if this were acceptable in a book on homemaking. Later, it turned out that one group of bookstores, associated with Evangelical Protestant thinking, refused to rent a list of its member stores to be circularized by the publisher. Some individual stores in the group, however, did stock the book.

A third staffer said the book needed copy editing and the typography of the original book was less than perfect and suggested resetting the book. The difference of opinion was settled when the publisher and the market manager opted for using the book, "as is," with minor resetting. The irrefutable evidence of a self-publisher's selling twelve thousand books on her own seemed like a pretty good omen and F & W moved ahead with *Sunshine.* As soon as book production was ready to begin, an interesting

290

development surfaced. The printer of the original edition agreed that the copyright belonged to the author but claimed the negatives and plates were his physical property. As a result, a new set of negatives was made from the printed pages of the original edition, and new printing plates, in turn, were made from these.

Commenting on this matter, Mrs. Nye said, "The original printer had the impression, probably because I was neither too careful nor too aware of the contract I signed, that the plates belonged to him. Although I paid for them, he was convinced they were his property." If you self-publish, your contract should state who owns the physical material from which the book is manufactured: color separations, negatives, plates, tapes, art, design, graphics. There is no hard-and-fast rule about who owns what, but it can be to your advantage to own outright all the materials from which your book is made.

In its approach to selling *Sunshine*, F & W took the position that *Sunshine* was the love child of Beverly Nye, and sales would promptly appear in the wake of her future TV appearances. Mr. Wallace wrote to me:

> The success of *A Family Raised on Sunshine* is Beverly Nye. Where Bev Nye has been exposed via TV, radio and lectures, the book is selling well. Where she has had no exposure, the book is not moving. She is unusually good on TV and has a natural way of promoting her book as she does a show. In our city, she has been on the *Bob Braun Show* on a weekly basis for the past five months.
>
> We have tried to maximize her exposure by working with a publicity firm in New York. Several weeks before Bev is scheduled to be in a city, we call our sales representatives, and they call on the major accounts and wholesalers to make sure the books are in stock. We also follow up by telephone to see how the books are moving and to get reorders. This is the first time I used the telephone to this extent, and it seems to be working effectively. Jeff Lapin has been supervising the day-to-day details on this project.

The man who handles the details, Jeff Lapin, was introduced to book publishing through calling on wholesalers. While nosing around the offices of Ingram, the large wholesaler, he learned that for the modest fee of $450 a week, the forty people at the Ingram order desk would be supplied with a brief sales pitch, focusing on one book. This sales pitch was given to the dealer after his order had been written down: "Thanks, Mr. Herbert, for your nice order. I'll see it gets shipped early tomorrow, and we'll pack it carefully. Incidentally, we have something new you might want to order. . . ." Then followed a sentence or two about a particular book.

Jeff recommended that F & W take the $450 gamble and Ingram accepted *Sunshine* as the book that would be plugged on the order desk one week. At that time, three hundred copies of *Sunshine* were being purchased by Ingram each week. During that one week, when forty people on the order desk plugged it, nineteen hundred copies were sold; the following week, seven hundred.

As a self-publisher, or a small publisher, you may want to know what it takes to have a book of your own placed into the sweet-talking mouths of forty order takers of a wholesaler. The cost of 450 bucks a week is not the half of it. You will be asked: Do you have four thousand books on hand to deliver promptly? If word of mouth keeps your book moving, as it did *Sunshine*, can you get delivery of five thousand more inside of three weeks? If you can answer yes to the above, the main question follows: does your book have wide sales appeal? Indeed the order desk can sell almost any book, but will the public buy that book from the dealer? If they don't, the wholesaler gets the books back! And next time, the dealer won't be so quick to listen and to buy. And the wholesaler will ask: what will you do to encourage the public to enter bookstores and ask for your book? Just being one title among three thousand others stacked on the shelves isn't enough.

The fee of $450 a week is subject to change depending on the season, the wholesaler, the number of people on the phone desk. More publishers apply for this service in the autumn and winter months than in July or August. The ploy works well for some books, not for all. Why not for all? It could be the sales pitch itself, the timing, or connotations that the title brings to the dealer's mind—of a couple of losers with titles that sound just like this one. If you have a book already in five hundred stores, with a proven batch of reorders, all recent, and your sales curve is rising, the person to write to at Ingram is Art Carson. As the wholesaler sees it, the gamble is not yours, but his. He is the one who takes the rap if the book doesn't move after the dealer buys it from him. So the jobber is highly selective.

A three-dollar retail price will work against a book offered to a wholesaler for this kind of promotion, as the jobber's gross profit per book is under 40 cents.

This type of jobber-publisher promotion is relatively recent, and, in our next edition, we will report on additional jobbers who offer it.

Like all true stories with a happy ending, this one about Beverly Nye just keeps on going. One year after *Sunshine* became a national bestseller, she completed her second book, *A Family Raised on Rainbows*. The initial print order was thirty thousand, and the week the books were delivered, F & W had orders for twenty thousand books. *Rainbow* seems likely to break into six figures at the end of one year.

The tidbit nobody expected came from radio station WLW's Bob Braun, who suggested that Beverly tape a five-day, thirteen-week series. Beverly wrote her own script and taped sixty-five shows (five days by thirteen weeks), three-and-a-half to five minutes each, open end. WLW offered the open-end series (advertising could be inserted at the beginning and at the end) to radio stations across the country at five hundred dollars for the sixty-five-show package.

Who gets a royalty on each syndicated package sold?

And whose books get a little plug here and there?

You may wonder to yourself, as I did, how many women in this world who are unknown, unsung, and without previous writing and publishing experience, could duplicate Beverly's experience? I think that there must be several score and that most of them would be great at anything they did. I don't think money means all that much to the Nye family, as Ray is young, healthy, and a good wage-earner with a fine career behind him and a long one still ahead. What matters most, I suspect, is the outpouring of love from Beverly in her TV appearances and the response that came from her audience.

Beverly's two books continue to be a family affair, and that's the way she and Ray like it. Her daughter helped type both books. Now that fan mail is heavy from various TV shows and from the radio stations that bought the thirteen-week syndicate rights, the kids help sort and keep records on the fan mail.

Between her TV appearances and her radio plugs, *Sunshine* and

Rainbows will surely sell six hundred thousand copies within five years. I asked Beverly if the big newspapers and magazines had reviewed either book. What did the *New York Times*, the *Washington Post*, *Cosmopolitan*, or *Time* have to say?

"Nothing," said Beverly. "They haven't heard about it yet, I guess."

"SMALL-TIME OPERATOR"

Few people would have thought Bernard Kamoroff would ever be a writer, let alone a successful self-published writer. A certified public accountant, balancing someone else's books, poring over ledgers, and filling out tax forms, he awoke to the day when he had his fill. Retiring to the small northern-California hamlet of Laytonville, he grew a beard, dressed in denim, and began to relax and enjoy the scene. The CPA in him, however, melted but slowly, and Kamoroff found himself looking about for a means of maintaining his self-esteem while doing something that came naturally.

This turned out to be writing a book originally titled *How to Be a Small-Time Operator and Stay Out of Trouble*. Feisty, determined, confident, Kamoroff may have surprised the world, but not himself, by watching his firstborn gross three hundred thousand dollars, the first four years, on sixty-two-thousand sales.

After deducting living expenses in Laytonville, Kamoroff finds himself ready to launch a small publishing business and has two new titles coming up. Is he really smart and talented, a fine writer, a great salesman? Or, is his charm the ability to express simply what other people want to know? Or both? See what you think. Here is his story.

Small-Time Operator was my first attempt at writing. I had a lot of business experience as a CPA, helping novice businesspeople get started. From ten years of dealing with these people, I learned how to explain technical stuff in everyday English. I acquired my writing skills from composing long letters to distant girl friends.

The clarity of my book was greatly enhanced by my long-time friend, a university English teacher, who had no business experience (and no editing experience, either). He'd read a sentence and tell me he didn't understand it, or he wasn't sure if I meant this or that. The sentence would be rewritten. We'd argue for hours over a word or phrase.

It took almost three years of research, writing, giving up on it, dusting it off again for more work, packing it away to build my house, digging it out once again, rewriting and rewriting some more before I finally declared it "done." I wasn't going to write one more word.

From its inception, my book was a complete concept. Physically it had a large-format, magazine-type layout. There was plenty of informality (this book and a sharp pencil are all you need to keep track of your business for a year), and samples of different kinds of ledgers. I figured it would be fun this way and make me more money. (It was and it did.)

When the manuscript was in the early stages, I wrote Doubleday, told them my ideas about the book, and asked if they were interested. No. They thought it might make a good magazine article. Another New York publisher wrote to say the market was supersaturated with start-your-own-business books.

A small California publisher agreed to publish the book but then realized he didn't have the money (and shortly thereafter realized he didn't have the energy, and quit publishing altogether).

A friend, however, convinced me to publish the book myself: do it the way I wanted it done, keep control, and keep all the profits, too. He introduced me to his printer's rep (from Braun-Brumfield, in Ann Arbor) and to his one-and-only distributor (Bookpeople, in Berkeley) and convinced me there was nothing to it. Well, as you know, there's quite a bit more than nothing-to-it, but I've been a do-it-myselfer since grade school, so I thought being a self-publisher was a natural.

No one except my English-teacher friend and my typesetter read the entire manuscript. A lawyer helped with the corporation chapter; my insurance agent helped with the insurance chapter; an accountant looked over the tax and employment sections.

The first printing of five thousand copies cost eight thousand dollars, three thousand dollars for prepress preparation—design, editing, typesetting, paste-up, illustrations, and cover—and five thousand dollars to the printer. The book was printed by Braun-Brumfield on a sheet-fed offset press. I sent them camera-ready copy. From that, B-B printed and bound the book—eight-and-a-half by eleven, 192 pages, three-color, coated cover—shrink-wrapped, boxed, and shipped to California for a dollar a copy (November 1976—today, it would cost about $1.50 a copy).

I raised the money from friends and relatives (seven people), offered them a percentage of the profits if there were any, zip if the book went bust. My agreement with all of them was for two printings only; after that, the book was 100 percent mine.

At first, I sent out only a handful of review copies. One of my review copies, a Xerox of the camera-ready material, went to *Library Journal* and resulted in a beautiful review. At the same time, the *San Francisco Sunday Examiner* (largest circulation in northern California) did a feature story on me and the book—I talked my way into their office and talked the editor into it. Between these two gold mines, I sold out the first printing in just a few weeks.

That was in November 1976, and sales have been great ever since. The book has now been reviewed in thirty publications—most of them found me and wrote requesting copies; anyone who asked for a review copy got one. The book is being constantly updated, so I continue to send out review copies. Word of mouth, however, has probably been responsible for most of my sales (other than to libraries), especially sales to various business and professional organizations.

At the start, I dealt exclusively with Bookpeople, Inc. (2940 Seventh St., Berkeley, CA 94710). They were my only wholesaler to bookstores for a year and a half. I slowly expanded to other small distributors/ wholesalers (and eventually to Ingram and Baker & Taylor as well). Ingram carries one thousand copies of my book in their warehouses (there are three) and sells four thousand copies a year to bookstores. Their best sales for my book are in the spring. I now work with about a dozen wholesalers.

I also have the same number of mail-order distributors and a rep who sells books to stationery stores. For me, these are specialty outlets since that's where small-business people buy supplies. Most of my distributors contacted me. Two small book clubs also picked up the book, both resulting in only a few sales.

In June 1980, the book went into its ninth printing with sixty-two thousand copies sold and sixty-eight thousand copies in print. It earns me a living up here in the wilds of Northern California where jobs are scarce. I don't have my "spring list," which I push like hell for six months, and then drop in order to push my "fall list." For four years I worked one book, my own.

Publishing, including self-publishing, is also "show business"; there is something slightly magical about it, and it draws people. The most fun I've had in publishing is meeting a lot of people, all of them happy to meet me. It's not the same thing as, say, owning a grocery store and hiring clerks and stockboys to work for you. Not the same thing at all.

Sometimes a self-publisher is invited by a large Eastern publisher to allow the latter to lease complete national distribution rights. It looks wonderful. There you are: collecting royalties, no more clerical details, no selling or financing. I find this kind of distribution arrangement is very limiting for someone like me. The big publishers demand exclusive distribution rights and then you are at their mercy and their whim, and bound by their energy, and their reps' interest in *your* book. And you are certainly lowest man on the totem pole when their own new fall line comes off the press.

I subscribe to lots of periodicals—*Publishers Weekly* and a half-dozen business magazines mostly—and I comb every issue for likely leads. Leafing through them, I look for someone who might want a review copy, someone who's running an entrepreneur-type organization, a likely mail-order operator, a new business school or seminar, a banker who advises small business. I write to all these people and offer complimentary review copies if they're interested. Occasionally, I just mail them copies cold.

It's obviously a slow process, but it all adds up, and it never requires a lot of my time.

My outfit, Bell Springs Publishing, is a one-person operation. I spend ten to twenty hours a week filling orders, posting books, doing promotion and seeking new sales, keeping track of inventories—who's not paying his bills, juggling the bank account. I exhibit at the ABA Convention every year—the only business travel I do. I occasionally do a radio talk show if I'm in the city. And every year I completely update the book for changes in tax laws, SBA loan rates, and so forth. The book is always current.

Bell Springs's second book, now being written (co-authored by me), is "We Own It: Starting and Operating Cooperatives, Collectives, and Other Employee-Owned Businesses, A Practical Manual." Publication probably next year. My third book, as yet untitled, is about starting and running partnerships, which I'm also helping to write, and I plan to keep both of them current, too.

THE BOOK MARKET

Small-Time Operator *is available, postpaid for $8.50 (Bell Springs Publishing, P.O. Box 640, Laytonville, CA 95454).*

TAKE A REFRESHING DIP

If you ever ran a church social, you know a few of the things that happen to people. Mrs. Benson agrees to lend her silver tea service, a thing of grace and beauty. On the afternoon of the event, she delivers it to the church-social chairman . . . only to be informed that someone else will pour.

She takes her tea service back home.

The town's famed pastry cook, who made the luscious raisin-chocolate-nut cookies last year that sold out at 60 cents each, refused to make even one this year, because the church-social chairman wanted the recipe included with each cookie.

Ever heard of a temple or church self-publishing a book? And running it by committees with zero publishing experience? What would you say the odds were of such an experiment working?

The self-published book that I am documenting came into being when a temple Sisterhood board wanted to raise a little money, and, to perform this task, the ways-and-means committee needed a project. The executive committee was consulted and replied: "Print a cookbook," a pretty commonplace decision in women's organizations, as more than two hundred cookbooks are printed annually by local groups.

Having given themselves a purpose (to raise money) and a direction (printing a cookbook), the women went to work with a will. The project started when the president of the Sisterhood, Joan Goldsmith, placed a notice in a local paper: "We are planning to print a cookbook. If you think you can help, give us a call."

Six women phoned and asked, "What can I do?"

In women's organizations, the standard reply is: "Come to a meeting." At the first meeting, Joan asked: "If we actually do a cookbook, what direction should it take?"

The ways-and-means chairwoman answered: "The church cookbooks I've seen seem to take the same route. Everybody is asked for a favorite

298

recipe. But, when this is printed, it doesn't give a cookbook unity, and there isn't any real theme. Can we improve on this?"

One of the women present, Barbara Rosenberg, agreed: "I have been giving cooking classes for several years, and even some of the good cookbooks I recommend don't have a theme—something that is theirs alone."

"What do you think we should do?" Barbara was asked.

"In my cooking classes, I ask for suggestions for the next semester. The most frequent request is for appetizers, party starters, hors d'oeuvres."

Another lady said she had fourteen cookbooks, but appetizer recipes were hard to come by.

Barbara looked around her, paused, and said, "I think we can print a cookbook about appetizers."

"Hey!" called out one woman, a free-lance writer, Jean Chimsky, "I've got a title: 'In the Beginning.'"

And so it was.

The first two questions were: (1) Should it be a Jewish cookbook? (2) If we are doing this to make money, shouldn't we make our book attractive beyond our membership? Should our book have an international, universal appeal?

The questions touch on the essence of book publishing: Should a book be parochial? Should it reach out to the national market? How can it be made universal?

Another woman, whose name was lost in the minutes, asked: "Does everyone send in her favorite recipe, and all we do is print it, or do we do something different?"

The first decision was to do what everyone at the meeting wanted to do: print something unique—something not found on the shelves of stores, and that led into the idea of an hors d'oeuvre cookbook. To make the book "special," they decided to deal with a cookbook fact: Most recipes are adaptations of a basic formula. There is hardly a truly original recipe. Take the old Jewish standby of matzo balls that float in chicken soup. The "secret" of the float is in adding ingredients with a specific gravity of less than one (water). Eggs are separated into yolks and whites, and the whites are whipped as one means of getting air into the batter mix. Using less matzo meal per ball, as opposed to using a lot, is also part of the standard method. All this was discussed sagely, cryptically, and with authority. The uniqueness of a matzo-ball recipe, it was agreed, was in its proportions.

Having reached one unanimous agreement—that all recipes are adaptations of a basic formula—the ladies present regarded one another favorably and decided to work together. The next decision was easy as well as vital: to accept some, not all, recipes submitted, and to allow the editors of the cookbook the privilege of alteration to create a unity of direction.

Recalling the first steps, Barbara Rosenberg says: "When we sent our letters for best recipes for hors d'oeuvres and soup, we got many similar ones, but the charm was we didn't have to choose between yours and mine."

Although a page in the front of the book makes acknowledgment to each of the 125 local cooks who submitted recipes, no recipe is signed. There were two reasons for this: "If a mistake were made, the cook who was misquoted would raise hell; also, a person who bought the book and read it would say: 'This isn't Jane's recipe—it's my mother's.'"

Barbara adds, "We wanted the book to be salable everywhere. If the recipes were signed by a lot of names no one ever heard of, it would be hokey. Right then and there, I really believed I could sell this book if it were all we wanted it to be."

I asked Barbara if she had selling experience. "Sometimes I help out at my husband's furniture store in Kentucky, and I can usually keep a customer talking until they can get a salesman."

Did this lack of experience enter her mind as being a block? Let's hear what Barbara has to say:

No, because, initially, we had only two ideas to sell our cookbook. Send a letter to our Sisterhood members, and call on local bookstores. Our first letter would make a prepublication offer of the book for $4.50 instead of $5.50. For promotion, all we had in mind was to place a coupon in the book to make it easy for people to buy extra copies for gifts if they liked what they read. As for style, we went for art déco, which to me means sort of gingerbready and the opposite of stark.

Editorially, the big thing was our decision to edit the recipes, since they were not signed. So the editing errors rested on our shoulders, not on the cooks who sent in their recipes. Our goal, of course, wasn't to change the recipe, that is to change one cup of flour to one and a half, or to add raisins instead of nuts, but to give the book a consistency in reading style so it didn't look as though 125 women had sent in separate recipes written in 125 different conversational styles. We wanted the directions so simplified that a rank amateur would have success with the same recipes that would also appeal to a creative cook.

In physically producing the book, our first decision was to have it set in real type, instead of having the material typed on an IBM carbon-ribbon typewriter. The latter was less expensive, and our committee members could have done the typing, but the book would have looked *heimgemacht*—home-made—and not like a real book taken off the shelves of a bookstore. We were after that kind of dignity in appearance.

To save costs, we did our own proofreading and our own paste-ups of the pages. Two hundred pages of typeset material would have cost about ten dollars a page, but we shopped around and found a small typesetting plant that was "slow in summer" but still wanted to keep their work force employed. Our job helped keep one person on the job for about six weeks, and we did get a good price. That's an essential in self-publication. You just can't walk into a big printing plant and order a book. You have to shop around and see what parts of the job you can do yourself and what parts you can pass out to companies who will give you a low price. The danger is in fragmenting the job so that responsibility for delivery of a unified, attractive book gets lost along the way. We went through the whole printing process, helping out at every step where we could save labor costs.

We bought one newspaper ad, and it produced eight hundred prepublication orders. While the book was being printed, we sold three hundred copies to local bookstores, but we didn't start to sell books to the stores until we had what our printer called "brown prints." These turned out to be blueprints made from the negatives of the actual pages. We read these for final corrections and then made a formal paste-up copy for the printer so there was one master copy that showed how the pages flowed in the book. To sell our book to book dealers, we pasted up one extra master copy.

In seeking a lower price, we made the mistake of going to a very small printer. Most printers have presses that print thirty-two, or sixteen or even eight pages at a time. Our printer was able to print two pages at a time. A real Snow-White-and-Seven-Dwarfs operation, if there ever was one. Not including our own hours of free work, the cost was $1.75 a copy for a two-hundred-page book, five and a half by eight and a half, with a one-color cover. The books were spiral bound so the cook could open her book flat on the kitchen table. We never thought to ask the printer how many books he could spiral bind in a week. It turned out that any cook could bake as many loaves of bread in a week as that printer could bind books. But, unknowing about all this, when we received our first shipment of thirty books, we rushed out to show them to the local media.

It worked like a charm.

The books were reviewed immediately, and people went into the bookstores to buy copies.

There weren't any.

We got three hundred more books, and then our small printer had an unforeseen breakdown on his press. In the end, we got the books in dribbles. I remember walking into one department store that had ordered twelve books and received none. I carried a shopping bag filled with books, and, as I spoke to the buyer, someone walked up to us and said, "Barbara, are you still trying to peddle those books?" The buyer looked at this person and said, truthfully, "We need all the books we can get. Calls come in every day." I felt like Salesman Sam, and my smile unfroze a couple of weeks of pained exasperation.

After we had a stock of five hundred unsold books on hand, out of our original order of three thousand, and had sold all the local stores that we seemed likely to sell, the shoe was on the other foot, and we looked around for new worlds. Up to now, we had no trouble selling *In the Beginning* to the stores. We knew them, they knew us, and we both knew our product had local interest.

But if we were ever to do what we started out to do, "make a little money for our Temple," the sales had to come from beyond home base. We all knew this from the word "go"; that's why we edited the recipes to give them uniformity and make them easy to follow, and that's why we sought to make the book universal in its application and in our layout and design to avoid a hokey look. But the excruciatingly slow delivery of our books, and our lack of gumption to take one deliberate step to sell the book nationally, nailed us to a purely local operation for the first three months.

I made the first move toward getting national sales when my husband took me along on a business trip to Chicago. He didn't seem surprised when I packed some of our books in our luggage. I called on the *Tribune*'s food editor, Joanne Will. Showing her the book, I asked if she would care to keep a copy and look it over for reviewing. She accepted it without any particular comment. I carried an extra set of our local reviews, which I left with her. It was my first call at a big-city newspaper office. Many publishers' representatives had preceded me, so, really, it depended on the book, not on what they thought of me. I left there feeling no one was going to point a finger and say, "Look at the amateur showing a book." I took a bus back to the Loop and called on bookstores near there: Carson Pirie Scott, Marshall Field, and a half-dozen little stores, including a cookware shop. One call, to the B. Dalton store, opened up an entirely new horizon. I learned about chain bookstores, local managers, and book buyers located at the headquarters of the chain.

Encouraged, I went from B. Dalton to a Walden store, where, by chance, I met the Midwest manager for Walden. He directed me to Walden's buyer for paperback books at their home office at Stamford. His easy pleasantness gave me the feeling that our book was on its way. I was not cut down in any way, because this was my first day of calling on bookstores, or of even learning that very day that chain bookstores had special buyers for special kinds of books.

Following my husband's business trip to Chicago, I went to visit my family in Glencoe and, while there, called on bookstores in nearby suburban Chicago towns. I found everyone agreeable, interested, never brusque. My confidence in our book rose.

On returning home, I told my experiences to our co-chairwoman, Roselyn Dave, who shortly after went to San Francisco with her husband and had a similar experience in getting reviews in the *San Francisco Examiner* and in selling *In the Beginning* to cookware stores and bookstores.

Now we had varied material to show the paperback-book buyer of Walden at Stamford. This consisted of reviews from Chicago, San

Francisco and other papers, plus copies of a few unsolicited fan letters from people who had bought the book. About a week after mailing this package, which included a copy of our book, I phoned this buyer at probably just the right time. It was eleven-thirty, and I read some of the recipes from *In the Beginning* to him. He said he was hungry, and the hors d'oeuvres sounded delicious, and he agreed to give me a token order for fifty Walden stores with each store to get three to five copies. I mastered levitation then and there, and I floated around the house.

When the formal order arrived, I wondered about the Walden dealer who would receive our three or five books. I tried to focus on him, instead of on our book or myself. I composed a letter, to go with each package of books, informing the local Walden manager that our book had been selected by their national paperback buyer because of its reviews and universal appeal.

I suggested that the manager take a copy home and let the cook in the house try it out; also, I asked if the manager would display the book in a high-traffic area.

Then I enclosed a return envelope and asked the manager to send me the name of the local newspaper's food editor and promised to send *In the Beginning* to this editor for review.

This worked well, and we sent review copies to all the food editors whose names came to us in this way. This, then, became our pattern: when a store ordered, we asked the manager for the name of the local food editor and shipped off a review copy, usually mentioning that a local store was stocking the book.

Barbara showed me an oversized scrapbook, ten inches thick, containing reviews from several hundred newspapers.

Well-known writers, whose books become blockbusters and sell seventy-five thousand copies through trade stores, sometimes receive one hundred reviews. Yet here was physical evidence of several hundred reviews in one huge scrapbook and another blank scrapbook on a workbench, being readied. The simple, functional merchandising idea just described, involving the dealer and the food editor, plus the love and energy of the Sisterhood members, gave this book the kind of unrelenting sock that only self-publishers seem to have.

I asked Barbara how she got merchandising ideas.

No matter what anyone says to me [she answered immediately], no matter how fine the print of something that comes into our home, I try to make a connection between that and *In the Beginning.* "Ah-ha," I say.

We also sell books by direct mail and rent lists. It started by our giving a copy of *In the Beginning* to a country-club manager. He sent us a lovely letter saying he had never had a book on his chef's kitchen library that he could turn to and find hors d'oeuvres recipes, for sure, because that book was devoted to appetizers and nothing else. He found our recipes useful and began to serve some of the dishes at club parties.

With his permission, we made a copy of his letter and sent it to food-management magazines along with a review copy. Then we bought, from a mailing-list company, a list of country-club managers and offered our book at the retail price of $5.95 plus one dollar to cover postage and packing.

We also phoned what seemed to be the most likely magazine in the field, *Country Club Management,* spoke to the editor, got him interested, and sent off a copy. He then advised us that *Country Club Management* wanted to sell the book through its own monthly book page, and this was our first customer of this kind. Since then, we added several others, including the *Wooden Spoon* and *Paragon.* Both are household and cookware catalogues, and each has sold two thousand copies.

We were now ready to try a mailing list of all trade bookstores, and in this way we began to have national distribution. We also tried to get jobbers. On a trip to New York City, I called on the bookstore managers of Macy's, Gimbels, and Bloomingdale's. Two of these stores wanted the book, but they preferred to order from a local distributor, Dimondstein; the third orders direct.

Our first three thousand books were sold within three months, and we ordered three thousand more, but this time we went to a printer who could print more than two pages at a time and who could deliver the entire order within sixty days. Having a supply of books on hand feeds energy to you, because there are the books, and all you have to do is sell them.

We have a secret weapon, Millie Tieger, who writes our sales letters and circulars. I am no writer. I'm into selling, and, when we get ideas on new ways to sell, I pass these on to Millie, and the whole thing comes back, lucid and literate. I think a self-publisher can do many things alone, but a spouse, or a friend, or a partner makes for fewer demands on the skills of one person.

We have printed seventy-seven thousand books and are now planning our next print order, which should take us close to one hundred thousand.

[I asked Barbara whether she had any special attitude toward selling.]

Yes, we gear our approach to the other person's values and needs. For example, in order to get publicity for *In the Beginning*, we send built-in columns to newspaper food editors that are easy for them to use. To give our material timeliness, we send it out on a seasonal basis: Passover, Easter, Christmas, and so forth. In our capsule review, we tie in appetizers that are geared to the season. Along with this hand-tooled publicity, we also offer to mail a complimentary copy of *In the Beginning* if the food editor wants to review it. Our offer also includes a copy of the book at a reduced price if the food editor doesn't want to review the book but would like it for a home kitchen library.

In some of the cities where we sold books to well-known department stores, such as the Federated Stores in Dallas and Houston, we asked the store if they would care to inquire from their local TV station whether one of our editors might give a TV demonstration of preparing and cooking appetizers. An affirmative response was received on this from Cleveland, Green Bay, Madison, and Columbus, in addition to the two Texas cities.

If the store doesn't reply, we phone either the program director or the host of the station's good talk show. However, when the store does it for you, they have some clout because they often use TV advertising.

Our success is due to a dedicated group of talented volunteers. We have just started offering a free counter-display unit with each twelve books, and, while this is old hat to all the larger publishers, it took us a while to get around to it. We will soon enter our sixth year of selling *In the Beginning,* and probably each year will allow us to develop more promotions that will interest and help dealers and the media. Can anybody else do the same thing with a self-published book either personally or as part of a community organization? I don't think any of us at the Temple Sisterhood are that special, but our book really was . . . and is.

To order In the Beginning, *send $6.95 plus one dollar postage to Rockdale Ridge Press (8501 Ridge Rd., Cincinnati, OH 45236).*

22

An Idea for a Self-Published Book in Your City

LET'S GET UNDER WAY by giving our idea a title: "A Children's Guide to (name of your city)." You've seen many city guidebooks for adults. A guidebook for children is the same except that its emphasis is on places that interest children.

Editorially, a children's guide is unusual in one respect. It is written for the child reader, yet is usually bought by the adult. Often the child will read the guide and select the places to visit. This gives you a dual reading audience, but direct your writing to the child reader.

If you live in Trenton, Oklahoma City, Windsor, San Francisco, Toledo, Lansing, almost any place sheltering over two hundred thousand people, you can take a special delight in writing such a book. If done well, it can be revised every year. You can expect to sell from five hundred to fifteen hundred copies per one-hundred-thousand population.

How to begin?

Off the top of your head, write down six places that children would like to visit in your city. There are always a few you can name right away—the zoo, the county parks, pop concerts, waterside resorts, special parts of the downtown area, a bird preserve, nature center, historical sites, gift days (jackets, caps) at professional sports arenas, a donut shop that shows visitors how donuts are cut, shaped, fried, and glazed.

We've started!

Now, decide the age group your guide will appeal to. Nine to twelve—

is that okay with you? Show your starter list of places to the presidents of several PTAs. What other locations do they suggest? What ones on your list do they approve? What do they have against some of the others?

Visit three teachers in each of the grades from which your guide will pull most of its readers: fourth through eighth grade, maybe the ninth grade, too. Show the teachers your list of places for children to visit. What places do they have to add? What places give them negative vibes?

Balance familiar standbys like the local conservatory with enough new, generally unknown information, so that your guidebook is fresh and worth its price. Don't be afraid to list things that can only be done by a group of ten or more, such as visiting an automated bake-and-flash-freeze pie factory. School and church groups are looking for places to take groups.

Now visit some special-interest people and get their reactions: the head of the county park system, the president of the Friends of the Zoo, the director of the city's public-works system, which may include the waterworks and transportation system. Does the latter sponsor a visitor's tour bus?

Local Girl and Boy Scout council headquarters are well informed about the interests and needs of children at various age levels. Troop and pack leaders are constantly searching for new ideas for their troop programs and are a good source of ideas. They are potential customers, too. Ask their advice.

Every targeted place for a child's visit needn't be a skating rink or a kite-flying promotion. An environmental group may schedule tours showing pollution of the area's water, air, and land. A traffic-court judge may encourage child visitors. An orphanage for preschool children may welcome eighth-grade boys and girls to bring them into community work. The city's director of public playgrounds may have rich surprises for you, as may the local heads of various sports activities and museums. Ask each for leads that may direct you to additional places where children can have a good time, learn something, enjoy the day and develop a greater rapport with the adults who take them in tow. Does a local ice-cream factory allow tours? Do they offer samples?

In two months you'll have a list of one hundred interesting places for children to visit and things to do at each place. Showing your list to civic-minded citizens who have a good critical sense may allow you to add three places and cut out twenty-three, bringing you down to eighty.

Now you start to think like a publisher.

If each one of the eighty places requires four pages to describe, that's a 320-page book, and the retail price will almost have to be eight or nine dollars, even if it's a paperback. That's high for a children's book. Would three pages instead of four do the job? Or perhaps you can cut the list to fifty places. That gives you a 150-page book. Or, you can list the entire eighty, but give forty of them one page each and the others two pages each. That's a 120-page book. The cost of two thousand such books would be under twenty-five hundred dollars, and the book could carry a three- to four-dollar retail price, paperback.

If you allow one or two pages for each place the children visit—what do you put on these pages?

You could tell why this particular place is included in the guide. What is its value to the child, its charisma? Describe some things to do and mention the admission or other charges.

Your descriptions should be written for the child, but key in the adult as to why he or she should take a group of children, or just one child, to this lake, amusement park, or public garden. What do you want the child to get out of it? Get the reaction of several children for your guide. It will be so much fun, so delightful to quote them. Sometimes the quotation can be in type, sometimes in script, as written by the child, in printed letters, or maybe colored crayons. That helps make it real to the child who receives the guide as a gift.

Should your guide be illustrated?

There's an opportunity! How about adding a subtitle to your guide: "Illustrated by Children"?

Perhaps twenty of the places described in the directory can be illustrated by children's art. Where do you get the art? One way to start is by visiting the art-curriculum directors of public, parochial, and private schools. They will provide you with introductions to some art teachers at the grade level of your book, and the art teachers will know the talented students in their classes. Maybe some art teachers will make a project out of it and ask the students for their responses in drawings or paintings.

That would take care of art for twenty of the places. For pace and variety, another twenty can be illustrated photographically.

Who should take the photographs?

THE BOOK MARKET

If you want them made specially for your book—and that's the way to go—it will require at least three weeks' time for the photographer, who will have to make no less than a hundred shots. So his investment is considerable. You will have to offer him a flat fee with no royalty, or repayment of out-of-pocket expenses plus a royalty. Shooting twenty places, making five shots of each, plus showing you contacts of each of the five, with a five-by-seven blowup of forty shots, is worth around two hundred to five hundred dollars for time, expenses, and materials. Be sure you buy all rights to all the shots, or you may be setting up a competitor.

When you have a half-dozen of the places written up and laid out with photostats showing where the text goes, where the children's art and photographs go, and what the headings say, you'll want to show this to people you think will buy the book as well as to children, art teachers, and the special-interest people who operate the parks, resorts, museums, arenas, pop orchestras, and so forth.

Here you want to listen carefully to what you hear and then make your own judgments. If you are unwilling to finance the venture yourself, at what point do you approach a selected local publisher? Not too late! You want to show him enough so that he realizes you are serious and intend to go ahead, but not so much so that if he wants to suggest a different tack and you like his suggestions, your guide won't be too far gone to make the change.

The publisher you want should be solvent, dependable, experienced in local distribution, and have a reputation for treating people fairly. Without that, you'd be lost, as your guide is really an annual to be brought up to date regularly. So you want a permanent relationship.

Prior to publishing this yourself or offering it to a publisher, you'll want to show your stats of a half-dozen selected places to the city's newsstand distributor, a few trade bookstores, several children's librarians and teachers in charge of buying books for elementary schools that have bookstores, and, of course, to parents who are potential customers, and to some children. A dozen affirmative letters will influence the publisher. And, if the letters are convincing, you may want to be the publisher yourself, especially if it looks as though you have a red-hot annual in your hands.

312

What if your town already has a book with this title? If the book is good, forget the idea, because two good guides are one too many for most cities. What if there is a book like this in another city? If so, select a title that is different from the one already in existence, even though you would not be competing in Oklahoma City, for instance, with a children's guide currently being published in Kansas City. There are enough words in the dictionary so you can create your own original title.

What if there is no book publisher in your city and you don't want to self-publish? Try a local bank or a building-and-loan association that seeks to do a widespread consumer-lending and home-mortgage business, or a well-established store specializing in children's clothing, or an insurance company whose home office is in your city and whose policies are aimed at young marrieds.

Does this type of book appeal to you? It's a ready way into the book market. The writing itself as well as the research is on the same level as doing any kind of first-class book. But because it's a local product, with local circulation, doesn't mean—to use Barbara Rosenberg's word—a *heimgemacht* job. You perform at your highest level. The mixture is sincerity, enthusiasm, modesty, patience, resolve, and (I think) an admiring spouse. A successful self-published book doesn't have to be a world beater with a capital B. All it requires to give you a financial lift and turn you into a local celebrity is a functional idea, with wide acceptance, executed on a professional level. That means good copy and good graphics. Such a book in a city of 400,000 can sell from two thousand to five thousand copies a year at three to four dollars each and lead the way into other publishing enterprises.

In the preceding chapter, did you note the experience of Beverly Nye? Her initial venture, *A Family Raised on Sunshine*, burgeoned into a taped series of homemaking ideas sold to radio stations. Then she wrote a sequel, *A Family Raised on Rainbows*, which is outselling the amazing record of her first book, and she followed this with a monthly newsletter, *Sunshine Notes* (subscription, twelve dollars a year), which gives household and cooking hints and ideas. It hasn't stopped there, and I don't expect it to stop for some time yet. The latest from Beverly is that she has a mail-order store called "The Pantry," in which she offers such items as "patty" molds at 99 cents each, or a dehydrator for $149.00.

THE BOOK MARKET

Beverly started as a self-publisher with a functional idea that she made into something original by her own phrasing. If you don't already have a children's guide in your city, this could be a candidate to introduce you to self-publication.

23

Tracking Down a Printer

FINDING, IN YOUR OWN BACKYARD, a commercial book printer who specializes in small press runs isn't easy, and you may have to select a printer who is located some distance away, with whom you can do business by mail or phone. Sometimes, however, you can locate the printer you want within a two- or three-hour drive by using one of the resources that follow.

You might start off by writing to The Printing Industries of America, Inc. (1930 North Lynn St., Arlington, VA 22209). PIA is a trade organization of commercial printers, and some of them do small-press-run books. The idea is to get the PIA to help you locate the printer you want either locally or within a convenient distance. The organization is made up of thirty locals, and each goes under a regional name: for example, The North Carolina Printer's Association. If your inquiry to PIA looks businesslike and "worthwhile" from the point of view of your becoming a customer of one of their members, it will be forwarded to one of the thirty local organizations nearest you; or PIA may write you directly and give the address of their nearest local. For best results, a visit to the local office, rather than a phone call or a letter, is best. Set up an appointment. Don't go in cold, as the local PIA manager might be on the road or have a meeting scheduled. The local manager knows the printers in his territory better than almost anyone, and, once he gets to know you and understand your goals, you are more likely to get a good personal steer.

THE BOOK MARKET

In your letter asking for an appointment, state in two or three paragraphs the editorial nature of the book you plan to publish. You might enclose a one-page outline. Don't send a sample chapter. State the page size, type-page size, number of typed eight-and-a-half-by-eleven manuscript pages, kinds of illustrations (pen drawings, photographs—color or black and white), whether you are interested in a hardcover or paperback binding, and the press run. Explain that you want an appointment to discuss the nature of your printing job. Hold your letter to one page, and the only enclosure you will want (and this is optional) is a one-page outline of your book.

If the nearest PIA local is five hundred miles away, it may not be worth the candle, but, if it is within a convenient drive, you can learn a great deal from the local PIA manager. He is a printer's pro and usually a social as well as a technical person. Should you receive an appointment, take along a dummy of the book you have in mind, showing type page and page size and number of pages. If possible, the dummy should be made of the paper you want to use. You can indicate the kind of binding you want by bringing along a book that is bound similarly to what you have in mind: hardcover, paperback, spiral bound. Some hardcovers open flat, and so do some kinds of paperback books. Your sample should indicate the kind of binding you prefer. Also bring a printed sample showing the kind of dust jacket you want, not in regard to design, but in regard to whether it is printed in one color on colored paper, or in one, two, or four colors on white stock.

By giving your visit to the PIA local manager a specific approach, you can expect the kind of serious, forthright attention given to potential customers.

The local PIA manager is not a salesman and cannot favor one printer over another. He works for all the association members in his territory, and his main job is to convey information on labor and new equipment, as well as to provide a forum for printing-trade discussion among his local members.

The local manager knows all the members of his organization, and he knows printing, so, if you give him a well-thought-out plan of what you want to buy, he may be able to match your goals with one or two of his PIA members.

There are only twelve printing centers in America, and most of these are in large metropolitan areas where magazines, catalogues and books are published. Relatively few cities have printers in their area who can, under one roof, do all the production jobs required to produce either a hardcover or a paperback book. Usually, a printer will "farm out" parts of the job to someone else. Binding, typesetting, artwork, graphics design, even trimming, collating, and folding would rarely be under the single roof of one printer who makes a specialty of small press runs. That's why a chat with the local PIA manager can be helpful.

A natural drawback to using the fine facilities of the PIA is that they have only thirty locals, and some of them are far away from some Western, Southern, Northwestern, Northeastern and North Central states. However, there is a second organization in the printing trade called International Association of Printing Craftsmen. It is made up of craftsmen who work for commercial printers. Many of these craftsmen are executives of their printing companies. They have no local offices, but they do have 116 affiliates in the United States and Canada. The Craftsmen group, as they are called, will not send the name and address of the nearest affiliate. However, under certain circumstances, they may forward your request for the name of a printer who specializes in small press runs to their affiliate, if they have one, who is within the driving range you mention in your letter.

The Craftsmen group is not an organization devoted to getting printing leads for its members. It is more interested in printing techniques and quality control. However, a letter from a self-publisher that has some substance to it (*i.e.*, it sounds businesslike, intelligent, and specific and is neatly typed on printed stationery) would normally be forwarded. If you don't get an answer from the local affiliate within three weeks, you have to assume they don't have a member within the driving time you mentioned, or, for reasons of their own, they put your letter aside. Forwarding "leads" is not their work. But the Craftsmen group has helped certain self-publishers, and that's why we include their name and address. Write to Jack Davies (International Association of Printing House Craftsmen, 7599 Kenwood Rd., Cincinnati, OH 45236). Mr. Davies is the secretary of the association and is very knowledgeable on printing.

What do you do if neither of these leads comes through? There are a number of alternatives.

THE BOOK MARKET

Your very best bet is to have a comfortable, personal talk with another self-publisher, and there's a neat way to arrange this. Len Fulton's *International Directory of Little Magazines and Small Presses* (P.O. Box 100, Paradise, CA 95969) is now running almost five hundred pages, and the last thirty are for you. These pages contain a geographical listing of all publishers of little magazines and small presses. In some states, there are only a straggling few (Wyoming, two; Delaware, three). Other states have a real goose-pimple rash of them (California, four hundred, New York, three hundred). Write down the publishers within a convenient drive of your home. Then, consult the editorial listing of the book-manuscript needs of these publishers, and you will get an idea of which publishers most appeal to you. Their phone numbers are usually given, but, since you are really asking for a half-day's time, it might be wisest to write instead of phoning for an appointment. If you write, it would be a nice idea to enclose a sample chapter along with a one-page outline. A few of these publishers own their own presses, and some of them do "outside" work for other publishers.

Another way to get in touch personally with other self-publishers is through *Coda*: Write to Poets & Writers Newsletter (201 West 54th St., New York, NY 10019), and ask for the name and address of the nearest local writers' affiliate of the National Endowment for the Arts and the Arts Council of your state. These locals rise and fall with federal and state budgets, so you can expect some problem in finding a local within a convenient drive. If you do locate one, address a letter to the local office manager and explain that you would like to talk with some writers who are self-publishers and who might direct you to a printer specializing in small press runs. The employees who are part of NEA's locals are usually pleasant and enjoy giving assistance. Generally, they have an amateur standing as far as book publishing goes but are definitely a useful resource.

You have four other bets. The *New York Times* (daily edition as well as the Sunday *Book Review* section) includes classified ads devoted to printers who handle small press runs. *Writer's Digest* (9933 Alliance Rd., Cincinnati, OH 45242) also publishes advertisements of such printers, as does *Small Press Review* (P.O. Box 100, Paradise, CA 95969). A sample copy of *Small Press Review* is one dollar. You might ask Ellen Ferber, the editor, if she would care to suggest a printer in your

318

area whom you might write or interview. If you do this, state your requirements to Ms. Ferber just as you would to PIA. The larger subsidy publishers, such as Vantage Press and Dorrance, will also act as a book manufacturer, without the added cost of sales promotion and marketing activities.

There is one more place to go in your quest for the best printer for you. *Literary Market Place* lists more than one thousand book publishers, and, at the end of the editorial section, there is a geographical index. Will the production manager of Simon & Schuster provide you with the names of nearby printers who might handle a small press run? Probably not. But how about the small book publisher who is issuing three to six titles a year? He's not much larger than you are and may be established only four or five years. You can be pretty sure that he started out with small press runs. To track down this particular fellow, you can readily put your finger on the book publishers in your geographical area and then consult the editorial listing of each to find a relatively new book publisher issuing a handful of titles or less. Now you will be more likely to run into a production manager who remembers back when. He will probably help you.

Here, too, in your letter asking for an appointment, be as specific in your inquiry letter as in the one suggested to PIA.

The last idea in your quest for a printer is to consult your local Chamber of Commerce or Better Business Bureau. If you can get two or three names and addresses of customers of small-press-run book printers and then communicate with these customers, it may be a learning experience.

24

The Retail Bookstore

THERE ARE SIX tested ways for the self-publisher to secure orders from the nation's four thousand retail bookstores. Here they are:

1. Sending sales letters by mail to the retail bookstores and backing these up with telephone solicitation.
2. Employing salesmen who call on bookstores.
3. Securing jobbers to stock your book.
4. Advertising in magazines read by store owners and managers.
5. Mounting a separate campaign to sell your book to chain bookstores.
6. Promoting your book with enough push to walk customers into selected bookstores and thus encourage the owner to order from you.

A self-publisher with one book to sell can use the first method alone (direct mail plus telephone backup) and make a success of it.

However, he'll need other things going for him. An editorially sound book is the first requirement, but there are others, too, and without them there is really no contest. The retail price must be competitive with similar books; the book should be attractive to look at, functional (a cookbook is easier to use when it opens flat), and reasonably well timed with the current book market. (Remember the bomb-shelter books?)

When these requirements are met, retail orders can be had in large numbers by a self-publisher who gives out with a consistent sales effort and whose book is editorially better than average. Every year, twoscore new self-publishers enter the field with books that sell in excess of twenty thousand copies. They bubble and thrive on the venture. Sometimes they develop a small royalty book-publishing business of their own. If you and your book are a good team, how do you start to sell your book to the bookstore?

You start, as always, with a cordial and sincere attempt to know your customer. Who is your customer? The owner? The manager? The store's book buyer? Large trade stores have more than one buyer. One buyer may handle only new cloth-bound fiction; another buys nonfiction, while a third works with paperbacks. If you owned a large bookstore with three thousand titles in stock, could you expect one person to evaluate every kind of book offered for purchase: fiction, juvenile, nonfiction, reference, art? The buyer gives each new book, or its dust jacket, a three- or four-minute appraisal. Actually, the dust jacket is all that the buyer sees; rarely does the publisher send a complimentary copy of the book itself. If that happened on a regular basis, the bookstore would receive ten thousand copies of forthcoming titles each year.

Let's think about the buyer. Each month, he receives circulars, letters, catalogues from several hundred publishers. Perhaps he will receive ten a day in the slow season and forty a day when the spring and autumn catalogues are released. The buyer is hired to buy. But he is supposed to buy only what will sell. His job is to devote a few intense minutes to studying the dust jacket, considering the reputation of the author, the viability of the field about which the book is concerned, the description of the book itself and then, by comparing it all, he comes up with a turn-down or an order. What if he orders six books and they fly out the window on arrival? That means a dozen orders lost while the clerks wait for a new supply. What if he orders twenty-four and they sit? Buying is part feeling, part guesswork and mostly experienced judgment.

The main thought in the buyer's mind is how the book will affect the reader and where the book should be placed in stock. What if it's a book on a new subject that is not in the news, or a book on a highly specialized subject? How will the clerks know where to put it on the store's shelves so a reader, browsing for something in that field, might discover it? If the book is in a popular category, such as cooking, will the reader request this one, or can the store get along with its present inventory and use its investment dollars for something else?

To the buyer, the retail price you choose for your book matters only when it is out of line with a comparable book of its size and number of pages. The discount matters when it is chintzy compared to the competition, or when the return policy is stiff. Generally, a self-publisher will allow a 40 percent discount much earlier than will a mainline publisher *; giving forty off for an order of three books is a kind of a "welcome, come on in" salutation.

To the buyer, the name and reputation of the publisher matters less than it ever did, because so few publishers limit their selections to high literary quality. The overall appearance of the book, the title, the name of the author, the subject matter, and its timeliness each mean more than the publisher's imprint.

The unknown, self-published author has one hard strike against him. No one has ever heard his name. However, nothing prevents him from having a good-looking book, a popular title, timely subject matter, a competitive price, a slightly better discount, a simple and favorable return policy, and a sales letter that is personal.

Each one of these seven factors is vital. When combined positively in your favor, they are overwhelming. This explains the success of many self-publishers.

When the buyer receives a sales letter, circular, or catalogue, he concentrates on it in relation to his own particular job. You can't expect the nonfiction buyer who happens to receive your circular to scissor out the portion devoted to fiction and pass it along to an associate buyer. For this reason, as a self-publisher, you want to place the name of the buyer of your particular kind of book on your envelope. In most cases, you won't know this.

What then?

---

* It is not unusual for a mainline publisher to offer a 25 percent discount, cash with order, for a single book; 30 percent discount for two to three books, 33⅓ percent discount for four to five books. A 40 percent discount may start with ten books. Postage is added to the bill. When a dealer orders from a mainline publisher, he very quickly mounts an order of twenty-four copies, since the publisher has several hundred titles.

THE BOOK MARKET

Simply write in the lower left-hand corner of the envelope an indication to the store's mail clerk as to where your letter should be delivered, thus:

Attention: Cloth-bound fiction buyer
or
Attention: Cloth-bound nonfiction buyer
or
Attention: Paperback buyer
or
Attention: Reference book buyer

This technique increases the chances of your sales letter getting to the right person.

Let's skip ahead and ask: What do you do when you get an order? You fill, bill, and ship. Anything else?

Let's see what your competition does.

At a large publishing house, the receipt of an order for twenty-five copies is devoid of emotion. At Harper or McGraw-Hill, the person who opens the mail sees the order as a piece of paper to be processed. The marketing manager sees it as part of a summary of the day's "take." The publisher sees it, a month later, as part of the cash receipts, or he sees it included in the dollar value of accounts receivable.

At Harper and McGraw-Hill, it didn't used to be that way. Once upon a time, they were little people who overflowed with joy from an order for twenty-five books. Make that fifteen. That emotional bang has left them.

I pray it never leaves you. As a self-publisher, you have what the large publisher lost many mergers ago. You're a unique individual who wrote, published, and now sells his own book. Fire yourself up—it's your privilege and reward.

If direct mail works so well in helping the self-publisher establish national trade-store distribution, how do you get your hands on a list of trade stores? There are many sources. A good start is the reference book called *The American Book Trade Directory*. It is available in any large library and is a good place to begin your acquaintance with trade stores. Visit with it for an hour or two to get a personal feel for the trade-store market.

A handy place from which to secure your list of trade stores is Sal Vicidomini, of R.R. Bowker (1180 Avenue of the Americas, New York, NY 10036). The direct line to him is (212) 764-5223, and Sal likes to answer his own phone.

You can rent Bowker's four-thousand-trade-store list for under $160. You are not entitled to Xerox the list and retain a copy for future use. If you want to mail the list a second time, you will have to rent it a second time. Will Bowker know? Yes. It is their prerogative to place decoys in the list you rent, and, if they ever get two letters from you addressed to the same decoy, that is the end.

The cost of renting the list of four thousand selected bookstores includes addressing the names on pressure-sensitive labels so that you may easily affix them to your own envelopes. Bowker maintains the right to approve a mailing piece before they rent a list, and, if you are a first-time renter, they may require this.

The 4,000 selected bookstores are a merged list of (1) 2,400 selected retail bookstores; (2) 2,100 chain bookstores; and (3) 1,500 department-store book departments. When these three lists are merged, and duplicates are eliminated, the final list boils down to 4,000. The list includes the store name and address only.

Should you shoot right out with a 4,000 mailing?

Yes, if you have done promotional mailings before.

No, if this if your first shot at doing it yourself.

In the latter case, regardless of your personal finances, move deliberately, testing as you go. You might start off by consulting *The American Book Trade Directory*. Copy off the names of three hundred retail bookstores along with the name of the particular buyer you want to reach, and the address.

There is a time lag between the day the *Directory* receives its information and the date you consult it. Up to 15 percent of all the names and addresses may change. Therefore, you want to identify the persons you will address by using their titles. Don't write, "Ms. Sally Jones, The Book Shelf." Address your envelope to "Ms. Sally Jones, Cloth-Bound-Fiction Buyer, The Book Shelf." If Ms. Jones has left, and the mail clerk is new, your letter will be delivered to the current cloth-bound-fiction buyer.

What if you can't find a copy of *The American Book Trade Directory*?

THE BOOK MARKET

Your library may have a shelf full of yellow-page telephone directories. Each has a section headed "Book Dealers, Retail." The names and addresses of bookstores that advertise here will give you a starter list.

If you have a friend who owns a large retail bookstore and attends book dealers' conventions, ask if he can secure the names and addresses of dealers who attend.

Your library may have the last fifty issues of *Publishers Weekly*. In each issue, you will find a dozen names of owners or book buyers of prominent retail bookstores and the name of the city where they are located. That's five hundred first-class names.

Isn't this a sort of cheesy way to do business? I began just that way, and, almost fifty years later, when I got to a new town, I sought out the yellow pages of the local telephone book to see if there were listings of book retailers whom I didn't know. There was always at least one. I copied it down. There was always one viable new prospect, even though I was now mailing well over one million direct-mail pieces a year.

When *Publishers Weekly* was routed to my office, I looked for names of owners and book buyers at trade stores that I didn't recall being on our own list and copied them and asked my secretary to check them against our computer list.

The dream list you want is not for rent. You assemble it one name at a time. You can rent large lists, but you piecemeal together small lists to add to your main prospect file. You keep everlastingly at it so that it bristles with the kind of prospects you personally want. For instance, if you are marketing a religious book, then you'll want to subscribe to *Christian Bookseller* (396 E. St. Charles Rd., Wheaton, IL 60187) or *Book Store Journal* (2620 Venetucci Blvd., P.O. Box 210, Colorado Springs, CO 80901). A sample copy of either is one dollar. Many specialty book fields have their own trade papers with good leads for you. If you add three names a day to your list, from a variety of special sources, it means you freshen your list by one thousand prospective customers a year.

How many orders do you need from every hundred names on your list to show a profit when you send out direct-mail pieces? That depends on the retail price of the book, the discount you give the dealer, the cost of printing the book, and the cost per hundred of your mailing pieces.

If you can produce one complete mailing piece for 25 cents, your cost per hundred is $25. If four trade-store buyers respond, and you can average three books per order, you will sell twelve books out of every hundred circulars mailed. If your book costs $3 to print and retails for $10 and you give the dealer 40 percent off, you bill the dealer $6 for each book you ship, plus the postage. Let's add it up.

Outgo

Cost of mailing 100 pieces at 25 cents each	$25.00
Cost of printing 12 books at $3.00 each	36.00
Total cost of publishing, selling and shipping 12 books*	$61.00

Income

12 books billed at $6.00 each	$72.00

Profit (or Loss)

Total income per 100 circulars mailed	$72.00
Total cost of 100 circulars and 12 books sold	61.00
Profit per 100 circulars mailed	$11.00

If you carry that kind of result through 4,000 retail bookstores, you will sell 480 books (12 books sold per 100 stores = 480 books sold to 4,000 stores) and collect $2,880 (480 times $6 = $2,880). Your costs will be $2,440 ($61 times 40 = $2,440). Profit of $440.

A lot of work for pennies?

Not so.

Out of 4,000 retail bookstores, you did business with 160 to make $440. That leaves 3,840 to go. What it boils down to is that a response of four orders out of every hundred, with an average of three books per order, may well justify another mailing. You can also see how one order for twelve books can change the profit picture, especially if one order in eight is for twelve books. That increases the profit by 25 percent.

---

* Outgoing postage is added to your bill.

THE BOOK MARKET

Let's back up and consider what goes into a mailing piece.

Usually it contains a letter, a circular, an order blank, and a return envelope.

What should each piece say?

A good way to get yourself going is to take your book to a few local trade stores whose owners you know. Give them a copy and ask if you can come back and ask some questions about a mailing piece you want to send to retail bookstores just like their own. Not many publishers ask this of a retail-bookstore owner, and he won't quite know what to say. Actually, this isn't his business, and, therefore, his advice is suspect. However, he can get you thinking, especially if he will do a little thinking himself. Allow him a few days to read the book and then come back for his advice. Probably he will not have read the book at all. Bookstore owners are not readers. They are experienced glancers. They will scan the dust jacket and break the book open at five or six places (and these are not random places, either, but spots for which they have an intuitive feeling that something must be going on here or else the book might be a dead one). At these places, they will read a few paragraphs. More would be remarkable.

The dealer's judgment can be shallow for your purposes, but the route he follows to get there could be valuable. Here's a key to what he thinks.

"It's sort of thin." (The book is overpriced.)

"Browse around the store. Our cloth-bound juveniles are around the corner to your left." (Your book doesn't look like our other juveniles.)

"Take a look at our other home-décor books." (The book seems noncompetitive.)

"I'm not sure about your title." (Your title doesn't tell him the category under which it should be shelved.)

These remarks have one thing in common. The dealer didn't have to read the book to make them. It would be hard for him to work up enthusiasm for a book he has barely scanned—but often that's the most you will get. Nonetheless, show your book to as many dealers as you have the patience and energy to seek out. After the dealer has said what he has to say, ask this: "If you had to sell this book to other dealers, how would you go about it?" Again, the answer may be the easiest thing that comes to mind to brush off someone who is taking time. You could hear:

"Get jobbers to stock it."

"Have salesmen show it to dealers."

"Put ads in the papers so customers come to the store and ask for the book."

So far you have drawn a blank on getting ideas for your circular.

Thank the dealer for helping you, and say there is just one more thing. Will he please show you one or two direct-mail campaigns from book publishers that he thought were okay?

This is easy and he may do it. Now the payoff.

"Would you please tell me why you liked this particular direct-mail piece and how many books you ordered?"

Out of three calls to dealers, you should be able to collect several mailing pieces from other publishers and, perhaps, a few comments from the dealer explaining why he liked them. You can't press him when he says: "This one gives me the facts I want," or "You can read this one quickly." The dealer is not a teacher. But he's worth your time. Study the direct-mail campaigns you pick up. If they bore you, that's good. Separate the reasons why and write them down. How would you change it so that, as far as you personally are concerned, it would be interesting, not boring? If you like one campaign, can you single out your reason? Perhaps you can introduce this factor into a letter, order blank or circular of your own.

Look at each direct-mail piece with the eye of someone seeing it for the first time. That's how the prospect sees it. Make some written notes of your responses, so, when you compose your own campaign, you have some start-up ideas.

If you spend a few days dogging dealers, you will find a few dealers— or maybe just one—who is willing to put his heart and mind into the subject and be helpful.

What if no dealer helps you out?

Then move down one step and select three or four trade-store clerks who have held their jobs for several years. Offer each one ten dollars to read your book and submit some ideas on how to sell it to bookstores. These are clerks, not publishers. They have never sold a book in all their lives to four thousand trade stores. Then why ask them? Most retail book clerks are not salesmen. At best, they know the stock and can courteously show the customer the books the store has in the area of the customer's interest. It's gambler's luck: two shots at ten dollars per.

THE BOOK MARKET

You have a third probe. If you live in a town of at least one hundred thousand population, the local bookstores are visited by book salesmen. Try to get in touch with two or three, and ask their assistance. These "travelers," as they are called in the trade, call on all dealers in their territories. They don't write letters or prepare circulars.

But they are appreciative of anyone who comes to them for advice and may give you as much as an hour's time of an evening. The salesmen won't read your book. They don't read their own. But they can give you the feel and the emotional, personal, and color side of the business. You can lift their spirits by asking about the time they worked hard and long on a sale and, then, finally made it. You may hear more than you want to hear, but, if you are fortunate enough to get a book salesman talking, it will shoo you into the human side of the business.

Perhaps you know someone in the advertising or promotion business. Here, your friend will probably read your book. As an advertising man, he has been taught that he has to know his product and his market. Perhaps even the questions he asks of you will be useful.

These research ideas will help you start your letter, circular, order blank, and envelope.

When your copy is written, bring it to an artist to design, lay out, mark up the size and kind of type desired, and indicate the color and placement of the illustrations.

Can't the printer do this?

A printer is not a designer, nor a typographer. To lay out, mark up, paste up, and indicate where the illustrations will drop for your letterhead, circular, order blank, and return envelope, an artist will charge from fifty to two hundred fifty dollars. It is money well spent. Before hiring the artist, meet with him to establish some kind of rapport. You want to see what he has done. You may want to show him circulars and letterheads you have seen elsewhere that you like. Explain why you like them. Reach for a meeting of minds, as well as an extension of your own knowledge.

If you and the artist agree on a price, ask to see a "rough" first. If the total fee is one hundred dollars or more, you may want an agreement that if you don't like the rough, you can pay the artist 15 percent of the total agreed price and have an amicable parting.

What sort of logic should be brought to bear on the trade dealer in the direct-mail campaign you send to him? To answer this, put yourself in the dealer's shoes, and figure out what you would want to know. How about these for starters?

1. What is the title, who is the author, and how much does the book cost?
2. What kind of person will buy this book?
3. Why will someone pay money for it?
4. Where should this book be shelved in the dealer's store: with cookbooks, astrology, or what?
5. What discount is offered to the dealer, and is the book bound in cloth or paper?
6. Do any national jobbers stock it?
7. What sort of companion books might the buyer of this book purchase? Does your book lend itself to the dealer making a "cheese-and-cracker" sale?
8. Can the dealer return unsold copies in six months for a cash refund?
9. What did the reviews say?
10. Is co-op newspaper advertising available on a fifty-fifty basis? (You supply suggested art and copy. The dealer places the ad at the local rates and bills you for half the cost. Usually a co-op ad runs from three to six inches by one column.)

Does anything else belong in the circular, letter, or order blank that doesn't pertain to the above ten points? I learned an eleventh item while attending a meeting of twelve salesmen who traveled for a Toronto jobber. The jobber's salesmen had been called in off the road to listen to eight publisher's representatives describe their spring lines. The jobber intended to buy a large number of these books, perhaps twenty thousand, and his twelve salesmen were going right back on the road to sell them.

For the eight publisher's representatives (of which I was one), it was a plum call. Each of us expected an order well into the thousands. To the surprise of my host, I asked to go on last. My reason was that none of these other publisher's representatives, at that time, was aware of the success of my operation; I suspected they would not all hang on till the last day, and, the less you tell another publisher, the better.

After three days, the twelve jobber salesmen had their ears bent. I don't think they knew one title from another. I listened to crack sales managers from Crowell, Harper, and five other publishers and wondered how they expected the salesmen to concentrate on so many titles, hour after hour, from Thursday till Saturday noon.

When my turn came at eleven o'clock Saturday morning, I thanked the jobber's salesmen for selling my two titles last year. Then I requested permission to "go around the circle" and ask each salesman to recount an experience in making one sale for either *Writer's Market* or *Artist's Market* to one Canadian trade store or college store.

The first thing I found out was that the salesmen had been bottled up and wanted to talk. After several jobber salesmen told their experiences in making sales on my titles, I made a summary of their ideas, and that was it.

Can you apply this experience?

Involve the dealer in your book. Find a way to get him to relate to you, to your title, or to the subject of your book. A short letter that accomplishes this will be a winner. If you could transmit some kind of human emotion, it might be better than a strictly business letter that is sell-sell-sell, with emphasis on "send your order now." Without being corny or discursive, can you come up with a way to relieve your letter by your own humanness and your own personality? Can you give the dealer a "reward" for reading your letter by offering him an idea, a piece of information, a technique in shelving or window display? Be as sincere as you know how, and think of the dealer in his own terms.

If direct-mail campaigns are to be your main method of getting distribution, how often should you produce them? I recommend three large mailings a year, plus one "pepper letter" a day. The pepper letter is something I think I invented. It consists of a daily shot of three to thirty letters to individuals, dealers, jobbers, libraries, or anybody else that you happen to think might buy your book and for whom you can construct a lead that fits his interests.

The lead should be about the recipient, not about you or the book. If your letter goes to thirty people, you may want to have it multilithed and then filled in with the proper name and address. Hand-sign it and add an individual handwritten postscript. "Hey!" you say. "Thirty fill-ins. Thirty handwritten signatures. Thirty individual postscripts. That's work!" Yep. You do it if you enjoy it. Some days, thirty such letters are manageable. Other days, three will be your limit.

If the pepper-letter idea interests you, you'll need an overrun of your dust jacket and your other campaign enclosures: the circular, order blank, and return envelope. One of the reasons you want an order blank is that it saves giving the discount information in your letter and thus makes your letter shorter. Just refer the dealer to the enclosed order blank that "gives full details on discounts and return privileges." I suggest a 25 percent discount on one book, 33⅓ percent on two or three books, and 40 percent on orders for four and over, along with full return privileges of all salable books when returned within six months. The self-publisher of one title needs a more attractive discount to counter the fact that the dealer doesn't like to order a few books from one single publisher. He prefers to order sixty at a crack from one source. This explains why the dealer prefers the jobber. The discount is less, but so is the paperwork.

Here is one example of a pepper letter.

The example I have chosen is really just another "special offer," but it is written so that it sounds individual. To get your lead, you need to do some research. Let's say that you have the names and addresses of four trade stores in Boston along with the names of the buyers of your type of book at each store.

By using the Sunday edition of the Boston newspaper, plus the yellow pages of the telephone book, you assemble thirty names and addresses of people in Boston who you believe are creditable customers for your book. You don't just copy down names and addresses—you think it out with care and ingenuity. This particular pepper letter combines an offer of personal assistance for the dealer along with a "special offer." Try the following letter on two dealers. Wait six days. To get a "feel" for what is happening, make a phone call to the first two stores and ask the buyer if it's okay to go ahead. Here's the suggested letter:

Dear——:

I spent the day doing something for you and I hope my work will help you sell books. I compiled a list of thirty prospects in Boston for my new book, ———, which is described in the enclosed circular and dust jacket.

The first three names on my list of thirty prospects are ———, ———, ———. [Then indent, and repeat the name of each person and your reason for believing this person is a prospect for your book.]

I would like to send a letter to each of these thirty prospects describing [Title of Book] and give your name, address and phone number as the trade store that has it in stock and also in the window.

I hope this will help you move six copies within ten days.

In addition, I offer you a 40 percent discount for your order for six or more, and one book free if you order ten or more. Books are returnable in six months when in salable condition. Please see the enclosed order blank.

It will give me great pleasure to encourage people to come to [name of store] and I want to thank you for considering this idea.

Cordially,

Why does this kind of letter pull orders?

To understand the reason, let's watch the action as the owner of a trade store opens up the place. It's 9:00 A.M., and there are no customers. In the basement, four boxes of books, weighing from twenty-five to forty pounds each, wait to be unpacked and shelved—not shelved just anyplace, but where they will be among books of their own kind. The dealer has a backache and doesn't feel like opening boxes and carrying the books from the basement to the first floor.

He starts to look at the morning mail. There are six bills, four statements, three catalogues and nine circulars asking him to buy books. A computerized first-class-mail letter calls his attention to somebody's national advertising campaign, and a one-line, filled-in letter with an indifferent match announces a change in discount schedule.

No one offers an idea. No one offers to do a single thing for him except to sell him something.

The door opens, and a customer comes in.

"Excuse me, sir, I'm parked outside. Do you have change for a quarter?" The phone rings.

A jobber has just received a stock of a current bestseller. How many does he want?

He says he'll take six.

The library calls. They want the same bestseller, and they'll take six. He calls the jobber back on the jobber's WATS line, but it's busy. He tries again. Still busy. He debates about whether to call at his own expense. Instead, he sends a note to the jobber to increase the order to twelve.

He gets up and walks along the aisles counting stock. He's almost sure two picture books have disappeared.

The phone rings.

The local paper wants to know if he will use an ad in the weekend edition.

The phone rings.

Does he want an outside window-washing service?

A man enters and starts to walk around the store.

A woman enters; she sees the man, and takes his arm. "Come on; we're late. We've no time to be here."

The two leave.

Would you be willing to stand across the street for one hour and count people going through his front door? Do many publishers do this?

No.

Why not?

They know it all, abstractly but not emotionally. To feel it yourself, stand across from a dealer's store and experience the whole thing.

While you're doing that, the publisher is selling rights to his best books to book clubs who will sell them by mail, in competition with the dealer, and at a cut price. The publisher is disposing of poor sellers to remainder houses, which will offer them by mail, to consumers, in a discount catalogue. And the publisher is vigorously producing mail campaigns of his own to sell his books directly to consumers.

Does this help you understand why the above pepper letter gets a decent response? The dealer is ripe for it. Finally, someone offers to do something for him that will bring traffic into his store—customers who come to the store asking for a specific book—not for change for a quarter or to browse when it's raining.

Will every pepper letter get an answer?

No.

Will one pepper letter out of two get an order?

No chance.

Will the pepper letters pay for themselves?

THE BOOK MARKET

Yes and yes some more. The key is to produce three to thirty daily. In every letter, talk about the dealer and offer to do something for him.

When do you use the telephone?

Before you send out your first sales letter to a large list of trade stores, find out the names of four bookstore buyers of your kind of book and have these four letters hand typed and hand signed. Six days after mailing your letters, phone the buyer and ask what he thinks of your letter and circular. One buyer won't remember it, another didn't see it, a third is out of town, and, when you speak to the fourth, the whole wide world of trade-store book distribution will rise up and communicate to you. Repeat this with every large mailing you make. It lets in the good sunlight.

When you receive an order for twelve books, phone the buyer to thank him personally. In appreciation, offer a free copy for window display. When you say thank you, sound as if you mean it. Which dealer in Sioux City did Marc Jaffe, publisher of Bantam Books, or Howard Kaminsky, of Warner, call today? You have one thing in common with these two gentlemen. They are publishers. And so are you. When a publisher phones a dealer to thank him for an order for twelve or twenty books, he is a standout to that dealer.

A publisher is a publisher, no matter how few titles he issues annually. Every time you introduce yourself over the telephone as Bob Brown, publisher of Brown Books, you are at that moment the overlord. Act with dignity, do business favors for dealers, and they will speak of you not as a tinhorn publisher but as a grand guy who's a decent person to do business with.

Play it straight and great, and you will love the dealer response.

How about the other ways to get dealer distribution?

Two of them, jobbers and chain stores for instance, receive separate chapters in this section. Certain methods such as hiring salesmen and placing trade advertising are beyond the self-publisher with a small press run. But you can blow up a storm by bringing customers into individual dealers' stores—not by hundreds, not even by scores, but by two or three a month.

They'll love you for it.

When you can secure three or four dealers in one town, the local promotion you do helps all the dealers. A customer may get a letter asking her to buy a certain book at the Book Tree, but her charge account is with Books and Things, and that's the store she'll call to order the book.

When Viking Press writes a dealer to say they will use a full-page advertisement in the *Book Review* section of the *New York Times,* and follow that with a page in the *New Yorker,* and follow that with full-page ads in *Time* and the *Smithsonian,* the dealer has to order. Otherwise, he will have customers who ask for the book, and he won't have it in stock. If this happens three or four times to the same customer, the dealer has lost him.

The self-publisher can't offer heavy advertising. But he can do something else, of his own making, that will perk up the dealer's ear. If the self-publisher can fill both sides of one sheet of typewriter paper with brief quotes of reviews from small magazines, country weeklies, small-town dailies, and community papers, the dealer will be attentive. He knows a grass-roots whir when he sees or hears it. And it impresses him.

A self-publisher of a good book can get a large volume of the kind of reviews mentioned above. And when those reviews are quoted briefly, filling one sheet of paper on both sides, it sounds like an awful lot. Not of drivel from jerk papers, but of a groundswell in public opinion. The dealer is attuned to recognizing this sort of thing and doesn't make fun of it. Go after this kind of publicity. If your book is good, you'll get it in reams.

In his own way, a self-publisher of a good book can make a living anyplace he cares to light, and, who knows, he may have another book on the fire.

25

The Specialty Store

ALMOST ANY SPECIALTY STORE can become an outlet for your book when the store's merchandise matches up with your editorial content. Among retail specialty shops that regularly sell new books are camera stores, museum gift shops, and health-food stores. Today, twenty thousand specialty stores sell new books.

In the arts-and-crafts field, for instance, several publishers issue a dozen titles a year and supply metal bookracks to retailers for convenience in displaying their books. Jobbers who sell foodstuffs to the health-food stores also supply racks of paperback books containing a varied line of reading matter on the value of natural foods.

If your book is in a specialty field, such as gardening, photography, crafts, or gourmet cooking, visit local specialty shops in your field, and get the names and addresses of publishers or jobbers whose bookracks you see. Perhaps a publisher will take on your book and distribute it nationally, or a jobber will add your title to his line.

If you can't make the deal you want, you can call on the stores yourself to sell your book, or you can use direct mail.

Let's say you are doing a ninety-six-page, illustrated paperback titled *How to Add a First-Class Cupboard to Your Home for under $130*. Some people who need more cupboard space have found out that a cabinet-maker wants around three hundred dollars for the job. As a result, they are thinking about doing the job themselves. Perhaps their first step is to visit a local lumber dealer to see if something is available in the way of plans or a how-to book.

When a book of this kind is in your mind, you want to get inside the head of the lumber dealer, because he is an important outlet. How will your book help him in his lumber business if he gives it display space? That is what he wants to know, and that is just what you want to tell him when you sell him your book. If the dealer has one hundred customers a week, he might sell three books a month.

Even before you get the words out of your mouth describing your book, he'll object to it on two grounds (neither of which has anything to do with its editorial content). He may say he has no room for it or that people will "walk off with a copy."

Don't answer his points. You need a different comeback.

In this case, show the dealer a one-column, four-inch newspaper advertisement that he can publish in his own community newspaper with a headline:

ALL THE LUMBER
you need to add a
complete cupboard to
your home for $130

Includes hand-made, standard-sized unstained door, complete with hardware, plus an easy-to-read how-to book on cupboard making, with complete plans.

Now, you're thinking about him. You are offering him a package and also a new idea for his regular newspaper ad. He hates to write ads and keeps on using the same ones. You gave him a new one with a new idea. You might also show him a suggested list of materials to go with the hundred-and-thirty-dollar package.

But, hey, you say, wait a minute!

The ad doesn't mention the title of my book or my name.

That's right. You are selling lumber, and that's why the dealer is listening to you instead of helping a clerk wait on trade. This kind of approach will more often result in a sale of twelve books instead of a dealer saying, "Well, I'll try two of them."

You thought about your customer first, yourself second. This is the approach that works with specialty stores.

All retailers have a soft spot in their hearts for a book that works their side of the street. The paperback edition of *Natural Foods Contain No Poisons* went on display at fifteen hundred health-food stores within four months after publication. Its wide distribution came about because the self-publisher found a number of food jobbers who were already calling on these stores. "The nice part about an item like this," one health-food store jobber told his retailers, "is that it doesn't have to be refrigerated, frozen, or kept out of the sun."

Specialty retail stores selling new books are five times more numerous than trade bookstores. Take bicycle stores, for instance. Been to one recently? About one-fourth of them sell books, as Ten Speed Press, a publisher of cycle books, quickly discovered. This small-press publisher issues six to eight titles a year. Naturally, they promote their own cycle titles first and have no strong desire to job other people's books, yet this is the type of lead that could blossom for a self-publisher of cycle books seeking a distributor.

To get wider distribution for a specialty book, you can go outside the publishing industry. If you have a book on canoeing, you might try one of the canoe manufacturers, and, if yours is forthright, instructive, and makes the reader want to own and use a canoe, then maybe a manufacturer will want a special edition for himself. If your book promotes the whole idea of canoeing, what could be a better idea?

Some books are duds at specialty stores. Poetry, novels, autobiographies, books of short stories, essays, biographies, literary criticism, political and historical studies, economics, and juveniles are examples.

Others, however, actually leap into the specialty outlets. Consider the case of *The Last of the Grand Hotels*. This elegant, illustrated, "coffee-table" book, priced at $24.95, relates the good life of high tea, tennis, golf, swimming, relaxing in cushioned wicker chairs, magnificent buffet luncheons, al fresco dining and well-appointed suites. People who stay at one grand hotel are curious about others, because they know people who spend a season at the Greenbrier or the Pocono Inn.

What better market spot for *The Last of the Grand Hotels* than the cashier's counter next to the newsstand at any of the eighteen spas pictured in this book?

Ask yourself this question: in relation to my book, what kind of retailer would push it? Where will it parallel his interests?

341

THE BOOK MARKET

If you have a book in progress, and you describe it to a specialty retailer, and in so doing you run over five minutes, he will start to half-listen. Sometimes, a better way is to hand the specialty-store owner a brief outline of your book and ask if he would want to sell it when published. Drop by in a few days to get his response.

An off-the-cuff, quick answer is hardly what you want. You need to persevere with the specialty-store owner to get him to comprehend the purpose of your book and then let him determine how he might be helped if his customers were to read your book. Doing this kind of research takes your time and his and may indeed switch your thinking around. On balance, if you can get three or four specialty-store owners to read your outline, their response is worth hearing.

While publisher of *Modern Photography* magazine, I developed a line of photo books, because our magazine was already on sale at nine hundred camera stores. This gave us a quick start on distribution. But what if you are a self-publisher of one photo book, and you don't publish a photographic magazine? In this case, your route to camera-store distribution might start with a visit to a number of camera stores to find out the names and addresses of jobbers of photo materials. Perhaps one of these jobbers will handle your book. A trade magazine in the camera field, for instance, publishes an annual directory issue that lists camera-store jobbers. There are two hundred trade magazines with directory issues, so you have access to names and addresses of jobbers in most specialty fields. *Writer's Market* devotes several hundred pages to the trade journals, and most of them publish a directory issue.

A good reference source that will help you locate trade magazines that publish annuals is *Standard Rate & Data*, available at downtown libraries or at any large advertising agency. Its trade-journal section cites those magazines that publish separate directory issues. *SR & D* categorizes all the trade journals, so it is easy to look up the field that interests you.

Professional people, such as small-animal veterinarians, tree surgeons, or disco-dance teachers, are willing to sell a book that makes their own life easier. Consider the vet who stocks the self-published paperback *How to Worm the Small Dog*. For 95 cents, it gives the complete illustrated story of worming. By referring his customers to this book, the vet saves the time of answering the same old question day after day. "It serves me well," "Doc" Edmond Woodward told me.

342

If you can't get a jobber or publisher to sell your book to specialty stores and you can't visit the stores personally, direct mail often works.

In your sales letter, how do you approach the dealer? First learn what is in it for him? How will the book create a greater interest in the store's merchandise?

Your direct-mail campaign follows the general idea described in the method of reaching the trade dealer by mail. Where do you get the names and addresses of specialty stores? They are available from several score of direct-mail-list companies. The New York City and Chicago yellow-page telephone books have a category devoted to mailing lists, and many libraries shelve them. Here are three direct-mail companies that offer lists of all trades: National Business Lists, Inc. (1001 International Blvd., Atlanta, GA); Buckley-Dement Direct Mail Advertising (555 W. Jackson Blvd., Chicago, IL 60606); Dunhill International List Co. (2430 West Oakland Park Blvd., Ft. Lauderdale, FL 33311).

While specialty stores don't sell nearly as many books as trade stores, because their main interest is not books, they are a profitable addition to the bookstore outlets that handle your self-published book. Think of it as a means to move fifteen hundred to two thousand additional copies.

Do the books of mainline publishers that deserve specialty-store distribution get it?

No.

The mainline publisher with a chance of increasing the sale of one title (retailing for eight dollars) by fifteen hundred to two thousand copies at specialty stores may decide not to bother with it. It costs too much to prepare a separate sales letter, circular, and order blank. And the travelers won't go out of their way to call on one store, when all they have to sell is one book. When orders from specialty stores come to the publisher, they hit a block. That's because there aren't any more handwritten filing-card systems at large publishers. They process orders by computer. To add a separate computer category for a few hundred dealers ordering three to twelve books each, and then to discard the list after using it briefly, won't provide the income to meet the high cost of computer time.

The specialty store is a "natural" for the self-publisher who wants to widen his distribution and has a book—usually nonfiction—that appeals to a particular retailer, because it promotes his merchandise.

26

The Book Jobber

THE DAY-TO-DAY OPERATION of the book jobber is almost unknown among self-publishers and among small publishers as well. To many of these enterprising people, the jobber is their lifelong dismay. Once a jobber buys a book, they feel he should go out and sell it to the dealer.

This concept appears to be so reasonable that few will argue it. The real fact is that if you walk into any independent trade store, 40 percent of the books you see are passed through a jobber on their way to the store. But no jobber has salesmen on the road plugging individual titles.

What the jobber does is to make the trade dealer's life easier.

If you are an average trade dealer in St. Paul, and you stock five hundred new hardcover titles, you get your books one of two ways. You order them from a large jobber. Or you order from the individual publishers. If you use the latter route, you will find yourself writing sixty separate orders and mailing each to a different publisher. You might try to make it easier by phoning in the orders. Ever dial twenty long-distance calls in a row? "Sorry, circuits are busy." "Our order-desk lines are busy. Please hold."

When the books arrive from the individual publishers, there is a shower of boxes of all shapes and sizes. Then comes the physical chore of opening each one and matching the contents against the original order. Each publisher has his own discount schedule and his own return policy. In general, these are alike, but, in their particulars, they vary at every point.

When it comes time to return unsold books for credit, you type a separate packing slip for each shipment and box up the books. If only two books are returned to one publisher, the cost of postage, packing, and clerical details is greater than the credit. After returning books to sixty publishers, fifty will send a credit slip, which you enter into your ledger. However, three of the credits contain an error. Patiently, you write and tell them so. The other ten, however, don't answer at all. So you send a follow-up: "Where is my credit?"

What a nuisance!

The book jobber makes all this easier.

He warehouses thousands of different titles and has three hundred to one thousand copies of the better sellers of all publishers and twenty-five to fifty copies of slower movers. The big, successful jobbers ship an order two days after it is received. Large jobbers have a WATS line, and at their phone-order desks are twenty or more people taking orders. These order-takers have been taught to be appreciative of an order, to make a pleasantry during the conversation, and to volunteer a suggestion for an additional title.

What's so wonderful about that?

Surprisingly, the order desk at many publishers' offices is staffed by people who manage to be cheerless and uninterested. I think I know why this is so. The chief operating officer at publishing shops, the "main gink," as they sometimes say in the order room, has not thought to call his own number from a trade store and place an order for six of these, nine of those, twelve of the other ones, and on and on, and listen to the response at the other end.

Why has the jobber been more human and more successful?

The jobber makes practically all of his money from the trade dealer. His business is wrapped up in one kind of customer, and he fights the hardest for their orders. But the publisher has many different kinds of major customers: book clubs, paperback houses, remainder companies, libraries, direct-mail responses. The trade dealer is only one.

One jobber, Ingram Book Company, led the way in using modern technology to show the trade dealer visually how books of all publishers could be ordered from one source. Ingram accomplished this by supplying trade dealers with a biweekly microfilm of their complete stock, showing not only the titles, but the names of the authors, the list prices, and how many copies of each were ready to ship.

When the dealer finds himself low on copies of a well-moving title, he puts the Ingram microfilm on a reader and immediately sees whether Ingram has this title in stock and how many copies are available. Other jobbers copied the idea.

By comparison, this makes ordering from sixty separate publishers a bothersome chore.

The jobber performs these services for the dealer and publisher:

1. The dealer may order one book or one thousand from one source. When the jobber supplies a microfilm and a reader, the dealer need only look up the title in one place instead of consulting a different publisher's catalogue for each title.
2. To the dealer, this means one order, one bill, the receipt of fewer packages, and one place to return unsold books.
3. The jobber's order desk can be reached by WATS line.
4. The discount the jobber gives to the trade dealer is slightly under that of the publisher. The discount is based on the amount of books ordered. Jobbers offer from 33 to 40 percent off the retail price of the book in most cases. Sometimes, a trade dealer's order for perhaps eight hundred books of mixed titles will push the discount to 42 percent.
5. As far as the publisher is concerned, the jobber earns his own large discount (about 50 percent) because of the size of his order. In addition, the jobber's credit is better than the credit of the average dealer. There are always one or two weak jobbers, but publishers quickly spot them because they don't pay up until they are phoned. When payment is promised and then delayed, a limit can promptly be placed on the credit extended. The jobber's credit is easier to track, since there are four thousand trade dealers and fewer than twenty jobbers with large volume.
6. Because he has only the trade dealer to consider, the jobber thinks about him all the time and comes up with many helpful ideas. One, for instance, is a starter list of titles, selected from all publishers, for trade dealers just starting up in business. To get the dealer on his way, some jobbers will prepay the shipping charges on the first order, which amounts to an additional 1 or 2 percent discount. Other jobbers, in order to help a new dealer get going, will make calls to twenty publishers asking if the publisher will

grant five books free if the dealer orders one hundred or more assorted titles from that publisher. This can amount to one hundred free books, and, if they retail at eight dollars each, that's a gift of eight hundred dollars. The jobber then fills the order.

7. The publisher fights hard to get the jobber's business. He much prefers it to orders for six, twenty-four, or fifty books from individual dealers. Yet, the dealer pays the publisher six dollars for a ten-dollar book, and the jobber pays five dollars. The enthusiasm to gross one dollar less per ten-dollar book is explained below.

While the dealer usually orders fewer than two hundred books at a time from any one publisher, the jobber's orders to the same publisher are large—often over two thousand at a crack. Well, which would you prefer if you were a publisher? Two hundred small orders that have to be filled, billed, shipped, acknowledged, and collected, or one very large order from one company? The cost of processing two hundred orders compared to processing just one order almost wipes away the difference in the discounts. As mentioned, the jobber's credit, on the average, is superior. And, of course, the travelers earn less commission* when they sell books to jobbers, because the volume is higher and the travel time is less.

These reasons are all a publisher needs to prefer the jobber as a customer when compared to the trade dealer.

As you can now see, when you examine the matter from inside the jobber's head, he isn't going to pick up one book (out of twenty thousand), ask his secretary to hold all calls, and spend the morning reading it, then get enthused and order someone out on the road selling this title to dealers. The main work of the jobber's promotional people is to explain to dealers the value of a particular jobber's service: the greater number of titles and better return policies he has compared to a competitor and the promptness with which the order is shipped.

If this helps you understand what it means to be a jobber, you can come even closer by examining his awareness of literature and philosophy. In this connection, think of him as being just like the fellow who runs an auto-parts business. He may be able to quote Joyce, or the Bible

---

* Many book publishers pay their travelers 5 percent commission on sales made to jobbers, and 8 to 10 percent to individual trade stores.

by chapter and verse, but, in his auto parts catalogue, he keeps this pretty much to himself. Politics or poetry may indeed be the book jobber's private concern, but, in his business, the main idea is to buy the books that will sell the most copies to the most people and to fill, ship and bill promptly.

But why mention this?

Because jobbers regularly receive sales letters asking them to take on a book for intellectual, moral, or patriotic reasons.

When you offer the jobber your book, he wants to know who will read it and why, how big your market is and what evidence you have, the list price, what people say about the book and who these people are. A dust jacket is often regarded as ample evidence of what the book looks like. The page size, number of pages, weight of the book, and kind of binding are submitted as interesting data. If the book has been on the market for a few months, the jobber will be pleased to look at a sheet that lists, in any given state, names of dealers who have ordered and the dates and precise number of reorders. Xeroxes of these orders and reorders may be enclosed in a separate envelope in case the jobber wants to examine them.

Giving this kind of information is regarded as a good sell. When you own the evidence—show it.

Can part of your sales story touch on the intellectual or the emotional appeal of your book? The closest you might come, and still be practical, is to sketch the reader's reaction. The jobber relates to books that make people *feel*—books that change their pulse rate, that dry their lips, or make their breath come short. If your book does any of these things, and you can touch on it conversationally and work it into your sales letter in a sentence, by all means do it.

In selling *Writer's Market*, for example, I felt that a significant feature was that it covered thirty-five hundred paying markets, regardless of religious, political, or philosophical differences in their editorial content. I believe this is a contribution to a free press, and a free press means a freer people. I worked this idea, in one sentence, into some sales letters. But I trotted it out toward the end of the letter as a throwaway idea and not as a reason to buy the book.

If yours is a knowledge book, or deals with how-to or self-help and you can get over briefly, but effectively how the reader is put into a more positive and informed state of mind by your book, this is worth a sentence if it is done easily and without making a heavy claim.

All people—jobbers, too—are social animals, and each has a key that unlocks him, quite aside from making a profit. It's nice to see if you can fashion such a key, especially if you can do it with your left hand and not parade it as though asking for approval.

As a self-publisher, there is a conclusion you can draw from the dealer-jobber-publisher relationship. Since most books ordered, by both dealer and jobber, are on full return privilege, the publisher is everybody's anchorman.

If the dealer orders directly from the publisher and fails to pay, the publisher is stuck. If the dealer pays for the books and they fail to sell, he returns them, and the publisher has to pony up the refund. When the jobber runs into a nest of dealers who are deadbeats, his payment to the publisher is slow in arriving. When the jobber pays promptly, but his dealers send the books back because the public doesn't want to buy them, the jobber whooshes them back to the publisher for cash or credit.

That's why the publisher (whether mainline or self-publisher) deserves the largest return for the capital and creativity he invests. He assumes the greatest risk.

Is there something in the fact that the publisher takes the greatest risk and deserves the greatest profit that the self-publisher can apply to himself? Yes, indeed.

You want to prepare yourself for the exigencies of the business by forthright pricing. What if a dealer pays for six copies of your book and returns two and one is shelf-worn and can't be resold? What do you do? You eat it. What if the jobber orders fifty, pays for them, returns forty, and says, "No calls, sorry; please send refund check"? These realities need to be taken into account in your pricing.

How do you go about doing this?

When the time comes to price your book—that is, when you have in your possession the printer's dummy of what your book will look like— ask the artist for a rough sketch of your cover if it is a paperback, or a dust jacket if it is a cloth-bound book. Then compare its physical appearance with books of similar subject matter.

What's the most you can charge and still be competitive?

If you have to charge two or even three dollars more than the competition, will your book stand up in the marketplace?

There are a few things you can do to reach for a higher price. Perhaps you can add sixteen blank pages, such as blanks before opening each chapter, blanks that face some of the front-matter pages, three blanks at the end of the book. Will adding sixteen pages give the book a bit more substance? Can you pep up the title—improve the cover—take a greater risk by increasing the press run in order to reduce the cost per book, and thus be able to sell it for less and in this way be more competitive?

If you can't do any of these things, you can review the editorial assets of your book. Consider how you would answer these questions.

1. Is my book reasonably original and does it have something that others in the same field do not have editorially? What makes my book competitive?
2. After I give the dealer a 40 percent discount, what is the spread between the cost of one book and the amount the dealer pays me? Is there enough (at least three dollars for a cloth-bound book) so that I have some money to spend for selling costs?
3. Does my pricing allow for exigencies: returns, nonpayment by some dealers, higher-than-anticipated sales cost?

You are taking the biggest risk of all concerned. Your bookstore customer may risk six to ten dollars to buy your book; the printer risks your taking off and not paying him; the dealer and the jobber risk shelf space. Because you are the main entrepreneur, you deserve the greatest profit. However, when you implement the kind of pricing that insures a profit, do you remain competitive with other books in your field?

A hard question?

Answer it with courage and common sense.

If you plan to sell your book through trade stores, your pricing needs to allow enough margin to get the customer into the store to ask for your book. Some dealers will order ahead of demand. Normally, the jobber won't buy a book and then try to sell it to dealers. The jobber holds up his orders until dealers order from him. Large jobbers, however, do issue catalogues, as noted in the list at the end of this chapter, and this does promote books they have already bought.

There is one interesting ploy by which certain jobbers promote one particular title—for a fee. They provide the people on their phone-order desk with a four- or five-sentence sales pitch describing one title. It is read to the dealer after his order has been phoned in. When a jobber has fifteen people on the order desk, and each one accepts thirty orders a day (a slow day), that's four-hundred-fifty times this sales pitch is given to a dealer. The fee for putting your sales message into the dealer's ear varies with the number of people taking orders. It may be as low as fifty dollars a week and as high as six hundred dollars.

If a sales pitch is given to four-hundred-fifty dealers in one day, will forty dealers each order three copies? That would mean 120 books sold in a single day, or six hundred in one week. If the charge for this service is six hundred dollars, that means an extra sales cost of one dollar per book. And worth it!

Will a jobber take on your book?

He has two standard *no*'s ready for any self-publisher who asks him this question. The *no*'s are self-protection against books from self-publishers he does not know.

The first *no* is a basic one. The jobber will say: "I can't give materials, handling equipment, and a separate warehouse bin to a publisher with one title. There's not enough in it for me." The second *no* is just as basic. The jobber will say: "I'm not getting calls from dealers for this book. People aren't asking for it. If the dealer buys it and the book doesn't move, he won't buy the next book we put through the phone desk."

Can you break through? Yes, of course, assuming you have a good book with a competitive price. Your path into the order room is paved with human relationships.

Usually, one person is in charge of the order room. Maybe, by a chance visit to the jobber, you can meet this person and show your book. Or, maybe you can learn the person's name and send a copy. Maybe one of the young women on the phone desk will tell it to you. At Ingram a few years ago, the woman in charge of the phone-order room selected, on the basis of her own tastes, a book that she asked her people to plug to dealers after the dealer finished giving his order. There was no charge. She did it because she liked the book.

Today, some jobbers sell this kind of sales effort as a service to publishers.

What if you are a thousand miles away from the closest large jobber, and the cost of a two-way trip is out of the question? How do you get started?

Well, the best way is straight up. You might begin by making a station-to-station call to find out who the buyer is for your kind of book. Then try this kind of letter:

Dear——:

I have published a new book, _____, and sent you a copy today. Enclosed are several pages of brief quotes from reviews. [No need to apologize when the reviews are from almost-unknown publications as long as you have them in quantity. Thirty favorable reviews say something positive about your book.]

Also attached is a sheet listing twenty dealers with the dates of their first orders, the amounts ordered, and the dates of the reorders and the amounts.

Perhaps you'd be willing to take _____ home to read. If you like it, please let me know if the workers on your phone-order desk would mention it to trade dealers after taking their order. I would expect to pay for this assistance.

[Then add a brief, personal, complimentary quotation about the jobber based on an interview from a local trade dealer. This cannot be ad-libbed or done loosely. You have to go out and get a quote that's spare and lucid.]

Sincerely yours,

_____

Wait ten days.

If there's no answer, send a carbon of your letter and write on it, "Hope you got my book, _____, and will have time to read it."

Wait five days. Then phone person-to-person and see what you can accomplish.

This kind of shot is worth the effort with several jobbers. Pick the jobber about whom you hear the most good things from your local trade dealers.

Is this kind of letter a peck on a granite rock?

Yes and no. On a dollars-and-cents basis, the buyer knows, if he orders two hundred books from you, it's no big deal for him, and, really, it is just a sort of nuisance. But, like everyone else in this world, he has come to wonder "how big is good and how big is bad?" A self-publisher struggling to market his book that has grass-roots strength (thirty reviews, reorders from twenty dealers) can't be all bad. That's how he'll think of it to himself. You'll find jobbers whose buyers are sympathetic to this kind of approach and who will respond affirmatively and enjoy doing so.

Lists of jobbers who handle books are available. Most of these lists include newsstand wholesalers who distribute magazines and paperbacks, on a consignment basis, to newsstands, rather than jobbers who handle trade books exclusively. Three reference books will help you with starter lists: *The American Book Trade Directory, Literary Market Place* and *The International Directory of Little Magazines and Small Presses*. The latter includes an elaborate list of wholesalers who handle books of small-press publishers. It is worth looking over and contains numerous small, regional wholesalers with whom you can do business. Most small, regional jobbers do not have the volume to support a phone-order desk of three employees.

Here are some jobbers with whom I have done business and found excellent. No company lasts forever, so check these names with your local trade dealer.

The Baker & Taylor Company
1515 Broadway
New York, NY 10036
(212) 730-7650

A clear vision of B & T's activities may be had by reading their three house organs: *Directions, Forecast,* and *Book Alert.* You may have to phone to learn the current departmental address and the person to write to secure a copy.

Baker & Taylor has four regional offices, and, if you are near any of them, stop by to learn something about logistics. The regional offices are at 50 Kirby Ave., Somerville, NJ 08876; Gladiola Ave., Momence, IL. 60945; Mt. Olive Rd., Commerce, GA 30529; 380 Edison Way, Reno, NV 89564.

Baker & Taylor, owned by Grace Chemical, has a complex organizational setup and impeccable credit. They are poor correspondents. When they approve of what you say by phone or letter, you'll get a prompt order.

Bookazine Company
303 West 10th St.
New York, NY 10014
(212) 675-8877

A good idea of this large jobber's activities may be had by looking over three of their house organs: *Bookazine Weekly, Bookazine Bulletin, Bookazine Children's Books.* This jobber is strong in the East.

Bookmen, Inc.
519 North Third St.
Minneapolis, MN 55401
(612) 333-6531

A regional jobber selling mostly in the North Central part of the country, plus Illinois.

Bookpeople, Inc.
2940 Seventh St.
Berkeley, CA 94710
(415) 549-3030

A relatively small jobber with under ten thousand titles, Bookpeople is active with small-press publishers and issues a catalogue in summer and winter called *Small Press Catalog.* They also produce a *Complete Catalog* in spring and fall, and have a monthly, *The Bookpaper.* Founded in 1968, many of its employees are younger and more expressive than those with the older, larger houses. Bookpeople is well oriented to West Coast dealers.

Brodart
1609 Memorial Ave.
Williamsport, PA 17701
(717) 326-2461

For many years Brodart has specialized in supplying libraries with systems and supplies, as well as books. Their West Coast office is at 1236 S. Hatcher St., City of Industry, CA 91748; the Canadian branch is at

THE BOOK MARKET

109 Roy R. Blvd., Braneida Industrial Park, Brantford, Ontario N3T 5N3. Recently Brodart has been on the acquisition road and bought up a number of jobbers, including Dimondstein and Book Distributors. The latter were the main source of new books for the Little Professor chain. Brodart is now committed to selling trade stores as well as public and private libraries, school and college libraries. Their book-buying originates from three separate sections: new books, juveniles, and paperbacks.

> Gordon's Books
> 5450 N. Valley Hwy.
> Denver, CO 80126
> (303) 572-7761

This is a small regional jobber and I found them willing to cooperate with a publisher. They issue a house organ, *Update: Book News from Gordon's*. If you are in this area, Gordon Saull, the owner, or David Youngstrom, the book buyer, might give you an appointment if you send your book along ahead.

> Ingram Book Company
> 347 Reedwood Dr.
> Nashville, TN 37217
> (615) 361-5000

One of the two large jobbers. They stock twenty thousand titles and have three branch offices: 8301 Sherwick Court, Independence Park, Jessup, MD 20794 (near Washington, D.C.); 1820 130 St. N.E. Bellevue, WA 98004; 16175 Stephens St., City of Industry, CA 91744. If you are in the area of their branch offices, stop in. The branches are primarily warehouses but will give you a picture of how a jobber operates. Most trade dealers will have an Ingram Microfiche System. Ask the store manager if he has time to show you how it works. Ingram is a sound, progressive jobber with excellent credit.

> United Book Service
> 1310 San Fernando Rd.
> Los Angeles, CA 90065
> (213) 221-3111

United is a regional jobber working the West Coast area and most of the mountain states and Texas.

Jende-Hagen Bookcorp.
Box 177A
Frederick, CO 80530

Included here is one specialist to indicate the presence of such jobbers. Jende-Hagen Bookcorp. stocks books of Western Americana. They issue two house organs, *Colorado and the West,* and *The Quarterly Endsheet.* Look over their house organs before offering your book.

These jobbers are the ones with whom I have done business. The full list of jobbers is many times longer and includes three types not useful to most self-publishers. These are:

1. Local jobbers who supply magazines and paperbacks on a consignment basis to newsstands in their area. A few own bookmobiles that visit schools and libraries. You can't lose anything, and the chances are that you will learn a lot by visiting the newsstand jobber in your community. Any local newsstand will give you the name and phone number. Among the eight hundred local newsstand jobbers, about a dozen have built up a sideline selling hardcover books, usually special titles that fit their area and their outlets.

2. There are about one hundred specialty jobbers, and one of them, Jende-Hagen, appears on the above list to show the tiger's stripes. Specialist jobbers include those who devote almost all their energies to schools and libraries, or to exporting and importing, or to scientific and medical books, and French, German, and Spanish language books. One small jobber specializes in backpacking, trekking, and walking (Bradt Enterprises, 409 Beacon St., Boston, MA 02115).

3. Drop-ship jobbers. A drop-ship jobber requests the publisher to ship the order and bill the jobber. Most publishers go along with this, but some ask for cash with order and allow a discount of 33 percent or less. An advantage of drop-ship business is that the publisher gets his hands on the name of the customer, which interesting fact is denied him when a stocking jobber orders. Sometimes a small publisher or self-publisher can build a good personal relationship with a drop-ship jobber, and this adds another pleasantry to the day and may build up a sale for a dozen books a month, sometimes much more.

27

The General Newsstand

CAN A SELF-PUBLISHER who has created a paperback of wide general interest publish it himself and get it distributed on the one hundred thousand newsstands in America? The answer is a conditional *yes*.

An inexpensive way to start is with your local newsstand wholesaler. If your paperback book is accepted by him and goes well, try another wholesaler in a nearby town and then a third. If 70 percent of your newsstand test distribution at three wholesalers is sold within three months, you are ready to think about the risk of printing enough copies to place your paperback on sale at twenty thousand newsstands that will take up to six copies each.

The paperbacks on sale at general newsstands are called "mass paperbacks" and have common denominators. The cover price is often $1.50 to $3.95, sometimes a bit higher. The editorial appeal is meant to include about one person in ten who can read well enough to get through a book of several hundred pages. The books are commercially printed and are made to be read and thrown away. Although they do cover all subjects, three-fourths of them deal with mystery, romance, sex, violence, fantasy, adventure, and self-help. Generally a sellout is unknown, but often a paperback sells 80 percent of its total distribution. Usually a sale of 65 percent is regarded as good.

My own first experience in the lion's den occurred in 1929, when I got the idea for a paperback annual to be called *The Writer's Yearbook*. As I write this, it has completed its fifty-first annual edition, but then it was an unpublished idea.

I combed *Who's Who* for the names and addresses of the famous authors whom I wanted to write for the first issue and offered each an idea for an article so the publication would have unity and hang together. That evening, I wrote a one-paragraph *précis* to describe its editorial goals. Driving back downtown that night, I taped it to my boss's desk. My first baby was born, I thought.

The next morning it came back to me with a big NO drawn through my single paragraph, and below it, my boss had signed his initials: Ed R. About five inches of white space separated his initials from my *précis*. In frustration, if not in good sense, I ripped off the top of the sheet of paper, and in the blank space underneath, and just above the initials of my boss, I typed:

> During my absence, Mr. Mathieu will be in charge of the publishing plant.

That afternoon, Ed R. left for six weeks in Europe, which gave me time to produce the publication and get it printed and distributed.

I worried whether my letters to the various authors would produce material, so I followed each one up with a telegram and a phone call. In my letter, after my signature, I wrote the title "publisher," hoping that would have some sort of residual, magnetic effect.

The articles from a baker's-dozen famous authors actually came in, and I had them set, made a dummy from the galleys, and ordered fifty thousand copies with a cover price of 35 cents. One Sunday in April, with four weeks gone of my allotted six weeks, I took the Limited for New York City and, bag in hand, went from Penn Station to 131 Varick Street to see Mike Morrissey, the president of the American News Company.

The American News Company owned several hundred branch offices, with warehouses at each, and had newsstand franchises at all railroad and bus stations and at several passenger airports spotting the country. If you wanted to publish, you drove up to the News Company and waited your turn.

Mike Morrissey, the president, started as a newsboy and was a tough egg. He also was a redheaded Irishman with a soft heart—if you could find it. His word was all you ever needed. And he saw everyone who came to his door. I got to the door and Mike waved me in.

He smiled. "What you got?"

I told him all about the *Writer's Yearbook* and, putting the dummy on his desk, began to reel off the list of authors who had obliged by sending articles: "Edgar Rice Burroughs, Upton Sinclair, Albert Payson Terhune, Faith Baldwin. . . ."

"Market's too small. Not for the News Company." The raised palm of his hand stopped my words. His head shook slowly, negatively, and he picked up a pen to sign a letter.

Across the room, I saw a door with its top half of clear glass. On the glass was lettered: Alan Gould, Chairman of the Board. Through the glass I saw a baldheaded gentleman who had to be the legendary Mr. Gould. Picking up my dummy, I bounded through the door and into his office.

"Mr. Gould, here is my first publication. There's been nothing like it. It's original and a winner. You'll be selling it forever—an annual, 35 cents a copy, for writers. Please take it. It's my first shot. Mike didn't say yes. Will you look it over, sir?"

Mr. Gould looked me up and down.

My father was a *Schneider* for a very conservative tailoring house and, I wore, that day, as always, a tailor-made blue serge suit, white shirt, dark-blue tie, and black, highly polished shoes. I was all of twenty-two, and my hands were moist, and I knew I was going to stutter.

Mr. Gould pressed a button and picked up his phone. "Mike, can I come into your office?"

He took my arm and we went back into Mike Morrissey's office. Mike looked at me impassively and nodded to Mr. Gould.

"Give the kid a chance. Maybe he'll do something good sometime. Take fifty thousand and give them to the better stands. The book isn't so hot, but let him get a start. What the hell?"

Mr. Gould left and Mike looked straight at me.

"We'll take fifty thousand. Your dummy says 35 cents retail. You'll get twenty-one cents. You pay the postage going out. Unsold books are 100 percent returnable; all you get back are the covers. We keep an annual on sale for five months, because it costs too much to push them around for redistribution for one whole year. How much will you lose on a 50 percent sale?"

I thanked him for his offer, wrote down what he said, initialed it, and put it on his desk, and floated out. If Mike said it, I knew it was a contract. When I got to the elevator, an office boy handed me the dummy (my only dummy) that I had left in the office.

Fifty-one years ago, I wasn't exactly a self-publisher, but I did go in cold, and the same thing can be done today. If the distributor likes your product or, for some reason of chemistry or future self-interest, is willing to put up with you, the whole thing can be done more or less the same way.

Placing a paperback on the newsstands is the riskier side of book publishing, and yet, within limits, I believe any self-publisher who has a first-class product and believes in himself can put it over.

Should you do it with your own self-published paperback, and where do you start?

First, let's consider the logistics, for this must be understood before the whole thing makes sense. There are a half-dozen national distributors of mass paperbacks, and the names and addresses of four of them appear at the end of this chapter. If they should ever take you on, they begin their work by supplying you with a galley list of more than eight hundred local, independent wholesalers. Opposite the name of each appears the number of copies the publisher is to ship to that wholesaler. After the publisher ships his copies, he bills the national distributor, who guarantees the credit of each local wholesaler. The publisher does not receive any payment from the national distributor until ninety days after the books have been placed on sale. This first payment is based on a checkup of the sales made by each local wholesaler. The final payment is based upon the copies shipped, less the covers returned. That is the net sale.

The actual newsstand distribution starts when the local wholesaler receives your paperback. Let's say you send him three hundred copies; however, he serves four hundred newsstands. Which newsstands should receive your paperback? And how many of your paperbacks should go to each of the newsstands that is selected?

A small fortune rides on the pencil of the local wholesaler's clerk who makes this notation for you. It's a job you can't do yourself, because you don't know the particular character of each newsstand in every town and city. The small publisher and the self-publisher must leave this vital chore to the clerk assigned to the job. Sometimes it is well done; sometimes it is botched.

The mainline paperback publishers, however, have field men who call on each local wholesaler, and often the field men take a galley list of all the local newsstands, jot down the number of copies of their own books to go to selected stands, and mark an O after the name of the stands to be skipped when this particular paperback is distributed.

Only those publishers who issue ten or fifteen paperbacks each month can afford the cost of employing one man to cover the main wholesalers in each well-populated state.

Are there ways of getting improved newsstand distribution other than employing field men?

I tried two and both work.

I wrote to several *Writer's Digest* subscribers in each city and asked if the *Yearbook* was on sale at the four largest newsstands in their town. I supplied an answer form for that purpose and offered to pay a small fee. When the answers were negative, I wrote to the local wholesaler, sent him a copy of the answer form, and asked that the *Writer's Yearbook* be placed on sale at these stands. Then I sent a copy to the national distributor and asked him to forward my replies to his own promotion man and see that the local wholesaler complied.

I still have a letter from one former national distributor (Fawcett) whose manager wrote me when he retired:

> I was awful nasty to you about all that correspondence you dumped on me for so many years but I want you to know it is the only thing that allowed your *Yearbook* to make a 75 percent sale. Don't let them talk you out of doing it.

The first year I published the *Writer's Yearbook*, I worked closely with our own local wholesaler and rode his delivery trucks to learn what it was all about. That first year, I stayed close to the wholesaler's operation, studying the monthly checkup reports to see what kinds of stands could sell the *Yearbook*. The next year, I helped this local wholesaler write a descriptive letter that explained the kind of distribution the *Yearbook* needed. When I shipped books next year to eight hundred newsstand wholesalers, this sheet was included.

If your paperback is a one-time shot, and you have no former year's records to work with, an alternative is to supply the local wholesalers with your own vision of the kind of stands that should receive your paperback. This means showing your paperback to many kinds of newsstand owners or managers and getting their responses as well as meeting some of the publisher's field men and asking for a helping hand. These field men are social people; they know each other, they know all the wholesalers, they know the drivers and the locations of the better stands. The best way to introduce yourself to the business is to make friends with one of the field men, travel with him for a part of a day, and see his solution to each problem that comes up. Doing this several times will give you a feel for the action.

When Ed R. returned from Europe and found the *Writer's Yearbook* on sale at newsstands, he bought a copy and threw it at me. "Look what your competitors did while you slept your tail off."

I opened my mouth, but no words came out.

He laughed.

"Look," he said. "You got away with it. Okay. Now I want you to go to see Dimpfl [the local manager of the News Company] and spend a little time in their return room. Just take it all in."

I did, and it scared the hell out of me. The great newsstand sellers of the day were stripped and their front covers laid out in huge piles on the one-hundred-by-two-hundred-foot floor of the return room. That's the dead end for books that don't sell. It's the other side of publishing, and not to know it is to be an innocent.

Spend a bit of time in your local wholesaler's return room. You won't be stripped; you'll come out alive and, if you are a publisher, with a good spirit.

What kind of a net sale will your paperback need? If you can't make a small profit on a 50 percent sale, you're in trouble. On a paperback that retails for three dollars, the publisher receives from $1.45 to $1.65 from the national distributor for each book sold, the difference being determined by who has the most of what the other fellow wants.

In the event you decide to test your paperback with two or three nearby wholesalers, and they are willing to go along with you, you almost have to figure your costs based on a large press run, say seventy-five thousand minimum, even though you may print only fifteen hundred copies for your test. The theory of the test is that, if all goes well, and your sale is 70 percent or better, and, if your wholesalers speak up for you, a national distributor may take the book on. The only reason he won't is if he backs away from one-time publishers. He wants a publisher who will deliver a salable product on a regular basis. So, in your approach to the national distributor, you need both a bird in hand and a few tricks up your sleeve. Mr. Gould didn't take on the *Writer's Yearbook* because he thought American News was going to make a fortune out of it; he took it on because, as old as he was, he was thinking about tomorrow.

In this respect, national distributors are like publishers. They need talent, too. Today's publishers sometimes fold and die, so national distributors sniff the wind for new publishers who can ship them salable books on a regular basis. Will any of them think that you have that talent in you? To them, that's as important as the self-published book you just completed.

The hazard of mass-paperback publishing, for the small publisher and the self-publisher, is lack of control at the newsstand level. The retailer who owns the newsstand isn't going to police his paperbacks to see that each one gets a full-cover display, nor will he make sure that every one remains on sale for an allotted period—say three or four months—or even thirty days. The corner druggist's newsstand is the unsung kingpin in paperback publishing. He offers free display space to your paperback for a limited time, and, then, unless it starts to sell, it's a goner.

As a business, the newsstand nearest you is usually a stable operation (with potholes). When the druggist is asked by the local newsstand wholesaler to pay his bill, and the druggist is short of cash, he may say to the waiting truckdriver: "Leave me two hundred new paperbacks; no more. Pick up the rest." In this way, the druggist uses his unsold paperbacks to reduce his bill. If the truckdriver is in a hurry, he sweeps up several hundred paperbacks without too much individual checking. Some of these are redistributed to other newsstands that will take them; the others are stripped.

When the local wholesaler is behind in his bill, and the national distributor puts a squeeze on him: "No money, no books," the wholesaler may simply "cream the stands" and ship back just about everything that sells for over $1.95 in order to reduce his own bill.

Does it happen often?

No.

Does it happen ever?

Yes.

How can you prepare yourself for this sort of contingency? What can you do to preserve the dignity of your product and keep your distribution intact if you are hit by a wholesaler who has to raise cash and sends a whole load of stripped covers back to the national distributor to help pay his bill? What can you do to prevent some local druggist from ordering the wholesaler's truckdriver to: "take everything off my stand except two hundred dollars' worth of merchandise"?

The answer to both questions is nothing.

Just before Christmas, Valentine's Day, and Easter, many newsstands put greeting cards in front of their paperbacks and magazines, covering up one kind of merchandise to give display to another.

What can you do?

Nothing.

The local wholesaler and the national distributor try, of course, to keep the better sellers on sale. At different levels, they punish, one way or another, the occasional operators who substitute bad management for good sense. As a mass-paperback publisher, you have to live with the built-in risks of general newsstand distribution if you elect to go this route.

There are other traps that bleed the publisher. The newsstands at airports, for instance, demand a greater percentage of "take" from the list price, because they say their franchise fee is so large. And the owners of some stands demand free copies from the field men to give front-cover display to certain periodicals.

The general newsstand is no more, no less, of a jungle than the world of gas stations or pro football. For every piece of incompetence, greed, or self-indulgence, there is an answer, sometimes a good one, and sometimes the best you can command at the moment. Large fortunes are made from the hundred thousand general newsstands, usually by the national distributor, frequently by the wholesalers, and often by the large publishers. The newsstand operator does not get the lion's share. As a self-publisher with a first-class product, you can work your paperback into national mass distribution. You have a fair chance at a profit and some assurance of an easier reception on your next venture.

I thought it might be interesting to ask Dick Rosenthal, the grandson of Ed R., if he would supply a list of four national newsstand distributors, and he obliged.

If you get three local newsstand wholesalers to distribute several hundred copies of your paperback to seventy-five or more newsstands in their area and the local-newsstand wholesaler reports a sale of 65 percent or better, one of the following companies may want your paperback for national distribution. Should one of them say "yes," the initial press run requested would be in the area of one hundred thousand. Books are supplied on consignment.

Now that you've made the hard swallow, here's the list.

Independent News Co.
Contact: Sol Himmelman, Executive V.P.
75 Rockefeller Plaza
New York, NY 10019

International Circulation Distributors
Contact: Gale Fleming
250 West 55th St.
New York, NY 10019

Kable News Co.
Contact: Frank Cerminaro
777 Third Ave.
New York, NY 10017

Select Magazines, Inc.
Contact: Dwight Yellen
229 Park Ave. South
New York, NY 10003

28

The Triple-A Newsstand

IN ALMOST EVERY CITY of one hundred thousand population or more, you will find stores whose entire merchandise consists of magazines and paperbacks. These stores are sometimes called triple-A stands.

They do more paperback and magazine business in one day than an average general newsstand does in one month. They do it because they have such a large, varied stock that anyone wanting to buy a special kind of magazine or mass paperback is pretty sure of finding it here. These stands are well managed. Magazines and paperbacks are their main business, not a sideline.

Triple-A newsstands hold a special charm for the small publisher and the self-publisher. They pride themselves on "full coverage" of magazines and on having unusual books that tie in directly with the magazines they stock. That's your key in selling books to these stands.

The traveler, as the book publisher's salesman is called, doesn't visit them, because they stock few cloth-bound books. However, the field men who work for the major paperback houses haunt the triple-A stands, because that's where the action is.

To sell your book to these stands, you will want to consider the owner's point of view. For instance, would you agree that a book on literary criticism or ancient history would not appeal to him?

He has so few magazines on these subjects, he doesn't attract enough customers who might buy books in these areas. Take poetry, for instance. His customers for poetry magazines may number a half-dozen a month. So a book of poems turns him off, not because of the subject matter, but because so few people who would buy this kind of book enter his store.

What if they did?

Then you'd have him.

When a triple-A-newsstand owner pulls a few hundred customers into his store to buy poetry magazines, you can bet your last sheet of typewriter paper that he will want some books about poetry to put alongside his poetry magazines. That's the logic the triple-A-newsstand owner understands. How do you put this logic into your sales pitch?

If you are doing this by letter, you want to realize that managers of these stands don't read. I don't mean they can't read; rather, I mean that reading is not their favorite pastime. They are busy with the details of tending racks that need refilling, of halting thieves who walk off with their merchandise, of keeping an eye on the clerks who make change, and of helping customers find what they are looking for. The stands have long hours. Many are open twelve hours a day, six days a week, and the turnover of help is high. As a result, the morning mail gets short shrift, unless your letter happens to arrive on a blowy winter day when no one is coming in the front door. Checks and bills receive attention. The rest is only scanned.

Yet this retailer has a great deal to offer you. Give him understanding, and the two of you will be a team. He has an educated eye for spotting merchandise that will interest his "regulars" and considers it part of his job to display items side by side that have a common theme. As a retailer, this is his strong point, and that's the thrust to use.

Let's take the basic idea of how to sell the triple-A newsstand and apply it to a book on the stock market. I did one with the title *Investing Your Capital at Ages 30, 40, 50, 60, 70—A Thoughtful Plan for Each Age.* The long title almost covered the entire front cover of the book. Jerky and bumbling though it is, the title made it easy to sell to the triple-A stand, even though it's a ten-dollar cloth-bound book and these stands won't carry six titles in this price range.

How do you start your sales letter to the owner?

In your lead sentence, remind him of the periodicals he sells in this field: *Wall Street Journal, Barron's, Business Week, Forbes, U.S. News & World Report, Fortune, Money, OTC News.* A general newsstand may handle two or three of these. The triple-A stand has them all. But that's just the beginning. Because they are a high-traffic newsstand, they have several hundred customers each month who buy periodicals that deal with investments. Some of these customers are experienced investors, while others are groping for a way to invest thirty dollars a month. The triple-A stand gets its share of each.

That's your hook.

Your sales letter may begin:

Would you say that your customers for *Wall Street Journal, Barron's, Forbes, Business Week, Money, OTC News,* and *Fortune* are in the neighborhood of two hundred a month, or more?

That's why I am enclosing a dust jacket of *Investing Your Capital at Ages 30, 40, 50, 60, 70.* . . . You can move two to three copies of this neat, practical book each month. And make four dollars on each sale.

With this lead, the only other thing you need is a sentence referring to the "enclosed dust jacket that tells your customer what the book's about." At the end of your short letter, include this thought: "Place two copies of this book alongside *Barron's* or *Forbes,* and you'll sell them." This type of short sales letter will succeed.

Why?

Because you aren't stretching a point to suggest to the owner that with the town's best prospects for investments coming into his store regularly he can sell two or three copies a month of the book described.

Let's look at another book and see how we can sell it to this kind of large newsstand.

An unknown woman in a small town in Oklahoma has a dozen tiffs with her husband in one month. Some she patches, some she can't. She wonders: How do these tiffs start? Could any have been stopped before they grew? Surprised at her thoughts, she starts to write them out. Over the next six months, she writes 160 pages of copy with the title—you guessed it—"How to Mend a Tiff with Your Husband." A local community paper uses part of it and she receives appreciative fan mail. She sends the fan letters and several chapters of her work to a high-school friend who is a marriage counselor. He makes some suggestions. She shows the entire 160 pages to her pastor, to her husband, and to her friends who come to play bridge Tuesday afternoons. On a visit to Oklahoma City, she visits a triple-A newsstand and asks the owner if there are any magazines that might tell her how to mend a tiff with her husband.

He hops to it, this being his job. In two minutes flat, he collects eleven magazines and gives them to her. Embarrassed, she buys three and walks out. Next day, she is back, "just looking." She visits an Instant Print Shop and inquires if they will print her booklet. Yes, indeed. Five hundred dollars buys six hundred.

Will it sell to the triple-A stands?

Granted certain conditions, it can't miss.

If it is agreeably designed and modestly priced—say two dollars tops—bound in paper, and eighty to ninety-six pages with a two-color cover, she can be pretty sure of getting one-fourth of the triple-A stands to try it right away, especially if she carries with her the front covers of four big national magazines in this very field that these stands sell. A 40 percent discount lets the dealer buy her paperback at $1.20. If twenty stands reorder in ninety days, she has authentic ammunition to use on those stands that didn't order the first time they were asked.

If a stand in one city moves one hundred copies in six months, it would be worthwhile going to that city, calling at the office of the local newsstand wholesaler, and meeting any of the field men who represent major paperback publishers and who happen to be there at the time. Would they like to recommend this book to their home office? Jake's, on 10th Street, sold one hundred copies in six months. That's a pretty good report card.

Self-help is the best kind of book to offer these stands.

Do these two examples set your mind to working on a title you can write for these stands, or give you an idea of how to sell your own self-published book to this market?

Where do you get the names and addresses of the triple-A stands?

You can start by looking at your library's shelf of yellow-page telephone books, under the heading "News Dealers." The news dealers listed here are the town's largest.

Triple-A stands are a beautiful market for the small publisher when the book parallels the editorial interest of some magazines with good sales. The book's style should be popular, possibly journalistic, and easy to read.

If the stands do well with your book, you can send a Xerox of their reorders to book buyers at large bookstore chains as evidence that you have a fresh new title that is catching on. The logic here is that what happens on newsstands portends what will happen in bookstores.

The logic of the triple-A-newsstand owner is that, if he sells three hundred copies of ten different magazines in one specific field, he knows he can sell a few books to these same customers. And, instead of making 30 or 40 cents on a sale, he'll make several dollars, if it's a hardcover, or at least 80 cents if it's a paperback.

Show him a book in a field in which he sells a lot of magazines, and he'll hear you out.

29

The Chain Bookstore

THE MAJOR CHANGE in book retailing over the past fifteen years is the growth of chain bookstores. Today, one hundred chain operations criss-cross the country and vary in size from four to six hundred stores each. Their combined sales are 60 percent of all trade bookstores, and the day is approaching when the independent bookstore will be a small segment of the industry.

How did this come about? Why are the chains taking over?

The story begins long before the new local chain store opens its doors for business. It starts with nationwide location studies seeking to pinpoint heavy metropolitan traffic patterns of reasonably affluent shoppers who are believed to be book buyers. When this fortunate location is found, it is compared with other available spots, and the best one, in terms of traffic pattern, sufficient space to shelve forty or fifty thousand dollars' worth of books, a fair rental, good parking space, and low-profile competition, is leased.

If all works well, the store remains; if not, the chain performs surgery. They close Fort Worth and open in Duluth. Or Jacksonville. The commitment to a location is based on what the chain is able to draw from it.

The local merchant who seeks to open a retail store works in a different way. He has no way to compare his location with thirty others and pick the best. The size of his store fits the size of his pocketbook, and, if the store can shelve twenty-five thousand dollars' worth of books, that's the best he can do.

This approach to location and number of square feet of selling space makes him less competitive, but the real killer is the diffidence in applying fundamental retail mathematics. One example will explain it:

A trade store purchasing books directly from publishers and jobbers receives an average discount of 37 percent. With this discount, a ten-dollar book costs the dealer $6.30 and leaves a gross profit of $3.70 on a ten-dollar sale. At this crucial point, the prospective dealer need ask two questions: (1) Exclusive of the cost of books, how much are my other expenses? (2) When my gross profit is 37 cents on the dollar, how much gross income do I need to cover my expenses?

If the dealer opens his store with a retail stock of twenty-five thousand dollars in books, and they turn over four times during a period of one year, the annual gross sales will be one hundred thousand dollars, leaving the dealer with thirty-seven thousand dollars to pay for all expenses except books.

Total gross sales in one year when a retail stock of $25,000 is turned four times	$100,000
Cost of books sold when the discount averages 37 percent	63,000
	$37,000

Allowing fifteen thousand dollars for himself, the dealer in the above illustration has twenty-two thousand dollars left for rent, utilities, supplies, advertising, store maintenance, insurance, a part-time helper, and the cost of postage in bringing the books to his store. On this kind of projection, he can float.

However, can a retail bookstore turn its stock over four times?

Rarely.

Is there an alternative?

Yes. A larger store with fifty thousand dollars' worth of books in stock that turns over twice a year would equal a $100,000 gross income and allow almost the same gross profit: $37,000. Another alternative is to start with $40,000 in books and attempt to turn the stock over two and a half times. This, too, would deliver $100,000 gross income and $37,000 gross profit.

But a start-up stock of that value is more than the small independent merchant can swing, so he goes ahead anyhow, hoping against hope that, with a smaller store and a start-up stock of close to $25,000, he can somehow manage to grow and prosper and make out during the first lean years.

Each week three independent trade-book dealers drop out because the stock is too small, and their turnover of stock varies from one to two. The chief exceptions are the several hundred big-city department stores that maintain a book department through which their store traffic flows. The book manager, recently promoted from corsets, or basement bargains, is schooled in turnover. The store's top-level management never allows him to forget that, when his department's turnover drops under two and a half for more than two seasons, he will be dropped, too.

If things continue as they are going, the independent bookstore, with the exception of locally operated department-store outlets, and about eighty retail book merchandisers in metropolitan centers, will vanish from large cities and be located only in smaller towns where the traffic isn't inviting to the chain. The eighty big-city merchants with independent bookstores could really have been anything they wanted in retailing but happen to like owning and operating the independent bookstore.

In the smaller towns, the surviving independent bookstores are copying their metropolitan peers. They work very hard on these points: (1) their store hours are longer, often including evenings and Sundays, especially those bookstores located near a cluster of expressway motels or in county seats; (2) they patiently build individual card files of customer preferences and do a heavy charge-account business based on phone calls to the customer on new titles; (3) to pep up turnover, they do more physical inventory and to make the return of dead stock easier, they order largely from jobbers; (4) the store lighting is improved, and remodeling makes room for more titles; (5) to improve their profit margin, the small-town bookstore adds non-book lines offering a 50 percent discount; and (6) to increase store traffic, some of them emulate the Little Professor chain by installing a splendidly large magazine display.

The independent bookstore survivors are born-again merchandisers. Their number is fewer, but they have a definite spot for themselves in book distribution.

Meanwhile, the chain store that has grown from doing under 5 percent of the bookstore business to 60 percent, and increasing every year—what do they do that's so smart?

Really, they are not all that smart. But they seem to be aware that with a retail stock worth twenty or twenty-five thousand dollars, the turnover an average store can expect is too low to make a profit. So the chain puts a different kind of package together, and it works. It starts with a location selected from the best that can be found anywhere. Then, the store's selling space has to provide room for at least forty thousand dollars in retail stock, and, in mainline stores, this runs over fifty thousand dollars. With this much stock, and a turnover of two, a profit is close at hand. But that's not all. The chain store does four more important things to push its bottom line into the black.

They order around 85 percent of their stock direct from the publisher, and, because the orders are large, they receive a 50 percent discount. The remaining 15 percent is ordered from jobbers, and, because of the large orders, the discount is 40 percent and sometimes a shade better. Their average discount is close to 48 percent. This gives them a gross profit of nearly 48 cents on the dollar, compared to 37 cents earned by the independent retailer. On one hundred thousand dollars' worth of business, that's eleven thousand dollars more.

With location, large stock, and greater discount, the chain-store operation is off to a great start. But there is more in their arsenal.

Just as you can't play the market and hit a winner every time, no book buyer is perfect either. He buys books that sit on the shelf. If 10 percent of the stock fails to turn over more than once a year, this can knock the socks off a dealer's goal of a two-and-a-half turn. The chain's local manager regularly reports wallflowers to his home office so they can be replaced.

Finally, the chain doesn't expect people to walk in and buy because they have nothing else to do on Monday morning. They go after prospective customers with newspaper and broadcast advertising, and, during the holiday season, they send attractive catalogues to the nation's book buyers. One chain shipped its prospective customers 4 million Christmas catalogues.

That's their entire ticket, and it's a good one. Backing it all up is a small, close-knit management that heads up each chain and has no sympathy for a loser.

How do you sell books to chains?

You begin by getting some kind of drop on the buyer.

You have to do that, because the buyer has already been busy getting a drop on you before you ever call on him or write. Each chain produces a weekly list of its better movers. The buyer studies his list of national winners as well as a list of sectional reading preferences. He brings this information, along with his past experience, to every buying decision he makes. And he makes plenty. Every book that is sold or returned must be replaced, or the stores go out of business in four months. The buyer has to buy, or the whole shooting match is *kaput*.

That's your edge. The buyer is paid to buy, and he has to buy.

Most chains do their book buying at chain headquarters. A few place only the initial order and allow the managers of their local stores to go from there.

We are now ready to explore the tactical means of selling books to the one hundred chain-store buyers. In almost every case, the purchase orders for new titles, as well as reorders, come to the publisher from the chain's home office. About 5 percent of the local chain-store managers send their reorders directly to the publisher. Which chain-store local managers have this prerogative? No such list exists. Therefore, direct your sales efforts to the chain's home office. If you ever receive a reorder directly from a local store manager, you can include that person on your list of prospects.

In the main, think in terms of getting your orders and reorders from the home-office buyer at the chain's headquarters.

Because of space limitations, a store can shelve only a fixed number of books, and, therefore, orders can be written only when inventory control provides room for a new shipment.

I was invited to observe one method of chain-store inventory control. The system begins with the local manager's receiving a bundle of printed inventory cards with instructions to fill them out every four months. After the cards are punched to show the number of each title in stock, this information is fed into a small computer. Via a telephone jack the results are ticked to a computer at headquarters. Similar information flows in from the other stores in the chain.

While I was observing this clerical task, the chain's headquarters computer phoned back a message to the local store:

**Send list of all titles that failed to sell
one copy in the past 120 days at your store.**

The store manager plugged in the telephone jack and supplied the fatal list.

That night, before going home, a headquarters supervisor ordered the computer to print out all titles that failed to sell one copy at any store during the last 120 days. The next morning a printout showed that seventy-eight different titles had failed to sell a single copy at fifty-two different stores. The seventy-eight titles represented six hundred books that had paid no rent.

All that day, the computer and the chain-store supervisor worked together to pinpoint poorly selling titles. That evening, the home-office chain-store supervisor ordered the return of titles that had failed to move, or were very slow movers. Because they were not shelf-worn, the chain store received full credit from the original publisher or the jobber from whom they were ordered. A small part of the unsold books were shipped to geographical locations where inventory reports showed good sales for these titles.

Within three weeks the returned titles were replaced with new ones that the chain's buyer hoped would do better.

If you ever get unsold books back from a dealer and they look new, you may think: "Why didn't he keep them on sale for another three or four months?" The dealer feels that if he were to do this, the books would not be acceptable for return. In addition, the idea of keeping four books on sale for six months, and selling only two, gives the retailer a weak turnover and ties up capital.

When you're the manager of a retail bookstore, you tend to pass over the name of the publisher, even the author. What concerns you is: Can I afford to continue to give it shelf space? Is it ruining my turnover, maintaining it at the same level or pushing it up?

Does that help you answer the question "Will the chain-store buyer pay attention to my sales letter, circular, or order blank?" Isn't he too busy jockeying all his different horses to bother with one small publisher? Look at it this way: When the stores of one chain return 15 percent of their total inventory because it is not selling, it is the buyer who may be replaced.

Each book circular dropped unheeded by the buyer into the wastebasket, each book he orders, each book he reorders, represents a small piece of his future with his company. If your book has a reasonably wide appeal, if your envelope is addressed to the right person and your letter, circular, and order blank make professional sense to the buyer, you will receive the attention you require.

Let's start to sell a book to a chain and see how we can go about it. To begin with, we want to communicate with the right person at chain headquarters. If we could peep in the door, we might see twenty to eighty office employees. Of these, maybe two are authorized to buy your particular book. How do you go about finding your buyer? One way is to trust to luck and address your letter to the company. Will this work? In theory, it should. The mail clerk finds it no great task to see that an envelope addressed to "John Given" is placed in his basket. A mail boy picks it up and delivers it to John. That's easy. But how about a letter addressed to People's Book Chain? There may be thirty just like it in one morning. It's chancy to ask the mail clerk to match each circular with the right buyer.

At the end of this chapter are the names and addresses of chain-bookstore companies. Here's how to reach the *right* buyer for *your* book at *each* chain.

1. In the lower left-hand corner of your envelope, write "Attention: Hardcover Book Buyer." Or, an improvement, "Attention: Hardcover Book Buyer: MYSTERY," or whatever genre covers your book. Or, "Attention: Paperback Fiction Buyer," and so forth. Although not perfect, this beats addressing your mail to the company alone.

2. Write a letter to the chain and address it to "Secretary, Hardcover Book Buyer," or "Secretary, Paperback Book Buyer." Describe your book in a sentence or two, and ask for the name of the buyer of this type of book. Enclose a stamped, self-addressed envelope, but no circular or order blank. If your stationery is simple, the graphics in good taste, your typing is neat and your letter short (five lines), you can count on a 50 percent response. Try four chains before writing to all. If you receive no response, ask some local booksellers and, if you can get to them, some travelers, what they think of your letter.

3. Speak with the telephone operator at the chain and ask for the name of the buyer of your type of book. Then ask to be connected to this individual's secretary. If the secretary is in, verify the information you have just received.

Once you have the correct name of the buyer, write a letter that briefly describes your newly published book. Tell where it should be shelved, the kind of customer who will be most likely to buy it, the list price, and the discount. If other chains have ordered, you might mention their names and the amount ordered. Have you secured good reviews and publicity? Enclose some and refer to this in your letter. Include a circular, order blank, and dust jacket.

But how do you know where your book should be shelved and who will be most likely to buy it? Can you visit some outlets of the chain to which you are writing? Or could a friend do it for you? Show the local chain-store manager your book, some reviews, a circular. Where would this store shelve it? Why? Would this manager want to stock it? What are the reasons? Including this kind of information and quoting two or three store managers allow you to speak a language familiar to the buyer.

If you receive an order, what do you do for an encore? Or, when you don't get the order, what do you do for a follow-up?

At this point you can let your ingenuity shine.

Let's say your book is titled *How the Tone Deaf Can Learn to Sing in Perfect Pitch.* * Who would be the best customers? People who *are* tone deaf, as well as music teachers who constantly run up against would-be students who are tone deaf.

In your follow-up to the chain buyer, offer to send a mailing to three hundred individuals in the music field, whose names and addresses appear in the current yellow pages of the phone book in one city where this chain has three or more stores. Enclose a sample of the suggested letter, which describes your book and its usefulness to the prospect and gives the chain's local store addresses and phone numbers.

Do big publishers do this?

You bet your life they don't.

This kind of hard sell is beyond their reach. Labor costs too much. Can you afford it? The small publisher is ideally situated for doing just this sort of thing.

If you go ahead with an idea like this, you will want to do some research first. Show your suggested sales letter to three or four people who would be among those included in your mailing. Get their reactions. By quoting their comments in your letter to the chain's buyer,

---

* Title of a book-in-progress by William L. Mathieu.

you give off the amiable sound of a sincere salesman whose interest is in the buyer. The safer you make it for the chain-store buyer to say "yes," the more certain you are of receiving the order.

Who pays for mailing the three hundred letters and circulars? You do. If you do most of the work it will cost sixty dollars. All you ask is for an order of five copies each from the chain's local stores in the one city in which you make the mailing. A thoughtful self-publisher will first show the local chain-store managers the actual mailing piece and get an opinion. If it's affirmative, quote it in your letter to the chain's buyer. If it's very negative, go back to your drawing board. That's the reason for research. Let's say the book *How the Tone Deaf Can Learn to Sing in Perfect Pitch* includes two mini-disc LP records. The entire book costs you $5.00 to produce and sells for $15.00, giving you a gross profit of $3.70 on each sale you make to the dealer at 42 percent off list. On 25 books, you'd be making a gross profit of $92.50 and then spending $60.00 to help bring the consumer into the store. The large publisher shakes his head and walks away. To you, it's the wedge that opens the door. If you do nothing, you rely on walk-in customers to discover your book or on local publicity and reviews to pull in the customers. If you are fortunate and receive an abundance of the latter, the local chain store may work with you on a cooperative newspaper ad in which you pay 40 to 60 percent of the cost of the ad, and the store pays the balance. This is a good way to bring customers into the store. Be prepared to create a series of efforts to bring customers for your book into the trade store in order to get word-of-mouth advertising started. You don't have to do this for every sale, but in each city you have to prime the pump.

I did this for years on different books, and it worked most of the time. As word-of-mouth advertising took over, my work load on each book became less. The point is that you can't rely on a two-hundred-store chain to get steamed up over five stores each ordering five copies of your book. That's a nothing deal for them. It's up to you to make it shine.

But how about all the other books on the shelves of each store? How are they sold? Some of these are advertised by the publisher, some of the authors are well known from previous books, some have been lifted by publicity from columnists, reviews, and TV talk shows, and some books don't sell at all and are returned. Think about doing positive things for your book that pull customers into the trade store asking for what you have just written and published. When you do that, you become the publisher most likely to succeed.

Most small publishers, never having owned a trade store, don't grasp the mentality of the retailer, who stares at a thousand different titles on his shelves every day. There they sit, a merged blur in his eyes. Some days, he rearranges the titles. Two of this one, four of that one, twenty of another. Can he afford to advertise a book that has sat in his store, unbought, for a month? And if he were to advertise it, and it were to sell out, how long would it take before he could get a new supply?

Can you rely on any retail bookstore, whether chain or independent, to think about you and work for you on an individual basis, to advertise for you, to teach the clerks about your book? The only route for the self-publisher is to dig up ideas and front for his book. For him, Job One is to sell the chain; Job Two is to help the chain with practical promotion devices that the local manager agrees will bring customers into his store asking for your book. The advantage in doing this for the chain store, compared to doing the same thing for one independent retailer in Perry, Georgia, is that your success with the former can be translated into orders for other stores in the chain. When you work for a single retailer in one city, or even when you combine a campaign to promote your book among five independent retailers in one city, you start over from the beginning when you broach the same campaign in the next city.

There is another side to all this. Marjorie Holmes points it out. She asks: "How can a writer do all this work and still write? Don't you have to be either a publisher or a writer?" People like Marjorie are natural-born authors. She is on her fifteenth book. That would take me forty-five years, allowing time to color in the spaces for gardening and tennis. Writers who do only one or two books can enjoy the good feeling of causing their works to sell and, perhaps, become successful small publishers. Marjorie is right: an author cannot do a book a year and, at the same time, hard-sell each book. A self-publisher is committed to writing and selling his first book.

The list of chain stores that follows does not include the eighty small satellite chains that radiate from flagship department stores. These chains came about as downtown department stores branched beyond the suburbs to outlying towns.

Two mailing-list companies, Dunhill International List Company (44 Park Ave. South, New York, NY 10016) and Walter Kraus Company (48-01 42nd St., Long Island City, NY 11104), offer lists of department stores with book departments. Each list sells for around forty dollars and contains between 650 and 900 names and addresses.

Neither list includes the name of the book buyer, nor is the name and address of the flagship store that buys for its satellites singled out. How do you get this? The way I know is the way I used to do it: use a direct-mail campaign that sells your book to one of these lists. The buyer will use his own order form, which lists the book departments in his immediate division, and check the stores to receive your books, and then sign his own name. In not too long a time, you'll have a first-class direct-mail list.

The book department of a mainline department store is usually the largest in town, pays within thirty days, and is capable of giving the largest order of any local store. It's worth a lot of effort to get the local flagship stores of each department-store chain to handle your book. All told, this represents about three hundred first-class retail book outlets including the better outlying stores.

Few department-store chains employ home-office buyers who order for all book departments in their chain. That's why you build your own list of regional department-store buyers who buy for the stores in their area.

The pragmatic way to begin writing individual sales letters to any chain-store book buyer is to call on some of their nearby outlets. Think of it as a research call rather than a selling call. Warm up in this way and feel loose and easy as you speak with the local store manager. Let your mind focus on this person, his interests and point of view, and you will find yourself selling books.

HOME OFFICES OF BOOKSTORE CHAINS

Atticus Book Stores
1020 Chapel St.
New Haven, CT 06510
(203) 562-7722
13 stores

B. Dalton
(A Division of Dayton Hudson Corp.)
9340 James Ave. S.
Minneapolis, MN 55431
(612) 887-5548
500 stores

THE BOOK MARKET

Barnes & Noble
105 Fifth Ave.
New York, NY 10003
(212) 675-5500
38 stores

The Book Cache
436 Fifth Ave.
Anchorage, AL 99501
(907) 277-2723

The Book Market
1200 N. North Branch St.
Chicago, IL 60622
(312) 440-4470
18 stores

Bookland
Industrial Park
P.O. Box 219
Florence, AL 35630
24 stores and 5 card shops
(Located in Alabama, Georgia, Florida,
    Mississippi, Louisiana, Tennessee,
    Maryland, Virginia)

Bookland of Maine
(Owned by Portland News Company)
P.O. Box 1728
Portland, ME 04104
8 stores

Brentano's
(Owned by Macmillan Company)
586 Fifth Ave.
New York, NY 10036
(212) 757-8600
31 stores

Crown Books
3301 Pennsy Dr.
Landover, MD 20785
14 stores

Dillard Department Stores
900 West Capitol
P.O. Box 486
Little Rock, AR 72203
42 department stores with book departments

Doubleday Book Shops
673 Fifth Ave.
New York, NY 10017
(212) 953-4828
28 stores

Gateway Books
6305 Baum Dr.
Knoxville, TN 37919
(615) 584-6141
50 bookstores; 32 card shops

J. K. Gill
2725 NW Industrial St.
Portland, OR 97210
(503) 226-4611
39 stores in Oregon, Washington, and
    California with book departments

Honolulu Book Shops, Ltd.
1450 Ala Moana Blvd.
Honolulu, HI 96814
(808) 941-2274
3 stores, all on Oahu

The J. L. Hudson Company
1206 Woodward
Detroit, MI 48226
11 stores, 10 in Michigan, 1 in Toledo,
    Ohio

Hunter's Books
(A division of Books, Inc.)
463 N. Rodeo
Beverly Hills, CA 90210
(213) 274-7301
22 stores; 2 in Washington, 8 in San
    Francisco Bay area, 7 in Southern
    California, 2 in Arizona

Kaufman's
400 Sixth Ave.
Pittsburgh, PA 15219
6 branches

Kroch & Brentano
29 South Wabash
Chicago, IL 60603
(312) DE 2-7500
18 stores, mostly in the Chicago area

Laco Books
4 East Alexandrine
Detroit, MI 48201
(313) 494-0367
Medical bookstores: 2 in Michigan, 1 in
    Buffalo

Lauriat's, Inc.
10 Pequot Way
Canton, MA 02021
(617) 828-8300
13 stores

Little Professor Book Center
33220 Capital
Livonia, MI 48150
(A franchised operation)

Missouri Store Company
908 Woodson Way
Columbia, MO 65201
20 stores
(College bookstores)

Vroman's
2085 E. Foothill Blvd.
Pasadena, CA 91107
(213) 449-5320
4 stores

Walden
(Owned by Carter Hawley, Hale)
201 High Ridge Rd.
Stamford, CT 06903
(203) 356-7500
630 stores

Coles Book Stores
90 Ronson Dr.
Rexdale, Ontario M9W 1C1
Canada
151 stores in Canada
49 stores in USA

30

The Library Market

WOULD YOU BELIEVE our country supports more libraries than trade bookstores, religious bookstores, commercial publishers, and jobbers all put together? And, because the books are free and well chosen, the patrons who enter libraries number into the millions each day.

People must like to read—and pay taxes to support libraries.

The number of our nation's libraries is staggering. Here is the breakdown:

9,000 public libraries
1,400 county libraries
1,300 federal and armed-service libraries
1,700 college libraries
1,500 religious libraries
1,100 junior-college libraries
13,000 junior-high-school libraries
16,000 public-high-school libraries
45,000 elementary-school libraries
10,000 Catholic-school libraries
700 historical-society and museum libraries

The above list, which does not include branch libraries, goes on and on, one of the smaller categories being 450 music libraries.

The nation's libraries are an attractive market for good reasons. There are endless thousands of them and over 95 percent pay up without too much coaxing. Each one has an annual cash allowance for the purpose of buying new books, and, although this sum rises and falls, the steady demand for new books from libraries is always there.

The astonishing diversification among libraries permits many kinds of specialized works to have a decent shot at this market. Direct-mail lists of libraries are in plentiful supply and available for rental. In addition, the library jobbers who inventory tens of thousands of titles will promptly stock a title as soon as their library customers begin to order it.

When a self-publisher wants to sell a new book directly to the library market, his first requirement is a good list. One of the better-known sources for library lists is R. R. Bowker (1180 Avenue of the Americas, New York, NY 10036). Their list-rental manager is Sal Vicidomini. Bowker publishes *Library Journal* and each day the names of new subscribers enrich their rental lists. Another authoritative source of names is the American Library Association (50 East Huron St., Chicago, IL 60611). Write to Robert Hershman. A.L.A. is the main trade association in the field. They own three library magazines, and names of new subscribers are funneled to their rental-list department.

Other reliable companies that rent lists of libraries include: Customized Mailing Lists, Inc. (158-23 Grand Central Parkway, Jamaica Estates, NY 11432), Hugo Dunhill Mailing Lists, Inc. (630 Third Ave., New York, NY 10017), Fritz S. Hofheimer (88 Third Ave., Mineola, NY 11501), The Walter S. Kraus Company (48-01 42nd St., Long Island City, NY 11104), Curriculum Information Center (1726 Champa St., Denver, CO 80202), Alvin B. Zeller, Inc. (475 Park Ave. South, New York, NY 10016).

The above companies will send a description of their library lists on request.

Can you find out, in advance, if the list you are offered is the rental list you want? There is one way to sample a list before you rent it. Ask the list renter for all names and addresses in one or two zip codes covering an area in your city that you can call on personally. After you receive this sampler and call on each library, then ask yourself if these are the kinds of prospects you want to send your sales literature. If the sampling is reasonably good (70 percent consisting of the kinds of libraries you want to reach), then you can rent the list with confidence.

Will list owners accommodate you?

Sometimes, no, but it's worth the effort to try to get a zip-code sampling.

They offer two reasons against doing this: (1) The computer can't extract one zip code without running through the whole list, and this is as costly as renting the whole list as far as computer time is concerned. (2) Providing a one- or two-zip-code sampling for the sake of renting only a few thousand names is too much sales cost for too few dollars.

The list companies that compile their own lists of libraries, such as the A.L.A., or Bowker, retain a computer printout of all lists, so there is always a "spare" in case of fire. To pull this cumbersome master list out of the safe, find the particular zip code that one customer wants, and then have it typed out, is a drag. When I rented a list, I regularly tried to obtain the names and addresses of one or two zip codes that I could check personally. I was successful in getting the sample when the list renter hoped I would rent many names if my test was successful, or if I was a regular customer. It's still worth the effort to request it. It's your money that you are spending, and you have the right to be careful of it.

The great part about library mailing lists is that they come in so many convenient classifications. For instance, you can buy "all public libraries with an annual new-book budget of two thousand dollars and over," or you can buy only those with an annual budget of fifty thousand dollars, of which there are six hundred. Or, you can buy separate lists of private-school, public-school, or college libraries, or specialized libraries of law, medicine, and so forth, to suit your needs.

If you don't want to spend your money to rent a list of libraries, you can pick up enough names free to make a small test mailing.

Almost every main downtown library has a copy of R.R. Bowker's immense seventeen-hundred-page reference work, *American Library Directory*, now in its thirty-third year of publication. It contains a comprehensive list of thirty-three thousand public, college, and special libraries in the U.S. and Canada. Each entry contains the name and address of the library, some of its department heads, and its annual budget for new books.

Since this is a frequently used directory, you can't hang onto it for a whole day while selecting and copying five hundred names and addresses of libraries on your envelopes. But librarians are understanding. They may tell you when the book is least likely to be used with the agreement that you will give up the directory when another patron wants it.

The *American Library Directory* sells for $47.50 and is now published annually. The print is small, and you have to read the descriptions of

391

each library to select the one you want. When you rent a list, of course, the computer does this for you (and charges you, too).

To serve their clients who want to make a test mailing before shooting the works, mailing companies will usually rent one state at a time or let you order every *nth* name. Thus, if a public-library list contains ten thousand names and you order every tenth name addressed, your sales campaign would be addressed to one thousand public libraries. This provides a sampling of what you might get back in orders, should you decide to go ahead and mail the entire list.

Let's say you have a book titled *The Big O*, and it has been put together by yourself, a psychiatrist, and a psychologist. The book seeks to shed fresh light on human sexual desire. You, and your coworkers, feel fantasy illumines reality, and, with this in mind, your team interviewed seventy-five women of different ages and backgrounds on the kind of orgasms each wanted most to have. You got a five-thousand-dollar grant for the book and paid every woman interviewed fifty dollars and gave each of your two doctorate helpers one-fourth of the royalty. After the book is published you enter a library carrying some of the tapes, a copy of the book, and a transcription of one of the tapes. Will they look at it?

I asked that question of the head librarian at a large library. He sat a while, fiddling with the roll of tape I placed at his desk, then asked me to follow him. In the library's history department he placed in my hands a documentary written in 1845 by an English woman interpreter at a Turkish harem. Opening the book, he ruffled the pages for the lines he wanted me to read:

> Marya, the Sultan's doting mother, brought to him that day four veiled nubile virgins. He thanked her pleasantly and offered her a freshly made ice flavored with rose petals, and, waving the girls to a eunuch who guided them out of the royal chamber, he took an ice for himself.

Reading the lines, I looked up.

"But, sir, I mean, would your acquisitions librarian read *The Big O*, listen to the tapes, look at the transcription of one tape?"

"Maybe," said the head librarian. "We receive more offerings than we can get into. There's just so much you can do. But, when something appears to be fresh and interesting, we find the time."

Daily, each library receives five to thirty circulars and catalogues that describe various kinds of books. Even the most saintly, patient, healthy librarian can keep up with only part of the flow. Your work may have the mass appeal of the book described above, yet the librarian doesn't get excited about a book every time she sees a new circular. What's her point of view? You can pretty well spell out three things:

1. She wants books that will fit the tastes of her patrons. Big cities, small one-library towns and people in the Deep South, far north, West, all have reading tastes that are part universal, part provincial.
2. The library has to stay within its budget. If it spends too little, the budget may be cut next year to match last year's outlay. If it overspends, the money may be taken out of next year's budget.
3. When local book reviews and TV talk shows send library patrons to the information desk asking for some particular new book, then the acquisitions librarian will order it, because, if she doesn't, there will be complaints: "They've got every book there except what you want."

These generalities form a loosely planked base for understanding librarians. But which department of the library will need your book? And what does your book offer patrons of this department? That's what you want to talk about with acquisitions librarians who hold your book in their hands. If you make a friend while calling on the acquisitions librarian, send him a copy of your sales letter after it is written. If you pick up even one idea, it helps.

In addition to interviewing, there's another way to dip into the library field. Get copies of *American Libraries* (50 East Huron St., Chicago, IL 60611), *Catholic Library World* (461 West Lancaster Ave., Haverford, PA 19041), the *Horn Book Magazine** (31 St. James Ave., Park Square Building, Boston, MA 02116), *Library Journal* (1180 Avenue of the Americas, New York, NY 10036), *Media Library Services Journal* (127 Ninth Ave. N., Nashville, TN 37234), the *Pamphleteer Monthly*** (55 East 86th St., New York, NY 10028), *School Library Journal*† (1180

---

*The *Horn Book Magazine* is for the juvenile book departments of libraries.
** A review of paperback pamphlets and books.
† A journal aimed at school and public libraries.

Avenue of the Americas, New York, NY 10036), *Wilson's Library Bulletin* (950 University Ave., Bronx, NY 10452).

The *Booklist* and *Choice*, both published by the American Library Association (50 East Huron St., Chicago, IL 60611), are devoted mainly to reviews. In addition to these magazines, there are others you may run into as you interview librarians. If, for instance, you believe your book belongs in elementary schools, you might ask some of their librarians for the names of trade magazines they read. Reading them gives you a touch of the language and a feel for the librarian's attitude.

Let's look at the advantages and disadvantages of selling to libraries. Their credit is good, but almost never is payment made within ten days. Almost 90 percent take 120 days or less. In my experience, when I sold to a library located in a small, one-library town and sent eight statements for an overdue amount (usually under ten dollars), I then tried a certified letter. If that fails, what to do? Sometimes I tried a short note to the town's mayor asking what he might recommend I do to collect from the town's library. The mayor won't make the collection personally, nor should you ask him, but he doesn't want "Ella Mae to get the town in trouble because of $9.67." He might call the right person on the town's Emergency Board to get the matter settled.

About one order out of ten sent to a library remains unpaid after sixty days. The reasons generally are: (1) The library may request a bill in triplicate with a notary's signature on each. Sometimes, they fail to send this triplicate form to you; sometimes, when you fill out and return it, they lose it. (2) The library has overspent and is holding all bills until they receive a new budget allowance. These days, with municipal and county difficulties, the budget may be approved, but the funds are not physically available.

As you would expect, the mainline commercial publishers just love library orders when they come in big volume from a jobber. Selling one book at a time, however, is expensive, and, unless a book is an annual or has a decent markup allowing the publisher a gross profit of five dollars on each order, the motive to hustle after individual library orders is not there.

Fortunately for book publishers, Baker & Taylor and the other big stocking jobbers are there. The stocking jobber specializes in selling to all libraries and has warehouses spotted throughout the country in which thousands upon thousands of titles are warehoused. The stocking jobber asks the publisher for a 50 percent discount and sells to the library at full retail price or, sometimes, at 10 percent off, or at larger discounts for a volume order.

How can you get to the stocking jobber?

They are busy buying books and filling and shipping orders. They rarely answer mail from publishers seeking to sell them one book and do very little selling of individual titles. However, they offer libraries a very real and important service: "Send one order to one company for all the titles you need. Fast shipment. Prompt report on OP and OS" (out of print and out of stock). Doesn't that beat sending separate orders to two hundred different publishers?

I made my first sale to Baker & Taylor when they were on lower Fifth Avenue, and I was twenty-two, and the buyer was the same age. Over the years, this buyer bought hundreds of thousands of dollars' worth of books from me, and, during that period, I received two letters. One was a thank-you note for a present I sent him on the occasion of our twenty-fifth anniversary of doing business, and the second was a note from his home, twenty-one years later, saying he had retired.

Can you get these large stocking jobbers to be aware of you?

In a sense, yes.

For you, just as for the mainline publisher, it is easier to let the stocking jobber handle the order and also easier on your customer, the library. Some libraries won't order a book unless one of their jobbers handles it. They simply don't want to receive bills from several hundred publishers. It's too much paperwork. They like the idea of one house, one order, one bill.

To help the library along in their thinking, you can send an advance copy of the sales letter that you plan to send to libraries to Baker & Taylor and other jobbers of your choice, and in the sales letter and on your order blank, you can include the line: "Baker & Taylor, Brodart, Ingram, Book House, and Bookazine carry this title in stock." Then enclose a stamped, self-addressed envelope, and ask each jobber to return your sales letter with an okay.

If the jobber writes "okay" on your letter and returns it, you want to thank the jobber and return a Xerox of his okay, so he has a record. Sometimes, when you show a large stocking jobber an advance copy of the sales letter that you plan to send to three thousand libraries (fewer may be less inviting), and his name is included as a source of supply, he will return the letter with his okay and a consignment order for twenty-five books. Take it. You're in motion. That's good.

What you don't want is for the stocking jobber to return a library order unfilled. That's the reason you help him generate orders for your book. The simple statement in your sales letter that the library may order from certain stocking jobbers, or directly from you, knocks out the first "no" some libraries throw at a solicitation letter from a one-book publisher who asks them to order directly. Now they can include an order for your book when they order fifty other titles from one of the large stocking jobbers you name. It is this sales method that originally got my books going with stocking jobbers. When I offered to include their name in my sales letter and on my order blank, I had enough takers so that the very names of these big stocking jobbers gave my books substance. You can do the same thing for yourself. Stocking jobbers who work the library trade include:

Baker & Taylor
1515 Broadway
New York, NY 10036

Ballen Booksellers
66 Austin Blvd.
Commack, NY 11725
(Scholarly, scientific, medical, social
sciences and humanities)

Book House
208 West Chicago
Jonesville, MI 49250

Bookazine
303 West 10th St.
New York, NY 10014

Brodart
500 Arch St.
Williamsport, PA 17701

Gordon's Books, Inc.
4280 Columbine St.
Denver, CO 80216

Ingram Book Company
347 Reedwood Dr.
Nashville, TN 37217

Melton Book Co.
111 Leslie St.
Dallas, TX 75207
(Specializes in juveniles)

Midwest Library Service
11400 Dorsett Rd.
Maryland Heights, MO 63043
(Specializes in supplying college libraries)

The library magazines contain a small, unexpected nugget. Most of them publish classified ads, and occasionally you will see an ad from a librarian with experience in acquisitions who is looking for a job. This might be just the person who, for a modest fee, will review your sales letter, order blank, and circular.

Because of the cheaper postage, most sales campaigns sent to libraries are by third-class mail. The orders you receive from a third-class-mail campaign come back to you, somewhat in this fashion, over a two-week period, when one thousand letters are mailed. Returns per day: 1, 2, 4, 7, 3, 2, 2, 0, 1, 1, 0, 0, 0, 1. This would be a 2.4 percent return on one thousand letters. When your sales campaign is mailed first-class mail, the returns are strung over fewer days. If, within eight working days after you receive your initial order on a first-class-mail campaign, you still haven't made 2 percent, you can hang it up. If your sales letter suggests to libraries that orders for your book may also be sent to a jobber, the actual number of orders you receive directly will not be materially reduced. Per thousand letters mailed, you may get five fewer orders. But the jobber will receive up to ten, so your total number of orders is larger.

Why is this so? While some librarians won't order from a one-book publisher because of the extra paperwork involved, others may choose to encourage the one-book publisher with a direct order. As always, when you give people a choice, you get more business.

To whom should you address a sales letter when you wish to sell your book to a library? I asked this question of many different librarians, and none expected the publisher to know the name of the particular person at their library with the authority to buy your kind of book. That was a relief. "So, what to do?" I asked.

The replies were simple, direct, functional. Here they are:

1. "Address your sales letter to: *Order Department.*"
2. One librarian said: "Since our order department handles books and all other supplies for us, it would be best to send it to: *Order Department: New Fiction* (or whatever category your book is in)."
3. "Your sales letter should go to *Acquisitions Librarian.*"
4. "We are a large library with more than one acquisitions librarian. It would be best to send your sales letter to: *Acquisitions Librarian: Biology* (or, naturally, instead of 'Biology,' use the category of your book)."
5. "Our small library buys under two-thousand-dollars' worth of books a year, so your sales letter should go to: *Head Librarian.*"

While the five responses cover the library-book front, they do present alternatives. Which one would suit all libraries? The suggestion made in items 2 and 4 cover most of the bases nicely.

How do you get your sales letter started?

At any major department in a large library (History and Literature, Music and the Arts) the person in charge at the information desk knows what the public is asking for. Librarians pick this up quickly, and their alertness in ordering books people ask about maintains the heavy library patronage. Is your book devoted to a field in which most libraries have a major department? Can you tie your book in with questions people are asking at the information desk? That's a good way to begin a sales letter about your book.

There's a little-known ordering tactic in the library trade that will not apply to the self-publisher of one book but is useful to larger publishers. The idea was created by a librarian who was overcome by skepticism after reading hundreds of book circulars. On ordering some of the books, he found them a bit short of what he had in mind. His plan, now called "The Greenaway Plan," or, sometimes, "The Advance Copy Plan," permits a library to order one each of all books issued by a publisher at a high discount. Undesirable books are discarded; books suitable to the library are put into circulation, and, often, additional copies are ordered by large libraries.

To invite a library in on the plan, the publisher mails out his own "Advance Copy Plan." Each publisher's plan varies a bit, but the general idea is to offer a discount of 35 to 50 percent on each book, with only one copy per book being offered at this discount. In some categories (texts, science, large, illustrated art books) the discount may be reduced to 20 percent. In this way, the library is allowed to sample the works of many publishers. This works out especially well for the metropolitan library by providing a broad sampling from which to choose books for their branches.

And it works out well, too, for the publisher of fifty books a year whose advance-copy plan is accepted by two thousand libraries. This produces an annual order for one hundred thousand books at 50 percent off, with the promise of more orders to come at 10 percent off, if the books are acceptable.

That's nice for the publisher of fifty books or so. But how about the one-book entrepreneur? You will be interested to know that certain kinds of books are supported almost entirely by their library sale. What kinds of books would you say these are?

Libraries are not the great institutions they have become because they stock popular novels, topical nonfiction, and the classics of Western civilization. The central core of library appeal comes from their wide and judicious stocking of reference books. A main library has literally thousands of such titles and having them carded and shelved gives a library its proud wealth of factual research material. People know "where to find it," and that's where they go. By the millions, daily.

What does this mean to you?

If you uncover a field in which you can publish a topical reference work of sound value, with carefully checked facts and editorial depth, and your reference work justifies either an annual or a biennial edition, you can think in terms of selling two to three thousand copies (sometimes more) to individuals, and, after your fourth or fifth edition, you should have from three to four thousand libraries buying it on "serial" order. A serial order is a request to ship each new edition of your reference work until the order is cancelled. A publisher with a reference work of this kind has the opportunity of a lifetime gross annual income of thirty to forty thousand dollars, and, using this as his launchpad, he may add supporting new titles.

As a self-publisher, you can think in terms of selling your book of wide, general appeal to libraries, or you can go the other route and think in terms of publishing a reference work that will grow in quality with each new edition and gradually widen its editorial appeal as the years pass.

31

The Religious Bookstores (Can You Guess How Many There Are?)

A LOT OF PEOPLE feel comfortable shopping for something to read at a religious bookstore. They like the atmosphere, and the clerks understand their taste. The other customers are often individuals of their own choosing. The tone of the store is quiet, friendly, and open countenanced.

In big cities you may find downtown religious bookstores on the second-floor level; sometimes, when the stores are at street level, they are several blocks away from the high-rent district. Only a few are in the big malls. This is another way of saying the religious-store owner believes his customers will come to him.

They do. And in such large numbers that four thousand retailers have been attracted to open religious bookstores. They don't advertise a lot, and the ones located on the second floor are not so easy to find. It is interesting to note that almost all do a large telephone business and have a steady mail-order operation.

Before self-publishing a book in this field, give yourself the advantage of meeting some book buyers for religious bookstores. An engaging way to do this is to attend the annual convention of the Christian Booksellers Association. Last year's attendance was close to eight thousand. This includes the store owners and some of their departmental managers, along with their families, plus religious-book publishers and their staffs, book jobbers, and the specialists who sell church merchandise. The latter includes the big-ticket items that give a religious bookstore its increasing dollar volume: pew cushions, church pews, liturgical vestments, choir gowns, religious ornaments, framed pictures, and choir bells.

The large membership of the CBA makes a cheerful family affair out of its annual meeting, and after visiting one of these conventions, you'll have a better touch of the distribution that is possible for a religious book, including your own.

Around nine hundred religious books are published each year, but fewer than two dozen authors have a lock on the field, and their books sell everywhere. "Everywhere" in this particular case means the 2,800 or so retail stores belonging to the Christian Booksellers Association, the one thousand Evangelical Protestant bookstores that are not members of the CBA, and the fifteen hundred secular bookstores that have large religious-book departments.

Who are these authors whose names move religious books?

Seven of them are Marjorie Holmes, Ann Kiemel, Eugenia Price, Keith Miller, Burt Larson, Jo Petty, and Catherine Marshall. I asked Marjorie Holmes how many of her books have been sold and she said, "Golly, I stopped counting and even thinking about it when the total passed three million." She mentioned two other authors as being fine craftsmen as well as best-selling writers: Joyce Landorf and Joni Erickson.

You may want to acquaint yourself with these authors—not to imitate—but to learn what is arming and comforting, pleasing and cheering so many people and causing them to think along lines that ease their personal problems and put their own humanity in closer touch with God. Having grasped emotionally and intellectually what these writers are doing, find your own voice and go your own way.

That's what the big-selling writers in the religious-book field have been doing during the past fifty years. If you have the mind for it, go back to an earlier reading period and examine what was popular then. You might start out with the novels of Lloyd Douglas in the thirties and early forties. A lot of old ladies of both sexes got their noses bent out of shape on discovering the Douglas books at religious-bookstores. Today, however, Lloyd Douglas seems innocuous and old hat.

In the fifties, *Honest to God*, by Bishop J. T. Robinson, was very big and very controversial. Today his works are neither new nor startling.

Then why mention them?

There's a good reason.

Some Christian writers can take any ethical or moral question and relate it by chapter and verse to the New Testament. That, a book doth not make. To prove a point by quoting the Bible and then assume you've locked up your case is a kind of celestial mechanics. If that's your main ploy, there's little reward for it from the religious-bookstores.

The goal is to relate Christian teachings to real-life experiences in a way that relieves the narrative of triteness and righteous morality. It is no trick to write "God Is Love" on every page, only to discover the reader's mind is backing and filling and looking about for something else of interest, even as St. Anthony's mind was drifting while he was telling his beads in his cell. A novel's message is accepted when the reader personally comes to the author's conviction from the strength of the narrative. The crutch of a preachment means the author has little faith in the power of his own narrative.

The other bestsellers in this field are devotional books. They are really prayers to be read to yourself at night or in the calm of a late afternoon. One of the best known is Marjorie Holmes's *I've Got to Talk to Somebody, God*. Of the same stripe is *Plum Jelly and Stained Glass*, by Jo Carr and Imogene Scoley. These authors touch the religious-bookstore reader where he or she lives.

If devotional prayers or novels are not your preference, what kind of nonfiction would be easiest for a self-publisher to sell to the religious bookstore? I asked that of Gerald Battle, who carried the Cokesbury retail bookstore chain up to thirty-two stores, as their chief administrator and book buyer. Speaking conversationally, he put it this way:

> Inspirational, personal-witness stuff seems to be what is commonly offered. Any kind of Bible-reference book would be a waste of time. There are too many well-established things to buck. You can't run up against *Strong's Concordance*, *The Interpreter's Bible*, or *Young's Analytical Concordance*.

If someone had an especial expertise in fund raising; quantity cookery; organizing, directing, and constructing year-round programs for youth activities within the church, such a person might construct a useful book we could all sell. However, every general religious-book publisher would be interested in it, too, if the writer's reference point were up to date and the copy well written.

An author writing of experience in personal witness, inspiration, overcoming disability, disease, personal misfortune through a renewed reawakening, or of Christ-centered experience of Christian faith and belief fares better in the marketplace if such an author has some roots (however far removed or tenuous) in an Evangelical Protestant, name-brand religious faith.

I showed this statement to the book buyer of another chain. He said: "I will add something if you do not quote me by name. If your self-published book deals with Catholics, converted Jews, Mormons, Blacks—of whatever religious brand name—you will have a harder row to hoe in selling it to the Christian religious bookstore. The market there is largely white, Protestant, and Anglo-Saxon."

Can we be more specific about the religious-bookstore customers? Loosely speaking, you could say there are four main groups.

1. Some customers are fundamentalists in outlook. What the Bible says is literal fact and not to be deviated from in religious or ethical matters.
2. Some customers of religious bookstores are more liberal minded. They study the New Testament for its moral teachings but do not necessarily believe the Bible is wholly the word of God. One manager of a religious bookstore, herself a member of this faction, said, "The Old Testament gives us a poetic interpretation of events from which laws of human conduct may be drawn." The more restrained of the fundamentalists refer to these people as fence-straddlers.
3. Some customers are "charismatic" people who have received the "Baptism of the Holy Spirit" and often speak "in tongues" and believe in faith healing.

4. In the third chapter of the Gospel of St. John appear the words: "Marvel not that I say unto you, except a man to be born again, he cannot see the Kingdom of God." What is the experience that allows a man to be "born again"? The individual feels he has experienced an impartation of the Divine Light, a spiritual birth. With it, such people feel better equipped to work out problems common to humanity.

Of these four segments making up most religious-bookstore customers, how many are there of each? The practical answer depends on the manager, who attracts the desired customers by the choice of books and prominence by which certain ones are displayed, and by the manager's choice of church merchandise. In a very real sense, it is the reach of the manager that seeks out the charismatic people, the fundamentalists, the upper-middle-class, born-again Christians, or the liberal middle-of-the-roaders who seek spiritual growth without the strictures of some of the fundamentalist sects.

The emphasis on which of these four groups will be most attracted to the store depends, too, on its location: Compare an inland, small-town farming area in Georgia to downtown New Haven.

How are you to know which group to appeal to in your devotional book, your fiction, or even your how-to book on cooking for large church groups? All you can do is the best you can and then announce your book to the stores and jobbers in the field. The store managers know the audience of their choice, and they will buy what their customers want. You can't please them all. If you did, you'd have a 5 million sale and more money than might be good for you or your family.

What religious ideas do the customers have in common?

One manager who has been on the job since 1949 says,

> Most of my customers agree that intervention may occur in response to personal prayer. I believe in this, too, and I would say the same about every customer whom I know.
>
> After that common binding [he continued], there is room for more than one religious attitude. For instance, I believe in God's intentional Will. To me, whatever happens is God's Will. Let's say you run carelessly across the street and a car hits you. Most

of my customers, in this case, would say you got hurt because of carelessness, not because it was God's intentional Will to cause you suffering. "You have free will," they say.

The religious beliefs our customers share, aside from intervention and answered prayer, are not exactly parallel, but they are a better common denominator than you would find among the customers of any secular bookstore.

For writers of religious books, there is a relatively new magazine that has four or five excellent leads in each issue, of people who might help you with editorial pretesting. The magazine is *Today's Christian Woman*, and if your book falls into the editorial groove of this publication, you are fortunate. If one of the articles in *Today's Christian Woman* agrees with ideas in your own book, try a letter to the author of that article along the lines suggested in chapter 2. You might also turn to the book-review section. Do some of the reviewers reveal a warm interest in your subject matter? If so, try a similar letter to one of these reviewers, care of the magazine. *Today's Christian Woman* is published by the Fleming H. Revell Company (Old Tappan, NJ 07675). A sample copy is two dollars, but you're better off walking into a religious store and buying it there. As you walk in, let the whole of the store come to you. Observe it with an innocent eye, as though you are seeing it for the first time.

When your book is ready to sell, a self-publisher has seven major markets. They are: (1) the religious bookstores, (2) the jobbers selling to these same stores, (3) the churches that maintain book and gift shops, (4) religious-bookstore chains, (5) the religious radio and TV stations, (6) direct mail to individual buyers of religious books, and (7) the religious book clubs. We'll take up each in turn.

MARKETING TO RELIGIOUS BOOKSTORES

Your best place to buy mail-order lists that will get your circulars to the right stores in the Evangelical-Protestant religious book field is the Christian Booksellers Association, usually called the CBA (2620 Venetucci Boulevard, Colorado Springs, CO 80901). The executive director is John T. Bass. The person whose job it is to offer marketing services to publishers is Debbie Mockerman.

If you cannot attend the annual CBA convention, the next best thing is to ask Ms. Mockerman if she has an extra copy of last year's convention issue of the *Bookstore Journal*. It is a lively three-hundred-page trade journal and will supply the attentive self-publisher with leads for marketing as well as some leads for editorially pretesting your book. The price is $2.00.

For instance, you may be an Evangelical Protestant writer with an understanding and affection for many Catholic friends. This adds a special tone to your book. On page sixty-four of the *Bookstore Journal*'s 1979 convention issue is a beautifully practical discussion of the attractions that CBA stores have for some Catholics. The author, Ellen Freeman, is a graduate of St. Joseph's College, with a degree in Scripture from Notre Dame. For the writer of a very particular kind of book, this woman might be a lead for editorial pretesting.

There are personality squibs here and there in the *Bookstore Journal* that give the astute writer good marketing ideas.

Just as Bowker has a tight grip on trade-store lists, the CBA has the same on religious-bookstore lists. They offer two lists.

LIST NO. 1: This consists of approximately twenty-eight hundred members of the CBA and is rented only as a complete unit. Cost: $105. Each name and address is on a pressure-sensitive label. Peel off the label, press it on your envelope, and it sticks like a charm. The list is by zip code, so, if you want to test certain states, you can put the rest of the list aside until you get the results of your test. Usually, a return of anything over 2 percent is profitable when the average order is for four books. For discounts, you might want to be a bit more generous than the average publisher and offer 25 percent discount for one book, 33 percent for two or three copies, 40 percent for four to twelve copies, and 42 percent after that. Add the outgoing postage to your bill, and offer full credit for clean, salable books that are returned within eight months.

Nothing beats calling on a half-dozen bookstores first. This will bring you closer to the people who will read your mailing piece. When calling, show them your dust jacket or front cover and two-page outline. Look over their stores, talk to the book buyers. After you get home, put together the sum total of their affirmative responses so that, when you write a sales letter, you can couch it in words aimed at their point of view.

LIST NO. 2: This is the subscription list of the *Bookstore Journal* and is between sixty-six hundred and seventy-two hundred depending on the year and the times. The cost is $385 for renting the whole list on pressure-sensitive labels. The list is zip coded, and you can rent only the whole list. It includes six categories:

1. Secular bookstores with religious departments. Some examples would be Kroch's main store in Chicago, or the main store of Gill, in Portland, or Kaufman's, in Pittsburgh. This kind of selectivity of leading bookstores that stock religious books is not readily available elsewhere.
2. Members of the CBA. This comprises the twenty-eight hundred stores in list Number 1, above.
3. Christian bookstores that are not members of CBA but are subscribers to the *Bookstore Journal.*
4. Individuals who prefer to receive circular material at their home so they can read it at leisure. Sometimes trade mail gets bounced around at a large office, or is borrowed by someone while it is in the process of being routed.
5. Managers of individual departments in religious bookstores. This includes the manager of the record, greeting-card, or other nonbook departments. These managers often feel that the *Bookstore Journal* is hogged by the book department and they want their own copy. Do the nonbook managers interest you? You never know when a departmental manager will see a "cheese-and-cracker" sale in your book and want to display it with some of his other items.
6. Several hundred religious-book publishers and some jobbers are included in this list. One or two of them may be interested in distributing your book.

These lists are offered for one-time rental only and may not be copied.

The CBA (and most other companies that rent lists) will ask a publisher to submit a sample mailing plus one copy of the book itself, before renting the list. When the renter thinks the book or the mailing won't work with the list, he will decline. This protects both you and the list renter. Look on it as a healthy action.

Don't expect the CBA list (or any list, except one from the cemetery) to be even 95 percent correct. A store closes or is merged; a new owner buys the place and within a few months installs all new help. It takes a while before such changes can be incorporated into a list. Managers change employers or are switched to other departments. So don't get mad at your list if you make calls and find that no one by that name is there or the store itself has vanished.

The realists in the mail-order business are those whose employers, at one time or another, gave them a prime list such as CBA's and ordered them to call on every name within a dozen zip codes and make a written report on each name. The experience of this permanently nails every mail-order man into reality. I remember when I called upon every subscriber to *Modern Photography*, in Columbus, Ohio. We had over one hundred subscribers in that city, and I carried three-by-five cards showing the address of each. At the spot where the first one was indicated, the house had been razed. Another house was being moved down the street on rollers. I stood and stared at it. I dogged through the list, managing to find thirty subscribers at home, and I visited the photographic darkrooms of those who owned them and looked through their albums. I asked about the attitudes of our subscribers toward great photographers of the past and what effect their contributions had had upon the photographic work done by our readers. I brought home samples of our readers' work and their answers to my questions. It was a learning experience.

As a self-publisher, your time is your own, and what you learn is yours for the rest of your life. When you write your sales letter to the list you have rented, you might try to visualize one person and write directly to that individual.

There are two main ways to write your letter. One is to talk about your book and its value. The other is to offer the reader a reward for reading your letter in the sense of telling something spontaneously new, informative, and awakening about the religious-book field as of today. This has to come from a well of experience and research and out of the fullness of your own heart. This gives a floor to the whole of your letter, and, when you talk about your book, it carries more credibility.

In directing a mail campaign to people in this field, should you create some visual difference between yourself and other publishers by printing your stationery on pale-blue paper? Should you use typescript for your name and address? How about slipping a ball of italic type into your electric typewriter and inserting a blue carbon ribbon into the ribbon wheel? Not one bookstore buyer knows even half of the eleven hundred book publishers, but they all know what a book publisher's stationery normally looks like.

For this reason, the safe ploy is to use printed stationery that falls into the slot of what a bookstore owner thinks a publisher's stationery looks like. Otherwise, will he fault you at the outset for being an oddball?

If you have strong feelings on the matter, you can test three hundred letters, using watermarked, white bond with your name in black type—something like hand-cut Caslon about one-half inch high—and matching white envelopes. Then try another three hundred employing whatever style appeals to you. If in doubt, hire a graphics designer to do the neatest, plainest, simplest letterhead and envelope that you can induce him to turn out. Something just a cut above a nice, well-bred undertaker's or investment banker's stationery, safe and guaranteed not to throw the buyer before he gets into the contents of your letter.

If you send the religious-bookstore buyer a complimentary copy of your book, the chances of its being read are dim. The poor fellow simply has no time. He buys on intuition, and it's a very sharp intuition indeed. He examines the dust jacket (or the front cover in the instance of a paperback), the title, the number of pages, the price, the discount, the general subject matter, and, possibly, a two-page outline of the book.

That's why you want to check your judgment on important details with the best people you can get to as you progress with your book. Two of the most important details are pretesting either individual chapters or the entire book and employing a graphics designer to help you with the cover design and typography. When writing your sales letters, call on some individuals whose names appear on the list you are renting, and ask counsel. You want to know how a book like yours should be presented to hold the reader's interest.

If you do this, and have 20 percent talent and 80 percent perseverance, and your religious book is not dated, wordy, thin, or trite, you can expect to sell it profitably from the word "go."

SELLING TO THE JOBBER

By comparison with trade jobbers, the religious-book jobber chooses his titles from a narrow field. To learn the kinds of books any one jobber selects, send one dollar with a brief note on your publisher's stationery asking for a catalogue. You might add a sentence explaining that you have published a religious book and want to examine a current catalogue to see if your book fits in with their selections. The jobber doesn't send catalogues directly to consumers, because that would make him compete with his prime customer, the retail bookstore. You might also ask your friendly religious-book dealer to show you any jobber catalogues he has on hand. If you find your book is similar to a dozen titles the jobber now sells, that's great.

Phone the jobbers you select and ask for the name of the individual who buys your kind of book: fiction, devotional, biography, and so forth, as well as whether he handles cloth or paper, depending on how yours is bound.

Then send off a letter enclosing a dust jacket or front cover and a two-page outline of your book. If you have reviews, quote from them in your letter. If the reviews are good, send a Xerox of each. Have you had publicity? It doesn't matter where, as long as there is a great deal of it. A three-sentence mention in *Time* and the dropping of your name in a nationally syndicated column isn't nearly as good as twenty pieces of publicity that run five or more column inches each, no matter how boondocky you may think the publication. Publicity in volume gives off the sweet sound of a grass-roots swell. Jobbers, as well as retailers, are more impressed with vibes like this than with a one-time, one-page story about you in *Vogue*.

After mailing your letter, wait ten days.

No answer?

Phone the buyer person-to-person, and ask if he has had time to read your letter and wants to look over a copy of your book. Name the retail stores that have reordered. Say that you are available for autograph parties, and name the number of books sold at your last one. If you appeared on a religious radio station, tell how many books were sold, or how much fan mail the station received.

If you have a good quote from a well-known businessman in the field, such as an officer of the CBA, read it to the buyer over the phone. Moonbeams won't do. You need honest ammunition.

What size order can you expect from the jobber, what discount will he want, who pays the postage, and what action will the jobber take to sell your books when he receives them? A starting order might be ten to thirty books, and you may add the outgoing postage to your bill.

As a starting publisher, you might offer a 50 percent discount on the jobber's first order, regardless of its size. Usually a 50 percent discount applies only to an order of three hundred, or more. Terms for payment to you should be net, thirty days. It will help you to offer full cash or credit for all unsold books returned within eight months when they are in salable condition.

One significant difference between the religious-book jobber and the big secular one is that the latter has fifteen thousand different titles on hand and therefore can't sell individual titles. Once in a while, he will issue a flyer, but hardly ever a full-dress catalogue.

The religious-book jobber stocks a smaller number of titles and issues both flyers and catalogues. He may do a few things to sell your book. But the main reason any jobber gets a retailer's order is based on the jobber's discount, careful packing, promptness in shipping and filling orders correctly, his terms for payment and return privileges on unsold books, and the likelihood that he will have hundreds of books in stock that the CBA-type bookstore needs.

Let's look at one jobber's catalogue. Cicero Bible Press, in its thirty-fifth year, distributes books of seventy-five publishers, including Abingdon, Avon, Bantam, David C. Cook, Doubleday (paper only), Holt, Rinehart & Winston, Macmillan (paper only), Moody, Nelson, Oxford, Rand McNally, Revell, Stein & Day, Zondervan.

Cicero offers a toll-free telephone number so that religious bookstores may phone free to place an order. Their catalogue measures eight and a half by eleven inches and contains sixty-four pages in black and white plus twenty-four pages in full color. That is a lot of catalogue. Including printing, postage, addressing, and envelope, it costs two dollars to ship. On its plain, unpretentious cover is the slogan: "Supplying Christian literature to the nation." The catalogue describes only the better movers. Well over one thousand additional titles are not included. This means you have no assurance, should this jobber order from you, that your book will appear in his catalogue.

Every other month, Cicero sends to its retailers a list of "America's 100 top best-selling religious titles, based on our own private records of absolutely top-selling books and Bibles. There is no guesswork, no

412

favorites, only those titles that have proved themselves with thousands of bookstores across the nation."

In addition to their every-other-month list of top sellers, Cicero also offers a "list of 500 active titles which should be considered for dealers who wish to go beyond our 100 best sellers." The last dozen pages of Cicero's catalogue deal with nonbook items: communion ware, offering plates, plaques, framed posters, cards, trays, gift-wrap paper, stationery and calendars. An advertisement of one calendar states: "Setting forth God's World and God's Word reaching around the world with the Scripture" (retail $1.25).

Jobbing religious books is a business, yet, within a range of reference, it is a ministry, too.

Here are the names and addresses of some religious-book jobbers:

Arbor Distributors
772 Airport Dr.
Ann Arbor, MI 48104

Cicero Bible Press
Airport Rd.
Harrison, AR 72601

Distribution by Dave
7220 Owensmouth Ave.
Canoga Park, CA 91303

East Coast Christian Distributors
P.O. Box 4200
Somerville, NJ 08876

Riverside Book & Bible House
1500 Riverside Dr.
P.O. Box 1058
Iowa Falls, IA 50126
(Riverside does two interesting things in addition to distributing religious books. They refer to themselves as "a leader in the distribution of high discount closeouts." Also they state, "Riverside goes in on press runs with major publishers for especially selected and designed books.")

Unilit, Inc.
5600 Hassalo St.
Portland, OR 97213
(Unilit represents one hundred publishers and issues a 160-page catalogue.)

One other firm, not a jobber, may be mentioned here: Genesis Marketing Group (250 North Central Ave., Wayzata, MI 55391) employs a dozen commission salesmen who call on both trade and religious bookstores. Genesis Marketing Group sells books for a number of book publishers. Usually, a "commission rep," such as those who work for Genesis, asks for all the "ledger accounts." This means that the publisher is asked to pay a commission on all books sold to the trade in the commission salesman's territory, whether the salesman made the sale or not. The commission is around 10 percent of what the publisher bills.

This is paid after the publisher receives the money.

With a commission salesman working for you, it is more profitable to produce mailings to the trade because you have a door-to-door follow-up working for you.

SELLING TO CHURCHES THAT OPERATE BOOKSTORES

Not all retail religious bookstores are on Main Street or in the suburban malls. Some are housed in churches. Mostly, these are small bookstores with an adjoining gift department. They are staffed by volunteers, and a stock of 150 different titles would be a lot. The problem is not so much in selling them as in getting your mail into the hands of the right person, in the right church, whose members are interested in your subject matter.

The following nationally known rental-list companies may help you. Most have offices in major cities as well as the headquarters office, which is given here:

Customized Mailing Lists, Inc.
158-23 Grand Central Parkway
Jamaica Station, New York, NY

Dunhill International List Co.
444 Park Ave. South
New York, NY

R.L. Polk Co.
9801 Walford Ave.
Cleveland, OH

Research Projects Corp.
50 Clinton St.
Hempstead, NY

Zeller and Letica Inc.
15 East 26th St.
New York, NY
  (Zeller has a toll-free number.
  (800) 221-4112)

The cost of renting a list from any one of these companies, addressed on pressure-sensitive labels, is thirty-five to fifty dollars per thousand.

When describing your needs to a mailing-list company be very specific. For instance, call on the kind of churches through whose bookstores you want to sell your book. Then send the mailing-list company ten such names and addresses from, let us say, Atlanta. They can now check and see if they actually have in stock what you want to buy.

Do you always have to be this specific? Can't you just go ahead and hope for the best? Crapshooters, yes. Publishers, no.

GETTING ORDERS FROM RELIGIOUS CHAIN BOOKSTORES

There is a handful of religious-bookstore chains. Put together, they account for some two hundred stores. Each store is very much the manager's own domain, as he seeks to orient the area's Evangelical Protestant mores with the stock that he believes will have the right appeal. Home-office buying accounts for most of the stock in each chain, but the local manager is still allowed some leeway in ordering directly from the publisher, and, of course, he is the one who decides where and how to display the merchandise.

You can "get a handle" on the larger chain stores by talking with the clerks and learning the manager's interpretation of his customer's tastes. From this research, you can really write a personal sales letter to the home-office buyer. Use the same method as given in chapter 29 to get the name of the buyer. Following are some addresses of chain bookstore headquarters:

Baptist Book Stores
127 Ninth Ave. North
Nashville, TN 37234

Berean Bookstores
8121 Hamilton Ave.
Cincinnati, OH 45231

Cokesbury Bookstores
201 Eighth Ave. S.
Nashville, TN 37202

Logos Bookstore
746 South Crouse Ave.
Syracuse, NY 13210

Pathway Bookstores
1080 Montgomery Ave.
Cleveland, TN 37311

Provident Book Stores
616 Walnut Ave.
Scottdale, PA 15683

Tyndale Bookstores
336 Gundersen Dr.
Wheaton, IL 60187

Zondervan Family Bookstores
1420 Robinson Rd., S.E.
Grand Rapids, MI 49506

GETTING A BOOST FROM BROADCASTING

One of the better ways to publicize your book is to appear on a talk show sponsored by a religious radio station. You can give your book more public exposure this way than by using any other kind of media support.

There are 250 full-time religious radio stations, plus 1150 other stations that allot eight or more hours a week to religious programs. How do you get to them?

THE BOOK MARKET

The National Religious Broadcaster (P.O. Box 2254-R, Morristown, NJ 07960) publishes each January a 350-page directory giving pertinent data on the 250 full-time religious stations, plus similar data for the other 1,150 radio stations. This gives you the names, addresses, and staff members of 1,400 radio stations that are candidates to publicize your religious book.

The directory's geographical breakdown makes it convenient for writers who want to make personal calls on stations within an hour or two's drive of home.

The directory is available by mail from the National Religious Broadcaster from January to June at fifteen dollars. The price drops to eight dollars in July while the supply lasts.

Mark Bainer of the NRB says that about 90 percent of the 250 full-time religious radio stations are Evangelical Protestant and usually have a conservative approach. That is, their interpretation of the Bible inclines toward a fundamentalist direction.

Mr. Bainer advises that these stations are supported one of two ways: (1) *Listener supported.* You'll rarely hear, ". . . and now stay tuned for this important word," which turns out to be a pitch for a new cereal. Some of these listener-supported stations sell books or permit the authors who appear on their stations to offer copies at the regular list price. (2) *Commercially sponsored.* These stations sell advertising as their chief revenue. Sometimes they sell items over the radio that are of interest to their listeners. It is hardly news for such a station to sell two hundred books as a result of a talk show.

How do you go about getting your book on radio?

You need some kind of hook. For example, what is it that can be said about your book to interest religious people? Is there a message in the book that could be said succinctly? Is there a story connected with its writing? Have well-known people commented on it? What does the book have within it that is unique, original, thoughtful, or beneficial? Is there a human-interest story connected with its publication? Can you put some of this into seven minutes, rehearse it, and try it out on a friendly audience of one? After you've finished, ask for constructive comments. Can you try this again, this time before eight or ten people? How do they feel about what you said? Can you tape some book-talk shows from religious stations and play them back and learn from the experience?

When you're armed and ready, write to the program director or general manager of the station, and explain what you have to offer. Enclose a one- or two-page book outline and a dust jacket. You can vary the book-outline idea by using only the chapter titles, plus a one-line description of each chapter, for all chapters except one. For that one chapter, you might offer a seven- or eight-line description. In your covering letter, explain that the outline offers the scope of the book, and the one chapter, with its eight-line description, offers a better look into the contents of one full chapter.

If this brings no answer, then what?

Somehow, everyone in the radio business believes the people who want to appear on their programs are immune from the despair of turndowns and just plain silences. If you listen to other writers who have tried to get on radio programs, you'd think there were a plot to keep us out. There isn't, but it often seems that way. What do you do in the face of silence?

Try a second letter.

Then a phone call.

Then a personal call on the program director. You just barge in. "But," says the secretary, "you have no appointment." You say, "How about next week? May I have one, please?" And if you have the perseverance, you go back again. A writer crashing into radio is a cross between a pest and an amiable, resourceful salesman.

The program director is beset by humdrum people who give other people the blahs. Or so he says. In self-defense, he falls back on the credo of all program directors that went before him. He's convinced that dramatic style and originality and talent have something in common. It's called perseverance. He may be right, too. Or maybe he's lazy. Or overworked. In any event, the person who gets a book reviewed or appears on a talk show is sometimes invited in and other times he bulldozes, swarms, cajoles, or wiggles his way in. Looking back, it's always worth it. To illustrate their possible value to you, here are two listings from the directory published by National Religious Broadcasters. One is from North Dakota, the other from Ohio.

KNDR-FM
Box 516, Mandan 58554; (701) 663-2345; Central Dakota Enterprises; 1977; 104.9 MHz, 3 kw
Format: Beautiful music/Gospel

Rep: Savalli-Gates
Personnel: Harold Erickson, pres; Steve Benedict, gen mgr/prog mgr; Harlow Bales, coml mgr; Stephen Winzenburg, news dir; Larry Johnson, chief eng

WELX
Box 456, Xenia 45385; (513) 372-7649;   Net: MBS, Mutual Black
   H&H Bcstrs; 1968 (acq 1975); 1110 kHz;   Personnel: Harold J. Wright, pres/gen mgr;
   250 w-D   Phil Wright, coml mgr/news dir;
Format: Gospel   Marcenia Wright, chief eng

MAKING YOUR OFFERING TO A BOOK CLUB

If your book has wide general merit, offer it to one of the book clubs that specialize either in religious books or in "G-rated" books for the entire family that have religious overtones.

The religious book clubs themselves are eleven in number. In addition, two are family-type book clubs that occasionally select books with a spiritual content. The religious connotation cannot be narrow, as these two clubs have wide, general memberships.

It is expensive to submit a book to any club, so the efficient approach is first to ask for a current circular and then to choose only the clubs whose selections are in your realm of interest.

There are three ways to submit a book to a club.

The preferred way is to send a set of galley proofs as far ahead of publication date as you can manage, at least ninety days. If your front cover, or dust jacket, is not yet printed, and you can supply a well-done artist's sketch, you might include that. Some letter shops lease a Xerox machine that will duplicate drawings in full color. This, of course, is a lot cheaper than employing an artist to make a half-dozen cover color sketches for you.

The second method is to send a trimmed, collated, unbound copy of your book, complete with dust jacket or cover, as soon as you get it from the printer.

The third way is to send the complete book itself. All the clubs prefer to see a book ahead of its publication date.

With your printed submission, attach a letter offering your book as a club selection.

The information in this chapter is largely directed toward Protestant Evangelical religious bookstores, but the selection of book clubs that follows covers other religious sects.

Carl F. Weller
The Augsburg Reading Club
426 S. Fifth St.
Minneapolis, MN 55415
(Includes selections for adults, youth, and
  children)

Joseph A. O'Hare
Catholic Book Club
106 W. 56th St.
New York, NY 10019

Robert L. Fenton
Catholic Digest Book Club
405 Lexington Ave.
New York, NY 10017

Leslie Stobbe
Christian Book Club for Today's Woman
40 Overlook Dr.
Chappaqua, NY 10514

Christian Quarterly Paperback Book Club
4800 W. Waco Dr.
Waco, TX 76703

Steven F. Landry
Church Growth Book Club
1705 N. Sierra Bonita Ave.
Pasadena, CA 91104

Rev. Father H. L. Foland
Episcopal Book Club, Inc.
Hillspeak
Eureka Springs, AR 72632

Vern Rossman
Evangelical Book Club
175 Fifth Ave.
New York, NY 10010

Leslie Stobbe
Family Bookshelf
40 Overlook Dr.
Chappaqua, NY 10514
(This is part of the Christian Herald
  Association)

Neal Kozodoy
Jewish Book Club
165 E. 56th St.
New York, NY 10022

Florence Weissman
Judaica Book Club
68-22 Eliot Ave.
Middle Village, NY 11379

Julian W. Carr
Religious Book Club
175 Fifth Ave.
New York, NY 10010

John C. Drahos
Thomas More Book Club
180 N. Wabash Ave.
Chicago, IL 60601

THE BOOK MARKET

Shirley Brants
Unity Book Club
Unity School of Christianity
Unity Village, MO 68065

William G. Gohring
Word Direct Marketing Services, Inc.
4800 W. Waco Dr.
Waco, TX 76703

SELLING YOUR BOOK DIRECTLY BY MAIL

A direct mailing to church people with a definite interest in your type of book is a good way to test the public's response. For this purpose, you need a list of only five or six hundred. Using a smaller-sized list, say fifty to one hundred, including only friends and acquaintances, is not objective enough to indicate public response.

One good list to start with is a church membership or a list of people who belong to a regional church council. Perhaps you have friends who can help you secure a half-dozen church membership lists. If so, try several kinds of "test campaigns" to find out which produces the most orders.

If you are friends with your local religious-bookstore retailer, you might offer him a 30 percent discount on your book, which you deliver to him on consignment (he pays only for what he sells), and, in return for this, ask permission to mail a letter and circular about your book to this store's mailing list. The store picks up two profits: (1) Having committed themselves to no expense on unsold books or on the sales campaign, they can't lose and certainly will make some sales. If the store has a street-level window, ask for a book display for ten days following the date of your mailing. Also ask for a display of your book, close to the store's entranceway. (2) The store may also make a sale of another book or of some church merchandise to the customer who comes in to see your book.

If you show a profit here, you are ready to try a cold list. The mailing-list companies whose names and addresses were listed earlier offer list rentals of religious-book buyers. Names of this kind are secured from religious book clubs and from publishers who have done a big mail-order job with a religious book. Perhaps a publisher has sold one hundred thousand copies of a certain title. The list of buyers may now be offered for rental.

420

As a final attack on the subject, you might look over the catalogue of the large religious publishers and try to find a book somewhat similar to your own. Then write the publisher and ask if he sold this book by mail and, if so, whether the names and addresses are available for rental. The methods you learned in researching your own book while you were writing it hold good when you proceed to sell it.

32

The College Bookstore

THE NICE THING about college bookstores is that there are three thousand of them with 9 million student customers. Nothing else in the retail book field can compare to it. The entré to this market for the self-publisher is through books that students use as supplementary reading. During the academic year, more than 18 million books for supplementary reading are purchased by students at their college bookstores. On top of that, the college library buys several copies of books regularly recommended for supplementary reading, and this is a nice market in itself.

At the college level, an instructor "adopts" a textbook of his own choice and then requests that his students buy it. In addition, he often recommends two or three other books that are more narrative in style to supplement the factual information shoveled out by the class text.

If you're interested in this market, where do you start? You know the story about the man who built a doghouse. He had never seen a dog, and, for the entranceway, he built a round chute that came down from the roof. Maybe it's a dumb question, but how many college stores have you entered recently?

The three thousand college stores have many things in common. If you want to make a few calls to feel your way into their situation, pick the slow season, usually July, or one of the holiday periods, or simply a month before school starts. Call ahead, and make certain the store is open. Explain to the manager or the book buyer that you want to sell your book to college bookstores and wonder if you could look his place over to learn a few things first hand.

Normally, at these seasons of the year, the manager will say he is very busy (taking inventory), or very shorthanded (everyone's on vacation) but, if there's time, he'll be glad to say hello. Your answer is, "Fine! I want to learn a few fundamentals about college bookstores."

Assuring you that his store is not typical of most, he will usually invite you to come over if you wish. You do wish, and that's the invitation you want. Some authors who are accustomed to the research that goes with writing, but not accustomed to the research that goes with selling, will wonder if this trip is necessary, especially if it has to be repeated four or five times. Is there an easier way?

Usually it's easier to read about something than actually to make calls. Two trade magazines circulate to the college stores: *The National College Store Executive* (Box 788, Lynbrook, New York, NY 11563) and *College Store Journal* (528 East Lorain St., Oberlin, OH 44074). A copy of each gives you a start in the right direction.

There's another choice, not exactly easier, but with different possibilities. At the end of this chapter we list thirty regional college bookstore associations who are members of the National Association of College Stores.

What can be learned by visiting a regional officer of the NACS? To find out, I spoke with Patricia Stone, at North Carolina Wesleyan Book Store, Rocky Mountain, North Carolina. These regional associations are run by people who daily are in the midst of buying college books from publishers and selling them to students. It is often possible, without the aid of a flying tackle, to bring one of them to rest so that a conversation may ensue. Here's Patricia Stone:

We have what is almost a one-woman operation at our store. I have three clerks, two of them part time, and I also handle the post office. Our student enrollment is 850, the largest we have had in some time.

You asked how I go about buying books for supplementary reading. When a professor asks me to order fifteen copies of a book, that's easy. But I receive a lot of letters and flyers from publishers, and there's too much good information there just to throw it away because I don't happen to have a professor's recommendation for that particular book.

So, I read the publisher's letter and look over the flyer. Let's say it's in the math area. That's where we are weak in supplementary reading, and

I would sure read that flyer. If the letter and the flyer turn me on, and the flyer really tells me what's in the book and gives full details about the contents, I might order one copy and place it where the students can easily see it. If it sells, I order more. If it fails to sell in maybe three months, I return it.

I order one copy of a book only when I am not sure of it—there is no point in asking for a free copy as the publishers won't send it, although often they send an examination copy to a professor. The trouble about ordering one copy is the short discount of 25 or 30 percent and then paying the incoming postage and, in addition, paying the return postage if it doesn't sell. But often I feel the students have the right to know a certain book exists. And I order one copy to give the book a chance.

Sometimes a book is outside my area of knowledge. Maybe the book is supplementary reading on higher math—the development of the philosophy of math by Descartes. Then I take the letter and the flyer to a math professor and ask his advice.

When I order four copies, I expect a 40 percent discount.

Incidentally, some NACS members are community colleges, and they buy relatively few books for supplementary reading because they haven't space. The college market is big, but everybody in it isn't big. Out of three thousand colleges, including both two-year and four-year colleges, 1,260 have enrollments of up to one thousand. The small publisher will find our regional officers of the NACS to be friendly. If our advice is worth anything to you, we would like to give it. While I was president of the College Stores of North Carolina, it was my feeling then that anything we did to help the small publisher understand how we order books helped us all.

Can any of these three thousand college bookstores help the sales of your book? If college stores could increase your sales by 10 percent, then meeting a few store managers and browsing through their places will give you a comfortable feeling when you sit down to write a sales letter to them. You'll be comfortable, because neither the stores nor the managers will be strange to you, and you will have learned (1) what kinds of merchandise are sold (you won't believe it), (2) the kinds of discounts available to college bookstores (20 to 25 percent on texts, 40 percent on books for supplementary reading in lots over five), (3) how the store promotes and advertises, and, most of all, (4) (in order to get the manager talking) what the store's problems are.

Once the manager gets into the latter question, you'll find ways of tying the operational problems of a college bookstore into your own sales letter. When you do this, you often have a better sales letter. There are other good ways, of course, and your own research will suggest some.

Among the knowledgeable people on the subject of college stores is Russell Reynolds, general manager of the National Association of College Stores (528 East Lorain, Oberlin, OH 44074). Russ wears two hats, and both become him. As the paid head of NACS, he has the responsibilities of maintaining a twenty-four hundred membership, defining the problems of the industry, seeking solutions, upgrading the gross income and profits of the member stores, and raising their goals of service to the college. Second, the NACS is a wholesaler of books, mostly paperback supplementary texts, to the college stores.

Will the NACS wholesale a small publisher's or a self-publisher's book? Let's hear what Russ has to say.

We have thirty thousand titles in stock, mostly quality paperbacks. We wholesale them to the college stores. We stock a few hardcover titles, basically dictionaries and reference books. Very few of the books we stock come from publishers whose titles are under ten. To me, this is a real regret and frustration, because there are many fine books issued by small publishers.

Our twenty-four hundred college-store members know we stock the paperbacks of Avon, Anchor, Dell, Bantam, New American, and all well-known quality paperback imprints, but we have learned that the college bookstore buyers won't remember which small publisher's line we stock and we have too many titles in stock to print a catalogue.

There's a funny thing about book buyers at retail stores. They don't write letters. They feel their job is to order, not to correspond. So, if they get a request for a book issued by a publisher they don't know, they won't write us to see if we handle it. Orders for the books printed by small publishers just don't come to us, and we more or less bowed out of trying to stock these books because we couldn't convince the college-store buyers to check with us to see if we handled the particular ones they wanted, before they ordered directly.

A small publisher might visit one of our thirty regional offices. The people there can offer information on how quality books for supplementary college reading are bought and sold, and they can also offer names of managers of nearby NACS stores. There are small publishers in the field with a lock on an academic specialty they have developed, and some self-publishers are in the college market based on the pure merit of their product.

If I were a small publisher, I would try to introduce my book to schools that offer courses associated with my book, because that's where the publisher, the instructor, and the college store have a connection.

It's different in tapes or vitamins or sporting goods. Here, the manufacturer reaches out to the college market as a whole. And this market is huge. Harvard Co-op is first with their $30 million annual gross. Here are the other leaders. Most of them are on-campus multilevel stores:

University of California at
   Los Angeles
Brigham Young University
University of Washington
University of Texas

University of Southern California
University of Minnesota
Yale University
University of Wisconsin

Oregon State University

Sixty of our members do over $4 million gross a year. All together our stores do $330 million of which $210 million is in books. Out of our twenty-four hundred membership, perhaps five hundred do half the business. For the publisher of a book intended for supplementary reading, the prime market are the schools whose courses tie in with his book.

If you haven't been to college for a while, you'll find the bookstore has changed. Remember when State U had ten thousand students and Old Ivy had two dorms with two hundred double rooms each? Today, State U has forty thousand students, and Old Ivy has four thousand.

The first thing you'll notice when you enter a college bookstore is that books are just one item. T-shirts, pens, pencils, bike bags, pocket calculators, three-ring binders, tapes, sporting equipment, greeting cards, and popular paperbacks provide a general atmosphere that leads to impulse buying. It also leads to something else: impulse theft, and that's one of the common problems that college stores have all day, every day.

What are other common problems?

Half the stores report that textbooks are a loss (the discount is usually 20 percent). That's why books offered for supplementary reading are in a favorable light at college stores. The discount is double that of most texts—40 percent—when ordered in minimum lots of around five or six.

When the self-publisher offers a college bookstore a single book at a 25 percent discount—even if it is a book that the store will use for examination and experimental display—and the publisher adds the postage to his bill, you remind the store manager that he's going to lose money on this purchase, just as he does on textbooks. A simple order for one book costs the college stores something like ten dollars in labor charges to set up as a new account. This can defeat you.

How can you knock it down?

While selling to college bookstores, I used this order form:

Please check which method you prefer.

☐ Enter our order for one examination and experimental display copy at 50% discount. This book not returnable for credit. (When check accompanies order, book is sent postpaid.)

☐ Bill us for_____copies of _____ at $8.00 less 40% plus postage. Books are returnable for credit when in salable condition. Minimum order: four.

Truthfully, this does not reduce the store's labor costs in opening a new account. They still have to spend the ten dollars. But, people make their judgments partly on an emotional basis, and, when a bookstore manager sees you are trying to do the right thing for him, he leans your way. I opened eight hundred college-store accounts by using the above order blank.

With forty thousand students enrolled in a quarterly system of study, a state university will require one hundred thousand new texts a year (some used texts are bought), plus another one hundred thousand new books for supplementary reading.

The number of books sold for supplementary reading is not recorded, so only a guess can be offered. If you take the nation's undergraduate college enrollment and multiply it by two, you probably have the lowest possible figure for the number of books sold a year for supplementary reading: 18 million books.

How do you decide if your book has a future with the colleges as supplementary reading, and, if it does, how do you sell it to the college stores?

Start by visiting your library and asking to see some of the college catalogues of undergraduate curriculum. Now ask yourself this question: If I were an instructor, what course would I have to be teaching to ask students to buy my book? How many such courses like this are taught at college?

Let's say your book is on art. Byzantine art. Would your book be helpful to both students and instructors in any of the Byzantine or other art courses described in the catalogues you have examined? What other supplementary reading is available in the courses that best suit your book? At several college bookstores, examine these other books. Is yours competitive?

That's the decisive question. It's a lark to sell a great book for supplementary reading like Rachael Carson's *Under the Sea Wind*, which has gone into the deep millions. Almost nothing else can touch it. The decisive factors that control the sale of books offered for supplementary reading are the inherent editorial quality of the book itself, the number of courses offered in the subject that fit your book, and the student enrollment in these particular courses.

When three or four college instructors who teach courses that fit your book agree that it fills their needs, the direct-mail lists you want to sell your books are readily available.

College Marketing Group (6 Winchester Terrace, Winchester, MA 01890) manages to get their hands on all college catalogues, and from these they compile lists of most college courses taught, along with the names of the instructors and the names and addresses of the schools. The lists change every year, of course. Write to Glenn Matthews, President, for his catalogue of mailing lists of college instructors and the subjects they teach. The current catalogue lists 140 main subjects taught at the college level (Art History, Philosophy, Psychology, and so forth). Within each of these is a detailed list of the courses taught. For instance, under the main subject listing of Art History are twenty-nine separate art courses such as Art History, Modern Art Survey, and Byzantine Art. Here's how the *College Marketing Group* catalogue describes Art History courses.

Name of Course	Number of Professors at Junior-College Level	Number of Professors at Senior-College Level	Total
Art-History Survey	654	1,802	2,470
Modern-Art Survey	60	446	508
Byzantine Art	2	74	76

By leafing through the fifty-six pages of this catalogue you can determine the market your book has for supplementary reading.

The above lists rent for fifty dollars a thousand. This includes the instructor, college, and address. College Marketing Group also offers a list of 2,470 college stores at thirty-five dollars a thousand. Their list of college libraries includes the names of the acquisitions librarians.

Other large and able companies supply direct-mail lists of college teachers. Their lists, too, are divided by the subject matter of the courses they teach. The Educational Directory (One Park Ave., New York, NY 10016) offers a free catalogue on request. They reach any field of higher education, world wide. Educational Lists Company (17 East 22nd St., New York, NY 10010) has lists of teachers at all levels: grade through college. They also supply direct-mail lists of principals and department heads.

B. Klein and Company (P.O. Box 8503, Coral Springs, FL 33065) has a list of twenty-eight hundred college stores, and their price is thirty dollars. R. R. Bowker (1180 Avenue of the Americas, New York, NY 10036) has a somewhat larger list of thirty-five hundred stores selling books to college students. The Bowker list includes college stores on campus, plus some area trade stores that make a specialty of college books. Write Sal Vicidomini.

So, if your book has definite possibilities for supplementary reading at the college level, you have ready access to instructors who teach that kind of course and to college stores.

430

How do you crank up your first sales campaign?

Begin with three hundred letters to college stores, describing your book and mentioning the kind of course it best suits. You might address your letter to "Book Buyer, Supplementary Reading, Paperback—Law," or "Book Buyer, Supplementary Reading, Hardcover—Biology." If it works, good! If the first mailing doesn't pay off, try step two. Show your book to instructors who you believe will benefit through an increase in academic interest when their students read your book. What do the instructors say about your book? Any quotes you can use? Then do a letter to three hundred instructors, and describe your book and how it can help them in teaching this course. Ask if they will recommend your book to students for purchase at the local college bookstore.

You almost have to get your book into the hands of the instructor before he will recommend it. You can do this by offering one examination copy free, or offer it postpaid at 50 percent discount. College teachers are pretty good beggars. Most publishers offer free examination copies only to instructors of large classes in those instances when the publisher knows in advance that his book suits the course of study.

Enclose a return form that allows the instructor to advise you of the name of the course he is teaching, the number of students, and of the fact that he will recommend your book's purchase at the local college store if he approves the examination copy. (You can either offer it free or postpaid at 50 percent off.)

When the forms come back, you have a choice of two routes.

Follow up with the instructor, and ask if he will recommend the book. Or go straight to the book buyer at the college bookstore and enclose a Xerox of the instructor's return form to indicate his interest in your book. What can you expect from the buyer?

Will he order two hundred copies of your book because the instructor asked for an examination copy? More likely, he'll wait to hear from the instructor, or he may send you a token order of five books. Meanwhile, follow up with the instructor to learn his feeling on your book. Once he approves your book for supplementary reading, you have a pass that means an order from both the college library and the college bookstore.

When an instructor in the commerce college has three hundred students in a survey course, "Operating Your Own Small Business" (an invitation to the kind of home-run order that is the special delight of

Bernard Kamoroff in chapter 21), the college store will ask for a confirmation from the instructor.

Have you noted one special thing college bookstores have in common? Most of the books they buy are chosen for them by someone else: namely, the instructor. The college-store buyer selects his own pens, notebooks, and T-shirts, but, when it comes to books, most purchases are the direct result of the instructor's saying he will use the book.

When three or four instructors are using your book, maybe you can pick up additional quotes from both the instructor and some of his student assistants. This is a protein additive to your next sales letter. As you add quotes from instructors and T.A.s (teaching assistants), your letters command increasing attention, because it's not just you who's doing the talking, but also the people who have handled your book and been impressed with it.

Another way to get into the college market is to use the efforts of College Travelers (105½ Main St., Smyrna, TN). Write Tom Neff, President; phone (615) 459-5550.

Mr. Neff's company operates three trucks called Bookmobiles, and these are stocked with two thousand books. About half are suited for supplementary reading at the college level; the others are texts.

Each year, the bookmobiles call on three hundred colleges located in three areas: West Coast, East Coast, and Midwest. Prior to a book-mobile's visit to a college, a letter is sent to the instructors and the acquisitions librarian stating the date of arrival and location where the bookmobile will be parked. The truck is twenty feet long and seven feet wide and permits two lines of people to enter and inspect books. A bookmobile's visit lasts three days. When an instructor or librarian is interested in a book, he is given a card describing it and the terms.

I used the trucks of College Travelers to sell our books. My terms were a "limit offer" of one postpaid book at 50 percent off, cash with order; or one book only at 40 percent off, provided a college-purchase order, with a purchase-order number, and signed by an authorized individual, was sent to the publisher. We added postage on books that were billed.

After filling the order, we mailed the instructor a sheaf of ideas offering class assignments when our book was used for supplementary reading. The ideas included student quizzes and questions for class discussion, as well as questions for students who wanted extra credit for a short paper. We placed the instructor's name on a file card and, from time to time, forwarded other ideas that came to us from teachers who were using this book for supplementary reading. We also asked teachers who were using our book if they would care to suggest the names of other teachers who might be interested in it.

I used the bookmobiles for many years. My thinking was that they would produce the lead and I would make the sale. We did not expect any automatic orders because of our bookmobile exposure. We did considerable direct-mail follow-up work, including some telephone calls to instructors who sent us a card and taught large classes.

One year, I played tag-along with one of the trucks while it visited a large college. Over four hundred instructors and librarians entered the truck to inspect books during the three-day period it was parked there. Going through the truck myself, I noted some publishers supplied cards for their books, offering free examination copies to instructors. One of the bookmobile drivers advised me against this, saying: "They'll palm you poor."

The cost of getting your book on each of these three trucks visiting a total of three hundred colleges is ninety dollars when a book falls into the category of professional and reference books that are either too expensive or too specialized for class adoption but would be used, in some cases, as supplementary reading.

Before leaving the college campuses with their annual purchase of 18 million books for supplementary reading, let's reach out to touch a few students and professors.

Here's a short case history.

A young woman student transferred from Wake Forest, a small college, to a state university. At Wake, she had twenty-five students in her class, sometimes fewer. At her state university, she has 350 students in her biology class and 450 in chemistry.

I asked the arts and science dean at this state university how he felt about large classes. "It's expensive to hire ten teachers when one can do the job. When we hire only one teacher, we can afford a more capable professor, on the average, than when we bring in ten instructors."

My friend's biology professor uses a microphone, and his students sit in a large hall and take notes. There is no question-and-answer period at the end of the fifty-five-minute lecture. During three lectures each week, the professor explains the biology concepts for which the students will be held accountable on written tests. On Friday, the 350 biology students gather in ten small separate units with a T.A. who expands on parts of the professor's lecture that may have been difficult to understand.

I talked to the biology professor and he said: "In the class you attended, I have 350 students. If I flunk three hundred, the administration thinks I'm a lousy teacher; if I pass 340, they'll think I'm overpaid and my course is a snap. When a student asks for an interview, I try to grant it, but, over twelve weeks, the best I can do is meet with sixty students on a one-to-one basis, and that's a drain on my time. I keep trying to find ways to increase the students' motivation.

"My T.A.s are first- or second-year graduate students and inexperienced in teaching."

The professor walked over to a small model of a Bohr atom.

"You know about the atom?" He pointed to a group of electrons painted, at different levels, on a clear-plastic sheet that wound around the atom.

He pressed a button, and, inside the atom, a light revolved and the electrons appeared to shift levels, grow excited, and move faster. "What kind of button do I have? How do I excite the students?

"There are no buttons in teaching. You rely on yourself or, when you must, on something outside yourself. I am led into assigning supplementary reading to lift the students' interest. It's not that I want a supplementary biology book to teach biology. I do that. And my text does that. What I want from supplementary reading is something that will increase the students' interest in biology, and then, maybe, they'll be more willing to sort out and relate the facts in my lectures and pay closer attention to the text, which is accurate but not easy.

"To me, supplementary reading can do what I find difficult to do with a class of 350—get the students really wanting to learn a subject rather than memorizing enough to pass a test and then flushing it out of their minds.

"If all I do is teach content and assume they are interested, I know from experience that I am wrong. If I spend half my fifty-five minutes selling biology, I can't teach them too much. So, in my case, I rely on supplementary reading to bolster the students' interest."

Will your book help an instructor get more out of his classes? If he feels it will do this, he'll recommend it for supplementary reading. And keep on doing it.

Presidents of State and Regional Associations of the National College Book Stores

Alabama College Bookstore Association	President:	Shelby Harkins, University of Montevallo Bookstore, Montevallo, AL 35115
Association of Indiana College Stores	President:	Joe Fulmer, IUPUI Bookstore, Purdue University, Indianapolis, IN 4622
California Association of College Stores	President:	Paul Mares, University Bookstore, University of California at San Diego, La Jolla, CA 92093
Canadian Booksellers Association	President:	Bill Roberts, Shirley Lieshman Books, Ltd., 88 Metcalfe, Ottawa, Ontario, Canada K1P 5L7
College Store Association of New York State	President:	Gary B. Finch, Campus Store, Broome Community College, Binghamton, NY 13902
College Stores Association of North Carolina	President:	Patricia Barbour, Sandhills Community College Bookstore, Rte. 3, Box 182-C, Carthage, NC 28327
College Stores of New England	President:	Henry Gill, Knight Bookstore, Rhode Island Junior College, 400 East Ave., Warwick, RI 02886
Florida Association of College Stores	President:	David G. Roberts, Campus Shop & Bookstore, Florida Atlantic University, University Center, Bldg. 31, Boca Raton, FL 33431

Georgia Association of College Stores	President:	Geneva Womack, South Georgia College Bookstore, Douglas, GA 31533
Illinois Association of College Stores	President:	Larry A. Latman, Illinois Institute of Technology Bookstore, 3200 S. Wabash Ave., Chicago, IL 60616
Kentucky Association of College Stores	President:	Buddy Childress, College Heights Book Store, W. Kentucky University, Bowling Green, KY 42101
Michigan Association of College Stores	President:	Charles W. Ramseth, Student Book Exchange, Inc., 209 E. Bellows St., Mount Pleasant, MI 48858
Middle Atlantic College Stores	President:	Mary Bonach, Book Center, Univ. of Pittsburgh, 4000 Fifth Ave., Pittsburgh, PA 15213
Mid-States Association of College Stores	President:	Kenneth M. Donnelly, Meramec Community College Bookstore, 11333 Big Bend Blvd., St. Louis, MO 63122
Mississippi Bookstore Managers Association	President:	Jessie Phillips, Rebel Press & Office Supply Co., Inc., 1005 Van Buren Dr., P.O. Drawer 1096, Oxford, MS 38655

Mountain States College Stores Association	President:	Garrett E. Case, Ricks College Bookstore, Rexburg, ID 83440
Northwest College Bookstore Association	President:	Arlene Spencer, Wenatchee Valley College Bookstore, 1300 Fifth St., Wenatchee, WA 98801
Ohio Association of College Stores	President:	Hugh Edgar, Ohio Northern University Book Store, McIntosh Center, Ada, OH 45810
Rocky Mountain Skyline Bookstore Association	President:	Shirley L. Frayser, Community College of Denver Bookstore, 3645 W. 112th Ave., Westminster, CO 80030
South Carolina Association of College Stores	President:	Mrs. Bert Price, Winthrop College Store, Rock Hill, SC 29733
Southern California Association of Community College Stores	President:	David Ruston, Cerritos College Bookstore, 11190 East Alondra Blvd., Norwalk, CA 90650
Southwest College Bookstore Association	President:	Gene Rainbolt, Jr., McNeese State University Bookstore, Lake Charles, LA 70609
Tennessee Association of College Stores	President:	James C. Lippy, Memphis State University Bookstore, Memphis, TN 38152

Tri-State Bookstore Association	President:	Lloyd Frick, Augustana College Bookstore, Morrison Commons Building, Sioux Falls, SD 57102
Virginia College Stores Association	President:	Romeo L. Spratley, Virginia State College Bookstore, Petersburg, VA 23803
Western College Bookstore Association	President:	Peter E. Paskill, Portland State Bookstore, Portland, OR 97201
Wisconsin Association of College Stores	President:	David Olson, Trading Post, Student Center, University of Wisconsin, Platteville, WI 53818

33

The Christmas Book Catalogue

WHEN THINGS GO WELL for a self-publisher and his book begins to move, he feels like a runaway train headed downhill. And there's good reason. A moving book has a life of its own. Publicity, word-of-mouth advertising, and the tide of affairs form an elegant alliance that pushes sales up.

A few whiffs of this euphoric updraft cause some publishers to stop advertising. This is a sad decision, because it is the one time in the life of a book when each dollar spent for advertising brings great returns.

When your book has been on sale in at least five hundred stores across the nation, and you or your jobbers are receiving ten reorders a week, you are ready for a major step. This step is the use of Christmas book catalogues that trade stores stack on their counters or mail, free, to their charge customers. Most Christmas catalogues are eight and a half by eleven inches in size and contain sixteen to thirty-two pages. How do these catalogues come into being? Can you get your book into one or more of them?

Each year, a half-dozen Christmas book catalogues are published to promote the sale of trade books that go on sale three months before Christmas. In each catalogue, one hundred or more books of wide, general interest are described and illustrated. The space devoted to each book is paid for by the individual publisher.

The catalogue itself is sold to trade bookstores at somewhere between 7 and 15 cents a copy. This is less than the actual cost because of the up-front money paid by the publishers whose books are represented in the catalogue.

THE BOOK MARKET

Would you believe it—8 million catalogues are distributed during the months of October and November by trade bookstores to their best customers. These catalogues are one of the most effective means of advertising books. In my experience, they are the best.

Let's see how the Christmas catalogues do such a fine job for book publishers and how you can utilize the strength of a catalogue so that it performs to its utmost for you.

We also want to see who publishes these catalogues, how they are put together, how they are sold to bookstores, and what happens when the public gets its hands on one. Then, if you are interested in considering whether a book of yours belongs in one of these catalogues, we'll show how to use one of them as a war club.

One of the oldest and most respected book catalogues is *Book Chat*, published by Booksellers Catalog Service, of Chicago. They distribute eight hundred thousand copies to book dealers, who pay 5 cents to 13 cents a copy. The largest users of *Book Chat* are the eighteen Kroch and Brentano stores. William J. McCarthy, book buyer for K and B, assists the editorial board that selects books for *Book Chat*. After years of buying for the K and B chain, he has developed an ineffable touch that allows him to sense from a title, dust jacket, and author the prospects for a book's sale.

Vroman's, of Pasadena, has been buying *Book Chat* for thirty years. This year, they will mail nineteen thousand copies to their customers, starting around October 10. The copies of *Book Chat* that Vroman's uses carry their name on the front cover as publisher, an industry practice. The manager says: "We stock most of the titles in *Book Chat*. People who come to our store and ask for a title they saw in *Book Chat* sometimes buy other merchandise. One reason for this is that the catalogue comes to our customers just at the right time for early Christmas shopping."

That's what the Christmas catalogues are all about.

In larger cities, sometimes as many as three different catalogues are bought by separate stores. Once in a while, a large retail bookstore is undecided which Christmas catalogue to buy, and so it will buy two and split its mailing list. The disadvantage of this is that it forces the store to stock additional titles as the catalogues do not select the same books. The advantage is that the store gets an opportunity to compare one sales tool against another.

How do you get your book into a Christmas catalogue?

You start in mid-February by writing to the catalogue of your choice and asking for deadline, circulation, and costs. The cost to the book publisher for using any of the current catalogues varies from ten thousand dollars for one full page to $225 for one single unit. One unit measures around one-tenth of a page. Why such a disparity in the price? Looking at the circulation of these catalogues as they appear at the end of this section shows that the catalogue with a larger circulation commands a proportionately higher price per page.

The companies who produce Christmas catalogues include one jobber, several independent companies each with a large user as anchor, and bookstore chains who are associated with the catalogue producer. Each catalogue producer seeks the same thing: quality books of popular appeal that are produced by reliable publishers. Yet, within this frame, the catalogue producer often has one or two reference points of his own.

The current crop of Christmas catalogues includes a relatively new and very successful one sponsored by a jobber, Ingram Book Company. Is their point of view, in selecting books, similar to all the others? Is it slightly different? The similarity is in selecting books of quality and popular appeal whose publishers can be depended upon to keep the dealers supplied. The slight difference arises from the chief occupation of this Christmas-catalogue producer who jobs books nationally to all trade stores.

When a jobber produces a Christmas book catalogue, he expects to sell the catalogue to dealers who, in turn, will distribute them to customers; in addition, the jobber looks forward to supplying these dealers with the books described in the Christmas catalogue.

Would that affect the selection of titles?

Put yourself in the shoes of any jobber who decides to publish a Christmas book catalogue. As a jobber, you buy a five-dollar book for $2.50, and sell it for $3.05 to a book retailer, a 55 cent gross profit. That's a slim profit.

With this in mind, you can understand why any jobber issuing a Christmas catalogue would prefer a greater number of titles in an eight-dollar-and-over retail price range. In this case, he buys the eight-dollar book for four dollars and sells it to the book dealer for around $4.95, a 95-cent gross profit.

Each Christmas-catalogue producer has considerations of his own, and I find this both natural and interesting. The better you understand the other fellow's point of view, the easier it is for you both to do business.

The Paperback Catalog Service, for instance, produces *Paperbacks for Christmas* and also a second Christmas catalogue titled *Books for Giving*. The difference between the two is that the latter includes all the pages of the former, plus a four-page insert for hardcovers. It is offered to bookstores that stock both paperbacks and hardcovers. The National Association of College Bookstores is the big user of *Books for Giving* at Christmastime, but other general bookstores and chains also distribute it. As an added promotion to attract book publishers to *Books for Giving*, the catalogue is mailed to five thousand public libraries to induce them to stock the titles as suggested reading for their patrons. The total distribution of *Books for Giving* is 1.1 million copies. The cost of the smallest unit, which is about one-tenth of a page, is $850.

Paperback Catalog Service publishes another seasonal catalogue, *Paperbacks for Summer*, and the National College Bookstores use this one under the title of *Paperbacks for Leisure Reading*. The summer catalogue, too, has an optional four-page insert devoted to hardcover books. Dealers may order either version, and, as is the case with all book catalogues, their name appears prominently on the front cover, as publisher. The distribution is 650,000, and the smallest unit costs $550. In the book-catalogue line that Rex Coston, president of Paperback Catalog Service, is creating, he has trained his sights on a specialty— paperbacks—and one large customer—NACS. But, in accommodating dealers who sell hardcovers, he has added a punch to his original concept of a paperback catalogue.

It would be reasonable to expect that this catalogue producer has an attitude toward his editorial selections based not only on his big customer, NACS, but also on the nature of the other stores or chains he would like to have but hasn't yet sold. These are things the outside publisher cannot know, but it is useful to recognize that such considerations exist.

Let's look at one more.

The Christmas catalogue with the largest circulation is distributed by Amaranth Publications to 5 million book buyers, mostly by three routes: (1) through the five hundred stores of the Dalton chain, (2) through several hundred additional trade bookstores who are not members of the Dalton chain, and (3) by direct mail to approximately 4 million book buyers. The cost of the smallest unit is four thousand dollars.

At Christmas time the catalogues help the retailer bring in customers. They help the jobber sell more books to dealers and give the book publisher a splendid chance to promote his better titles to his best prospects. Finally, they allow the general public a leisurely look at an array of reading material.

The producer of one catalogue told me the following:

My main problem is logistics. In late February, we write all the book publishers and tell them how many catalogues we think we will sell to bookstores.

At that time, however, no publisher has a firm idea of the titles that will actually be on his Christmas list. He may have eighty tentative candidates for the Christmas book season and plan to publish fifty of them. Which thirty will he drop? He doesn't know. So, he orders the space he wants in our catalogue, but he can't name the books. We trust his judgment, with the right to reject his titles if we must.

Usually the publisher picks his best mover. That's great with us. But sometimes he picks a weak candidate just to see if our Christmas catalogue will do anything for its sale. If twenty publishers do that, we have a honky-tonk catalogue, and our selections don't sell. Next year, the dealers won't buy our catalogue. In self-protection, we urge the publisher to use only his best movers.

On July 1, all the publishers who ordered space in our catalogues are asked to send a dust jacket plus a description of each book they will advertise in our catalogue. They can do the description easily, but in July the dust jackets have not been printed. So we patiently pester the publisher and say, "Pretty please, for God's sake, get your dust jackets over here, as we are already on press." They know when we go to press, and, about a month after we swore we were closed, they get us an artist's sketch of the dust jacket.

Would our catalogue use a book produced by a self-publisher?

Not unless we had hard evidence that more than three hundred trade stores were handling the book, and reorders were coming in regularly. Copies of one hundred recent orders with dates on them would prove the matter; ditto with reorders. We might ask to see some reviews and the dates they were published. We simply can't afford to get stuck with duds. We get enough like that anyway.

For six straight years, I bought advertising space in all the Christmas book catalogues. No one else did this. Some years, there were eight catalogues; other years there were more. I learned a few things you might want to know.

The main question is whether your book is suited for this kind of advertising. If you have a perennial—something that moves in all seasons—and serves the reader as well today as last year or the year before, you have the ideal Christmas-book-catalogue item. Three books that fit this description are discussed in chapter 21. All were originally self-published, and two still are.

Another kind of book well suited to a Christmas book catalogue is an annual that moves all year and has earned a wide readership. There are dozens of such books. Some are annual reviews of photography; others provide journalistic coverage in fields such as finance and sports. Others are directories on widely popular subjects. Every time you sell one copy of a book like this, you add a prospect for next year's edition. Then there is the book of limited editorial interest: architecture, dolls, pocketknives, American glass, antique repairing, herbs, making it big in real estate from scratch, plus other hobbies and vocations.

This latter kind of book requires definite characteristics: (1) It must be informative, well illustrated, and priced competitively with anything on the market that is similar. (2) If issued by a self-publisher, he has to be able to buy it from the printer for five dollars and sell it retail for fifteen dollars. When the dealer buys such a book for nine dollars (40 percent of fifteen dollars) there is a four-dollar gross profit for the publisher.

Do you really need a four-dollar gross profit per book when there are hundreds of thousands of people with a sincere interest in each of the above topics? It takes considerable sales expense to locate your customers from the other 225 million Americans. That is why you need a large gross profit per book.

One way to turn a title into a "forever book" is to revise it editorially when it becomes dated and publish it periodically. This "dating" makes the customer want a new, updated edition, and it keeps the book alive. Unfortunately, this technique doesn't work with fiction or poetry, but it can be done nicely with many subjects, such as travel guides, investment programs, or hang gliders (*i.e.*, newly discovered, exciting terrains, names and addresses of all the hang-glider clubs, dates and classes of all the competitions, new models, and so forth).

How many additional books will you sell as a direct result of using a Christmas catalogue?

If you use one unit of space in a Christmas book catalogue, you can count on the sale of one book, and sometimes two, for every one-thousand copies of a catalogue bought by a dealer. That's 500 to 1,000 books sold per 500,000 catalogues printed in which one unit of space is devoted to your book. One unit of space in a catalogue that distributes 500,000 copies costs from $325 to $400 and occupies around one-tenth of a page.

It is extremely important to understand that you can't buy an advertisement in a Christmas catalogue and then sit back and wait for orders from the dealers who will distribute the catalogue.

There's work to be done as described below.

The Christmas-catalogue companies, bless their souls, provide each publisher who buys one unit or more of space with the names of dealers who buy the catalogue and the number of copies each orders.

Well, what have we here?

What we have is a lovely opportunity to get your money right back, and then some.

Following is a sales letter I sent by first-class mail to each bookstore that bought a Christmas catalogue containing a description of one of our books. Each store received three sales letters: one before it received the catalogue, another a week after it received it, and the third on the day after Thanksgiving. The first letter was mailed around October 1, immediately after learning the names of the dealers who would be receiving the catalogue.

THE BOOK MARKET

Dear ——:

Congratulations on purchasing one thousand copies of the
——— Christmas Catalogue to distribute to your best customers. I
hope you do well, and your inventory turns over faster because of the
traffic this catalogue will bring through your front door.
Your catalogue includes, on page —, a picture of the dust jacket
of ——— plus a description of the book. Herewith, a dust jacket is
enclosed for window use.
Have you been buying copies from your jobber? They now have a
large, fresh supply. You can also secure them directly from us.
[Then explain the kind of customer who will buy this book, where the
book should be shelved, and enclose an order blank and circular.]

Using a series of three such letters, you can expect orders for four
hundred books from each set of about 150 to 200 dealers, plus another
one hundred books for reorder in January. You cannot afford to depend
only on the customer to ask the dealer for your book. For you, much is at
stake. You need to get your book on the dealer's shelf. You start off by
reminding the dealer that it does him no good to buy and mail the
catalogue unless he stocks the books described in it. Naturally, he won't
stock them all. Between 75 and 150 books are described in each of the
Christmas catalogues. The dealer will stock at least half the titles,
sometimes more than half. But you have to do some pushing, too.

Do all the publishers who use the Christmas book catalogues do the
same thing; that is, do they each get in touch with the dealer by mail
and/or phone and ask for an order? They do not. Mostly, it is the large
publishers who use these catalogues, and to them this effort is a
miniscule one in relation to their whole operation. When they see the
list of dealers who are buying the catalogue, the most they will do is mail
copies to their travelers. The effort stops there.

Small, direct-mail campaigns are an anathema to the large publisher.
The bother of hand-addressing envelopes to two hundred dealers,
composing a single-purpose letter for such a small group, and, God
forbid, doing this three times to the same list, is regarded as redundant.
They want something that can be computerized and mailed to a large list
at third-class-mail postage rates. When you have a good book, and a
good markup, it's no trick to beat them at their own game by

personalizing your whole approach to the dealer, jobber, and individual. Way back when, that's how everybody started. But, today, your competitors, Harper, and Doubleday, and Simon & Schuster, are hard put to do these things. Their labor costs have gone through the roof.

As a self-publisher you have the edge, because the Christmas catalogues are a major promotion for you, and it is to your interest to work the list of dealers for every sale you can get. If you do as I did, and use each catalogue for just one book, the mention of this bold fact to any dealer is significant. Probably no one else in the country will be doing this except you. The moving train has gathered new speed. The dealer senses this at once, and it nudges him toward buying your book and giving it window and counter display. When you are in all the catalogues, it's pretty hard for any dealer to ignore your book as the splash spills over to all stores, whether or not they use a Christmas catalogue. In my own work, I developed a series of special sales letters for dealers who were *not* using the catalogues. Once these dealers recognized that many hundreds of active dealers in the country were mailing out or handing out a catalogue with one particular book advertised in each, they were more willing to stock this title.

I spent twenty-five thousand dollars a year on the Christmas catalogues and estimate my gross dollar return was a comfortable six for one.

A list of seven Christmas catalogues follows. Circulation and rates vary from one year to the next, mostly becoming higher. One unit is about one-tenth of a full page.

Amaranth Productions * P.O. Box 9471 Minneapolis, MN 55440	Contact: Joel Papa Circulation 5 million; 1 unit–$4,000
Book Chat Bookseller's Catalog Service A Division of Kroch and Brentano 29 South Wabash Ave. Chicago, IL 60603	Contact: Doris Laufer Circulation 700,000; 1 unit—$625
Christmas Book Catalog Brentano's 586 Fifth Ave. New York, NY 10036	Contact: Mr. Jess Joseph Circulation 300,000; 1 unit—$400

* This Christmas catalogue company is associated with the B. Dalton chain of bookstores.

THE BOOK MARKET

Christmas 1981
The Scribner Bookstores, Inc.
597 Fifth Ave.
New York, NY 10036

Contact: Jean Touroff

Circulation 300,000; 1 unit—$325

Cokesbury's Gift Books
201 Eighth Ave. S.
Nashville, TN 37202

Circulation 400,000; 1 unit—$400

The Ingram Gift Book Catalog
The Ingram Book Company
347 Reedwood Dr.
Nashville, TN 37217

Contact: Michael Zibart

Circulation 2.3 million; 1 unit—$1,000

Paperbacks for Christmas
Paperback Catalog Service
Roaring Brook Lake
Putnam Valley, NY 10579

Contact: Ann Sorg Coston

Circulation 1.1 million; 1 unit—$850

34

How to Sell a Self-Published Book by Direct Mail

THERE'S A POPULAR SAYING used by salesmen who rent mailing lists to publishers: "Anything that can be sold, can be sold by mail." It's mostly true, too. Diamonds, cemetery lots, islands, books, even sexual encounters of the unusual kind are successfully offered by mail.

Only one kind of book, however, ideally fills the bill for an exclusive, direct-mail sales plan. We'll discuss its nature and then name other kinds of books that can also benefit from direct-mail campaigns used to back up other sales programs.

A true story illustrates the kind of book that sells best by direct mail. A bright young man by the name of E. Haldeman-Julius married the daughter of a printer in Girard, Kansas, and, instead of busying himself by selling printing for his father-in-law, he created titles for "knowledge" books and ordered them written under contract. He called them *Little Blue Books*. Within twenty years, the small post office at Girard was awarded the rating of U.S. Post Office, First Class, due to Haldeman-Julius and his *Little Blue Books*, which were all sold by direct mail.

Haldeman-Julius asked my help in rounding up the authors he needed, and, when I visited his office he asked: "Which of my titles do you think sells best?"

Looking over his list, I couldn't settle on any one. "Ha!" he said, "I'll teach you something. Any *Little Blue Book* title sells best that starts off with the magic words 'How to.' Of my twelve hundred titles, *How to Be*

449

an Electrical Engineer outsells *The Love Poems of Ovid,* and *How to Stay Young* sells three for one compared to *The Life of Cleopatra.*"

That was fifty years ago, and when it comes to selling books by direct mail, the "knowledge" book is still the easiest and most profitable to sell. Consider the unlikely case of two radiologists who, in their own way, reinvented the wheel. Drs. Ben Felson and Morris Reeder put together the ideal knowledge book, and you can get the hang of its concept in one minute.

When an X ray passes through a part of the human anatomy on its way to a photographic plate, its path is impeded by bones, marrow, organs of the body, certain tumors, and many other things. When few impediments are in its path, the X rays burn darkly into the photographic plate. Thus, a dark blob on the photographic plate can be the result of X rays passing through lungs filled with air, while lighter blobs can be from X rays passing through bones or the heart or spleen. An X ray can leave hundreds of different kinds of shadows on a photographic plate, depending upon the parts of the human body it passes through. The Felson-Reeder book describes these shadowy blobs and offers various possible diagnoses of each. What a simple idea!

Are there other ideas like it? At least several hundred. The first one I saw was written by a pulp-paper writer, William Wallace Cook. He called it *Plotto.* After listing all possible components of a story plot, he organized a system that allowed the reader to combine selected parts into an original, bare-bones plot. The nice part about an idea like this is that you don't have to sell it. It sells itself.

In the case of Drs. Felson and Reeder, all they did was print fifteen thousand copies of their book, pricing it at thirty-five dollars. As these words are written, word-of-mouth advertising and direct mail have sold ten thousand copies. The book cost $4.50 to print and bind, and, as Dr. Felson explained it to me, it took "most of our lives to accumulate the knowledge and only five years to organize it." The reason I feel these two doctors reinvented the wheel is that the book's approach to its subject matter is basic and fits several hundred books yet to be written. Putting the idea for either *Plotto* or the X-ray book into a sentence, you take a given field and organize the knowledge within it in an easily grasped way.

A friend of mine is at work on such an idea. His name is Mike, and he

450

is a great tailor, a gentleman's tailor, as they say. So was his father; so is his son. Here's Mike's idea:

> What we don't have in tailoring today is knowledge. Nobody knows quality. I mean most customers, most mills, most tailors have no understanding of the elements that make up true quality in wool, silk, cotton, or cashmere, in stitching, design, lining, or the rest.
>
> In the whole field of tailoring, not one person in five hundred knows how to turn a shoulderpad and judge the handiwork. I want to do a book that explains it all.

Because my father was a *Schneider*, I took to Mike's idea, and we spent an hour going over the beginnings of a chapter outline.

"That would be one hell of a book," said Mike, "but I think I am a tailor."

Yes, it would be one hell of a book, and libraries, vocational counselors, tailors, mills, retail- and wholesale-clothing salesmen—the entire field would buy it. Who has the wit, the energy, the knowledge and the organizational ability to write it? I don't know, but the market is there. Mike's idea is directly related to the kind of book that Drs. Felson and Reeder wrote, and it is at this point that you begin to decide whether your book can be sold profitably by direct mail.

Let's think in terms that will clue you in on whether your book is a true candidate for profitable direct-mail sales. If yours is a knowledge book, you already have a good start, because you can charge a little more per one hundred pages than for poetry, fiction, essays, and juveniles. People will pay more for a book to improve their skills than for a book whose main usefulness is to give a lift to a leisure hour.

The lower the retail price of a book (juveniles, thin volumes of verse), the more difficult it is to sell profitably by mail, because it costs the same amount to mail a circular to ten thousand prospects whether the book sells for $4.50 or $14.50. And, because people buy more knowledge books than any other kind, there are more available rental mailing lists for people interested in electronics, farming, or any other knowledge subject.

If you intend to self-publish a knowledge book and sell it by mail, you want to make very sure it is competitive with what is already on the market in number of pages, illustrations, page size, price, and coverage of subject matter. Because direct-mail campaigns are usually backed up with a money-back agreement to return the buyer's money in fifteen days, you have to "go" with a product that stands up to the current competition. Or you may have to eat the returns. They become indigestible after the first several hundred. In fine, you start with quality. It doesn't have to be the world's greatest book or the one-hundredth greatest, but you'd better feel secure about its worth and have ample reasons for your confidence.

The work that goes into proving the worth of your book before publication is a good investment. A well-done knowledge book makes an author rich for life. Revised editions enjoy a comfortable initial sale from people who bought the first edition and found it first class. *How to Avoid Probate,* by Norman F. Dacey, sold over one million copies and now has a one-up clone titled *How to Avoid Probate—Updated.* The new edition started out with 125,000 built-in original orders from people who enjoyed the first edition or who had heard good things about it. A fine knowledge book is a serious and beautiful financial venture, and the author's profits are lifelong and substantial. You have a right to decide to give a book of this kind your very best.

Here are two other book ideas that relate to the basic formula of the knowledge book. A friend of mine, Henriette, is married to an ophthalmologist and is her husband's receptionist. In addition to greeting incoming patients ("Ring bell—Walk in"), she schedules the patients' next visits, fills out medical-insurance forms, sends bills, verifies surgery appointments, supervises the office details of three nurses, and packs a hot lunch for her husband in the event he can't leave the office. She is one of the great people in this kind of job. There are probably one thousand others, but, if you listen to doctors, they are few and far between.

Why do Henriette and her peers excel? What is their technique of organization and accomplishment? What is their on-the-job attitude? What can another person who holds down the same job learn from a book she might write to justify the doctors' buying a copy? An annual market of twenty thousand has always existed for this book among the nation's doctors. Will Henriette write it?

"I've been at this job for thirty-five years, and soon we will retire to travel and spend time with our grandchild. It's one thing to make room in your life for a career, and another to organize and write a book when your career is over."

As of this moment, Henriette's book is unwritten. If "How to Run a Doctor's Office" is produced well, it will be a permanent success.

My typist at Longboat Key is a homemaker by love, by vocation and by choice. I asked her what she did all day with her time, and the next day she prepared a three-page, single-spaced outline of her activities as a homemaker. Did she see it as a book? She saw it as a short article for *Reader's Digest*. As a book, its mail-order possibilities leave a book salesman limp with desire. The readable, definitive, knowledge book on this subject is still unwritten and unpublished. Look around you, and see how many examples of such classic knowledge books are needed and unavailable. Collect forty items that belong in one such book. Think in terms of what you might do in this field. A definitive, accurate, and readable knowledge book is a lark when it comes to selling it, but a millstone when it's a skim job.

Step one in a direct-mail campaign for a self-published book is to have a killer of a book before you start. Test the individual chapters, test the completed manuscript, and shoot for as many editorial reactions as you can through newspaper and magazine reviews and for public reaction with TV appearances. If this comes up roses, the direct-mail steps are simple. We'll give them right now and follow with a consideration of direct-mail campaigns as a back-up for sales work on books of verse, essays, fiction, juveniles, and so forth.

Some discussion of the points that follow appear in previous chapters, as direct mail is an integral part of book-selling.

STATIONERY AND ENVELOPES

Your prospective buyer sees your outside envelope and your stationery first. Put your best foot forward by employing a graphics artist whose samples of stationery and envelopes please you. No samples? Try another artist. For stationery, order a simple, clean design in one or two colors, preferably on eight-and-a-half-by-eleven paper matched to a Number-10 envelope. Use a pale-tinted paper, eggshell or dead white. What you seek is clarity and an expression of good taste through simplicity. Avoid script or sans-serif type; both are on the lower half of the spectrum for readability. Black ink is usually easiest for the eye to read. Green is harder.

Can a rule-breaking, creative letterhead and envelope be used successfully? Yes. But a near miss is disastrous.

ENCLOSURES

Each part of a book publisher's direct-mail campaign has a particular job to do, and the trick is to limit the work of each enclosure to one responsibility. In most cases, four enclosures make up a direct-mail campaign: circular, order blank, return envelope, and letter.

THE CIRCULAR

The task of the circular is to describe and illustrate the contents of the book being offered. Let's examine that word, describe. Instead of saying "The coverage is complete," select one chapter and tell what's in it and then give a concise breakdown of the other chapters. Instead of saying that a chapter is "very readable," take an excerpt and quote it. The circular informs by using specifics. Generalities are a put-off for the real thing. If you use a superlative ("the best illustrations on the subject you have ever seen"), examples of some illustrations should be included.

Testimonials and quotes of reviews belong in the circular. Favorable quotes from noted people and appreciative reviews increase the reader's willingness to buy. You might place these quotes in a separate box or panel so that they retain an entity of their own. The circular also requires these special facts: name and address of the publisher, title of book, retail price, name of author, picture of the book's front cover, number of pages, page size. In case of a large, out-size book, give the weight.

The circular should also provide space for the reader to order the book in the event that the other enclosures are lost and only the circular remains, or in the event the reader gives the circular to a friend or offers it to the local library. When your circular provides space for the reader to order, it can also be used as an enclosure in correspondence.

The final task of the circular is to explain the value of the book to the reader.

In writing your copy for the circular, try to be conversational without being familiar or using "in" talk. If you can manage it, a few touches of good humor are wonderful. The opposite of the right way to write is the style of most radio or TV commercials.

A book circular may be printed on two sides of an eight-and-a-half-by-eleven sheet, or on four similar-sized pages that fold to fit a Number-10 envelope. Two or four colors are better than one color. Too much small type with little or no white space is self-defeating. White space serves to give the eye a rest and makes the task of reading the circular appear less arduous.

ORDER BLANK

This is a separate enclosure, and it may be small in size—up to seven or eight inches wide and three or three and one-half inches deep. The single purpose of the order blank is to tell the reader that an order is expected and to provide the convenient means for doing so. Using a light-tinted stock allows the order blank to stand out. When a bolder color is used, it is harder to read the type on the order blank. Printing the order blank in either one or two colors is acceptable. Use only one side. Keep the copy simple. Don't give too many choices to the customer. Include a money-back agreement that you are willing to live with. ("Your money refunded in full by return mail when book is returned within fifteen days after receipt.") In the order blank, don't be cute about anything or allow the language to be ambiguous.

RETURN ENVELOPE

The purpose of the return envelope is to make it convenient for the reader to order. No selling copy need be used. The size of your return envelope should be about three and one-half inches by six and one-half. You don't want any enclosure that fits too snugly into your outside envelope because of the difficulty of insertion. The post office has become fussy about accepting odd-size envelopes, so, if you reach for something distinctive in size, check it out with your local post office.

THE LETTER

Most professional major-league pitchers can't even throw a pitch out without taking a wind-up. Warm up to your letter by drifting into it gradually. By the time you get to the middle of page two, you'll have the lead. It's easier doing it this way than by staring at the typewriter for an hour trying to get a lead that starts the letter on the run. If you have cased your list and called on a number of the people who will receive your letter, you have an image of some of the people to whom you are writing. That's good. Now concentrate on one such person, and write directly to that individual.

Normally, the person who is receiving your sales letter can't be expected to be enthusiastic about receiving your communication. What can you do to increase the reader's interest? Your letter can offer some sort of reward to the reader for opening the envelope and starting to "give it a read." The reward can be intellectual, philosophical, urbane, good-humored, story-telling, valuable data connected with the subject matter of your book; it can be erotic, or it can be just plain funny. Try to connect this "reward" with the reader, not with you or with your book. It's a sort of free float to attract the reader to whatever else you have to say.

There's no rule on long or short letters; rather, it's what you have to say and how you say it. If you can lay your letter aside for two weeks and then read and cut, it is sometimes a better letter. You can think of the circular as the steak and the letter as the sizzle.

How many orders per thousand letters mailed will you require?

Although every direct-mail campaign has its own special cost, and every book has its own production expense, it is fair to say that the average third-class-mail campaign costs 17 cents to 20 cents for each piece, including postage, when mailed in lots of five thousand.

Every publisher figures his own costs a little differently. If your book costs three dollars to print and sells for eight dollars, you have a five-dollar gross profit from each sale.

How many orders do you need per thousand letters to show a profit? By using bulk third-class mail, the entire cost of postage and printing is around two hundred dollars, or 20 cents per letter. Thus, when you sell an eight-dollar book, costing five dollars to print, you need forty orders per one thousand letters mailed, to reach your "nut" or break-even point. Let's see it as a bookkeeper would write it:

Income	Expenses
40 books at $8.00 each . . . $320	Printing 40 books at $3.00 each . . . . $120.00 Mailing 1,000 letters at 20 cents each $200.00 $320.00

In this case, all orders over forty from each one thousand letters mailed will show you a profit of five dollars each. But forty orders per one thousand letters mailed equals a 4 percent return. That's higher than would normally be expected. Somewhere between 1.5 percent and 3.5 percent is average.

How can you lower your break-even point?

1. A better mailing list might mean a higher percentage of returns.
2. A higher retail price might show a greater profit per sale.
3. A lower cost per book printed will show a greater profit per sale.
4. A more effective letter or circular might improve the returns.

Items 2 and 3 often appear easier to alter in the publisher's favor, and they account for the violent rise in the retail price of books and, simultaneously, in their reduction in quality. The number of editing hours devoted to each book are fewer, the weight and rag content of the paper are less, binding boards are less sturdy, and the total number of pages in a book is reduced when feasible.

There is no question that publishers are producing shoddier books at higher prices. Can you beat them at their own game by producing a better book editorially and having it manufactured to specifications of higher quality—and, if you do this, will the reader appreciate it?

That's a very fair question. When the self-publisher is the lover who cares, and his time isn't carded out at twenty dollars an hour, but given cheerfully and freely, he can occasionally beat the big-time royalty publisher by producing a higher-quality book both editorially and physically. This can mean employing and listening to objective, competent professionals whom you consult regarding book design, manufacturing specifications, and editorial quality.

You can do it yourself and do it better when you seek out standards of excellence and meet them at the upper limits of your talent. This, the big publisher does not do. That's his weakness, your strength.

Should a campaign be tested first?

Yes. If you have access to a mailing list of five thousand or more, test your mailing with five hundred. A test that is smaller than five hundred may not be a fair test, since your best prospects on the mailing list may not be evenly spaced at the rate of two, three, or four out of each one hundred names. Your best prospects may come in clusters, and, for that reason, a test of five hundred is just about the minimum. If you test five hundred and the results are profitable, can you go ahead with a mailing of twenty thousand? That can be a four-thousand-dollar gamble. It would be wise to make a second test, this time of two thousand, and, if that is profitable, shoot the works.

What do you do with your customer list?

Lots of things. Ask the people who ordered your book if they liked it. You may receive some fine quotes. Also ask if they would care to send you the names and addresses of several friends to whom you might send a circular. Or would they like to send a book as a gift? If it's a nonfiction book, ask if they have ideas for things to go into a revised edition.

POSTAL RATES

The cheapest postage rate for a direct-mail campaign is bulk, third class, and, as you would expect, a permit to use this is required. Like propagation, the right is denied to virtually no one. Don't be scared off because you have to wade into a government office and buy a permit. The cost is seventy dollars for the first year and forty dollars each year thereafter to renew it.

Your permit allows you to mail third-class bulk letters. The rates vary with the political winds and the effectiveness of the Washington lobbyists employed by the big mailers. Recently, the rates were 8.4 cents for each piece of mail weighing up to 3.278 ounces. Under this favorable rate, a minimum of two hundred pieces may be sent at one time, and the mail has to be separated and tied into zip codes. If you mail *under* two hundred pieces (with or without a permit), the letters need not be separated and tied into zip codes, but the cost is 20 cents per piece up to 2 ounces. When you plan to mail about five thousand pieces in a year, in lots of two hundred or over, a permit is economical.

The regulations for using permit mail are bewildering at first, and you will benefit from a question-and-answer session at your main downtown post office. Suburban or village postal people don't speak the language. The place to go is the "Weigher's Office" or "Third Class Mail, Bulk Section." The main-office post-office people are accommodating and well informed and understand how complex the rules appear at first blush.

One of the curious alleys of third-class regulations is that the cost of mailing one piece weighing up to two ounces is 20 cents, so that a one-ounce third-class-mail letter dropped off at the post office costs 20 cents, while the same letter sent by first-class mail costs 15 cents. How can this be so? If it worries you, think of what things must be like in Russia.

As a rule of thumb, figure that your third-class bulk-mailing costs will be a little less than one-half the total cost of producing a mail campaign in lots of five thousand.

MAILING LISTS

As a publisher, you have 90 million prospects available for use in selling a book by direct mail. The names and addresses of almost all of them may be rented from mailing-list companies. A million or two are not available from mailing-list companies but may be had free when both publisher and list owner find it useful to cooperate.

For instance, most trade bookstores will not rent their list of charge customers. Usually, the list is too small, and the mechanics of having it addressed are not available. But if the publisher supplies the trade bookstore with a lightweight mailing piece, the trade-store owner might enclose it when sending out bills, provided, of course, that he currently stocks the book. A sweetener in this case need be no more than one free copy of the book for window display.

To locate the various mailing-list companies, try your main library and ask to see the yellow pages of the telephone books from large cities, especially New York, Chicago, and Los Angeles. Another good source is *The Literary Market Place,* published by R.R. Bowker and shelved by most large libraries. In *LMP*'s chapter on mailing lists, the companies selected are those specializing in serving book publishers.

Here are the names and addresses of a few mailing-list companies:

Ahrend Associates, Inc.
64 University Pl.
New York, NY 10003

Ed Burnett, Consultants, Inc.
2 Park Ave.
New York, NY 10016

The Coolidge Company
25 West 43rd St.
New York, NY 10036

Dependable Lists, Inc.
257 Park Ave. South
New York, NY 10010

Alan Drey Co.
600 Third Ave.
New York, NY 10016

Dunhill International Lists
2430 W. Oakland Park Blvd.
Ft. Lauderdale, FL 33311

Saul Gale Associates, Inc.
5703 Kissena Blvd.
Flushing, NY 11355

The Kleid Company
200 Park Ave.
New York, NY 10017

Response Mailing Lists
Drawer C
Park Ridge, NY 07656

Alvin B. Zeller, Inc.
475 Park Ave. South
New York, NY 10016

Zeller & Letica, Inc.
15 East 26th St.
New York, NY 10010

When writing to a mailing-list company, submit a cover of your book, a two-page outline and a circular, and ask what lists of prospective buyers the company can secure for you. Most lists are available by geographical selection. The minimum lot offered for testing is usually three thousand. Rented lists may be used only once, and the names and addresses may not be copied for a second use.

The names offered by the mailing-list people are categorized for the convenience of the renter: millionaires, bankers, florists—there are over seven-hundred classifications. However, each list was assembled for someone else's purpose and may be imperfect for you. The best list is the one you build yourself, as discussed in chapter 24.

In addition to the big mailing-list companies that offer many millions of names, there are also hundreds of small specialty companies offering their very own customer lists to selected mailers. In selling your own list by direct mail, try to think of who might have the ideal list, and perhaps you can convince them to rent it to you.

The cost of renting one name and address from a mailing-list company varies from 3 to 5 cents. The addressing is included in this price and the list comes to you in geographical sequences so that, if you have a third-class, bulk-rate mailing permit, it is easier to separate into zip codes. Most list companies supply names and addresses on pressure-sensitive labels for convenience in attaching them to your envelopes.

Is it profitable to rent a mailing list? The only way to go is with a test mailing. If you produce a test mailing of up to three thousand and the test is profitable, and then you try a second mailing of five thousand and that is also profitable, you can usually anticipate a profit from using a large mailing.

Not every book lends itself to direct mail. Although the knowledge book is perfect for this type of selling, most other books can use direct mail only as a supplementary aid. Direct mail, for instance, can always be used to get orders from trade dealers and specialty outlets. If you have a catalogue of a dozen or more different titles and can divide the sales cost of your direct-mail campaign among each of these titles, it is then possible to sell a wide general line by direct mail.

But it is difficult to offer a single book, be it history, verse, juvenile, biography, autobiography, essays, literary criticism, folklore, or short stories, by direct mail to the consumer.

Take two of the bright, stunning books of the last few years: *The Snow Leopard*, by Peter Mathieson, and *Vida*, by Marge Piercy.

As a track for the reader to follow, the Mathieson book provides a trip through the Himalayan Mountains in search of the snow leopard. The main thrust of the work, however, is a different kind of search: a quest for inner discoveries that come to the relaxed open mind when it is in a state of solitude and well-being. The book is a glorious, even joyful experience.

The other book, *Vida*, is a novel about a group of political dissidents. They bomb and cause disruption and phone the media to take credit. They call themselves "The Little Red Wagon" and have no home, clothes, or money; no car, paintings, books, or savings, and very few friends. For recreation, they sleep with each other regardless of gender. They have no clear-cut dogma like a Seventh-Day Adventist or an imam to move the world into their way of thinking. They prepare papers about what they think is important, only to discover, in time, that their ideas change. The characters who people the book are by turn poignant,

461

courageous, naive, determined. Their agonizing, political involutions lead the reader not to disbelief but to caring for them as human beings.

I am a great believer in the literary value of these two books, and I can't figure out how I would sell either one of them by direct mail. I suppose the only way to promote them is through TV talk shows, coupled with trade-store displays for the week following the broadcast, and by publication of selected chapters in class magazines. But direct mail to the consumer, no.

There are ever-so-many fine books that do not lend themselves to direct mail. You may recall reading Salinger's *Catcher in the Rye* at school, as it remains a favorite with college English departments and sells a quarter of a million copies a year. But it would be murder to sell singly by mail.

So, if you wish to use direct mail to secure consumer orders for a self-published book, you have to start off with the right kind of book. We'll summarize its unique physical requirements.

1. Your book needs to be competitive with what is offered in the marketplace in price, size, coverage, and editorial quality.
2. The difference between your printing cost and retail price should be over five dollars. You are safer with eight dollars.
3. Your "nut" or break-even point, per one thousand letters, should be under thirty orders.
4. To the extent that you are depending upon direct mail to sell your book, you require access to mailing lists of prospective buyers in lots of no less than one hundred thousand in order to sell three to four thousand copies.
5. Test your direct-mail campaign before going into a large mailing such as twenty or thirty thousand pieces.
6. Visit with some of the people whose names and addresses are on your mailing lists to learn their reactions to your subject matter and circular.

Any knowledge book can be sold successfully by mail when the above six items can be answered affirmatively. Other kinds of books when offered singly (and with nothing else in the circular for the customer to buy) are seldom a prize package for a direct-mail campaign.

462

35

You Can Do It

THIS BOOK HAS practical information for author and publisher alike. Its idea is to defuse injustice. Instead of leaving things to chance, we need a firm grip on our own situations.

No author can control his publisher. He can, however, prevent his book from being abandoned by employing certain direct types of action. Some of these actions are open to only a few, others to all.

First in importance is producing the best book within the limits of your talent and energy. Second is pretesting before you show your book to a publisher. The third step comes in selling your book. Select a publisher who has some background for your kind of manuscript, as suggested in chapter 9. Together, these three steps are a great beginning.

There are two other steps, and they carry the author into a different area of direct action. The author, or his agent, needs to come up with the kind of salesmanship that secures a large, nonreturnable royalty payment in advance of publication. This induces the publisher to print a larger number of copies and to promote them with vigor.

When no sizeable up-front money is involved, the publisher may drag his feet. To be truthful, that is the easiest way for him to publish a book. He simply drags his feet while waiting for reviews and reorders. If they come in, good. If not, see you later. Suppose you are a publisher with two titles a day coming off your presses. Can you hire enough competent people to publicize every title with intensity, and can you assemble enough money to put ten or twenty thousand dollars into the initial advertising of each book?

THE BOOK MARKET

Sooner or later you would get down to what every large publisher does: You hit hard, at one in every twenty of the books you publish, then take a few healthy swipes at another one in every three. For the others, you wait and see.

Wait and see for what? Wait and see if six major media come in with hot reviews and whether half of the bookstores phone in reorders within three months after their initial order is received.

When reviews and word of mouth push up the sale, the author's battle is half-won. The publisher then opens his wallet and starts to spend money, even though he began with a minimal budget. The publisher's original stratagem looks like disinterest but is really a laid-back policy based on his own statistics. The figures tell him: Wait before you push. Unless you're suckered into it, the figures say, by your own gut feeling or a large advance, let the book do the talking before you do the spending. That's the gospel from Madison Avenue. It's based on the records and without regard for human flesh. Your strength lies in knowing this attitude and understanding how to counteract it.

As an example of how to counteract it let's look at the author whose prudent publisher gave him no advance. The book garners few reviews and not many more orders. Meanwhile, the publisher has placed fifteen hundred dollars into an advertising budget and, after spending two-thirds of it, has stopped. If your faith in your book is alive and well, you don't quit. Now is the time for the fifth and final step. You've simply got to give out with the battle cry and haunt nearby radio and TV talk shows, push local publicity, and prove what can be done in a controlled area— making sure your book is well distributed before you set the town afire. When well done, this final piece of direct action can turn your publisher around.

A literal example appears in chapter 6. Jane Heimlich, an unknown, unproved book author, took it upon herself to get her stalled book moving. And she did it, too. Maybe not spectacularly, but one heck of a lot more than would have occurred if she hadn't bent her mind and will to it. She worked within the establishment, consulting her publishers each step of the way, so they felt comfortable about it all. Three authors of self-published books mentioned in chapter 21 did the same thing and with sweet success. None of these authors had a grain of previous P.R. experience. If you can write a book, you know what's in it, and you know

464

yourself. Promote the two of you. Decide early to make local and regional promotional events happen. Do it with the advice and consent of your publisher's P.R. department, to verify that your book is on sale in the area in which your publicity will break.

Now what of the publisher? Why does he become disenchanted with 5, 10, or 15 percent of his books within a few months after publication and quit on them? Is he part of the theater of the absurd? Not at all. He is simply a different sort of fellow from what he once was. If the publisher of your choice issues books that are no great shakes when it comes to sales, major-media reviews, and publicity (when did he last have an author on *Today, Donahue, Carson, Griffin, Good Morning?*), you have to assume either his P.R. department or his books are suspect. Maybe in publishing he's a bit inept. This ineptness is just as true of motion-picture producers and major-league ballclub owners as it is of book publishers. The title they carry gets its weight from people other than themselves.

But what if that's the best publisher you can find? And no other one is in sight? If you accept the offer, do all you can to back up your book and start concentrating on your second book. The world is big, bright, and beautiful, and the book that only one small fish snapped at may be a learning experience. Move on.

Is there an excuse for the publisher's neglecting a title and allowing it to die, for contracting to publish a book, especially fiction by a new author, and then not budgeting a dime (*i.e.*, under two thousand dollars) for time, space, and publicity?

In neglecting a title, the publisher has lots of excuses. He has pushed books by new authors before and in most cases taken a bath. So now he carries a pop gun. He issues the book, puts his company's honored name on the binding, and then waits to see what will happen. This way he loses less, he says, than if he punches hard at every title he brings out. And he is so right.

So that's the bind, and, if you encounter it, you need to take the direct-action steps briefly outlined above.

Will things get any better?

Why should they? Publishing used to be run by relatively small businessmen who were just fair as business people but invested in book publishing as a way of life. It pleased their sense of fulfillment. And they loved it. If they took in a half-million dollars a year and paid themselves fifty thousand dollars in salary, and managed to put away another fifty thousand dollars in reserve (whether it be real estate, rolls of paper, equipment, or money), they were ecstatic.

Today's big publishers don't think in terms of grossing a half a million dollars. They are part of a big-business operation, and their division may be grossing twenty million or more, and the dollars they earn go to the parent corporation. That's why the publishing division was acquired. Not for glory, not for literature, but for dough. So, for the big people, things are not going to change unless three or four book-publishing divisions have a string of red years.

Will this happen? Why should it? Books are put together like merchandise: peanut butter, jeans, or a cola drink. The job is done by skilled merchandisers. While they do the hyping, the selling is passed on to the market manager. He is handed a product to sell, and its substance is not his first concern. Usually, he is not a book man. When his opinion is asked, he often hangs back unless the book is in a field that has a track record. The big books, the ones whose authors receive five hundred thousand dollars' or more advance royalty, are valued on the basis of the kind of hyping that can be pinned on them rather than their literary worth. The market manager has no great affection for reading or for the reading public. Many people feel this is one weak link in the publishing chain.

How long will book publishers continue to pour a lot of titles on the market and give most of their attention to a few? How long will this attitude prevail? As long as it is profitable.

It is possible the public will care less about reading. Presently, this is not so. The public is buying fewer hardcover books only because they cost so much, not because they are hastily conceived.

Is there a backlash in the offing? If there is one, it will probably come from another Henry Luce, another Harold Ross, or from the kind of people who produce *Rolling Stone*. They will be young, poorly financed, and will aim high. Some will succeed. My rationale for this is embedded in magazine-publishing experience. Within a few years after Luce published the first issue of *Time*, his only competitor, *Literary Digest*, went out of business. People bought *Literary Digest*, because nothing else was available, and, when they saw *Time*, the *Digest*'s day was over.

Judge, a popular humor magazine, went down the drain shortly after Ross brought out the *New Yorker*. It lasted as long as it did, because there was no other choice.

A new breed of book publisher, seeking primarily quality, can make a safe landing if he has the motivation, originality, and the flair of Luce, Ross, or editor-publishers like Helen Valentine and Enid Annenberg Haupt.

Eager, bright young minds will continue to enter book publishing. Not all of them will copy the books with the best track records. Some of them will publish what they want to publish for the utter joy of it. Crazies are like this, too, and we have our share of them. But sheer publishing talent, steered by an innocent eye and unbounded energy, may find the kind of books to set many readers free by the simple act of seeing freshly and by encouraging their authors to do the same. When will this happen?

This afternoon.

Tomorrow.

The day after tomorrow.

Consider what happened to General Motors, Ford, and Chrysler. Their losses for the year 1980 were gargantuan. They were more intent on making cars the same old way than in making some new kind of car. Are book publishers doing the same thing? Are they publishing books while putting most of their attention on ingenious forms of hype but with little concentration on the quality of the book or the untapped needs of the book-reading public? Even as the mind of the successful money-making publisher is on buying the kind of books he can hype and sell, the mind of the author reaches for the same kind of book.

Who is thinking of the buyer?

Maybe that is what you should do.

As an author, have faith in yourself. You aren't going to change the publishing business. It isn't going to milk itself just to nurse you. Accept that. Write your best sentence every time. Think about what you are doing and why. Take your time and do it well. If you have talent, a little wisdom, and you own yourself, no one can take these away from you.

A book publisher is neither your friend nor your enemy. He is part of the scene that includes you. Work with him with the knowledge that, although he is big and you are small, he is a dead duck in a world without writers.

Be the writer everyone wants. The writer who gives all of himself and writes what he has to say.

Index

THE BOOK MARKET